ORTHOPEDICS

Translated from the German Series:

**Krankengymnastik
Taschenlehrbuch in elf Bänden**

Edited by

**H. Cotta, W. Heipertz,
A. Hüter-Becker, G. Rompe**

Clinical Handbooks in Physical Therapy Management

H. Cotta
L. W. Friedmann
W. Heipertz
G. Koester
E. Marquardt
W. Puhl
G. Rompe
A. tum Suden-Weickmann

ORTHOPEDICS

English Language Edition Edited by
Linda A. Karacoloff, M.S., P.T.
National Rehabilitation Hospital
Washington, D.C.

translated by
Renate King, D.V.M.

AN ASPEN PUBLICATION®
Aspen Publishers, Inc.
Rockville, Maryland
Royal Tunbridge Wells
1987

Library of Congress Cataloging-in-Publication Data

Orthopädie. English.
Orthopedics.

(Clinical handbooks in physical therapy management)
Translation of: Orthopädie.
"An Aspen publication."
Includes bibliographies and index.
1. Musculoskeletal system—Diseases—Treatment.
2. Musculoskeletal system—Abnormalities—Treatment.
3. Physical therapy. I. Cotta, Horst. II. Karacoloff, Linda A. III. Title. IV. Series. [DNLM: 1. Bone Diseases—rehabilitation. 2. Bone Diseases—therapy. 3. Joint diseases—rehabilitation. 4. Joint Diseases—therapy. 5. Physical Therapy. WE 168 07621]
RD732.07413   1987   617'.3   86-28811
ISBN: 0-87189-625-7

English language edition, Copyright © 1987 by Aspen Publishers, Inc.
All rights reserved.

Aspen Publishers, Inc. grants permission for photocopying for personal or internal use or for the personal or internal use of specific clients registered with the Copyright Clearance Center (CCC). This consent is given on the condition that the copier pay a $1.00 fee plus $.12 per page for each photocopy through the CCC for photocopying beyond that permitted by the U.S. Copyright Law. The fee should be paid directly to the CCC, 21 Congress St., Salem, Massachusetts 01970.
0-87189-625-7/87 $1.00 + .12.

This consent does not extend to other kinds of copying, such as copying for general distribution, for advertising or promotional purposes, for creating new collective works, or for resale. For information, address Aspen Publishers, Inc., 1600 Research Boulevard, Rockville, Maryland 20850.

Originally published as *Orthopadie* © 1985 Georg Thieme Verlag,
Rudigerstrasse 14, D-7000 Stuttgart 30

Library of Congress Catalog Card Number: 86-28811
ISBN: 0-87189-625-7

Editorial Services: Ruth Bloom

Printed in the United States of America

1 2 3 4 5

Table of Contents

Publisher's Note ix

Preface to English Language Edition xi

Preface xiii

Chapter 1—Physical Therapy Introduction 1
    G. Koester

    Evaluation Results in Physical Therapy 1

Chapter 2—Congenital Systemic Diseases 11
    H. Cotta, W. Puhl, and G. Koester

    Evaluation Results in Physical Therapy 11
    Clinical Manifestations 12
    Physical Therapy 16

Chapter 3—Acquired Systemic Diseases 19
    H. Cotta, W. Puhl, and G. Koester

    Evaluation Results in Physical Therapy 19
    Clinical Manifestations 19
    Physical Therapy 22

Chapter 4—Deformities 23
        H. Cotta, W. Puhl, and G. Koester

    Evaluation Results in Physical Therapy 23
    Clinical Manifestations 23
    Physical Therapy 26

Chapter 5—Tumors and Tumorlike Diseases 27
        H. Cotta, W. Puhl, and G. Koester

    Evaluation Results in Physical Therapy 27
    Clinical Manifestations 27
    Physical Therapy 34

Chapter 6—Aseptic Bone Necroses 35
        H. Cotta, W. Puhl, and G. Koester

    Evaluation Results in Physical Therapy 35
    Clinical Manifestations 35
    Physical Therapy 45

Chapter 7—Aging Process of the Musculoskeletal System 49
        H. Cotta, W. Puhl, and G. Koester

    Evaluation Results in Physical Therapy 49
    Clinical Manifestations 49
    Physical Therapy 55

Chapter 8—Contractures 57
        H. Cotta, W. Puhl, and G. Koester

    Evaluation Results in Physical Therapy 57
    Clinical Manifestations 57
    Physical Therapy 59

Chapter 9—Inflammative Diseases of the Bones and Joints 65
        W. Heipertz and A. tum Suden-Weickmann

    Clinical Manifestations 66
    Physical Therapy 80

Table of Contents vii

Chapter 10—Diseases of the Spine and Trunk **87**
    W. Heipertz and A. tum Suden-Weickmann

    Structure and Function of the Spine 87
    Evaluation Results in Physical Therapy 89
    Postural Weakness and Malpositions 94
    Deformities 105
    Spinal Changes in Systemic Diseases 120
    Aseptic Bone Necroses of the Spine 122
    Scoliosis 127
    Degenerative Diseases of the Spine 150
    Spinal Syndrome 154
    Osteoporosis 172
    Spondylitis 175
    Bechterew's Disease 178
    Spinal Tumors 184

Chapter 11—Upper Extremities **189**
    H. Cotta, W. Puhl, and G. Koester

SHOULDER

    Evaluation Results in Physical Therapy 189
    Clinical Symptoms 192
    Physical Therapy 196

ELBOW

    Evaluation Results in Physical Therapy 209
    Clinical Symptoms 210
    Physical Therapy 211

HAND

    Evaluation Results in Physical Therapy 213
    Clinical Symptoms 220
    Physical Therapy 221

Chapter 12—Lower Limbs **233**
  H. Cotta, W. Puhl, and G. Koester

HIP JOINT

Evaluation Results in Physical Therapy 233
Clinical Symptoms 237
Physical Therapy 250

KNEE

Evaluation Results in Physical Therapy 285
Clinical Symptoms 289
Physical Therapy 297

FOOT

Evaluation in Physical Therapy 318
Clinical Symptoms 320
Physical Therapy 336

Chapter 13—Typical Orthopedic Surgical Procedures **357**
  H. Cotta, G. Rompe, and G. Koester

Surgical Procedures of Tendons 357
Operations of the Bones 359
Surgical Procedures of the Joints 363
Alloplastic Implants 366

Chapter 14—Amputations, Prostheses, and Orthoses **371**
  E. Marquardt, L.W. Friedmann, and G. Koester

Rehabilitation 371
Physical Therapy 401
Orthoses 413
Upper Extremity Orthoses 417
Lower Limb Orthotics 421
Spinal Orthoses 426

Bibliography **427**

Index **431**

About the Editors and Contributors **447**

Publisher's Note

Aspen Publishers is pleased to announce this series entitled *Clinical Handbooks for Physical Therapy Management*. These handbooks have been selected from a prestigious series entitled *Krankengymnastik*. Prior to the current edition, this German series was collected together as one single volume and it served as a standard text/reference for decades. Recently, the German editors, H. Cotta, W. Heipertz, A. Hüter-Becker, and G. Rompe, along with their publisher, Georg Thieme of Stuttgart, decided to issue the new edition as a series of ten smaller topical volumes to allow for greater flexibility in the use of the material.

We selected those volumes in the series that we felt were most appropriate to North American and other English language readers. Each volume we select is translated by a biomedical expert and then heavily edited for language usage. Finally, each volume is edited by American experts for content and appropriateness of coverage and terminology.

We are indebted to our experts who serve as Editors of our editions and to Susan Woll, PT, who lent her knowledge of content and language to all titles in the series. Special thanks to Dr. Lawrence Friedmann who joined Dr. Marquardt in a revision of his chapter 14 in *Orthopedics*.

These volumes will be distributed to readers worldwide. We hope the English language editions serve our readers as well as their German counterparts have.

Preface to the English Language Edition

For over a decade the specialty of orthopedics in physical therapy has undergone major growth and development. For this reason, the need to keep abreast of the latest approaches and techniques in orthopedic case management has never been more acute. Therefore, this first volume in the series, *Clinical Handbooks for Physical Therapy Management,* is appropriately devoted to orthopedics.

Written for the physical therapist, this book presents the management of orthopedic conditions based on the results of the physical therapy evaluation. Although based on the experience of German orthopedic surgeons, treatment methods outlined in the book are rarely regionally based. Each chapter is organized to provide guidelines for the development of a therapeutic treatment program and a goal oriented treatment plan based on the physical therapy evaluation results.

The therapeutic techniques presented throughout the book are not included to provide all possible exercise alternatives, but to broaden the pool of therapeutic techniques upon which a treatment program is based. Also included are recommendations for the management of clinical manifestations of the specific orthopedic condition being discussed in each chapter as well as recommendations for surgical versus conservative treatment.

In retrospect, the publication of an English language edition of *Orthopedics* would not have been possible without the commitment of many individuals other than the original contributors. Therefore, I would especially like to acknowledge Renate King, DVM, for her excellent translation of the German text, Margaret Quinlin and Ruth Bloom of Aspen Publishers for their patience and direction, and Dr. Lawrence Friedmann for his assistance in the revision of Chapter 14 for the English language edition.

Linda A. Karacoloff, MS, PT
Assistant Director
Physical Therapy Service
National Rehabilitation Hospital
Washington, D.C.

Preface

Orthopedics is the science concerned with the diagnosis, treatment, and prevention of dysfunctions and diseases of the musculoskeletal system: muscles, tendons, ligaments, joints, and bones of the trunk and extremities. This book presents a selection of the most important orthopedic diseases with a special consideration of the examination results available during a physical therapy evaluation.

The progress in the diagnosis of and particularly the surgical intervention for orthopedic diseases during the past 20 years has drastically changed the treatments given in physical therapy. As a result, this text on orthopedics has been completely rewritten. After several years of work, this book now meets present standards in orthopedics. Individual clinical practice and new advances in orthopedics will indicate changes that should be made in a subsequent edition and I ask the readers not to hold back their criticism or suggestions.

I thank the authors for their cooperation and their understanding. I feel especially obligated to the Georg Thieme Publishing House and not only to the many silent helpers but also to Dr. G. Hauff and Mr. A. Menge for so eagerly supporting our project.

Gerhard Rompe
Heidelberg

Chapter 1

Physical Therapy Introduction

G. Koester

This book offers therapeutic principles in conservative, preoperative, and postoperative orthopedics. Chapter 9, "Inflammative Diseases of the Bones and Joints," and Chapter 10, "Diseases of the Spine and Trunk," are based on experiences at the Orthopaedic University Hospital in Frankfurt, while the other chapters are based on clinical experience at the Orthopaedic University Hospital in Heidelberg.

The book does not claim to be complete, since there may always be therapeutic methods and experiences which are regionally based. We do encourage readers to let us know of any new ideas and facts that should be included in the next edition.

Physical therapy in orthopedics implies working with patients suffering from diseases and dysfunctions of the musculoskeletal system. The dysfunctions are usually manifested in obvious disabilities of which the physical therapist must be able to both observe and assess. In order to do this, one important requirement is the therapist's knowledge of normal physiology and of functional and topographical anatomy. Within the text the sections on examination results in diseases of the trunk and extremities also will describe important anatomical details. The purpose of these descriptions is to encourage more comprehensive assessment in this area by the therapist. This is especially true in Chapter 11, the section dealing with the hand which contains very specific information, since treating the hand is especially complex. Some other diseases will also be described more fully because they are seen more often by physical therapists. The sequence of therapeutic methods given throughout the text, especially during the postoperative phase, should not be considered absolute, but should be modified according to the needs of the individual patient.

EVALUATION RESULTS IN PHYSICAL THERAPY

The physical therapist evaluates each patient on an individual basis, taking into consideration the severity of a disease or deformity and the patient's general status. This evaluation is valid only for this patient.

The evaluation should always start with:

- Observation of posture and movements, including the affected area of the body without attempting to correct it; additional aids may have to be used, if necessary
- A request for an active, spontaneous correction
- An instruction for correction

This is followed by an evaluation of the function in the affected joints as well as the neighboring joints, testing active and passive mobility and movement against resistance. Active mobility and movement against resistance are evaluated by assessing the function of the contractile structures (muscles and tendons with their insertions). Passive mobility is evaluated by assessing the function of both the contractile structures and the noncontractile structures (joint capsule and ligaments). It is important to record the results on a standard evaluation sheet.

Based on the evaluation results collected the first day, a treatment program is set up by the physical therapist and specific treatment methods and techniques are chosen. The patient is reevaluated during treatment to determine the effectiveness of the program.

The evaluation results are documented by notes, for example, results of muscle tests (Table 1–1), and by graphs and tables, such as a diagram of the developing joint mobility over a period of time (Fig. 1–1). More sophisticated methods of determining the effectiveness of the physical therapy program such as the following can also be used:

- Photography
- Tape and video recorder; the course of the movement can be reproduced as often as necessary and used for corrections by repeated watching
- Biofeedback registering muscle potentials and showing the actual muscle work.

To complete the evaluation result, the following additional information is needed:

- From the patient: the duration of the disease or complaints, earlier physical therapy, subjective assessment by the patient about his or her condition, expectations regarding present or proposed treatment
- From the physician: special information about the referral for physical therapy, therapeutic goals and methods, operations, radiographs, endurance of the patient, etc.

Table 1-1 Documentation of muscle strength.

MUSCLE FUNCTION

Name
Diagnosis
Onset

Date of Birth

Floor/Room

0	- no reaction
1	- contraction, visible or palpable
2	- supported movement
3	- movement against gravity
4	- movement against light resistance
5	- movement against strong resistance
+	- no evaluation possible
S	spasticity
C	contracture

Record in red ink: 0, 1, 2

Record in blue ink: 3, 4, 5

Right

Date			Function	Muscle				Date			Left
			flexion	flexors							
			extension	extensors							
			lateral tilt, rotation	sternocleidomastoid							
			flexion	rectus abdominus lower portion							
				rectus abdominus upper portion							

Neck / Trunk (row labels on both sides)

Table 1-1 continued

Right											Left
Date					Function	Muscle					Date
					rotation + lateral tilt	external oblique abdominals					
						internal oblique abdominals					
Trunk					extension	erector trunci cervicalis					Trunk
						erector trunci dorsalis					
						erector trunci lumbal					
					pelvic elevation	quadratus lumborum					
Scapula					elevation	trapezius descending					Scapula
						levator scapulae					
					adduction	trapezius transverse					
						rhomboids					
					caudal shift	ascending trapezius					
					abduction	serratus anterior					
Name of the physical therapist					Remarks						Name of the physical therapist

Evaluation Results in Physical Therapy

Region	Movement	Muscle
Shoulder Joint	elevation and abduction	deltoid (anterior portion)
		deltoid (medial portion)
		deltoid (dorsal portion)
		supraspinatus
		pectoralis major and minor
		serratus anterior
		levator scapulae
		trapezius descending
	retroversion	triceps brachii caput longum
		teres major
		latissimus
	inward rotation	subscapularis
		pectoralis major
		teres major
	outward rotation	infraspinatus
		teres minor
Elbow	flexion	biceps brachii
		brachialis
		brachioradialis
	extension	triceps brachialis
	supination	biceps brachialis
		supinator
	pronation	pronator quadratus
Hand	flexion and abduction	flexor digitorum
		flexor carpi ulnaris
		flexor carpi radialis
		palmaris longus

Table 1–1 continued

Right						Left		
Date	Hand	Name of the physical therapist	Thumb	Finger	Function	Muscle		
					extension and abduction	extensor digitorum communis		
						extensor carpi ulnaris		
						extensor carpi radialis (longus and brevis)		
					Remarks			
					flexion	flexor pollicis longus		
						flexor pollicis brevis		
					extension	extensor pollicis longus		
						extensor pollicis brevis		
					abduction	abductor pollicis longus		
						abductor pollicis brevis		
					adduction	adductor pollicis		
					opposition	opponens pollicis		
					2.fi.	flexor digitorum superficialis		
					3.fi.			
					4.fi.			
					5.fi.			

Evaluation Results in Physical Therapy

	2.fi.	3.fi.	4.fi.	5.fi.		2.fi.	3.fi.	4.fi.	5.fi.		2.fi.	3.fi.	4.fi.	5.fi.		2.fi.	3.fi.	3.fi.	4.fi.		5.fi.		2.fi.	4.fi.	5.fi.		5.fi.		
flexion					flexor digitorum proficialis					lumbricales (I, II, III, IV)					extensor digitorum communis					interossei dorsales (I, II, III, IV)		abductor digiti V				interossei volares (I, II, III)		opponens digiti V	therapy opposition	Remarks

Table 1-1 continued

Right				Function	Muscle			Left	
Date								Date	
Hip				flexion	iliopsoas				Hip
					rectus femoris				
					tensor fasciae latae				
					sartorius				
				extension	gluteus maximus				
				abduction	gluteus medius and minimus				
				adduction	adductores				
				inward rotation	inward rotators				
				outward rotation	outward rotators				
Knee				flexion	semi-muscles				Knee
					biceps femoris				
				extension	quadriceps vastus latus				
					quadriceps vastus medialis				
					quadriceps vastus intermedialis				
					rectus femoris				
Foot				plantar flexion	gastrocnemius				Foot
					triceps surae				
					soleus				
				dorsal flexion	tibialis anterior				

Evaluation Results in Physical Therapy

Foot	supination	triceps surae																	
		tibialis posterior																	
		tibialis anterior																	
	pronation	fibularis longus and brevis																	
Toes	flexion	flexor digitorum longus																	
		flexor digitorum brevis																	
		flexor hallicus longus																	
		flexor hallicus brevis																	
		lumbricales																	
	extension	extensor digiti longus																	
		extensor digiti brevis																	
		extensor hallicus longus																	
		extensor hallicus brevis																	
	abduction	dorsal interossei																	
		abductor hallicus																	
		abductor digiti V																	
	adduction	interossei plantares																	
		adductor hallicus																	
Remarks																			
Name of the physical therapist																			

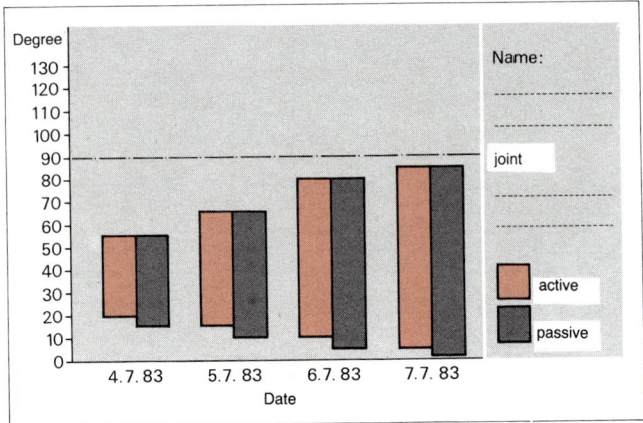

Fig. 1–1 Progression of joint mobility.

- From other professionals: nurses (general medical status), occupational therapists (status of patient's daily activity level), and orthopedic technicians (status of any immobility device, past or present fracture treatments, etc.).

The evaluation result is the prerequisite for developing a therapeutic treatment program and plan. The therapist should always support and motivate the patient as the patient begins to feel and understand new movements which have to be learned. Since restored and improved abilities should be used in daily routine as soon as possible, the patient's age and individual habits are taken into consideration.

Patients in an orthopedic rehabilitation hospital are generally not confined to bed for an extended period and generally have been able to prepare for their hospitalization. In addition to the usual personal belongings, patients should bring the following items with them to the hospital:

- A pair of comfortable, well-fitting shoes (possibly orthopedic shoes), even if they are not able to walk at the time of the admission
- A training or warm-up suit that can be worn outdoors
- Sufficient changes in underwear.
- Shorts and T-shirts
- Swimsuit and robe
- All aids that are presently being used.

Training mobility and independence is the best route to rehabilitation. Therefore, the patient should begin treatment as soon as possible after admission.

Chapter 2
Congenital Systemic Diseases

H. Cotta, W. Puhl, and G. Koester

EVALUATION RESULTS IN PHYSICAL THERAPY

Patients with systemic diseases suffer from dysfunctions of the musculoskeletal system, deformities, and malpositions. Because such patients exhibit such a variety of symptoms, we offer no special rules for the physical examination. Each evaluation must be matched to the individual, following the guidelines for each area of the body. Usually the following details are evaluated:

- Active and passive joint motion (passive motion must be tested carefully in most patients)
- Muscle strength, coordination, and endurance
- Posture
- Walking ability
- Function in daily routine and ability to help oneself
- Use of or need for additional aids.

The physical therapy evaluation and therapeutic program in occupational therapy are best scheduled at the same time. The patient's expectations regarding treatment should not be neglected, but should be discussed, preferably with the team that includes the patient, physician, parents, physical and occupational therapists, and orthopedic technician. Overly optimistic expectations should not be destroyed, but modified, and the importance of active cooperation of the patient and the parents should be emphasized.

Findings from the initial evaluation should be carefully recorded, since therapeutic success can only be proved if the initial evaluation results were thoroughly documented.

CLINICAL MANIFESTATIONS

The term "congenital systemic diseases" covers a variety of diseases and their concomitant symptoms. The manifestations of the diseases depend on which phase of skeletal development was disturbed at the time of onset. Congenital systemic disturbances and deformities are not necessarily obvious at birth; some become evident during infancy or early childhood. There is no general symptomatology behind these diseases, since the pathogenesis is unknown.

Skeletal Dysplasias Mainly Affecting the Epiphyses

Chondrodystrophia Calcarea (Chondrodystrophia Calcificans)

Origin. Unknown.

Symptoms. Cartilaginous necroses and calcifications of the epiphyses, which might regress until puberty, but which, in the interim, can cause deformities of the joint. Single bones can be affected, or there may be multiple lesions.

Treatment. Prevention of contractures. Possibly operative correction of articular malpositions; treatment of the early arthrosis.

Skeletal Dysplasias Mainly Affecting the Metaphyses

Achondroplasia (Chondrodystrophia Fetalis)

Origin. Unknown. Predominantly hereditary. Originates in the fetal stage during cartilage development.

Symptoms and Manifestations. Longitudinal but not circumferential growth of the long bones is inhibited. The diaphyses are bent and enlarged. There is slight thoracolumbar kyphosis, small facial bones, flat nasal saddle, relatively large occiput. Intellect is not affected. Tridental shape of the hand; height 100–120 cm.

Treatment. In children, attempt to direct the growth, especially the spine; prevention of contractures; therapy for the early arthrosis.

Disturbances of Bone Remodeling with Changing Bone Density

Osteogenesis Imperfecta (Osteopsathyrosis, Glass-Bone Disease)

Origin. Unknown. Disturbed periosteal (rarely also endochondral) ossification. The cortex of the long bones is thin owing to a decreased function of the osteoblasts, which results in bending and fractures. At the same time, odontoblasts (dental development) and fibroblasts (blue sclera) are affected.

Clinical Manifestations 13

Symptoms. There are two types:

1. Early (osteogenesis imperfecta congenita Vrolik): Numerous prenatal fractures; life expectancy not more than 2 years.
2. Late (osteogenesis imperfecta tarda; osteopsathyrosis Lobstein): Bones are brittle during early childhood and improve after the onset of puberty. There is bending of the long bones by multiple, often unnoticed fractures. Other features include malpositions of the joints and the spine, small facial bones, pale skin, blue scleras, impaired hearing of the inner ear (Fig. 2–1; see also Chapter 10).

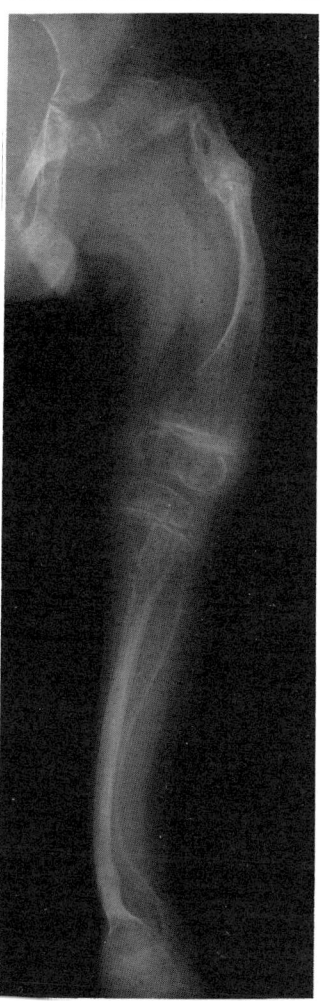

Fig. 2–1 Osteogenesis imperfecta type Lobstein. Coxa vara, femur varus, and crus valgum owing to bending and fractures of the bone. (H. Cotta: Orthopädie, 4. Aufl., Thieme, Stuttgart, 1984).

Treatment. Physical support and prevention of further fractures until puberty. Conservative fracture treatment is possible, since bone healing is accelerated. Osteotomy and intramedullary pinning (directed growth) are indicated in case of bending tendency.

Arthrogryposis (Arthrogryposis Multiplex Congenita)

Origin. Disturbance of muscle development or muscle innervation with congenital, nonprogressive limitation of the movement related to the soft tissue, mostly in the extremities.

Symptoms and Manifestations. Abnormal contour of the extremities, overall stuffed appearance, torso cylindrical or wedge shaped; absence of skin folds and lack of muscle or joint contours. Presence of skin indentations or "dimples" on the knee and elbow joints. No tendency to spontaneous improvement. Joints are frequently affected symmetrically. Their range of motion is limited not only in one direction, as in a contracture, but in all directions.

Treatment. The few remaining muscles (with their reduced number of fibers) need to be trained as early as possible and the joints must be exercised as much as possible, with active and passive motions, to counteract the tendency toward progressive capsular contracture. Corrective osteotomies may be indicated to provide for a more favorable functional position, or arthrolysis may be done, sacrificing the insertions of nonfunctioning muscles as a prerequisite for passive motion.

Marfan Syndrome (Arachnodactyly, Spider Fingers)

Origin. Hereditary disturbance in the development of the connective tissue.

Symptoms and Manifestations. Abnormal length of the body, delicately structured with extremely long fingers and toes (spider or Madonna fingers), flaccid connective tissue, hypotonic muscles, hyperextension of the joints, unstable joints, scolioses (see also Chapter 10).

Treatment. General muscle strengthening, posture training (scoliosis), avoidance of excessive stress, prevention of contractures and unstable joints, treatment of deformities.

Mucopolysaccharidosis IV (Dysostosis Enchondralis Epimetaphysaria, Morquio-Brailsford Disease)

Origin: Hereditary disturbance of the mucopolysaccharide metabolism.

Symptoms. Reduced growth, characteristic deformities of the lumbar vertebrae, dwarfism, epiphyseal growth disturbance and joint deformation (Fig. 2–2; see also Chapter 10).

Treatment. Prevention of contractures and treatment of early arthrosis.

Hemophiliac Joint *(Arthropathia Hemophilica)*

Origin. Inherited, recessively sex linked (males show the clinical symptoms, females carry and transmit the gene). Coagulation factor VIII is reduced in hemophilia type A; the less common hemophilia type B is characterized by a greatly decreased or missing factor IX. Depending on the severity of the coagulation disturbance, bleeding occurs in all tissues and organs and frequently in the

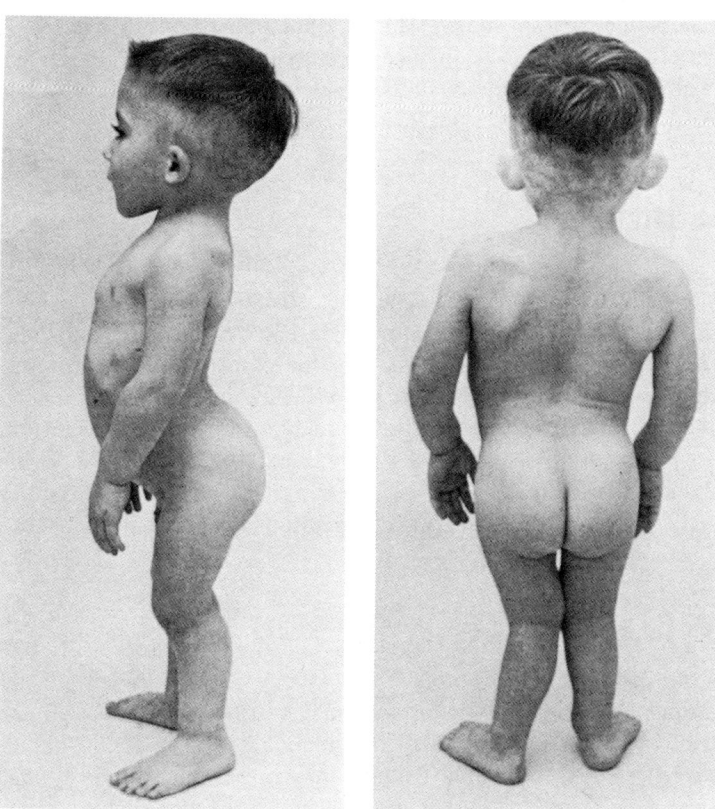

Fig. 2–2 Polytopic dysostosis type Morquio-Brailsford dwarfism, scoliosis, genu valgum, short extremities, disproportion between the size of the head and the size of the extremities and trunk (H. Cotta: Orthopädie, 4. Aufl., Thieme, Stuttgart, 1984).

joints, which can become severely arthritic as early as childhood because of enzymatic and metabolic damage of the cartilage and scarring of the joint capsule.

Symptoms and Manifestations. Knee, hip, elbow, and tarsal joints are most commonly affected. Initially, there is painful swelling of the joint; after repeated hemorrhages there is thickening of the joint capsule and, later, contractures. Malpositions, subluxations, and complete fusion may also occur. At the time of the acute hemorrhage the joint is tensed, and pain is caused by palpation or motion. Extensive hemorrhages can cause minor temperature elevations and leukocytoses owing to resorption. The spontaneous resorption of an articular hemorrhage takes from 3 to 6 weeks. Intraosseous hemorrhages with lesions of the growth plates can cause considerable joint deformities and skeletal deviations.

Treatment. Permanent substitution of the missing coagulation factor. Minor articular hemorrhages require compression and immobilization for a few days. Severer joint effusions need to be drained. Recurrent hemorrhages require synovectomy with intensive substitution of the missing coagulation factor. Contractures, malpositions, and arthroses are treated accordingly.

PHYSICAL THERAPY

In all systemic diseases the therapy is planned to maintain or improve remaining functions. The physician must be consulted in each case for the individual prognoses and possible precautions. Most of the cases require an extensive therapeutic program, which is divided into phases, since the trunk and extremities are affected at the same time. An exercise program needs to be designed for the patient to use independently, since the disease will last throughout his or her life. The patient should be seen at least once a year by the therapist to be sure the exercises are being performed correctly and for reevaluation of possible changes in the patient's condition.

Osteogenesis Imperfecta

In the treatment of glass-bone disease special care is needed to avoid further fractures. However, the joints have to be immobilized intensively after the fractures have healed. Consultation with the referring orthopedist is strongly recommended. It is important to use a progression of isometric, active assisted, and active exercises to strengthen the weak muscles. This will also help to prevent future fractures. In some cases, training in the use of orthoses and activities of daily living is also needed.

Arthrogryposis

With arthrogryposis, it is important to determine, as early as possible, which muscles are functioning in order to create (even in severely affected patients) conditions for active (although limited) movement. This requires an extremely demanding physical therapy regimen for the infant patient, since the progress during the first few weeks will determine (similar to congenital contractures, such as clubfoot) to what extent the remaining functional ability will be further inhibited by secondary contractions.

Hemophiliac Joint

Physical therapy for a hemophiliac joint usually creates special problems. The strengthening of the muscles and postural correction to compensate for the lack of exercise is the general goal. However, it is important that the joints be handled with extreme caution. Although the knee joints (and the lower extremities in general) are most often affected, the basic principle of strengthening with cautious handling applies to all other joints as well.

For Acute Hemorrhage

The joint should be supported in an extended position, if possible, and then a compression bandage should be applied. The leg must be kept elevated at all times.

During sufficient substitution of the coagulation factor (and after hemorrhage has been stopped), the patient should perform isometric contractions of the quadriceps muscle. A trial of ice application to the joint should also be performed; if tolerated, continue more extensive ice application. The patient should then begin careful active exercises, mainly extension; these should be increased depending on the result.

For Chronic Hemorrhage with Chronic Synovitis

An increasing flexion/extension contracture develops, which is caused by adhesion of the intraarticular and periarticular tissue, especially the upper recess of the joint capsule, and the fast atrophy of the quadriceps muscle. The range of motion can also be drastically limited.

A sensitive but intensive therapy program is necessary, to minimize further complications of the joint capsule, ligaments, and muscles (*see also:* exercise treatment in arthritis). The decreasing weight-bearing ability of the legs results also in bone atrophy and brittleness. A knee orthosis might be necessary to protect the joint. Mobilizing movements are attempted only under gentle traction.

Chapter 3
Acquired Systemic Diseases

H. Cotta, W. Puhl, and G. Koester

EVALUATION RESULTS IN PHYSICAL THERAPY

Patients with acquired systemic diseases as well as patients with congenital systemic diseases suffer from dysfunctions of the trunk and extremities. There are no general guidelines: each evaluation must be matched to the individual patient and must follow the guidelines for the areas of the body involved. Therapeutic success or the prevention or worsening can only be verified by comparison of re-evaluation findings with a well-documented initial evaluation.

CLINICAL MANIFESTATIONS

Rickets (Rachitis, English Disease)

Origin. Vitamin D deficiency, which results in an insufficient bony mineralization (osteoid tissue). The bone remains too soft to bear the weight of the body. Because of the availability of a balanced, vitamin-supplemented diet, rickets caused by vitamin D deficiency and resulting in severe skeletal deformities, such as scoliosis, kyphosis, coxa vara, and deformities of the lower legs, seldom occurs.

Symptoms. Seen during the period of accelerated growth, between 6 months and 3 years:

- Craniotabes: Skull remains soft and thin, and closure of the sutures is delayed; the expansive pressure of the growing brain causes head deformities (caput quadratum).
- Disturbances of the bony consolidation cause bead-like enlargement of the costal cartilage (Ricketty rosary).

20 ACQUIRED SYSTEMIC DISEASES

- Harrison's sulcus: Thorax is bell-shaped, with bilateral impressions at the level of the diaphragm.
- Kyphosis (humpback): The insufficiently mineralized vertebrae are deformed by the weight of the body.
- Leg deformities include bending and rotation (corkscrew leg; Fig. 3–1).

Treatment. Correcting bandages *prior* to the therapy with vitamin D_3 are useful in consultation with the pediatrician, since the soft bone can be corrected. After the onset of therapy with vitamin D_3 the axial deviations of the lower extremity can be corrected surgically after the florid phase (see Osteotomy in Chapter 13). Spontaneous healing is possible.

Renal Rickets

Origin. General disturbances of ossification based on a congenital or acquired renal malfunction.

Symptoms. See rickets.

Treatment. Correcting bandages *prior* to the therapy with vitamin D_3 are useful,

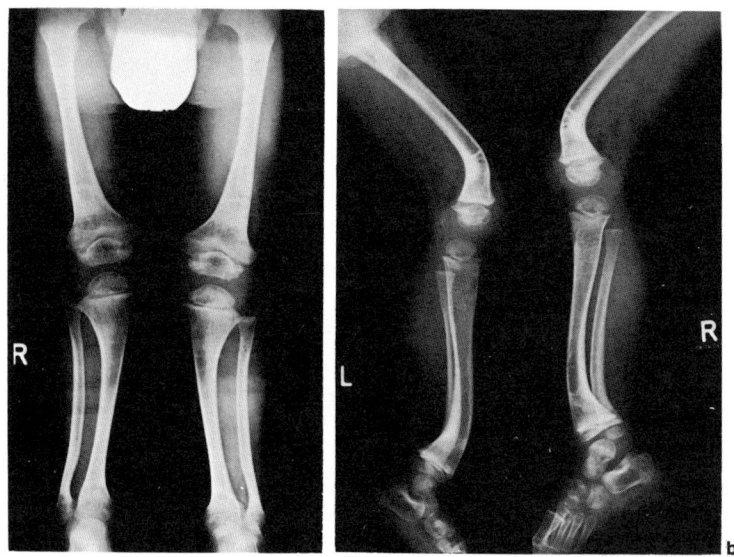

Fig. 3–1 Severe deformity of the lower extremity (H. Cotta: Orthopädie, 4. Aufl., Thieme, Stuttgart, 1984).

Osteomalacia (Adult Rickets)

In normal bone resorption the mineralization of new osteoid tissue is inhibited, and the bone gradually softens.

Origin. Vitamin D deficiency, unbalanced diet, lack of sunlight (ultraviolet light), malabsorption, intestinal disease, gastrectomy, hunger, disturbances of vitamin D metabolism or vitamin D resistance of the skeleton, kidneys, or intestine.

Symptoms. Slowly progressing skeletal deformity, dependent on the weight bearing.

Treatment. Balanced diet, vitamin D.

Osteoporosis

Origin. Age-related decrease in stability of bone, especially the spine.

As is true for other biological functions, bone formation regresses with increasing age, resulting in a bone loss. However, if the osteoporotic changes become obvious earlier (presenile osteoporosis), the bone atrophy becomes more obvious than is normal for the age and sex. Calcium deficiency and a disturbed protein synthesis (cortisone) can cause an osteoporosis. The origin of most cases of presenile osteoporosis is unknown.

Symptoms. Weight-bearing intolerance of the bone results in an initial deformity of the spine.

Treatment. Controlled weight bearing is the best stimulation for bone formation and prevents progressive bone atrophy. Medications given are calcium and antibiotics.

Paget's Disease (Osteitis Deformans)

Origin. Bone remodeling is slowed down, especially in males from age 40 on. There is increasing bone thickness but reduced weight-bearing tolerance.

Symptoms. Deformity of the long bones and enlargement of the bones (the hat, for example, no longer fits); finally spontaneous fractures occur; there are deficits in eyesight and hearing, symptoms of increased intracranial pressure that slowly progress. Spontaneous remission may occur. Thirty percent of cases are sarcomatous.

Treatment. Decreased weight bearing, prevention of fractures, medication (calcitonin), usual fracture treatment.

PHYSICAL THERAPY

The functions that remain must be maintained or improved in all systemic diseases. The referring physician must be consulted, since the course, symptoms, and prognosis vary with each individual case. An extensive exercise program is necessary, since the trunk and extremities are greatly affected, and the program has to be divided into phases.

Each patient should work out his or her own schedule, which can be done at home later on. The patient's exercise program is monitored once a year to avoid training mistakes and update the examination and findings. With rickets, the muscles are initially hypotonic but they react well to exercise during the time that the metabolic disturbance is returning to normal.

Exercise programs for patients with osteoporosis and osteomalacia are frequently limited because of pain, especially of the spine (spontaneous deformity of the vertebrae). However, because the weight bearing of the bone is the most important factor for the improvement of the (basically unknown) metabolic disturbance, a program that includes slowly increasing weight bearing must be started. It is especially important to motivate the elderly osteoporotic patient to rest only at noon and at night; however, the presence of existing deformities must be considered when establishing a rest schedule.

Chapter 4

Deformities

H. Cotta, W. Puhl, and G. Koester

EVALUATION RESULTS IN PHYSICAL THERAPY

The evaluation must be tailored to the individual patient (as is also true in systemic diseases). The therapist needs to determine if the deformity is minor or limited to one segment of the extremity and whether or not the deformity can be readily compensated. On the other hand, the entire musculoskeletal system may be so severely affected that the patient will never be independent and will always need medication, aids, and assistance.

There are two basic principles of the evaluation:

1. In infants and young children conduct a thorough passive and active functional test of the trunk and extremities, even if hampered by deformities of joints and muscles. Also evaluate the physical and mental development as compared with normal children.
2. In older children and adolescents the main concern is for independence in their daily living (school, leisure time, education) and for determining possibilities of functional replacements with or without additional aids.

In general, functional testing must be done before surgery or application of orthopedic devices.

CLINICAL MANIFESTATIONS

Congenital deformities can arise either endogenously or exogenously. They may or may not be hereditary, and they occur in various forms. Endogenous or exogenous deformities can cause the same clinical manifestations. The extent of

24 DEFORMITIES

the deformity depends on the time of the noxious effect, its duration, and its intensity. The type of the noxa can also influence the symptoms of the deformity.

The earlier the noxious effect occurs during the fetal development, the severer will be the deformity. Noxae during the development of the extremities will result in deformed extremities; peripheral deformities affecting only hands and feet originate from a noxious effect later in pregnancy.

There are two types of factors that determine the origin of the deformity:

1. Endogenous factors
   - Genetic mutation
   - Chromosomal aberration
2. Exogenous factors
   - Oxygen deficiency
   - Infections during the pregnancy, especially viral infections (rubella, measles, chicken pox)
   - Drugs and other chemical substances (dysmelia syndrome owing to thalidomide)
   - Incompatibility of blood types

Not all deformities are obvious at birth. However, even if they manifest themselves later (as in congenital dislocation of the hip) they are still unquestionably congenital. The deformities of the musculoskeletal system are classified as those of deficient or excessive development.

Deformities Caused by Deficient or Incomplete Development

- Amelia: Entire extremity missing (Fig. 4–1a, right arm)
- Peromelia: "Congenital amputation" (Fig. 4–1a, left arm, left leg)
- Phocomelia: Long bones missing; hands and feet attached close to body, resembling flippers of a seal (Fig. 4–1d)
- Ectromelia: Main group of deformities on extremities; combination of deficient or missing development of several long bones on one extremity (Fig. 4–1c)
- Split hand or foot: Regression of the phalanges II, III, and IV, including the related metacarpal resp. metatarsal bones (Fig. 4–1b)
- Syndactylia: Two or more fingers (toes) connected either cutaneously or osseously. The term "spoonhand" applies to fingers connected by skin along their entire length. Loose and thin skin between the fingers is also called web formation.

Clinical Manifestations 25

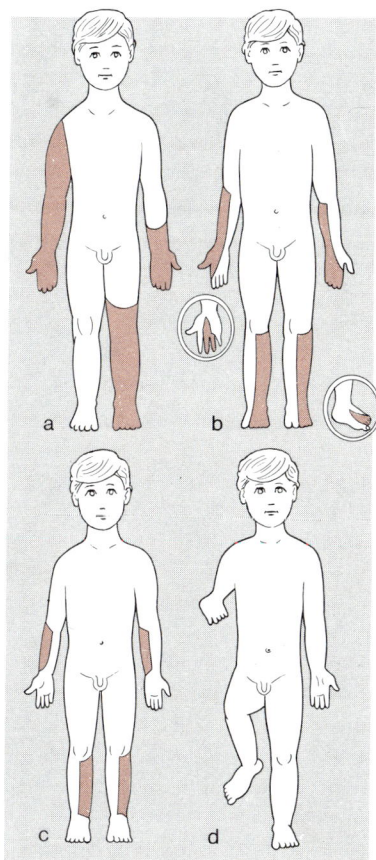

Fig. 4–2 Chart by Blakelslee of the different classifications of deformity in the extremities. In **a**: Deformity that is transverse through an extremity; on both sides is a complete lack of an extremity distal to the level of the congenital amputation. **b**: Deformity on the lateral portions of an extremity; complete absence on both sides of the pre- or postaxial part of an extremity. "A switch piece deformity." **c:** Ectromelia: A complete absence or deformity on a lateral portion of an extremity. The amputation is pre- or postaxial and there is an undamaged portion of the extremity distal to the deformity. **d**: Phocomelia: The absence of the central portion of an extremity combined with the shortening of that extremity.

- Club hand: In ectromelia, especially in combination with radial aplasia (Fig. 4–2); in congenital contractures.

Deformities of Excessive Development

- Polydactylia: More than five fingers, ranging from an initial doubling of the skeletal component (visible only by radiography) over a bifurcation of the fingertip to the double development of one or more entire fingers. All stages in between are possible.
- Partial Acromegaly:
  —True acromegaly: Enlarged segment of an extremity but with normal proportions

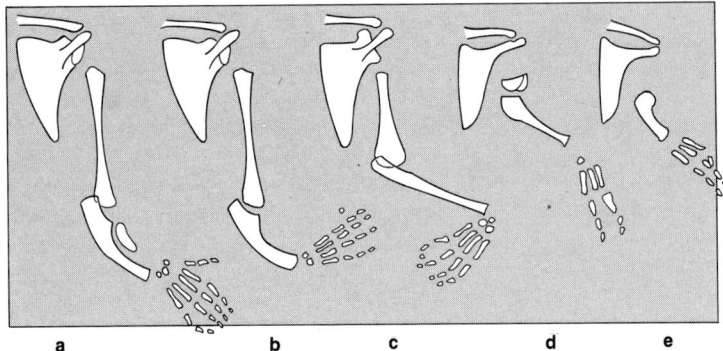

Fig. 4–2 Teratological sequence of radial ectromelia-dysmelia of the upper extremity.

—Pseudoacromegaly: Discrepancy between the soft tissue cover and the skeletal size.

PHYSICAL THERAPY

The therapy is demanding, especially in severely affected children, starting with infants improving the grip and touch of a deformed upper extremity with transition to active functional training, and training of replacing functions, such as the use of the feet instead of the hands. Contractures must be improved, or at least their progression needs to be halted, by use of splints. The training of posture and walking is started.

Treatment includes the entire body and is intensified gradually, at a rate that depends on the patient's age. The parents' cooperation is essential, and they are trained to participate in some of the therapy. Another area of consideration is the preoperative and postoperative treatment of patients undergoing orthopedic operations to improve or create function. Communication with the physician is mandatory, since those severely affected children are never treated routinely, whether treatment is conservative or operative. Contact with the orthopedic surgeon is necessary. The combination of orthopedic technique and physical therapy facilitates optimal care of the child.

Chapter 5
Tumors and Tumorlike Diseases

H. Cotta, W. Puhl, and G. Koester*

EVALUATION RESULTS IN PHYSICAL THERAPY

Before treatment a thorough discussion with the physician (in the absence of the patient) dealing with the type, severity, and expansion of the tumor is necessary. If the tumor is not completely benign, it is necessary to ascertain information about the patient's life expectancy, the extent of metastases of the tumor as well as expected metastases in the near future, and the weight-bearing capacity in the area of the tumor.

There are three types of treatment:

1. Operative: excision with sacrifice of a considerable amount of healthy tissue; amputation
2. Chemotherapy: interfering with the cell metabolism, affecting especially the rapidly multiplying tumor cells by cytostatics
3. Radiation therapy.

Frequently, pathological changes caused by the tumor are difficult to distinguish from changes caused by the treatment (e.g., induration, swelling, lymphatic congestion, scarring). Suspicious changes noted in the evaluation should be immediately reported to the physician.

CLINICAL MANIFESTATIONS

Bone tumors can originate from any type of cell that is involved in the formation of the bony structure. The tumors are best classified according to the tissue in

---

*With the cooperation of Dr. A. Braun, Heidelberg.

which they originate. The radiograph reveals whether the process is osteolytic or osteoblastic, which depends on the destructive or constructive ability of the tumor. However, this finding has no prognostic value.

The classification of tumors as malignant or benign is reasonable but not always possible and has led to the clinical terms "tumorlike lesions" and "semimalignant tumors." Semimalignant refers to a benign tumor that carries the future risk of malignancy. Tumors with a locally infiltrating growth but without metastases are called tumorlike lesions.

Some of the most common tumors are described in the following sections. The success of the treatment depends not only on an early diagnosis, but also on exact histopathological classification. Biopsies and histological examination are mandatory prerequisites before decisions can be made about the extent of the operation and the use of cytostatics or radiation therapy.

Benign Tumors

Cartilaginous Exostosis (Osteochondroma)

Origin. Cartilage or bone cells.

Symptoms. Bony-structured enlargement with a thin stem or wide base, growing into a soft tissue next to the growth plate. Certain growth disturbances and joint deformities can result from interference with the adjacent growth plate. Diagnosis is usually made during the accelerated growth period in puberty. The tumor may gradually compress vessels and nerves (Fig. 5–1).

Treatment. Operative removal of exostoses. The prognosis is favorable. A rare malignant transition should be considered if the tumor enlarges after puberty.

Multiple Cartilaginous Exostoses

Origin. Dominantly hereditary cartilaginous tumors, ossifying to exostoses.

Symptoms. Originating adjacent to the growth plate, "moving" toward the diaphysis during the longitudinal growth of the affected bone. Disturbance of the growth plate results in axial deviations and joint deformities. Metaphyseal enlargement (Fig. 5–2).

Treatment. Leveling of exostoses and correction of axial deviations. Prognosis is favorable; malignancy is uncommon.

Enchondromatosis

Origin. Metaplasia to cartilaginous tissue originating from the joint capsule. The enchondromas, connected to the capsule by a stem, can become free joint bodies by separation.

Clinical Manifestations 29

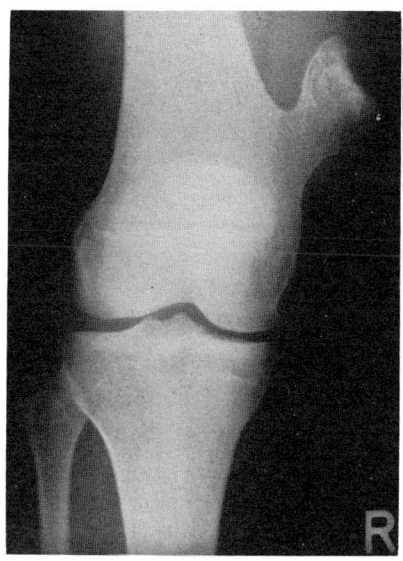

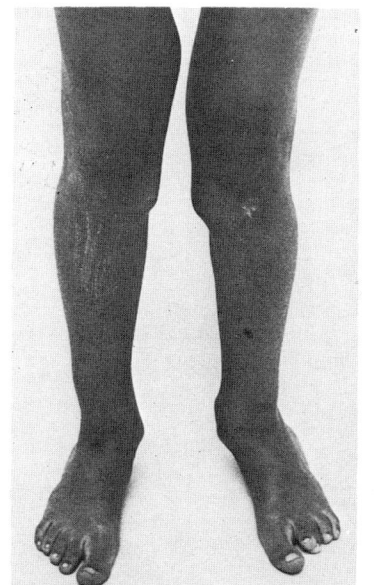

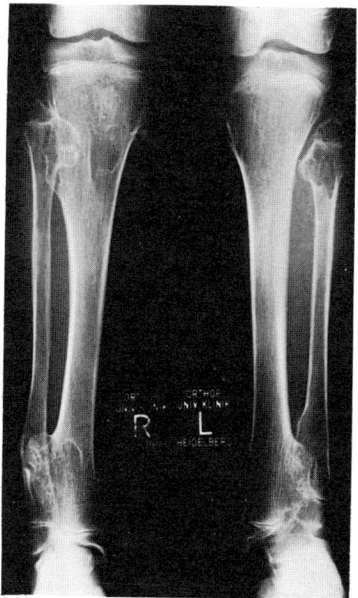

Fig. 5–2 Multiple cartilaginous exostoses (almost symmetrical) have resulted in growth disturbance of the lower leg and malposition of the proximal tarsal joint; exostoses on the area of the tibial head and the medial malleolus are bulging beneath the skin.

Symptoms. Unspecific joint pains, swelling, limited range of motion. Radiographs reveal free bodies that are either single and large or numerous and small (Fig. 5–3).

Treatment. Removal of the free joint bodies.

Ganglion

Origin. Cystic, tumorlike neoplasm, originating from connective tissue, lined by a capsulelike layer, containing a gelatinous, clear yellow fluid.

Symptoms. Occurs on joints, tendons, tendon sheaths, especially wrist, dorsal foot, knee, and toes. The tight, smooth-walled formations move freely underneath the skin and can grow to the size of a pea or an apple. Increased stress can cause additional swelling.

Treatment. Generous excision.

Solitary Bone Cyst

Origin. Nontumorous disturbance of cellular differentiation.

Symptoms. Cystic formation in children and young adults between ages 6 and 15. Its position is metaphyseal and does not exceed the growth plate. They are usually found accidentally by radiology for a pathological fracture.

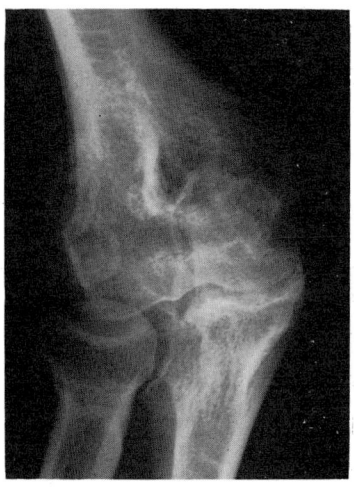 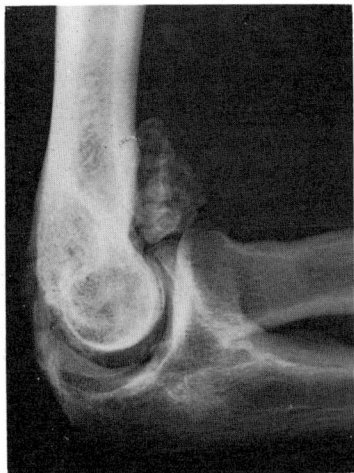

Fig. 5–3 Chondromatosis of the elbow joint. Calcified free bodies are visible in both planes. Chondromatosis caused early arthrosis, narrowing of the joint space, and osteophytes along the edges of the joint.

Treatment. Surgical excavation and filling with (autologous) spongy bone. Weight bearing is limited until bony consolidation is completed.

Osteoid Osteoma

Origin. Presently recognized as a tumor; previously considered a trauma or inflammation.

Symptoms. Piercing pain, especially at night, which can be controlled by aspirin. Radiograph reveals light oval areas surrounded by sclerosis.

Treatment. Operative excavation.

Tumorlike Lesions: Aneurismatic Bone Cyst

Origin. Venous thromboses or arteriovenous fistulas cause atrophy by pressure and cystic degeneration of the affected bone segment.

Symptoms. Long bones and vertebrae are mainly affected between ages 10 and 20. Recidivism is possible.

Treatment. Operative excavation, filling with spongy bone.

Semimalignant Tumor: Giant Cell Tumor (Osteoclastoma)

Origin and Characteristics. Originating tumor cells are unknown. Malignancy, grades I–III, occurs in 10 percent of cases, depending on expansion. Brown discoloration owing to extravasation of blood is observed; tissues are soft and delicate.

Symptoms. Unspecific pains close to the joint; swelling.

Treatment. Operative removal.

Malignant Tumors

Malignant Synovialoma (Synovial Sarcoma)

Origin. Synovia.

Symptoms. Swelling close to the joint, most often of the knee, hand, or ankle.

Treatment. Removal of tumor or amputation of affected limb, possibly in combination with chemotherapy or radiation therapy.

Osteosarcoma *(Osteogenic Sarcoma, Osteochondrosarcoma, Osteofibrosarcoma)*

Origin. Bone cells.

Symptoms. Occurs mainly in children and adolescents and is located on the metaphyses of long bones. Pains at night. Distinctive radiographic periosteal reaction (Fig. 5–4); primary metastases in the lung.

Treatment. After initial chemotherapy, operative removal or amputation. Occasionally it is possible to remove lung metastases successfully.

Chondrosarcoma

Origin. Cartilaginous tissue.

Symptoms. Occurs mainly after age 40. Radiographic calcifications (Fig. 5–5) and late metastases.

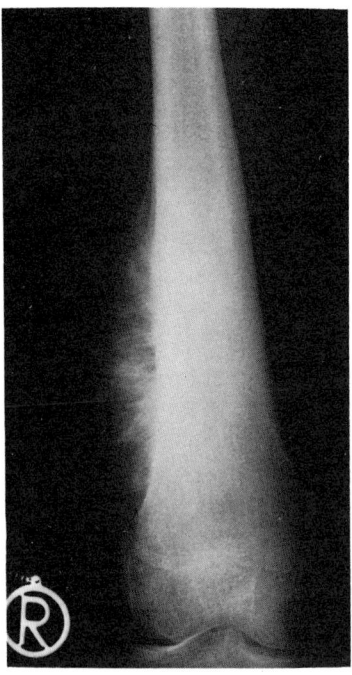

Fig. 5–4 Osteosarcoma. Distal femur of a 14-year-old girl; typical formation of spicules and diffuse sclerosis of the bone.

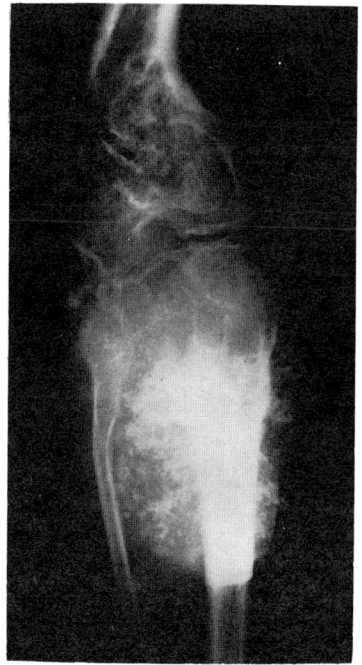

Fig. 5–5 Chondrosarcoma, proximal segment of the lower leg (posttraumatic destruction of the distal femur) (Figs. 5–1—5–5, H. Cotta: Orthopädie, 4. Aufl., Thieme, Stuttgart, 1984).

Treatment. Radical operative therapy is promising due to the late metastases.

Ewing's Sarcoma *(Undifferentiated Reticulosarcoma)*

Origin. Immature reticulocytes of the bone marrow.

Symptoms and Etiology. Most common in young persons between ages 10 and 20; mainly affects the long bones of males. There is pain, swelling, and fever. Often misdiagnosed as osteomyelitis.

Treatment. Chemotherapy, radiation, and surgery.

Bone Metastases of Malignant Tumors (Secondary Malignant Bone Tumors)

Origin. Cells of the primary tumor are disseminated hematogenously and are implanted into the bone. Carcinoma metastases are generally diagnosed by radiograph as osteoblastic, osteolytic, or mixed osteoblastic-osteolytic types. In persons over age 50, old bone metastases are more common than primary bone tumors.

Symptoms. Vary, depending on the primary tumor.

- For osteoblastic metastases: Prostate, mammary, and urinary bladder carcinoma
- For osteolytic metastases: Bronchial, thyroid, or mammary carcinoma; hypernephroma

Metastases are mainly found in areas of spongy bone. Spontaneous fractures are frequently caused by osteolytic metastases.

Treatment. Operative treatment is of limited use, since multiple metastases cannot be removed. Solitary metastases are excised radically. The loss of stability requires a supportive osteosynthesis, endoprosthesis, or orthosis.

PHYSICAL THERAPY

The treatment of malignant tumors (whether by physical therapy, irradiation, or cytostatics) causes tissue damage, appearing as an amputation or as a pseudojoint (resection arthroplasty). In some cases the defects are bridged by endoprostheses or orthoses. The goal of physical therapy is to prevent secondary contractures (caused by scar shrinkage) and maintain the remaining range of motion. Orthoses or endoprostheses should be used and the patients' ability to help themselves must be encouraged. Any clinical change must be reported immediately. Consultation with the physician is also required in cases of benign tumors, since the variable evaluation results mean also variable stability of the bone.

Chapter 6

Aseptic Bone Necroses

H. Cotta, W. Puhl, and G. Koester

EVALUATION RESULTS IN PHYSICAL THERAPY

Aseptic bone necrosis is a typical disease of the joints in children and adolescents. During its early stage, pain is the main symptom. Early osteochondrosis can only be revealed by radiography. During the course of the disease the range of motion becomes limited by a loss of congruency in the affected joint (Perthes' disease, osteochondritis, or osteochondrosis dissecans) or by axial deviation (epiphysiolysis of the hip). These conditions are considered to be prearthroses and have a tendency to contractures. Approximately 2 years after the onset of the disease, full weight bearing is allowed, as in an arthrosis. During the first year after the onset of the disease the weight-bearing ability is severely limited. Before treating children or adolescents, information about their weight-bearing ability must be obtained.

CLINICAL MANIFESTATIONS

Aseptic necroses of the bone are a disease complex, occurring during the growth period (or shortly thereafter, as in necrosis of the lunar bone and osteochondrosis dissecans). Young males are affected more frequently than young females, and the pathological changes are mostly observed on the epiphyses, metaphyses, and apophyses of the long bones, respectively, on the endochondrally ossifying metatarsal and metacarpal bones (Fig. 6–1; see also Chapter 10).

The necroses (Greek: *necros*, death) of the bone and cartilage are ischemic, aseptic, and of unknown origin. The necrosis results at first in a decreased weight-bearing ability of the affected area, with a concomitant risk of deformation under load. During the repair phase, vascular connective tissue from the healthy medulla or periosteum grows into the necrotic area, resorbs the dead tissue, and forms new

36 ASEPTIC BONE NECROSIS

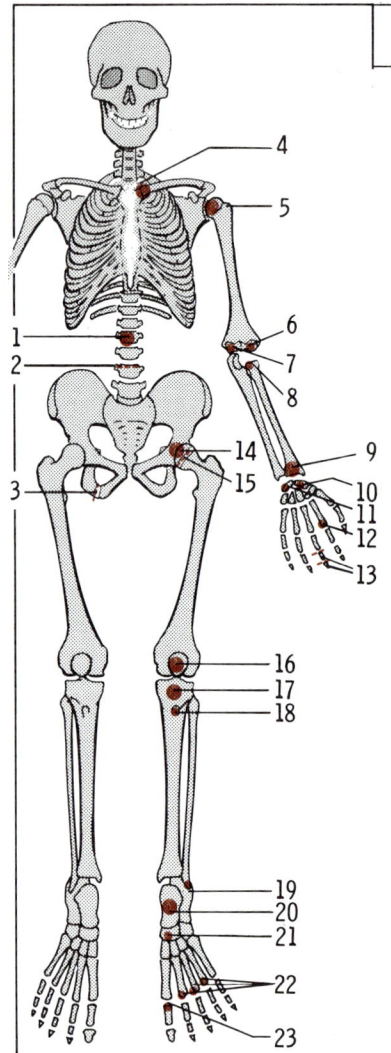

Fig. 6–1 Localization of aseptic bone necroses (H. Cotta: Orthopädie, 4. Aufl., Thieme, Stuttgart, 1984).

bone tissue. In the ideal case, complete healing in a young person can occur. This prognosis differentiates the aseptic necrosis in a young person from the disease in an adult. In an adult we mainly observe an idiopathic necrosis of the femoral head (see Chapter 12) and especially necroses owing to a posttraumatic blockage of the vascular supply, which is a dreaded complication in fractures of the femoral neck, talus, and the navicular (scaphoid) bone of the wrist. The disease is asymptomatic during the early stage and causes only unspecific complaints, which is important to

No.	Localization	Author
1	Vertebral body	Calvé
2	Vertebral edges and dorsal arch	Scheuermann
3	Synchondrosis ischiopubica	van Neck
4	Clavicle, sternal border	Friedrich
5	Humeral head	Hass
6	Capitulum humerus	Panner
7	Trochlea humerus	Hegemann
8	Radial head	Hegemann
9	Distal radial epiphysis	De Cuveland
10	Navicular bone (wrist)	Preiser
11	Lunar bone	Kienböck
12	Metacarpal head	Dietrich
13	Bases of the middle and end phalanges	Thiemann
14	Femoral head and neck	Calvé–Legg–Perthes
15	Proximal femoral neck and proximal growth plate	
16	Patella	Sinding–Larsen–Johannson
17	Tibial head	Blount
18	Apophysis of the tibial head	Osgood–Schlatter
19	Calcaneal apophysis	Haglund/Sever
20	Talus	Vogel
21	Navicular bone (ankle)	Köhler (I)
22	Heads of the metatarsals II–IV	Freiberg-Köhler (II)
23	Bases of the proximal phalanx of the great toe	Thiemann

keep in mind. The radiograph shows at first a structural density of the necrotic area and later a more irregular structure, owing to a simultaneous resorption and new formation of bone. The articular cartilage is not affected unless there is a deformation under loading stress.

Treatment basically consists of eliminating the weight-bearing stress and improving the blood supply before operative drilling and osteotomy of the necrotic area, to facilitate the ingrowth of vascular connective tissue.

38   ASEPTIC BONE NECROSIS

Perthe's Disease

Perthe's disease, aseptic necrosis of the femoral head, is the most common bone necrosis. Onset occurs between ages 3 and 9. Relative incidence in boys and girls is 4:1. It occurs bilaterally in one of five cases and lasts for 2 to 4 years.

Symptoms. Two stages are:

1. Early stage: The patient tires quickly. Complaints vary, depending on the stress. There may be a slight limping. Abduction and rotation of the hip joint are limited. Pain advances to the thigh and the knee joint.
2. Late stage: There is persistent pain, limping, disuse atrophy of the muscles on buttocks and thigh. Adduction contracture of the hip joint and increasing deformity of the femoral head with shortening of the leg occur (Fig. 6–2).

Treatment. Without treatment, severe contractures and joint deformities can develop, which can cause early arthrosis. Conservative treatment consists of

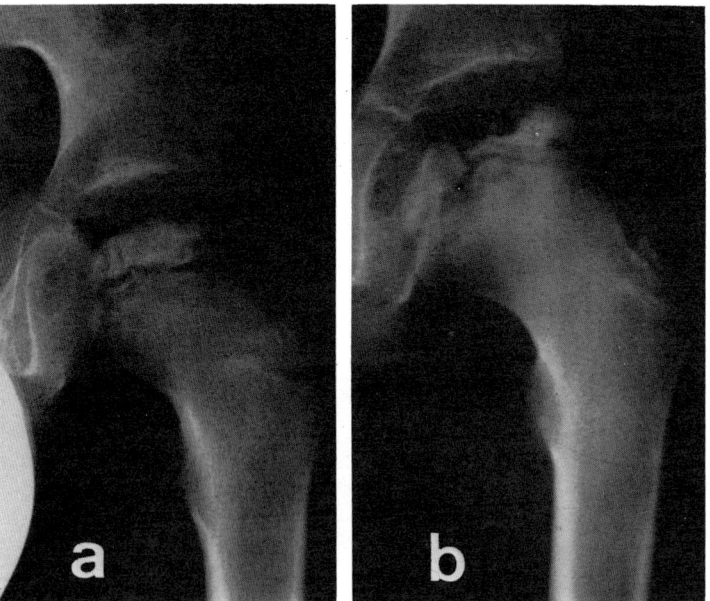

Fig. 6–2 Perthe's disease, radiological sequence. In **a:** Onset of stage II, flattening and increased density of the femoral head. **b:** Stage III, destruction of the sclerotic center of the femoral head, 20 months after **a.**

elimination of weight bearing (bed rest) until the bone structure of the femoral head appears, by radiography, to be normal. Extension or abduction and rotation, to center the femoral head within the socket, is done when applying a Thomas splint.

Operative treatment consists of improvement of the blood supply to the femoral head by implanting bone chips, drilling, or nailing (three-lamellar nail). Intertrochanteric varus osteotomy is done to stimulate the blood flow and simultaneously reduce the stress on the femoral head.

Epiphysiolysis of the Femoral Head (Epiphysiolysis Capitis Femoris, Coxa Vara Epiphysarea, Coxa Vara Adolescentium)

Origin. Aseptic necrosis of the proximal femoral epiphysis and metaphysis. Occurs during puberty in boys between ages 16 and 18 and in girls between ages 10 and 14. Boys are affected more often than girls at a ratio of 3:1. Incidence of bilateral disease is 80 percent. Complete lysis of the femoral epiphysis occurs in 10 to 15 percent of cases. Adolescents are mainly affected; their appearance

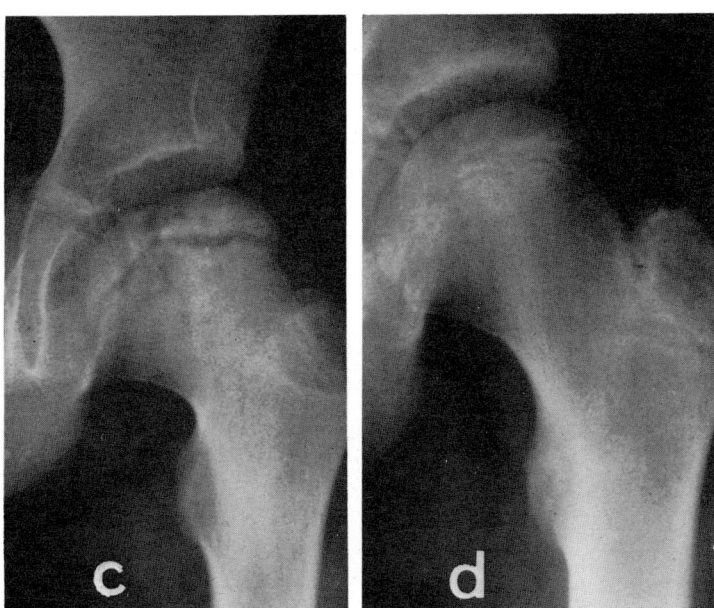

c: Late stage IV, restorative activity has not quite reached the normal structure of the femoral head, 8 months after **b. d:** Complete healing, femoral head flattened, normal bony structure, thickened femoral head, 36 months after **b.** Duration of the entire disease with conservative treatment is 5 years (from H. Cotta: Orthopädie, 4. Aufl., Thieme, Stuttgart, 1984).

results from a dystrophia adiposogenitalis (adiposogenital degeneration) or a eunuchoid overgrowth, which indicates hormonal imbalance.

The decreased weight-bearing ability of the proximal femoral growth plate results in a dislocation between the epiphysis and the femoral neck. The epiphysis of the femoral head is shifted backward and downward in 98 percent of the cases.

Symptoms. There are two typical courses: either the epiphysis shifts slowly or it dislocates suddenly.

1. Epiphysiolysis capitis femoris lenta: Slow shifting over weeks and months, causing a quick tiring of both legs. Internal rotation and abduction of the hips is limited by an increasing dislocation of the epiphyseal cap. The leg rests in external rotation. During examination of hip flexion, the thigh is forced into an increasing external rotation (Drehmann sign). In the bilateral disease the lower legs cross each other (with a 90° flexion of both knees) if the thighs are adducted (scissor symptom). The abductors of the hip become insufficient because of an elevation of the femoral neck.
2. Epiphysiolysis capitis femoris acuta: Acute disease can develop from a slowly progressing form or it can also suddenly appear without a clinical history. Acute dislocation of the epiphyseal cap (possibly in a minor accident) causes severe hip pain, weight-bearing insufficiency of the leg, and collapsing (similar to a fracture of the femoral neck). The radiographic

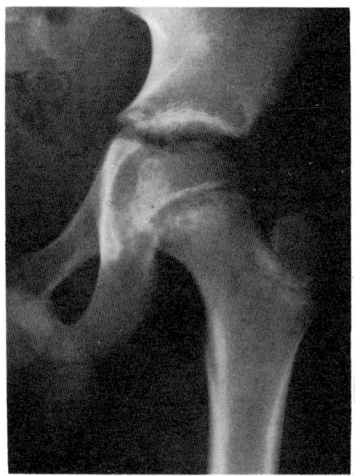 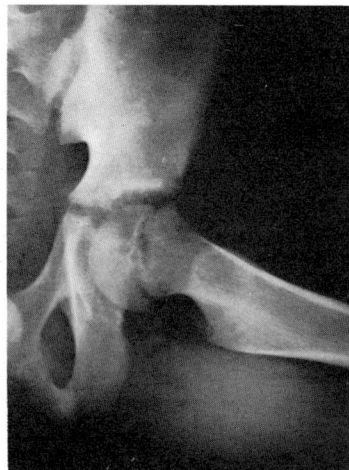

Fig. 6–3 a: Anteroposterior radiograph reveals only a minor varus position of the epiphysis. **b:** The Lauenstein position shows an obvious dislocation between the femoral neck and the epiphysis of the femoral head with the typical structural change of the femoral neck (from H. Cotta: Orthopädie, 4. Aufl., Thieme, Stuttgart, 1984).

findings from the usual pelvic view appear to be nearly normal, since the head is, in most cases, dislocated backward and downward. Another view in a Lauenstein position will reveal the typical dislocation (Figs. 6–3 and 6–4).

Treatment. Two treatments are:

1. Epiphysiolysis capitis femoris lenta: Fixation with a three-lamellar nail to a dislocation angle of 30° of the femoral head toward the femoral neck. Prophylactic fixation of the contralateral side. Weight bearing is possible after wound healing. A slight prearthrosis will remain. A dislocation greater than 30° is a prearthrotic deformity, which requires an intertrochanteric osteotomy according to Imhäuser (Fig. 6–5a) or, in severe cases, an intracervical osteotomy according to Wiberg (Fig. 6–5b).
2. Epiphysiolysis capitis femoris acuta: Closed or open reduction, followed by a fixation with Kirschner wires or a three-lamellar nail. A satisfactorily reduced hip can be partially loaded after the 4th week and completely loaded after the 12th week. There is a risk of a necrosis of the femoral head (as in a fracture of the femoral neck).

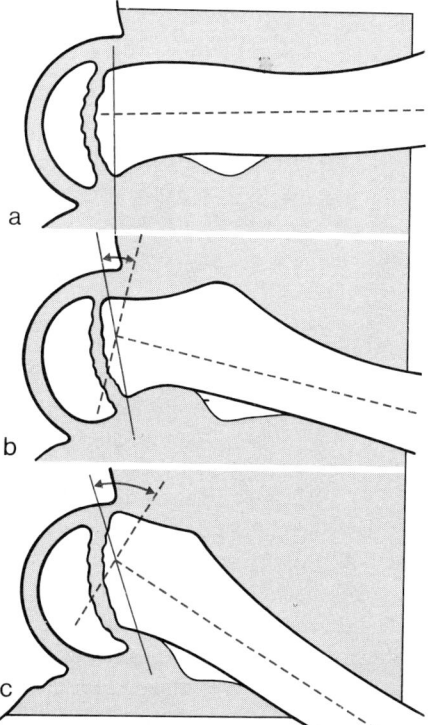

Fig. 6–4 Radiographic scheme according to Lauenstein. **a:** Normal result. **b:** Dislocation 25°. **c:** Dislocation 50° with distinct deformity of the femoral neck (from H. Cotta: Orthopädie, 4. Aufl., Thieme, Stuttgart, 1984).

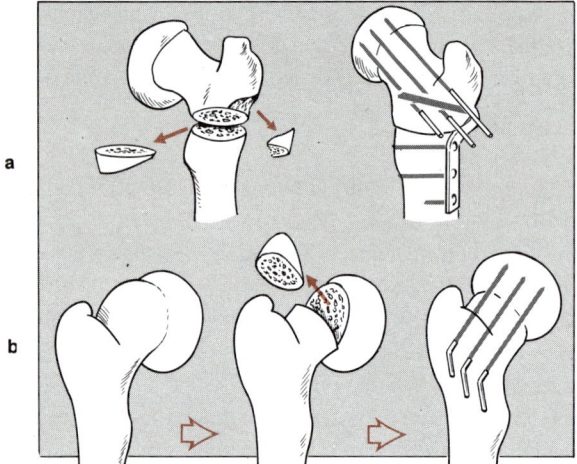

Fig. 6–5 Operative correction of an epiphysiolysis of the femoral head. **a:** Intertrochanteric two-dimensional osteotomy according to Imhäuser. **b:** Subcapital osteotomy (from P. Pitzen, H. Rössler: Kurzgefaβtes Lehrbuch der Orthopädie, 14. Aufl., Urban & Schwarzenberg, Munich, 1980).

Osteochondritis Dissecans

Origin and Etiology. Subchondral necrosis in the convex part of an articular surface. Reactive sclerosis of the healthy bony nucleus until there is complete demarcation of a bone-cartilage piece, which remains in its place or is separated completely into the articular space, where it can cause appropriate symptoms as a free body (or joint-mouse). It occurs generally in the knee, elbow, hip, and tarsal joints.

Symptoms. Prior to the formation of a free body there may be only minor pains, depending on the degree of weight bearing; occasionally effusion. Diagnosis can be made by radiography (Fig. 6–6). After the formation of a free joint body there is a sudden sharp pain and locking of the joint, which can sometimes be reversed by shaking the joint. The lesions on the articular surface can cause early arthrosis.

Treatment. During the early phase and the growing period, spontaneous healing is possible by placing the joint in a non-weight-bearing condition. In a progressive sclerosis or in older patients, treatment consists of implantation of (autologous) bone chips or spongy bone to facilitate a revascularization of the necrotic area by interrupting the sclerotic degeneration. Free bodies can be fixed by pieces of cortical bone (match size) or screws. In the hip joint the lesion can be shifted away from the area of main weight bearing by an osteotomy. Free bodies that cannot be attached are removed.

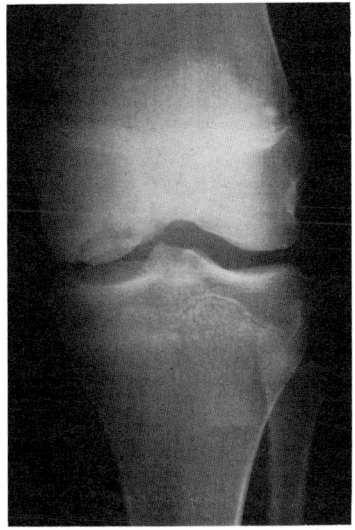

Fig. 6–6 Osteochondritis dissecans, medial femoral condyle (from H. Cotta: Orthopädie, 4. Aufl., Thieme, Stuttgart, 1984).

Schlatter's Disease (Osgood–Schlatter's Disease, Osteochondritis of the Apophysis of the Tibial Head)

Origin. Aseptic necrosis of the apophysis of the tibial head, in which the traction of the patellar ligament might be of some importance. Young males aged 2 to 15 years are affected most often.

Symptoms. Pains around the rough area of the tibia, especially during heavy use of the quadriceps muscle (as occurs in soccer playing) (Fig. 6–7a and b).

Treatment. Drastic reduction of weight bearing, possibly with a cast around the knee.

Osteochondritis of the Calcaneal Apophysis

Symptoms. Pains around the insertion of the Achilles tendon and the heel.

Treatment. Elevation of the heel by increasing the height of the shoe heel, reduced weight bearing. In cases of severer complaints, immobilization of the ankle in a cast in an equinus position for 4 to 6 weeks.

Osteochondritis of the Metatarsal Head (Köhler II Disease, Köhler-Freiberg's Disease)

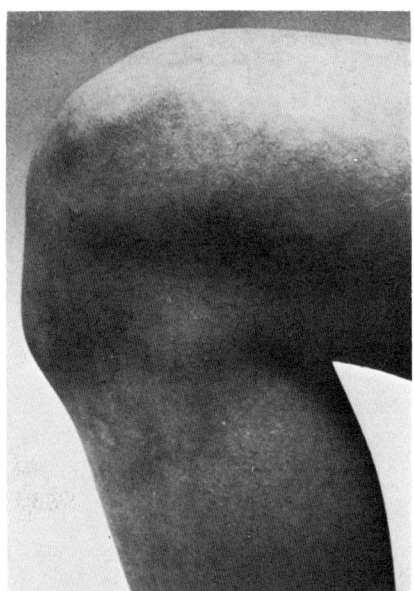

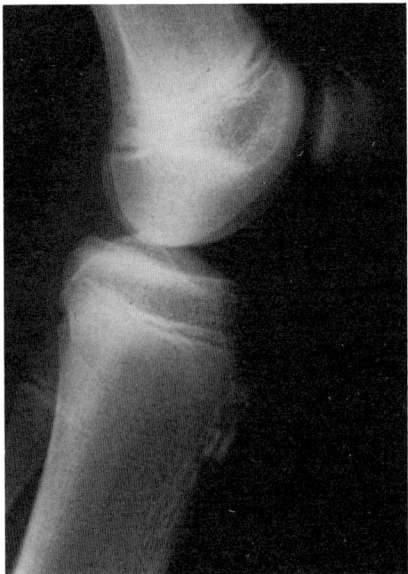

Fig. 6–7 Schlatter's disease. **a:** Swelling around the tibial tuberosity. **b:** Radiograph; segmentation of the apophysis of the tibial tuberosity (from H. Cotta: Orthopädie, 4. Aufl., Thieme, Stuttgart, 1984).

Origin. Aseptic disease of the second (rarely the third and fourth) metatarsal head, especially in a splayfoot, occurring most frequently in females.

Symptoms. Pains of the forefoot, depending on the degree of weight bearing, which can be located exactly at the affected heads of the metatarsals; characteristic radiographic findings (Fig. 6–8).

Treatment. Cast with an arch support; if complaints persist longer than the disease itself, the treatment is the same as for hammer toe.

PHYSICAL THERAPY

In the majority of aseptic bone necroses, treatment consists of a drastic reduction of weight bearing, which can be augmented by orthotic devices (such as arch support in the disease of the metatarsal heads or elevated shoe heel in a diseased calcaneal apophysis). Diseases of the apophyses and the bones of the foot do not

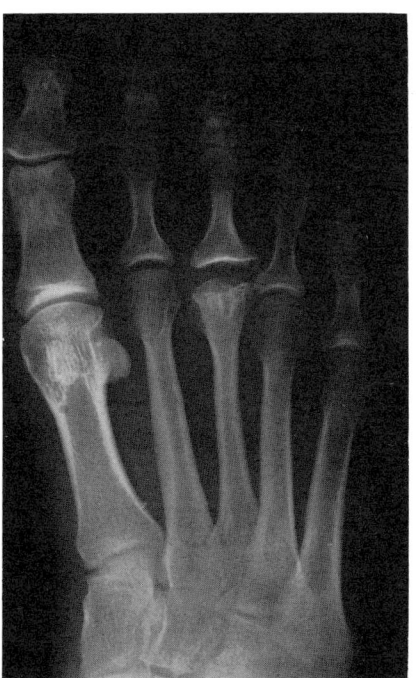

Fig. 6–8 Köhler II disease. The third metatarsal is affected; the head is flattened and broadened; enlarged basis of the proximal phalanx III by osteophytes (from H. Cotta: Orthopädie, 4. Aufl., Thieme, Stuttgart, 1984).

usually require physical therapy. Diseases of the hip joint, however, mostly require intensive treatment. Even with treatment, however, they often end in an arthrotic deformity, which will be discussed here in more detail.

Perthe's Disease

Conservative Treatment

During the immobilization period the patient is confined to bed. Therefore, to prevent atrophy of the muscles, all foot muscles and the muscles of the normal leg, without involving the diseased hip joint, are exercised, using active resistance. For the knee of the affected side, active exercises are done on the edge of the bed or in prone position, without involving the hip. Isometric contractions should be done for all thigh muscles and hip muscles on the affected side.

Physical therapy is limited to these basic exercises. Immobilization of the joint is the main treatment.

Application of Splints (Thomas Splint)

1. Ambulating and becoming accustomed to the apparatus.
2. Ambulation technique: The shoe heel of the normal side has to be sufficiently elevated. The affected leg with the splint should be approximately 1 cm shorter than the normal leg in a standing position. The leg with the splint is moved forward by elevating the affected side of the pelvis and by lateral flexion of the lumbar spine (abdominal, quadratus lumborum, and latissimus muscles). Walking up and down stairs is accomplished by first placing the unaffected foot on the next lower or upper step and then pulling the affected leg. The knee lock of the apparatus is loosened when the patient sits down. Ambulation is started with two crutches. Children generally ambulate without any aid after some time.

Postoperative Treatment

For more information, see Elongation Osteotomy, Chapter 13.

Epiphysiolysis of the Femoral Head

Acute Form

Fixation of the epiphyseal cap by Kirschner wires.
Position: Keeler splint and flap extension with 1 to 2 kg.
Postoperative (day 1): Treatment includes active exercises for both feet plus the leg.
After 1 week: Active (supported) flexion and extension for the affected hip. Isometric contractions for all leg muscles.

After 6 weeks: Ambulation with 5-kg weight bearing.
After 8 weeks: Increased weight bearing to 20 kg. Discharge from the hospital.
After 10 weeks: Reexamination. Increased weight bearing to 30 kg.
After 12 weeks : Full weight bearing, depending on the radiographic findings.

Pending slipping of the epiphysis or slipping of 30°

Nailing of the femoral head.
Position: Keeler splint and flap extension with 1 to 2 kg.
After 2 days: Active (supported) exercises; the nailing is exercise stable.
After 7 days: Ambulation with full weight bearing is possible, perhaps supported by a cane at first.
After 2 weeks: Discharge from the hospital.

Slipping of the epiphysis more than 30°

Osteotomy to correct the position (Imhäuser or Wiberg).
Position: Keeler splint with flap extension (1 to 2 kg).
After 1 day: Active exercises for both feet and the unaffected leg.
After 1 week: Active exercises (supported), flap extension only at night.
After 6 weeks: Ambulation with 5-kg weight bearing, depending on the radiographic findings.
After 8 weeks: Increased weight bearing up to 30 kg. Discharge from the hospital.
After 12 weeks: Depending on radiographic findings, full weight bearing is started.

Osteochondritis Dissecans

The postoperative physical therapy program depends on the extent of the diagnosis and the type of operation and has to be modified according to the affected joint.

Spongioplasty in the knee joint

Position: Cast for the upper leg.
After 6 weeks: Cast removal, mobilization, and activation of the knee joint, strengthening of all thigh and hip muscles, depending on the radiographic result; walking with 5-kg weight bearing. After a short introduction, treatment can be continued on an outpatient basis.
After 11 weeks: Full weight bearing based on a satisfactory radiographic finding.

Chapter 7
Aging Process of the Musculoskeletal System

H. Cotta, W. Puhl, and G. Koester

EVALUATION RESULTS IN PHYSICAL THERAPY

The active and passive parts of the evaluation procedure are designed to use differentiated techniques for the different tissue structures of the musculoskeletal system. The physical therapist learns with increasing experience to recognize age-related differences. During the evaluation it will become apparent whether the aging patient has kept himself or herself in good shape through fitness training, has been affected by long-term stress, or suffers from lack of exercise. Combining knowledge of the physiologic aging process and results of the individual's evaluation, the therapist will be able to set up a therapeutic treatment plan based on a correct understanding of the patient's situation.

CLINICAL MANIFESTATIONS

Aging of the Connective and Supportive Tissue

The connective and supportive tissue undergoes characteristic changes with increasing age. An understanding of these changes is essential for the evaluation of most orthopedic diseases. The connective and supportive tissue is highly differentiated according to its specific function. Specialized tissue systems are found in tendons, intervertebral disks, joint cartilage, bone, and muscle.

The tissue structures of the musculoskeletal system show typical wear and degeneration with increasing age. These changes contribute to clinical illnesses such as spontaneous tendon ruptures, disk lesions, osteoarthritis, osteoporosis, and decreased muscle substance. The micromorphology and biochemistry of the tissues consist of the same principal elements. The tissues are formed by cells, collagen, and amorphous intercellular substance; the bone contains additional crystalline structures (phosphate and apatite).

The intercellular substance of the cartilage, disks, and tendons consists mainly of sulfate–polysaccharide–protein complexes, which support the spatial network of collagenous fibers and fibrillar bundles and which determine the mechanical properties of the tissue, mainly through their ability to bind water. This ability is especially true for disks subjected to high pressure and for joint cartilage.

Not only do morphology and biochemistry share the same features, but the mode of nutritional supply is also similar. In the adult, the joint cartilage and the disks receive their nutrients by diffusion. Tendons, ligaments, and fasciae do have some vascular blood supply, but a considerable part of their nutrition is still dependent on diffusion. To a small extent this is also true for the bone. Optimum mechanical performance can be expected from the tissue only if the cells are able to resorb and synthesize the typical substances at the same time. The synthetic ability of the tissue can be limited not only by a decreased number of cells, but also by a decreased amount of nutritives. A decreased supply of nutritious substrates can be caused by a long diffusion distance. The initial result is a decreased synthesis and a molecular change of the tissue, followed by a change in the mechanical properties of the affected tissue and a restricted amount of diffusion owing to a higher density of the tissue.

In order to understand many diseases of geriatric orthopedics, it is necessary to ask which of the essential age-related changes of the tissue systems are known and which problems of the musculoskeletal system result from those changes. Tendons, ligaments, and fasciae contain a decreased number of cells per unit volume and lose mucopolysaccharides and water with increasing age. The number of elastic fibers also decreases. The mechanical properties of the tissue change in such a way that, with age, stretch resistance and durability increase and elasticity decreases.

The age-related loss of water and the increasing induration of the tissue cause a more direct impact (traction) on the collagenous tendon fibrils. A number of microtraumas can change a physiologic aging process into a pathological situation. The 10 to 15 percent reduction in water content interferes with the diffusion of nutritious substrates. This lack of nutrition and the reduced number of cells during aging result in decreased metabolism and the deposition of metabolic waste. Finally, the tendons are affected by necroses, calcifications, and ossifications. These so-called tendinoses are often painful. Calcifications within the tendon can be diagnosed radiographically. These areas of the tendons can rupture spontaneously from even minor impacts.

The same alterations are observed in the intervertebral disks. Their structure consists of collagen and polysaccharide–protein complexes with a high water-binding capacity, which creates the tight elasticity and is the basis for the function of the spine. The disks in a newborn are still directly connected to the vascular blood supply, but this connection gradually disappears and the disks become completely dependent on nutrition by diffusion. During the aging process the content of polysaccharide–protein complex decreases and the distribution pattern changes, accompanied by a 20 percent loss of water. The turgor of the disks decreases. These biochemical changes in the tissue cause a subsequent change in the micromorphology; the fine structure of the disk is lost, and cracks and sequesters start to form. The age-related decrease of turgor in the disks and the derangement of the tissue structure result in a variety of vertebral-related ailments.

Like the disks, the joint cartilage contains fewer cells per unit volume with increasing age, the polysaccharide–protein complex decreases, and the distribution pattern changes. The loss of water parallel to the loss of polysaccharide–protein complex causes increased density, which disturbs the diffusion of nutritious substrates. The permeability and elasticity of the tissue decrease with increasing age. The cartilage is less resistant to any kind of noxa. Each further decrease of the joint nutrition by trauma, immobilization, or vascular disease can result in a cartilaginous dystrophy and a subsequent arthrotic process. The ratio between weight bearing and weight-bearing ability is influenced unfavorably.

The bone tissue also undergoes regressive changes with age. Lack of exercise and disturbances in nutrition cause a reduction in bone remodeling. The trabecular structure changes; in particular, the transverse trabeculae decrease and the radius of the individual trabeculae becomes smaller. The cortical bone diminishes until severe osteoporotic changes occur. The bone system becomes unable to stand daily stress, and fractures start to occur.

As the largest organ system, the muscles are especially affected by aging. During the aging process the muscles lose their ability to adjust to various situations by opening, dilating, or increasing the pressure within the capillary system. This results in an accumulation of metabolic waste products in the less active and less well-supplied muscles, which causes nuclear destruction and hyaline degeneration. Finally, muscular tissue is transformed into connective tissue (myogelosis). The typical sites of muscle induration show the relation to the disturbed blood supply. The muscle insertions and the center of major muscle portions are most frequently affected.

The changes in the muscle tissue also affect the joints, in turn creating tonic changes and disturbances of the muscular blood supply. The dysfunctions within the "kinetic chain" occur in alternation: degeneration of one component always results in subsequent changes of all the other components of the musculoskeletal system.

Arthroses

Degeneration and wear of the intraarticular surfaces is called arthrosis, or arthrosis deformans. During the arthrotic process, inflammation of the joint capsule, soft tissue swelling, joint effusion, and pain can occur secondarily. The secondary inflammation of the joint capsule concomitant with the arthrosis is often incorrectly called arthritis deformans.

Origin. A variety of reasons are given for the development of an arthrosis. They can be reduced to a few basic mechanisms, which must be known in order to understand the pathological processes occurring in the joint and in order to choose between conservative and operative treatments.

The main characteristic of a healthy joint, the free gliding of the articulating surfaces, is gradually lost in arthrosis. Normal joint function depends on the integrity of the cartilage and the function of the capsule. The mechanical properties of the cartilage can be affected not only by age-related degeneration, but also by metabolic disturbances and during a joint dystrophy. The joint capsule, as the nutritional basis of the joint, undergoes age-related changes that can result in a restricted nutritional supply to the cartilage. Mechanical destruction of the cartilage is due to a disproportion between stress and durability of the intraarticular surface. The lesion can be caused by excessive stress on a normal surface, physiologic stress on a damaged surface, or physiologic use of a joint that is not lubricated sufficiently.

Excessive physiologic weight bearing can be related to congenital or acquired malpositions of the joint or can result from a joint fracture, healed in a malposition (prearthrotic deformity), or from injuries and a sudden development of an incongruity (meniscus rupture). Physiologic weight bearing can destroy the joint cartilage if its mechanical durability is reduced—for example, after a long period of immobilization—or during the physiologic aging process owing to metabolic disturbances. Physiologic use can also cause cartilaginous lesions if the lubrication mechanism of the joint does not function properly. This can occur in any kind of arthritis or in old joints, where the degree of polymerization of the hyaluronic acid in the joint (a main contributor to its lubrication) is reduced. Decreased quality and quantity of the hyaluronate–protein complexes must be considered in all diseases of the joint. All pathological situations have in common the disproportion between stress and the durability of the intraarticular surfaces. During joint motion the cartilage is torn at the surface, resulting in a primary lesion.

Not only primary mechanical but also primary enzymatic destruction of the cartilaginous surface is possible. Posttraumatic irritations and any type of arthritis increase the enzyme levels in the joint fluid. The number of granulocytes increases. Enzymatic activities originating from granulocytes, serum (hemarthrosis), and synoviocytes can destroy the cartilage. Clinical experience shows that arthrosis, like changes of the articular cartilage, can occur after arthritis. It can also occur after repeated hemorrhages into the joint cavity, in which case the enzymatic systems affect the intraarticular surfaces from the joint space and destroy them.

Enzymatic damage is also observed when cartilaginous cells die and release their enzymes, which begin to dissolve the surrounding cartilaginous matrix. The enzymes of the cartilaginous cells become pathogenetically effective. The chondrocytes die increasingly owing to the limited nutrition, which can result from diseases of the joint capsule as well as from generalized vascular disease. In addition, the nutrition of the joint is unfavorably influenced by joint immobilization. Because the blood circulation of the joint capsule is reduced and the joint motion needed to stir up the synovia as a transport medium is missing, the intracartilaginous flow of the substrate is inhibited.

After the primary mechanical or enzymatic erosion of the surface, the ensuing pathological development is based on the correlation between enzymatic and mechanical factors. The lesions interfere with the smooth gliding of the surfaces against one another, which causes even more wear (prearthrosis). The primary cartilaginous lesions are the origin of the arthrotic process, which is characterized morphologically by destruction of chondrocytes and the development of chondrocyte clusters. The enzymes and waste products set free by the cell destruction induce an irritation of the joint capsule, which in turn can interfere with the nutrition of the entire joint. The increased enzymatic activity in the joint capsule causes even further enzymatic destruction of the cartilage. The inflammation of the joint capsule causes pain, local symptoms of inflammation, a painfully limited range of motion, and, later, the development of contractures.

During the progressive destruction of the cartilaginous surface, the increased mechanical stress on the subchondral bone causes adaptive reactions and later destruction with severe joint deformities and malpositions. The destruction of the cartilage ends with abrasion of the subchondral bone, but the arthrotic process can result in a bizarre deformity of the bony joint components.

Symptoms. Arthroses are most commonly observed in the aging and the elderly and mainly in the joints of the lower extremity (hip and knee). They may also occur in adolescents and children (posttraumatic arthrosis, hemophiliac arthrosis owing to intraarticular hemorrhage, coxarthrosis after necrosis of the femoral head owing to epiphysiolysis, etc.). At first there may be only a cartilaginous friction in the joint. Later, pains are experienced during movement, especially getting up in the morning, which gradually decrease during the day, depending on the duration and extent of the stress. Muscular, capsular, and arthrogenic contractures may develop (see Chapter 8). Depressions and deformities of the intraarticular surface can cause malpositions, such as genu varum or genu valgum. Alterations of the joint capsule may not be apparent for some time, and there may be few or no complaints (latent arthrosis). However, the clinical symptoms may be distinctive (thickening of the joint capsule, local heat, pain on palpation or during movement, intraarticular effusion) and characteristic of an arthrosis (activated arthrosis). During the arthrotic process the development of severe stiffness in a malposition, abrasion of the cartilage, collapse of the intraarticular joint surfaces, overstretching of the capsular ligaments, and even complete instability of the joint is possible.

The loss of joint cartilage causes a narrowing of the joint space. The mechanical overload of the joint, in addition to the lack of cartilage, initiates a sclerosis of the subchondral bone and, later, the development of cystic spaces in the bony joint components. Severe joint incongruencies and complete blocks can occur if the cysts collapse. Osteophytes develop along the edges of the intraarticular surfaces. Finally, severe deformities and malpositions can result from the remodeled and partly collapsed surfaces (Fig. 7–1).

Treatment: Conservative Therapy. The general principles are as follows:

- Eliminate factors that can maintain or worsen the arthrotic process.
- Reduce the weight bearing of the lower extremity by one-third with the use of a cane.
- Encourage weight reduction.
- Treat diseases that can contribute to the development of an arthrosis (diabetes mellitus, varicosis).
- Avoid exposure to cold and wetness.

Joint immobilization is also allowed for a short period on the lower extremity by use of an intermittent flap extension under a traction of 1 to 4 kg.

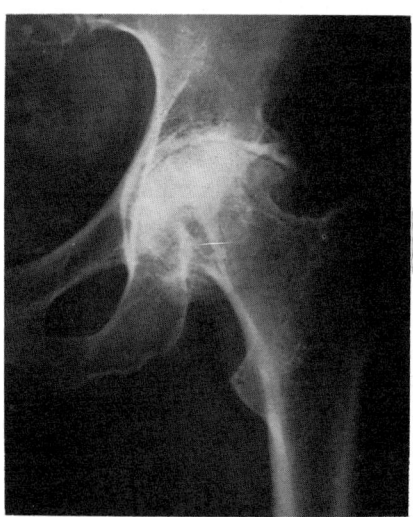

Fig. 7–1 Typical x-ray picture of an arthritic joint with narrowing of joint space and osteophytes on joint edges. There is also thickening of joint edges causing lightened areas on x-ray.

Medication. The painful inflammation of the joint capsules can be treated with antiphlogistic (antiinflammatory) drugs containing an analgesic component or with steroids, which can be given intraarticularly, or both. Side effects and contraindications must be considered. The arthrotic process of the joint capsule itself is treated with drugs that affect the deranged cartilaginous metabolism of the arthrosis (antiarthrotics). Further possibilities for drug treatment are alleviation of the painful tension by myotonolytics and psychopharmaceuticals.

Orthopedic Aids. Orthoses, orthopedic shoes, and supports to reduce weight bearing on the joints and eliminate painful movements are considered.

Physical Therapy. Heat (ice for the activated arthrosis), electrotherapy, ultrasound, massage, and exercises to loosen tensed muscles, stimulate general blood circulation, and improve range of motion in the joints.

Surgical Treatment. Depending on the situation, corrective osteotomies, synovectomies with or without additional treatment of the joint ("cleaning" and smoothing of the surfaces), partial or total joint replacement, joint resection, and arthrodeses are the procedures of choice.

PHYSICAL THERAPY

The possibilities for physical therapy are discussed in detail in connection with coxarthrosis (Chapter 12). The tissue structures should not be overstressed in exercises, and the intensity of the exercises should be determined by consultation with the physician and the patient's ability to tolerate them. Additional aids are recommended and the patient is trained, if necessary. Group exercises are encouraged. Besides the treatment related to the actual problems, therapy is also oriented toward activities of daily living. Elderly patients should preferably exercise initially in non-weight-bearing positions.

Chapter 8

Contractures

H. Cotta, W. Puhl, and G. Koester

EVALUATION RESULTS IN PHYSICAL THERAPY

Contractures are limitations of joint motion that cannot be compensated actively or passively. They can be determined by taking range-of-motion measurements. Chapter 12 deals with the specific examination of each joint.

CLINICAL MANIFESTATIONS

Contractures in one or more directions can be congenital or acquired.

Congenital Contractures

Congenital contractures generally affect several joints and are symmetric. As in clubfoot, there is often an inherited tendency. The tendency, but not the extent of a contracture, is congenital, especially contracture of several adjacent joints. Multiple contractures are frequently observed in families; however, the mode of inheritance is unknown.

Acquired Contractures

Usually only one joint is affected, except in systemic diseases (such as chronic polyarthritis, scleroderma), Sudeck's atrophy (which nearly always affects the entire extremity), or severe multiple trauma. Dysfunctions are caused by trauma, by inflammative or destructive processes, depending on the extent of the damage to the intraarticular or periarticular tissue.

Intraarticular Dysfunctions

- Joint stiffness: Ankylosis, synostosis, joint aplasia acquired after arthritis, dystrophy, destruction of the joint cartilage, congenital disturbances of the joint development
- Inhibited range of motion (joint locking): Partial free movement; acquired lesions of the intraarticular surface, free joint bodies; blocking of the intraarticular components against each other (like a jammed drawer); congenital in joint dysplasias
- Inhibited joint mobility by a disturbed gliding ability of the cartilage or the synovial fluid; chondropathies and arthroses; restoration of mobility in a destroyed or ankylotic joint is called a partial regenerate.

Periarticular Dysfunctions

The following types of contractures are related to the soft tissue:

- Capsulogenic, ligamentous: Primary shrinking of capsule and ligaments. Commonly acquired as a stiff shoulder of different origin or as stiff extension of the finger after an immobilization in an unfavorable position
- Myogenic: Congenital in aplasia, hypoplasia, and other developmental disturbances and in myopathies. Acquired by scarry adhesions (after muscle injuries); conglomerates of muscle, fascia, and periosteum (circulatory disturbances, infection); disuse (immobilization in a cast with muscle origin and insertion close together)
- Neurogenic: Result from dynamic imbalance
  —Spastic: Increased muscle tone with increased excitation of the alpha and gamma motor systems. The muscles stretch resistance can be interrupted by a stronger force (jackknife phenomenon) in congenital (myelodysplasia, spina bifida) and acquired paralyses; and in congenital (infant cerebral palsy) and acquired (hemiparesis) spastic paralyses.
  —Paralytic: Result from considerable flaccid paralysis, which progressively causes an imbalance by the dominating function of the nonparalyzed or only partially paralyzed muscles. Congenital in newborn paralysis (hereditary paralysis, Klumpke's paralysis); acquired in traumatic, inflammative, and degenerative nerve lesions
- Fibrinogenic: Mainly Dupuytren's disease and fibrosis (scar shrinking), which play a role in all periarticular contractures
- Dermatogenic: Scleroderma, but mainly scar contracture after burns
- Osseous: Bony restriction of the range of motion outside the joint by exostoses, rarely by axial deviation

- Heterotopic ossifications: Congenital (myositis ossificans congenita) or acquired (periarticular ossifications)
- Dystrophic: Posttraumatic symptoms (Sudeck's atrophy) or unknown origin (algodystrophy, reflex dystrophy) of symptoms of uncontrolled autonomous function
- Psychogenic or hysteric: Initially reversible under anesthesia.

PHYSICAL THERAPY

Conservative Treatment

The basic disease is treated first, if possible. The joints should never be immobilized longer than necessary. Nonimmobilized joints must be exercised daily. If there is an extended period of bed rest, the correct position of the extremities must be ensured to prevent development of contractures. The position of paralyzed extremities must be changed several times during the day. Flaccidly paralyzed and atonic muscles should not be stretched, but should be placed in a relaxed position, since the stretching would cause even more muscle damage and could limit the success of further physical therapy.

Prophylaxis is important. The following contractures have to be considered, since they are common:

- Equinus, caused by the pressure of the blanket
- Flexion contractures of the knee joint owing to the permanent support beneath the knee joint
- Flexion contractures of the hip from permanent support beneath the knee joint, soft mattresses that give under the buttock, elevated headpieces, and permanent elevation of the leg
- Adduction contraction of the shoulders from long-term bandaging in adduction position (airplane, Desault)
- Voluntary adduction of the shoulder done to prevent pain or paralysis of the shoulder abductors.

If extended immobilization of the shoulder is necessary and the development of a contracture is pending, the joint is placed in the most favorable functional position, which is generally the arthrodesis position of the joint. The nonimmobilized joint should be moved actively. Anxious and elderly patients need guided movements, and paralyzed patients need passive movement supported by the physical therapist.

In existing contractures, physical therapy can proceed along the following principles: facilitating procedures, active exercises, passive exercises, and active/passive exercises.

Facilitating Procedures

Goals of Therapy

- Stimulate blood flow
- Promote relaxation
- Alleviate pain
- Prevent edema.

Procedures. Active exercises are most important, using techniques according to proprioceptive neuromuscular facilitation (PNF); "rhythmic stabilization" close to the joint using a short lever or use of "hold-relax" for pain relief. The adjacent motions should always be included in the therapy program, especially if two-motion muscles of the lower extremity are involved.

- Ice application (reactive hyperemia and pain relief)
- Moist heat (if ice cannot be tolerated)
- Electrotherapy
- Massage, vibration
- Active exercise; edema is further reduced by active muscle work and elevation plus position change.

Active Exercises

Goals of Therapy

- Increase range of motion
- Strengthen muscles.

Techniques

- PNF
- Any active exercise to strengthen the muscles—both isometrically and actively, with and without use of weights.

Passive Exercises

Goal of Therapy

- Increase range of motion.

Techniques

- Use mobilization techniques only after a thorough evaluation has been done with correct identification of involved structures (loss of extensibility of joint capsule and ligaments)
- Use Quengel treatment with splint or cast (Fig. 8–1). In certain cases the technique is still indicated for contractures but only for shortened muscles. The joint motion must be free (Fig. 8–2).

Active/Passive Exercises

Goals of Therapy

- Increase range of motion
- Stretch muscle tendon
- Strengthen muscle.

Technique

- Passive phase is short and carefully done.

Example: Extension contracture of the knee, single phases of the exercise

- Quadriceps muscle is tightened against the therapist's maximum resistance until exhaustion.

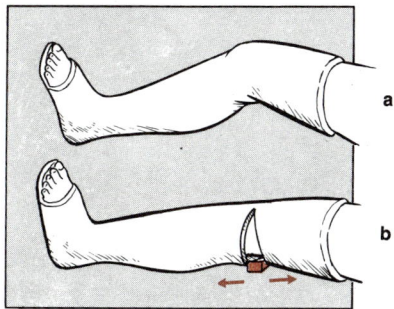

Figs. 8–1 a: Cushioned cast, which is split on the side of the flexion with a circular incision, **(b)** leaving only a dorsal bridge. Wooden blocks of increasing size are placed between the edges of the cast, the flexor tendon is stretched, and the malposition is corrected step by step (redressment in stages) (from P. Pitzen, H. Rössler: Kurzgefasstes Lehrbuch der Orthopädie, 14. Aufl., Urban & Schwarzenberg, Munich, 1980)

62 CONTRACTURES

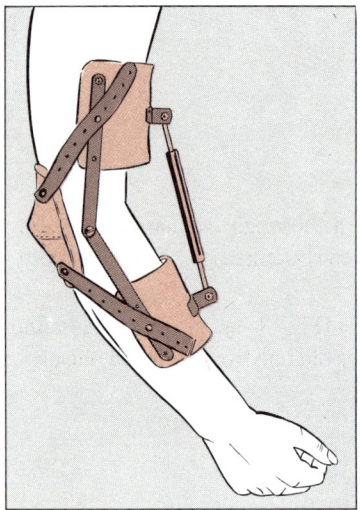

Fig. 8–2 Principal design of a Quengel splint applied to the elbow joint.

- Total relaxation is requested.
- Knee is actively pulled into extension.
- Position held against resistance at the end of the flexion range.
- Passive stretching is done by the therapist until the pain threshold is reached.
- From this final position, quadriceps muscle is tightened again. Repeat as above.

The exercises can also be repeated with applications of ice. The breaks in between should be sufficiently long so that the pain threshold is not exceeded.

The exercises can be done with movement around one axis or according to the PNF technique of contract/relax:

- Specific exercises to stretch the muscles are used for muscle shortening.
- Active/passive traction as an additional means of mobilizing shortened muscles is contraindicated in inflammation or effusion of the joint. Active/passive means that (a) the traction has an active and a passive component: the direction of the traction is passive, but the mobilizing force is active; (b) the traction is part of an active treatment (i.e., treatment of a contracture with ice application or hydrotherapy, followed by traction and exercises to strengthen the muscles).

Example

Figure 8–3 shows the position for the use of traction to treat an extension contracture of the knee joint. Holding position is in the restricted direction of motion. Flap and traction rope plus pulleys are applied vertically to the longitudinal axis of the long bone, which acts as a lever. The weight should only be as heavy as can be tolerated permanently with a relaxation of the muscle to be stretched. The treatment is started with a 5-minute traction, increasing to 20 to 30 minutes. The patient is not left alone during this time. The treatment should never be allowed to cause irritation of the joint. If irritation occurs, the treatment must be interrupted or modified. The effect of the treatment is controlled by measuring the range of motion at regular intervals and plotting the results on a graph or chart (see Fig. 1–1).

Joint Manipulation under Anesthesia

This technique is used only after intensive exercise treatment with various methods has been tried over an extended period but has not improved the condition. The only purpose is to interrupt the stagnancy of the exercises and

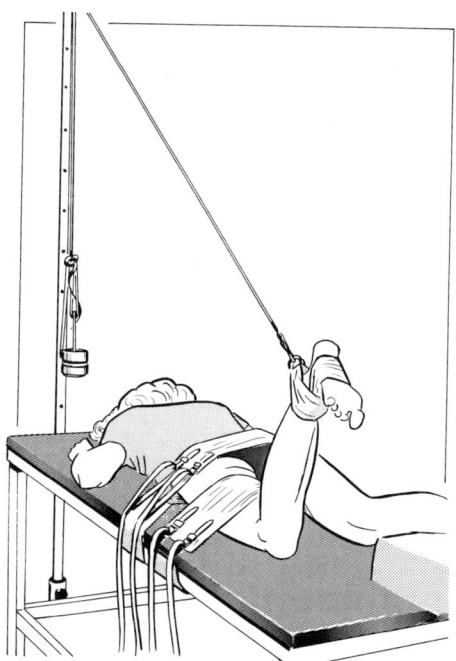

Fig. 8–3 Position for the use of traction to treat an extension contracture of the knee.

create better conditions to continue treatment. Whenever possible the therapist should attend the procedure to observe the result. While the patient is still under anesthesia, the extremity is placed in the desired position with pillows, splints, or traction. If necessary, a bivalved cast, which is especially suitable for mobilization of the knee joint, can be applied to maintain the new flexion position during the following days.

Careful active, assisted movement of the joint is started after the patient wakes up from anesthesia and while analgesic and antiinflammatory drugs are administered. The day after the manipulation the exercises are continued intensively, as are passive motions, changing positions, and ice applications. The active exercises are intensified with use of active resistive movements. Several daily treatments are necessary, which should not be interrupted even on weekends or holidays. Three days after manipulation, hydrotherapy is added to the schedule.

Operative Arthrolysis

An operative treatment is indicated in case of a complete failure of the previously outlined conservative therapy approach. Common surgical techniques include plastic surgery of the skin, elongations of tendons and fasciae, transections of capsules and tendons, and muscle and tendon transplants. Severe contractures cannot be treated sufficiently by surgery alone. They require corrective osteotomy, possibly with a concomitant shortening osteotomy. This is often the only way to achieve a correct position, weight-bearing ability, and use of the extremity.

Postoperative care depends on the type of surgery and needs to be discussed with the patient's surgeon.

Chapter 9

Inflammative Diseases of the Bones and Joints

W. Heipertz and A. tum Suden-Weickmann

An infectious disease of the bone is called osteomyelitis, or osteitis. These diseases are classified either as specific infections (tuberculosis, typhus, or syphilis) or as the more common unspecific inflammations (Fig. 9–1). Hematogenous and also exogenous acute osteomyelitis can lead to a chronic disease (secondary chronic osteomyelitis). Paget's disease, a disturbance of bone remodeling, is also characterized by inflammative reactions, and therefore is discussed in this chapter.

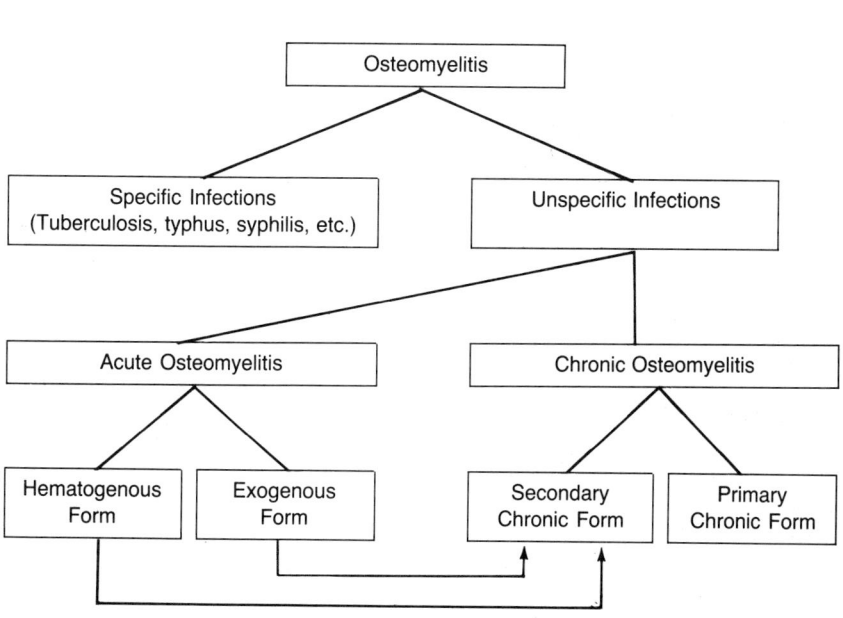

Fig. 9–1 Classification of osteomyelitis.

CLINICAL MANIFESTATIONS

Unspecific Osteomyelitis

Acute Hematogenous Osteomyelitis (Infant Osteomyelitis)

Origin. Infectious agents, transported by the blood, can grow in the bone because of the insufficient immunological defense of the newborn and the decreasing protection by maternal antibodies. The origin might be an infection of the umbilical cord, a pyoderma, or otitis. The metaphyses of the long bones are mainly affected. The infection spreads to the periosteum, causing subperiosteal abscesses and subsequent necroses owing to disturbed nutrition of the bone. Demarcation of the granulation tissue causes sequestration and more extended bone defects; osteolysis can include adjacent joints, especially the hip joint (Fig. 9–2).

Symptoms. The general symptoms are minor in an infant; after age 2 the osteomyelitis is accompanied by fever, general malaise, swelling, and local heat as signs of a serious infection. Acute hematogenous osteomyelitis is uncommon in adults; it causes less subperiosteal abscesses and sequestration but more extraperiosteal abscesses with the formation of fistulae and the tendency to turn into a secondary chronic form.

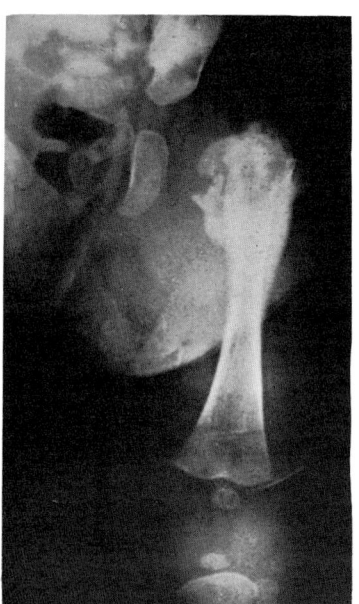

Fig. 9–2 Radiograph of the left hip and thigh in an infant coxitis (from H. Cotta: Orthopädie, 4. Aufl., Thieme, Stuttgart, 1984).

Treatment. The therapy in infants is immobilization of the affected extremities and antibiotic treatment, initially with a broad-spectrum antibiotic or a combination, which is continued with a specific antibiotic after the infectious agent has been identified. Overall, the general condition and the defense mechanism of the body is improved. In infants the necrotic area of the bone can be revitalized. In infants and older children the course and outcome of the disease are favorable, provided adequate treatment is given. Surgery can usually be avoided. Abscesses are split acutely rather than drained, to avoid a superimposed infection. In adults, surgery is indicated, such as excavation of an unspecific spondylitis (see Chapter 10), since it accelerates the healing process.

Acute Exogenous Osteomyelitis (Posttraumatic Osteomyelitis)

Origin. The acute exogenous form of osteomyelitis is caused by contact with infectious agents, usually during an injury. Compound fractures, periosteal lesions, subperiosteal hematomas, and sometimes even soft tissue injuries can cause exogenous osteomyelitis, the latter form being caused by penetration of infectious agents. Implants used in an operative fracture treatment are often the reason for an exogenous osteomyelitis.

Treatment. The course of the posttraumatic or postoperative osteomyelitis depends on the type, quantity, and virulence of the invasive infectious agent and on general and local blood circulation. Transition into a secondary chronic osteomyelitis is prevented by high doses of antibiotics, immobilization, and possibly surgical removal of the osteosynthetic material.

Secondary Chronic Osteomyelitis

Origin. Secondary chronic osteomyelitis develops from an acute endogenous or exogenous osteomyelitis. Local swelling occurs and pain increases; fistulous secretion begins to drain. Laboratory tests reveal an elevated erythrocyte sedimentation rate and progressive changes in blood cell count and differential. General symptoms worsen. Amyloidosis, which interferes with the function of internal organs, is a complication during a chronic course.

Symptoms. A sclerotic margin begins to develop around the bony osteolysis, to protect the healthy bone; sequestration is frequently observed (Fig. 9–3). Filling the fistula with a contrast medium and making contrast radiographs and tomograms can facilitate the evaluation of the fistula's size and shape and a possible connection to the joint.

Treatment. A secondary chronic osteomyelitis requires operative treatment under antibiotic coverage. The affected part of the bone is removed, sacrificing sufficient healthy tissue and excavating a depression (Fig. 9–4); a muscle flap with sufficient blood supply can be placed in this space to support healing. Chains with antibiotic-containing balls and filling spongy bone in large defects have proved

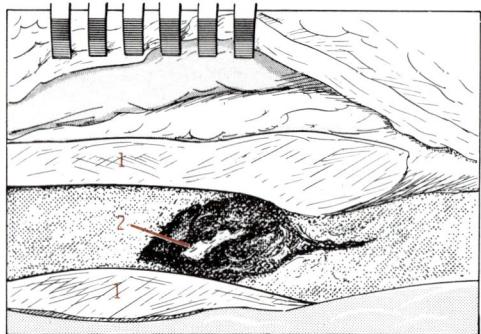

Fig. 9–3 Surgical site of a tibial osteomyelitis. 1, Sclerotic seam; 2, putrid abscess with sequestration.

successful (Fig. 9–5). Sometimes a drainage for rinsing and suctioning is also used (Fig. 9–6).

Primary Chronic Osteomyelitis

Origin. A primary chronic osteomyelitis occurs if the immunological defense mechanism of the body prevents the infection from spreading. This results in an encapsulated bony inflammation, called Brodie's abscess, and osteomyelitis sclerosans.

Symptoms. Brodie's abscess is found mainly in children and adolescents in the metaphyseal area of the long bones. The disease starts subacutely; the patient complains of pains, mostly at night, and describes a pulsating pain across the

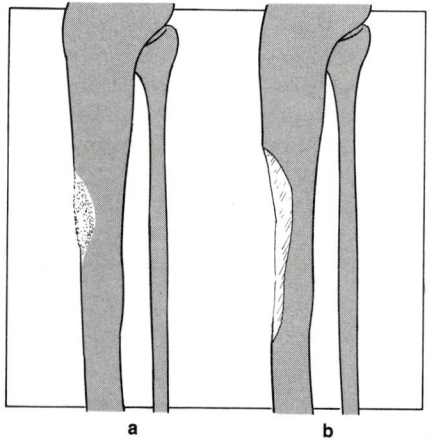

Fig. 9–4 a: Tibial osteomyelitis. **b:** Situation after the excision of the diseased area.

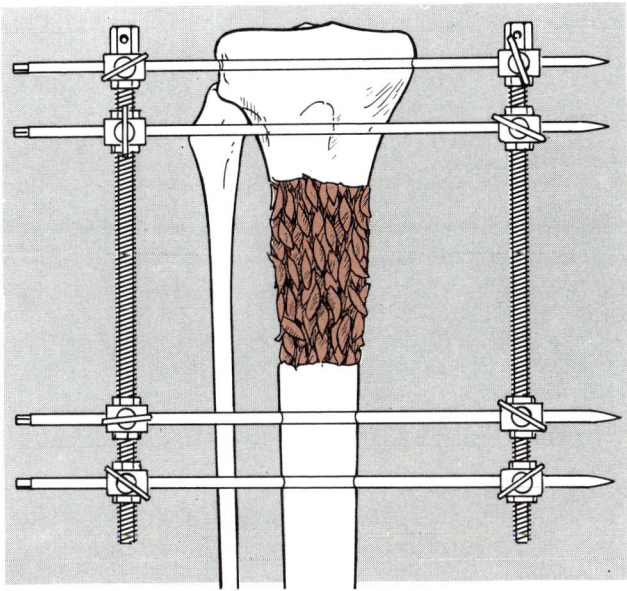

Fig. 9–5 Situation after the resection of an osteomyelitic bone segment and filling with bone chips. Immobilization with an external fixation device.

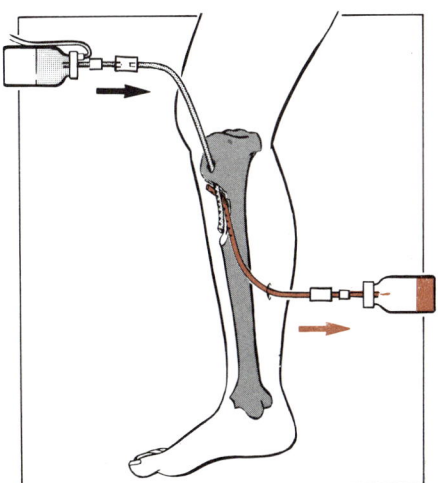

Fig. 9–6 Rinsing-sucking drainage of the excavated bone.

affected area of the bone. Radiography reveals a circular light area surrounded by a sclerotic seam, which must be differentiated from bone cysts, enchondromas, and beginning osteosarcomas. Osteomyelitis sclerosans affects the diaphyses of the long bones and can progress to the bone marrow. An osteoid osteoma must be considered as a differential diagnosis.

Treatment. Both types of primary chronic osteomyelitis require surgical intervention with removal of the diseased tissue, as described earlier (see also Figs. 9–4 through 9–6).

Specific Osteomyelitis

Origin. Specific osteomyelitis is caused by infectious agents, such as *Mycobacterium tuberculosis, Spirochaeta pallida,* or *Salmonella typhosa.* Tuberculotic osteomyelitis is most important; as an organ tuberculosis it is one of the late forms of this infection and usually develops hematogenously by spreading from pulmonary foci. The mycobacteria mainly settle in the spongy bone and the epiphyseal area.

Symptoms. The symptoms of tuberculotic osteomyelitis are initially unspecific; radiographic examination reveals a lighter area at the infection site and a calcifying atrophy of the affected skeletal part. The granulating or necrotizing osteitis can be accompanied by sequestration and formation of fistulae and by periosteal ossifications. The areas mainly affected are the spine (spondylitis tuberculosa; see Chapter 10) and the major joints. Spina ventosa is a special form in the area of the fingers.

Typical symptoms of this specific chronic osteomyelitis are elevated temperature and increased erythrocyte sedimentation rate.

Treatment. Specific osteomyelitis is treated by immobilization, antibiotics or tuberculostatics, supporting or activating measures (changing climate), and operative evacuation of the affected bone areas.

Paget's Disease (Osteitis Deformans, Osteodystrophia Deformans)

Origin. Osteitis deformans affects one or more bones. The etiology is uncertain, and today it is considered more a disturbance of bone remodeling than an inflammation.

Symptoms. The clinical symptoms are unspecific and resemble rheumatoid complaints; sometimes there are no symptoms. During the first stage, hyperemia is observed. Histopathologically, there is resorption of bone trabeculae with fibrous transformation of the medulla, accompanied by additional bone formation (mosaic structure). The bone loses its weight-bearing ability. During the second stage there is equal activity of osteoblasts and osteoclasts. During the third stage the bony sclerosis increases, the fatty medulla is transformed into fibrous tissue, and cystic cavities are formed by osteolysis, mainly in the spine and the tibiae (scabbard tibia; Fig. 9–7).

Treatment. Treatment is mainly symptomatic and includes the prevention of fractures (application of an apparatus, if necessary) and osteotomies in case of severe bending (see also Chapter 3).

Unspecific Arthritis

Arthritis is inflammation of a joint owing to various etiological and pathogenetic factors. It is classified as either unspecific (abacterial and bacterial) or specific (rheumatoid and metabolically related) arthritis.

Abacterial Joint Effusion

Origin. Abacterial joint effusions have various causes and range from serious effusion caused by overstress of an arthrotic joint (activated arthrosis) to hemorrhagic effusion in joint trauma. There can also be an underlying allergic reaction, in which repeated effusions occur in connection with a general infection ("cold of the hip" in a catarrhal infection). Younger and middle-aged patients are mainly affected. In women, joint effusions have been described in relation to the menstrual cycle.

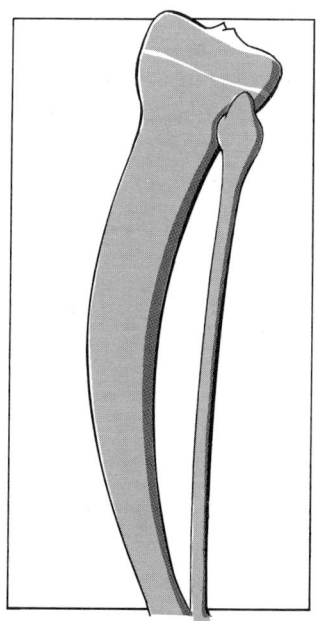

Fig. 9–7 Scabbard tibia in Paget's disease.

Joint inflammations during bacterial or viral diseases were once called rheumatoid (typhus rheumatoid); today they are named after the special infectious agent (*Yersinia monarthritis*).

Rheumatoid synovitis is caused by an allergic reaction, in which the specific antigen–antibody reaction causes an unspecific reaction of the joint capsule.

Symptoms. The joint capsule contains inflammatory infiltrates but no rheumatids (rheumatic nodules). Several joints are affected, with joint swelling by effusion or capsular swelling. Further signs of inflammation with related general signs are possible (fever, headaches, malaise) and may persist for several weeks. The radiograph does not initially reveal anything, but later shows a diffuse decalcification. Treatment is with medication (including antiinflammatory drugs) and with temporary immobilization in a functional position.

Recurrent abacterial effusions (Fig. 9–8) can cause not only immediate discomfort and reduced function, but also permanent damage by overstretching the capsule and ligaments and can result in an unstable joint. Local disturbances of blood flow can be caused by the compression of capillaries. The joint cartilage undergoes enzymatic destruction, which reduces the lubricating ability of the synovial fluid and is followed by a prearthrosis.

Treatment. Consider the underlying disease. An effusion is punctured for diagnostic reasons and to prevent capsular overstretching and cartilaginous damage. Intraarticular and periarticular inflammations and chronic polyarthritis produce a serofibrinous effusion. A hemorrhagic effusion indicates injuries of the capsule and ligaments or an internal lesion of the joint. However, recurrent intraarticular hemorrhage without external force is observed in hemophiliacs.

The therapeutic possibilities for recurrent effusions are numerous and variable, and physical therapy is important.

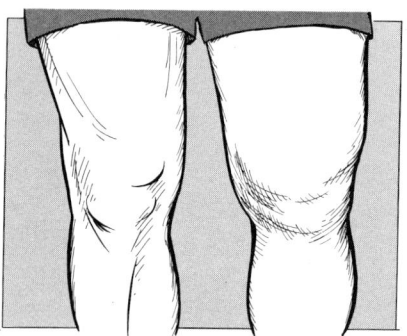

Fig. 9–8 Abacterial effusion of the knee joint.

Bacterial Joint Effusion

Origin. The infectious effusion of the joint—bacterial or purulent arthritis—is caused by the invasion of infectious agents into the joint space by way of blood (hematogenously), originating in the surrounding tissue, or exogenously. The main pathogenics are staphylococci, streptococci, pneumococci, *Escherichia coli* bacteria, and gonococci.

Direct contamination is possible not only through trauma or surgery, but also by diagnostic puncture or injection. Hematogenous infections might be due to such conditions as infections of the umbilical cord, otitis media, angina, purulent bronchitis, empyema of the gallbladder, and bacterial diseases of the urogenital system. Empyema of the joint can also be caused by disruption of an inflammative process close to a joint in an osteomyelitis, bone tuberculosis, or a periarticular process. The mostly monoarticular gonorrheal arthritis has an insidious onset and may cause an empyema; the generic (or general) infection might have occurred a long time before.

Symptoms. Bacterial arthritis destroys the cartilage and the bony joint components, which results in subsequent malpositions and contractures or fibrous and osseous ankylosis.

The affected joints are swollen, red, and hot. Weight bearing or motion is avoided because of severe pain. Range of motion is limited. The patient may feel ill in general. Fever, increased erythrocyte sedimentation rate, and leukocytosis with left shift are observed.

Radiographic examination reveals decalcification, possibly circumscribed osteolytic areas, and blurred contours of the intraarticular surfaces. Rheumatism, tuberculosis, and tumor must be excluded as differential diagnoses.

Treatment. Treatment consists of immobilization, antibiotics, punctures, and rinsing. As early as possible the position is changed and physical therapy is initiated.

Specific Arthritis

Among the specific inflammative joint diseases, tuberculous arthritis is prevalent. It is caused by dissemination of mycobacteria from a primary focus. Gonorrheal arthritis has become most serious.

The specific arthritis lueca occurs during the late stages of syphilis and mainly affects the sternoclavicular, knee, and vertebral joints. Other joints, such as wrist and ankle, can also be affected.

Joint Tuberculosis

Origin. Primary tuberculous arthritis is classified in both the synovial and the osseous form. Primary synovial joint tuberculosis is initiated by hematogenous dissemination; in the primary osseous form the specific arthritis originates from a bony focus close to the joint. A symptomatic joint effusion frequently precedes the penetration of the infection into the joint by a simultaneous reaction of the joint capsule. During the course of the arthritis the joint cartilage and the bony components are severely damaged.

Symptoms. Joint tuberculosis is mainly observed in children and young adolescents. Initially, it causes slight pain during weight bearing and during the night. Later, functional disturbances become obvious: limping, painfully limited range of motion, and muscle atrophy owing to disuse. Laboratory values indicate a chronic inflammation. Tuberculosis tests are positive. The diagnosis is confirmed by isolation of mycobacteria from the joint fluid, animal inoculation, or biopsy. Primary joint tuberculosis reveals, radiographically, a decalcification, osteolytic focus close to the joint, narrowing of the joint space, malposition, and destruction of the joint (Fig. 9–9).

Treatment. Treatment includes medication and surgical intervention with immobilization and avoidance of weight bearing until the specific inflammation subsides. Tuberculostatics and general support (climate change) are prescribed. The course of the healing, which takes years, can be accelerated by an operative evacuation of the focus. Synovectomy has proved successful in a primary synovial tuberculosis. Depending on the expansion and the course of the joint tuberculosis, resection of the joint and arthrodesis and sometimes also implantation of an endoprosthesis may be indicated.

Luetic (Syphilitic) Arthritis and Arthropathy

During the early and secondary stages of syphilis, unspecific (polyarthritislike) irritations occur, which respond to antiluetic therapy during the regression of the

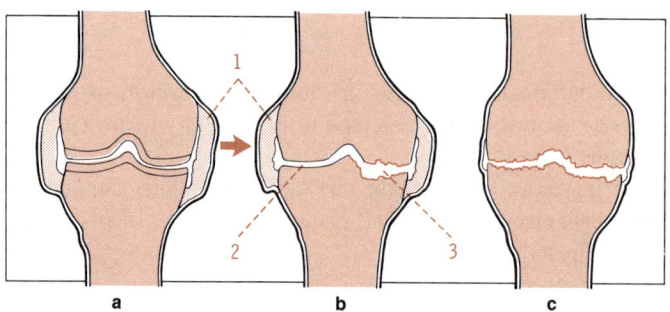

Fig. 9–9 Joint tuberculosis. **a:** Inflammation of the synovia(1). **b:** Inflammation of the synovialis(1), cartilaginous destruction(2), and bone destruction(3). **c:** Destruction of the joint, fibrous ankylosis.

syphilis. Luetic arthritis is characterized by capsular swelling and effusion during the late stage, and the exudate causes a positive Wassermann reaction. The formation of luetic nodules destroys the joint cartilage and can be verified radiologically in the transition zone between bone and cartilage. The arthropathy in tabes dorsalis is characterized by severe destruction of the bone, which causes destruction of the joint but, surprisingly, without any pain.

Rheumatic Arthritis (Joint Rheumatism)

Rheumatic arthritis is classified as either (a) acute joint rheumatism, (b) chronic polyarthritis, or (c) juvenile chronic polyarthritis (Still's disease). In addition, Reiter's disease and psoriasis arthritis are included. Rheumatoid arthritis is related to infections, with the exception of arthritis psoriatica, whose etiology is unknown. Several factors contribute, especially biological reactions related to the complex of allergic reactions.

Acute Joint Rheumatism (Polyarthritis Rheumatica Acuta, Rheumatoid Fever)

Origin. The rheumatoid fever is caused by an infection with hemolyzing streptococci. It becomes clinically obvious several weeks after the preceding disease (for example, angina, scarlet fever, erysipelas). The course of the disease may be asymptomatic or accompanied by severe clinical manifestations, such as inflammative reactions of the heart, blood vessels, lung, skeletal muscles, or skin.

Symptoms. Temperature of up to 40° C and higher may be present, as well as malaise, sweating, different degrees of pain in the joints, swelling, redness, and local heat in quickly changing locations. Children and adolescents especially are affected.

Infectious and rheumatic arthritis and osteomyelitis must be excluded as differential diagnoses. Radiographic examination of an acute rheumatic arthritis does not reveal any special results.

Treatment. Treatment is primarily conservative, with use of high doses of penicillin and subsequent long-term antibiotic prophylaxis to prevent reinfection. A pathogenic focus may have to be localized and treated (excised), such as tonsillectomy in recurrent tonsillitis. Antiinflammatory drugs and cortisone are also used. Pain usually responds well to salicylates. Bed rest is necessary until the acute symptoms subside; then physical therapy is initiated.

Chronic Polyarthritis (Primary Chronic Rheumatism, Progressive Chronic Polyarthritis)

Origin. Chronic arthritis may be caused by several factors, especially allergic (autoimmune) reactions. Constitutional factors and disturbances of the nervous system can also be involved. Climate, physical and mental stress, hemolyzing streptococci, staphylococci, mycoplasmas, or viral agents are also responsible.

Symptoms. Chronic polyarthritis is mainly found in middle-aged female patients. The small joints (finger, second and first phalangeal joints, first phalangeal joints of the toes) are affected first. Preceding clinical symptoms include a tendency to sweat, quick mental and physical exhaustion, suppressed appetite, weight loss, paleness of single fingers, and acrocyanosis. During the course of the disease, inflammatory episodes increasingly affect the general condition and the swelling of the joints (local heat, pain, stiffness). The disease of the joints progresses from distal to proximal.

With chronic polyarthritis, rheumatoid and infectious arthritis, gout, psoriasis, polyarthrosis, and tumors must be considered as a differential diagnosis.

In chronic polyarthritis the joint capsule, tendon sheaths, and mucosal linings are affected by an exudative-inflammatory process. Less frequently included are the pleura and the pericardium. Necroses can develop in the heart muscle, bone, and skin. A proliferative inflammation of the synovial membrane develops, accompanied by fibrinous exudation and tissue necroses. Along the synovial folds a granulation tissue develops (pannus), covering the joint cartilage and causing destruction of the cartilage and parts of bone components. During the chronic form, contractures start to develop, which can turn into a fibrous fixation of the joint or ankylosis. Later, the tendons in the area of the tendon sheaths undergo destruction and rupture.

Chronic polyarthritis is divided into four stages. Stage I is characterized by an inflammative thickening of the joint capsule and by joint effusion without limited range of motion or deformity. Stage II progresses to limited range of motion, muscle atrophy, inflammation of the tendon sheaths, and rheumatoid nodules. Stage III interferes considerably with the use of the affected extremity. Joint deformities, muscle atrophy, and limited range of motion are obvious (Fig. 9–10). Radiographs reveal early osteoporosis, narrowing of the joint space, and peripheral erosion during the second stage, which progress to erosion and destruction of the bone, malpositions, and subluxations during the third stage. Stage IV is characterized by partial painful stiffness, bony ankyloses, extreme axial deviations, and partial or complete functional loss of the extremities (requiring nursing care). The radiograph reveals bony decalcification, severe deformations of the joints, axial deviations, and elimination of the joint space (Fig. 9–11).

Treatment. Consider the location and the stage. During episodes and flareups of the disease antirheumatic drugs and cortisone are applied (or administered intraarticularly). Physical therapy is important for maintaining and training of function. Splints or other aids are used accordingly. Early synovectomy has proved successful as a surgical treatment. Late synovectomies, joint replacement and arthrodeses, and resections are considered in order to relieve pain and improve function (Fig. 9–12).

Clinical Manifestations 77

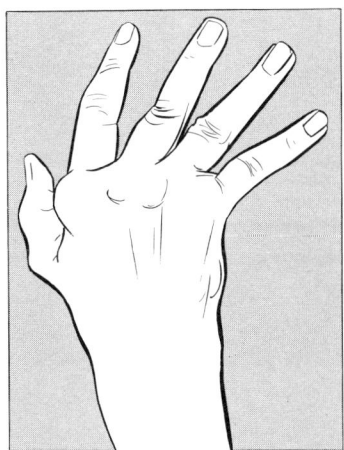

Fig. 9–10 Hand deformity in chronic polyarthritis. Ulnar deviation and malpositions of the joints in the long fingers, inflammative swelling, especially of the metacarpophalangeal joints.

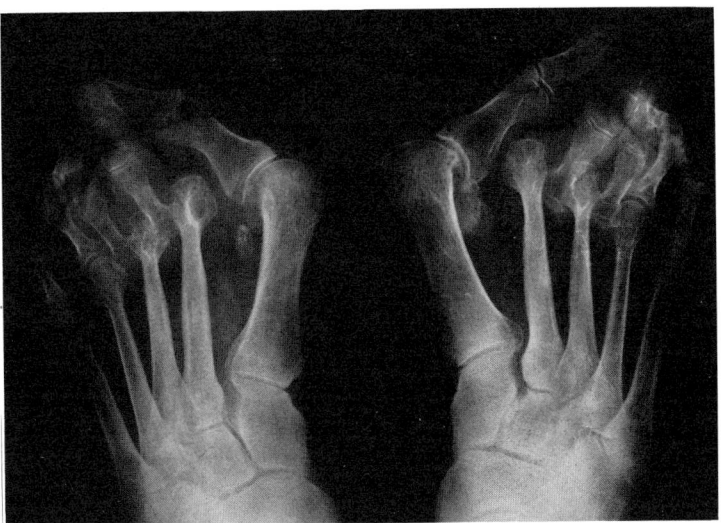

Fig. 9–11 Radiograph of both feet of 56-year-old female showing progressive rheumatic changes of the metatarsophalangeal joints.

Still's Disease (Juvenile Chronic Polyarthritis)

Origin: The etiology of Still's disease is unknown. There are two types: one resembles chronic polyarthritis in adults and has a good prognosis. The other

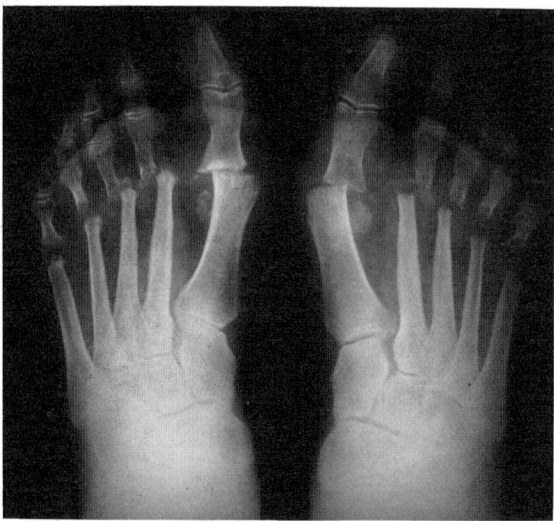

Fig. 9–12 Radiographs of the same patient after resection of metatarsal heads.

---

form, Still's syndrome, is a chronic polyarthritis in connection with swelling of the lymph nodes, spleen, and liver; myocarditis; pericarditis; and skin erythema. The mortality is 20 percent.

Symptoms. Still's disease starts with fever and swollen joints, including the joints of the cervical spine, jaws, end phalanges of the fingers, and iliosacral connection. Frequently, coxitis is the predominant manifestation. Secondary growth disturbances are noticed. The clinical symptoms can be dominated by complications originating from the internal organs.

Treatment. Antiinflammatory agents, such as cortisone and salicylates, are used in treatment. The joints mainly affected might require synovectomy. Contractures are prevented or corrected by physical therapy and use of positioning.

Reiter's Disease

Origin. Reiter's disease occurs mainly in males between ages 30 and 40 and is considered to originate from infectious and allergic reactions.

Symptoms. Reiter's syndrome is characterized by polyarthritis in connection with urethritis and conjunctivitis. The time period between a preceding infection of the urogenital system and the outbreak of Reiter's syndrome can vary from days to months.

The laboratory values indicate an inflammatory process (elevated erythrocyte sedimentation rate, and leukocytosis, which is also present in the joint fluid). The radiographic examination is unspecific. Symptoms of an arthrosis can be found after longer duration of the disease.

Treatment. The affected extremity must be weight bearing for a period of time without immobilization. Repeated position changes and exercises are indicated. Antiinflammatory drugs and antibiotics may also be administered, depending on other symptoms. Healing can be complete within several weeks; however, in some cases it can take several months, or recidivism can occur.

Ankylosing Spondylitis (Bechterew's disease, Strümpell-Marie-Bechterew's disease)

Ankylosing spondylitis is a rheumatic disease of the spine, which is discussed in Chapter 10. The Bechterew type of the disease is limited to the spine, but the Strümpell-Marie-Bechterew type also affects the large joints, especially the hip joints. Throughout the course of the disease the accelerating stiffness and malposition of the joints are treated with physical therapy. Developing ankyloses can also be treated operatively by endoprosthetic replacement.

Psoriatic Arthritis

Origin. This type of arthritis occurs frequently in families. It is based on metabolic disturbances and allergic and immunopathological processes. During its onset the typical skin symptoms are not always present. The clinical picture resembles chronic polyarthritis and arthritis urica or even polyarthrosis, depending on whether the onset is acute or subacute.

Symptoms. The typical symptoms of psoriatic arthritis are effusion, capsular swelling, and red and hot skin areas of the affected finger and toe joints. The disease causes pain and loss of function and progresses in single episodes. Frequently the sacroiliac joints, intervertebral joints, and paravertebral ligaments are also affected in an asymmetric distribution. Periostitis and peritendinitis can also develop. Bony destruction and proliferation are diagnosed radiographically.

Treatment. The disease is essentially treated as rheumatoid arthritis.

Arthritis Related to Metabolic Disturbances (Gout, Pseudogout, Chondrocalcinosis)

Among the types of arthritis related to metabolic disturbances, gout (arthritis urica) is most important. It occurs during middle age. Laboratory analysis does not always show elevated uric acid levels. In this general disease, urate crystals are deposited in the cartilaginous tissue. The affected joints (initially the metatarsophalangeal joints but also the tarsal, elbow, and knee joints) appear swollen, red, and painful, with a limited range of motion. Considering a differential diagnosis, it is important to keep in mind that in gout, mainly the distal finger joints are affected, whereas in polyarthritis rheumatica, mainly the metacarpophalangeal joints are affected.

Arthritis urica causes osteolysis during a chronic course. Radiographs reveal narrowed joint spaces and decalcifications.

Pyrophosphate gout (pseudogout) matches arthritis urica in most clinical features. It affects several joints, particularly the knee joints. Pyrophosphate crystals are deposited in the joint cartilage.

Chondrocalcinosis causes radiologically evident calcifications.

PHYSICAL THERAPY

Osteomyelitis

The physical therapy during or after an osteomyelitis is matched to the site and stage of the disease and the individual symptoms. It is aimed at strengthening the muscles that are atrophic from immobilization and at a careful mobilization of the affected joints.

The exercises are never passive, and the therapist must observe the patient carefully for any signs of adverse reactions. There is always the possibility of recidivism, which should not be increased by forceful manipulation of a pathologically limited joint.

Abacterial Joint Effusion

Treatment is usually started after the initial drug therapy, which helps to reduce the irritation of the joint. Sometimes it is necessary to start physical therapy during acute symptoms that are recurrent because of the underlying pathological condition.

Evaluation Result

Redness and swelling are observed around the joint, later accompanied by atrophy of the quadriceps muscle. The range of motion is limited, with restricted extension and painfully inhibited flexion. In longer-lasting diseases the joint becomes unstable owing to insufficiency of the capsule and ligaments.

The following measurements are taken:

- Circumference of the thigh 10 and 15 cm above the cranial edge of the patella. The lateral joint space as a reference point is not available, since it cannot be palpated on a swollen knee joint.

- Circumference of the patella (upper edge, middle part, and lower edge).
- Range of motion of the hip, knee, and ankle joints.

All measurements are compared with those of the unaffected side.

Goals of Therapy

- Reduce or eliminate the joint effusion
- Strengthen the muscles of the affected knee and the affected leg
- Train stability and mobility of the knee under increasing weight bearing.

Techniques

- Active movements of the ankle against resistance
- Isometric exercise of the affected leg
- Isometric exercise of the quadriceps muscle (Fig. 9–13)
- Active (supported) movements in supine and prone positions
- PNF patterns using "slow return" and "repeated contraction"
- Weight-bearing exercises in standing and walking
- Application of ice.

Both static and dynamic exercises are done with an ice wrapping. After an initial test of the reaction (three times during the first treatment) the wrapping can stay in place during most of the treatment (15 to 20 minutes), being changed several

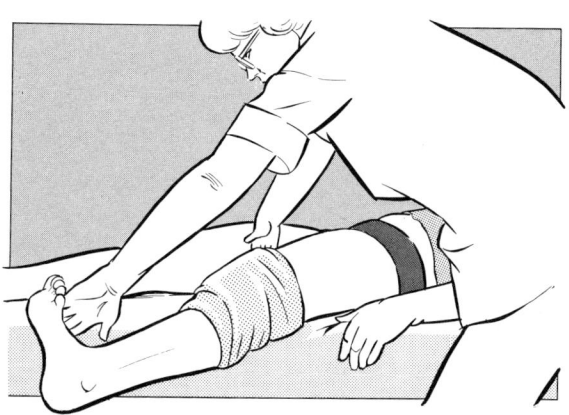

Fig. 9–13 Active motion against resistance.

times. Long-lasting application of ice without any activity is not recommended, since negative reactions (additional irritation) have been observed.

Weight bearing should be increased gradually and carefully. The circumference should be checked before and after each treatment to document the results of the treatment.

Chronic Polyarthritis

Patients with chronic polyarthritis frequently undergo orthopedic treatment during the progressive stage of the disease. Depending on the situation, conservative or surgical methods are chosen.

In order to be effective the therapist must know the principles of the disease process and the preoperative and postoperative therapy. In the following section the basis of conservative treatment in chronic polyarthritis and after synovectomy is discussed.

Evaluation Result

Progressive polyarthritis affects many joints, which must all be examined. It must be determined whether the joints are presently in an acute period of inflammation. If so, they may be swollen; the skin across the joint may be red or pale, glassy, and hot. Movements are possible (if at all) only with considerable pain or with help. The evaluation procedure must be done carefully and may initially remain incomplete regarding function.

Typical malpositions of the joints found on evaluation are:

On the Fingers

- Ulnar deviation in the metacarpophalangeal joints (Fig. 9–10)
- Buttonhole deformity (flexion of the interphalangeal joint, extension of the distal phalangeal joint)
- Swan neck deformity (hyperextension of the interphalangeal joint, flexion of the distal phalangeal joint)

On the Wrist

- Ulnar deviation and possibly volar flexion

On the Metatarsophalangeal Joint of the Great Toe

- Hallux valgus

All joints may have a limited range of motion. The muscles are accordingly atrophic and contracted. In addition to thorough joint evaluation, a functional assessment is made of the patient's remaining abilities, especially regarding his or her independence in activities of daily living. To help determine whether the patient can manage alone or with the help of others or additional aids, the patient's own assessment must be obtained and objective data gathered.

Many polyarthritic patients suffer for a number of years and must withstand frequent or permanent pain. Attitude toward the disease is an essential factor in the assessment of long-term patients, and it has to be considered more than in other patients with respect to the development of a therapy program.

Goals of Conservative Therapy

Independence is supported by the following goals of therapy:

- Pain relief
- Improvement or maintenance of function in the affected joints
- Compensation for functional deficits
- Performance of daily activities
- Facilitation of impaired functioning with the use of aids
- Psychological support

Techniques

Physical and occupational therapies are important. The therapeutic schedule is designed according to the evaluation results and the patient's present condition (acute episode or chronic situation).

- *Position.* The joints must be placed to rest in a functional position. The tendency to stiffness and contractures is high, requiring a functional position rather than a non-weight-bearing position. For example, the knee joint is not supported by a pillow, since this would cause a flexion contracture of the knee and hip joint, and weight-bearing ability would be considerably diminished.
- *Hot and cold packs.* During the chronic stage use warm baths or hot packs; during the acute episode cold packs are indicated.
- *Treatment of the joint.* Each joint is moved actively and passively until the pain threshold is reached. In an already existing malposition move the joint into a corrected position under traction.
- *Dynamic exercises.* The newly gained range of motion at involved joints is maintained or increased through active use of the muscles overlying the joint.

Complex movements of the extremities are practiced to enable performance of daily activities.
- *Changes in position.* Changing the position of the body (lying down, standing up, sitting down) is necessary, as well as climbing stairs and ambulation with additional aids if needed. Canes and walkers are especially useful, for they can be adjusted to the patient's height and can be equipped with special handles or platforms.
- *Hydrotherapy.* A variety of exercises can be done successfully in a warm tank or therapeutic pool, where the patient feels pain-free and stimulated.
- *Exercise program.* An independent exercise program should be designed for each patient in addition to all other treatments. It must be simple enough to be done at home and must include movement of each joint so that range of motion can be maintained and possibly improved. Experience shows that especially severely handicapped rheumatic patients have surprising energy and independence, which only needs to be encouraged.

Examples of exercises are related to the procedures discussed and depend on the treatment of one or several joints.

Early and Late Synovectomy

The physical therapy of early and late synovectomy involves the following goals:

- Utilization of the joint that has been improved by the surgical procedure
- In an early synovectomy, complete functional restoration of the joint or at least, as in a late synovectomy, restoration of function as good as that before the operation.

Physical therapy starts on the first postoperative day. Initially, treatment is limited by the postoperative bandages but is oriented toward the affected joint and the affected extremity, which is considered a functional unit. The extremities are placed in splints and the position of the affected joint is changed after several hours. The optimum range of motion can be reached only if the postoperative treatment is pursued immediately and vigorously. In case of severe pain, analgesics may be administered before treatment. The application of ice might also be helpful and is recommended, as soon as permitted by the removal of some of the postoperative bandages.

During the first few days the exercises must be supported. Muscle tone is achieved by isometric exercise. As soon as possible, the exercises are intensified by resistance. Complex movements are added later in preparation for coordination activities and activities of daily living skills training.

After a synovectomy, the goal of physical therapy should be aimed at restoring the function of the joint, for example, extension of the knee joint.

Arthritis Related to Metabolic Disturbances

Physical therapy of metabolically related arthritis is the same as in rheumatoid arthritis.

Chapter 10

Diseases of the Spine and Trunk

W. Heipertz and A. tum Suden-Weickmann

STRUCTURE AND FUNCTION OF THE SPINE

The spine consists of several tissues combined in the formation of the axial skeleton, the main component of the musculoskeletal system. The spine plays an important part in statics, dynamics, and proprioception; it also protects the spinal cord. Last, but not least, it serves as a means of emotional expression. Disturbance of one spinal function affects other functions of the body.

The shape of the spine might be compared to a bent feather. In posterior view it is straight; in lateral view it is curved slightly in an S shape. The combination of solid components (bony vertebrae) and elastic components (discs, ligaments) allows motion in all directions with a high degree of stability. Owing to its location above the sacrum, the spine is included in the statics of pelvis and legs. The load put on the spine by the trunk, shoulder girdle, and upper extremities is increased by the head, which is balanced freely with a wide range of available motion.

The shape of the vertebrae differs within the spinal segments (cervical, thoracic, and lumbar). The intervertebral disks together with the vertebral joints and ligaments form the so-called mobile segment (Junghanns) (Fig. 10–1).

Ligaments are passive elements of fixation that connect the components of the spine. The back muscles are the active elements; they are divided into a superficial group, developed from the upper extremities, and a deep group, consisting of autochthonous muscles. The erector spinae muscle runs from the pelvis to the transverse vertebral process and to the ribs and connects the single vertebra with short fibers. The abdominal muscles work synergistically in an upright position; they work antagonistically to the back muscles when the trunk is flexed.

Malfunctions of the spine lead to disease. In segmental disturbances the close relation of the spine to vessels and parts of the central nervous system is most important. The nerve roots, with their surrounding tissue, leave the spinal cord through the intervertebral foramina. The autonomous nervous system also plays a

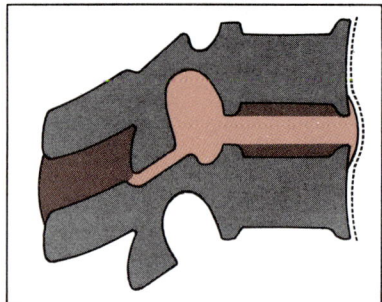

Fig. 10–1 Mobile segment according to Junghanns (between two vertebral bodies with arch and spinous process: intervertebral disk, foramen, small joints, interspinous ligament).

role in dynamic malfunctions. The clinical symptoms are varied and require a thorough examination and correct interpretation of the results (Fig. 10–2).

Symmetrically functional examination techniques and exactly defined tests are usually preferred in diagnosing malfunctions of the spine, in which results are only prerequisites for the diagnosis and not the diagnosis itself. In addition to clinical evaluation and examination of mobility, postural changes are determined and replication of pain during movements is evaluated. Differential diagnosis requires careful examination and critical evaluation; this is obvious in comparing the clinical results for hypermobility and hypomobility, which are different only in points 5 and 6 in Table 10–1.

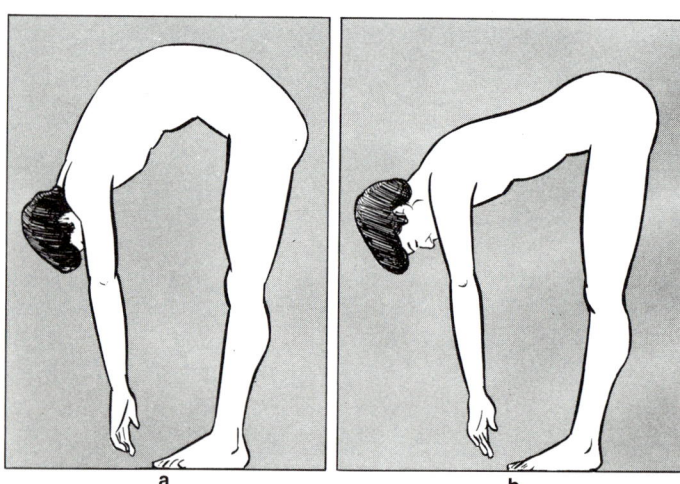

Fig. 10–2 In **a:** Flexion of the trunk shows good curvature of the spine. **b:** Stronger flexion of the hip joint can mask the malfunction of rigid spine.

Table 10–1 Clinical results in hypermobility and in a block

Aspect	Hypermobility (increased segmental mobility)	Block (decreased segmental mobility)
1. Pain	Locally spreading Projection pain Pseudoradicular Autonomous	Locally spreading Projection pain Pseudoradicular Autonomous
2. Muscles	Tensed	Tensed
3. Subcutaneous tissue	Swollen	Swollen
4. Pain on palpation	Positive	Positive
5. Overall motility	Increased	Limited(?)
6. Segmental motility	Increased	Limited

EVALUATION RESULTS IN PHYSICAL THERAPY

Evaluation of a patient with a spinal lesion always includes consideration of posture and movements. The postural and functional status can be assessed only by observing the patient in a standing position. The examination room must be of sufficient size to allow the patient's posture and motions to be evaluated from a distance, and a good light source is necessary to avoid shadows, which could be mistaken for an asymmetry. A simple aid to having the patient take a standing position is to place a board on the floor with footprints painted on it, on which the patient places his or her feet.

The initial evaluation is time-consuming, and the patient must stand still for some time. In attempting to maintain this posture, the patient may become tense and rigid and experience a drop in blood pressure. It is helpful to let the patient walk a few steps occasionally during the evaluation procedure. At first the patient's general posture is observed (firm, relaxed, flaccid). Observation of a single plane of the patient's body at a time may reveal significant deviations from the norm.

Frontal Plane

- Weight bearing on the legs
- Pelvic shifting
- Lateral deviation of the spine

Sagittal Plane

- Weight bearing on the legs
- Pelvic position
- Deviation of the spine

Transverse Plane

- Position of pelvis and shoulder girdle to each other

Next, the posture is evaluated in detail. This requires an ability to observe, which is done by a systematic comparison of bony landmarks of the body on both sides. Because the lower extremities are the basis of the posture, they are examined first. Then the patient, wearing only shorts, in a room with ample lighting, is observed. He or she stands on a level floor (feet at the same level), in a resting position. Initially, the patient is observed for general impressions of frame type, posture, and difference between resting and standing position. Then the following specific observations are made.

Dorsal View (Fig. 10–3a)

1. Position of the heels
2. Position of the lower legs (possibly circumference)
3. Level of the folds in the popliteal space
4. Position of the thighs (possibly circumference)
5. Height of the gluteal folds
6. Posterior superior iliac spines
7. Iliac crests
8. Waistline
9. Position of the spine
10. Thoracic shape
11. Level of the lower angles of the scapula
12. Position of the scapula
13. Distance between scapula and spine
14. Height of the shoulders
15. Position of the head.

Ventral View (Fig. 10–3b)

1. Feet—longitudinal and transverse arch
2. Position of the great toes
3. Patella
4. Possibly position of lower leg and thigh
5. Position of the greater trochanter
6. Anterior superior iliac spines
7. Iliac crests
8. Lower thoracic border, epigastric angle, thoracic shape
9. Position of the sternum

Evaluation Results in Physical Therapy 91

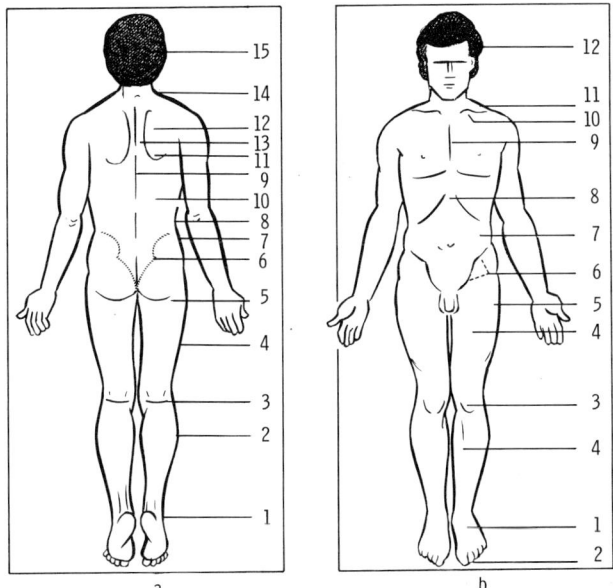

Fig. 10-3 Posture chart—dorsal and ventral views.

10. Position of the clavicle
11. Shoulder level
12. Position of the head.

Lateral View (Fig. 10-4)

1. Weight bearing of the feet
2. Position of knee and hip joints
3. Position of the pelvis
4. Lumbar spine
5. Thoracic spine
6. Cervical spine (head)
7. Postural reactions: legs, trunk, head.

The observation is completed by analzying the positions of body segments to one another, starting caudally in a standing position:

- Hindfoot to forefoot
- Lower leg to longitudinal axis of the foot
- Forefoot to thigh

92 Diseases of the Spine and Trunk

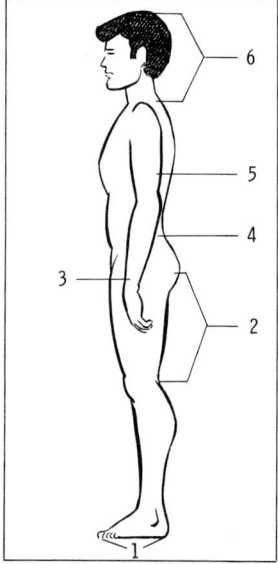

Fig. 10–4 Posture chart—lateral view.

- Pelvis to thigh
- Lumbar spine to pelvis
- Thoracic spine to lumbar spine
- Cervical spine to thoracic spine
- Head to cervical spine
- Shoulder girdle to the thorax, thorax to position of the arms.

The evaluation proceeds from lateral to ventral to dorsal. The assessment of posture is a necessary but time-consuming procedure. Frequent practice accelerates the procedure, and the feedback received also influences one's effectiveness in other areas of the evaluation.

The mobility of the spine must be examined in three dimensions: flexion/extension; lateral flexion of the cervical, thoracic, and lumbar spines; rotation of the cervical and thoracic spines.

Lateral deviations and rotatory malpositions are noticed in a flexion position, while standing in front of or behind the patient. A tangential view of each spinal segment can be checked separately, while the patient gradually moves from hip and spine flexion into an upright position. Minor, but important, deviations can be detected in this way. In the lateral view of trunk flexion, hypomobile segments show up as uneven curvature of the spine.

The patient's gait must also be evaluated in a spinal examination as well as other activities, such as bending down, lifting and carrying objects, and changing positions. The following measurements can also be taken to complete the evaluation:

- Chest expansion—circumference of the thorax measured at three levels: beneath the arms, at the tip of the sternum, and 5 cm caudally in a neutral (resting) position while inhaling and exhaling
- Vital capacity
- Deviation from a plumb line dropped from the back of the head (Fig. 10–5)
- Distance between the fingertips and the floor during forward flexion of the spine (including hip flexion)
- Distance between the fingertips and the floor during lateral flexion of the spine
- Height in sitting and standing positions
- Schober sign: Mark the spinous process of the fifth lumbar vertebra and make another mark 10 cm cranially. If normal range of motion exists, the distance during forward flexion increases approximately 5 cm.

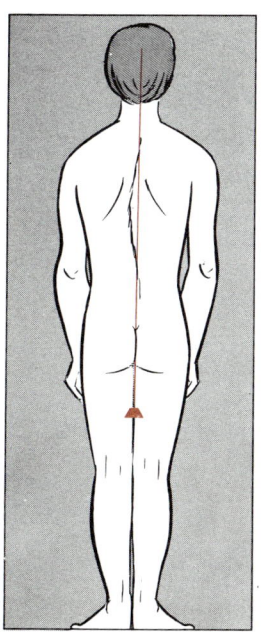

Fig. 10–5 Assessment of the posture—perpendicular line, dorsal view.

- Ott sign: Mark the spinous process of the seventh cervical vertebra and make another mark 30 cm caudally. If normal range of motion exists, the distance during flexion increases 2 cm.
- Distance between the chin and the sternal notch during flexion/extension of the cervical spine in centimeters (no normal values available).

The joints of the proximal and distal extremities are examined, if necessary. A detailed examination result must be obtained if a posture is based on foot deformities or pareses of the lower extremities.

The upright position shows the strength of the erecting muscles. The strength of single muscle groups is determined by carrying out a manual muscle test. This may be done by testing muscle according to segmental innervation.

Because the visual and functional results of the examination of posture and mobility overlap or supplement each other, palpation follows afterward in this evaluation procedure. Muscle tone, tensions, indurations, and contractures are also evaluated.

Physical therapy of diseases or lesions of the spine is similar. Each of the following sections is as complete as possible in itself and serves as a source of reference. For this reason some repetitions or similarities of the exercise examples cannot be avoided.

POSTURAL WEAKNESS AND MALPOSITIONS

The upright position of the human requires the muscles to work against gravity. A postural weakness exists if the upright position with the arms extended forward cannot be maintained for at least 30 seconds (test according to Matthiass). Posture is also influenced by the actual ability of the muscles, by mental status, and by constitutional factors. The spinal curvature and shape of the back undergo specific development from the time of birth. During the first year the wide kyphotic curvature of the thoracic and lumbar spines increases, whereas a physiologic lordosis of the lumbar spine starts to develop as soon as standing and walking are learned. Finally, the three physiologic spinal curvatures—cervical lordosis, thoracic kyphosis, and lumbar lordosis—are complete (Fig. 10–6).

Depending on the muscle work, Debrunner distinguishes the following normal positions:

- Habitual posture: resting tone, middle thoracic kyphosis, and lumbar lordosis; the perpendicular line from the vertex of the thoracic kyphosis touches the sacrum
- Resting position: tiring of the muscles, decreased muscle tone, diminished attention causes increased thoracic kyphosis and lumbar lordosis; the perpen-

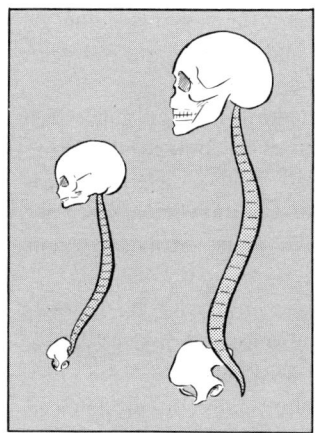

Fig. 10–6 Curvature of the spine of a newborn **(a)** and in an adult **(b)**.

dicular line from the vertex of the thoracic kyphosis touches behind the sacrum (relaxed position)
- Upright position (request to straighten up as much as possible): actively stretched spine and decreased pelvic tilt; the perpendicular line from the vertex of the thoracic kyphosis touches the sacrum or slightly in front of it
- Scoliotic position: lateral deviation of the spinous processes owing to a tilted pelvis or pain; not to be confused with scoliosis, which is characterized by fixation of the lateral deviation.

Lateral deviations (not fixed) are also observed in an "insecure posture," especially during periods of accelerated growth and in combination with diseases, which weaken the general condition.

An actual position is only part of the entire process, the antagonism between gravity and the body's own forces. Therefore, the evaluation of posture and the definition of the results are difficult. Posture is a dynamic process, even if it means maintaining a status. The degree of disease varies in postural deviations, which can be corrected; it is minor, for example, in weak posture resulting from lack of performance but with intact functional ability. Weak posture based on an emotional disturbance or insufficient physical training is more questionable and may be a symptom of endangered health. Deterioration of the posture and malpositions are definitely serious signs of disease.

Malpositions are based on pathological changes of the spine. They are usually characterized by limitations of mobility and by axial deviations. The extent of the disturbance is worsened by lack of exercise.

Owing to constitutional irregularities in the structure of the axial skeleton, the vertebral body is changed; there are uneven edges and laminae and decreased intervertebral spaces, which cannot be compensated any longer.

Malpositions are classified as kyphosis, kyphosis/lordosis, and a flat back (Fig. 10–7). Unlike postural weaknesses, malpositions of the spine resulting from a congenital tendency cannot be completely corrected. Without adequate treatment they tend to worsen. Because of a continuous disproportion between weight-bearing ability and weight-bearing stress, the spine develops secondary lesions and early signs of wear.

In a kyphotic back (humpback) the shoulder girdle is protracted, the thorax is flat, and respiratory efficiency is decreased. The physiologic thoracic kyphosis increases owing to the effects of gravity and muscle weakness.

In kyphosis/lordosis the thoracic and lumbar curvatures are more pronounced, the pelvis is tilted forward, and the abdominal muscles are flaccid. The body bulges forward (Fig. 10–8).

In a flat back the physiologic curvatures are less pronounced than normal. The lumbar lordosis can be eliminated or even changed into a slight kyphosis. A flat back limits the weight-bearing ability in adolescents and adults more than a kyphotic back.

Physical Therapy

The therapy program consists of intensive exercises. Over a long period additional orthopedic aids or corrective splints can be used together with therapy, depending on the severity of the malposition (Fig. 10–9).

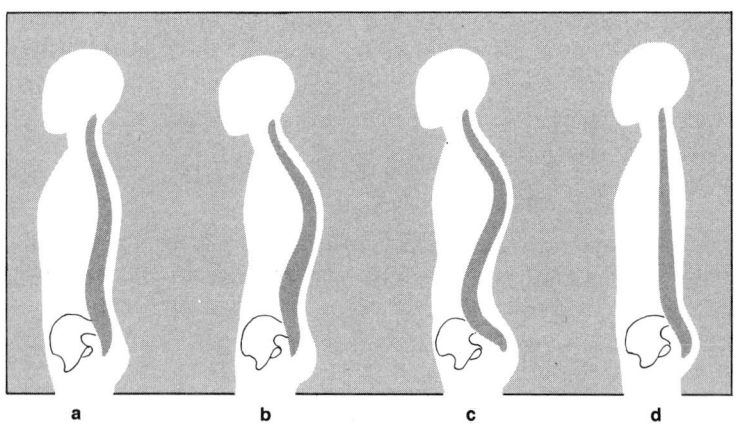

Fig. 10–7 The human posture. In **a**, normal upright position; **b:** kyphosis; **c:** kyphosis/lordosis; **d:** flat back.

Postural Weakness and Malpositions 97

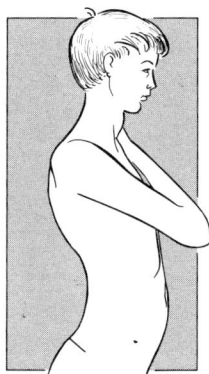

Fig. 10–8 Distinct kyphosis/lordosis in an adolescent.

Swimming and horseback riding are especially suitable therapeutic sports. Special gymnastics should be offered in school, although regular exercise lessons for all schoolchildren would be even more advantageous to counteract the deterioration of the posture caused by long periods of sitting.

Many children and adolescents do not exercise more than twice a week, which is not enough to correct their posture. Together with their parents, they should be taught how to exercise on their own in addition to the exercises done as part of their therapy. The therapist should check on the success of the home exercises at regular intervals. A prerequisite for a regular fitness program is a choice of interesting exercises. A suitable piece of equipment for home exercise is a therapeutic ball.

Goals of Therapy

- Train the entire person in posture and movements.
- Motivate the patient to be active in exercises and sports.

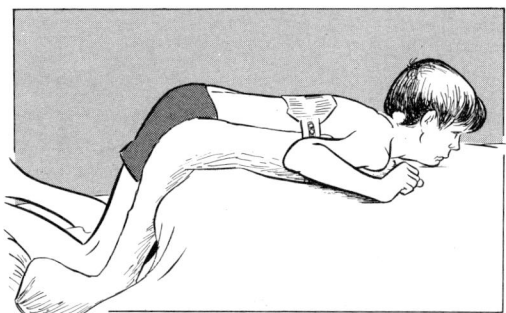

Fig. 10–9 Open corrective cast to compensate the pathologically increased thoracic kyphosis.

Specifically:

- Improve muscle strength and coordination.
- Exercise within limitations.
- Correct deformities.
- Teach new movement and position patterns.
- Offer suggestions for changes in activities of daily living.

Techniques

Children with weak posture should be treated only in small groups. Children with malpositions can also work in small groups, provided they undergo additional corrective treatment. Because physical therapy can be successful only if it is applied regularly over an extended period, the children must be motivated so that they look forward to attending the lessons.

The sessions are started with an upbeat warm-up, walking, and running routine, including exercises for the feet and extension of the trunk. Then the muscles of the abdomen and back are exercised in a prone/supine position, on all fours, sitting on the heels, kneeling, and in a standing position. Exercises for the feet and respiration are scheduled in between. The exercises are modified by using equipment such as a rod, heavy ball, or rope and might be accompanied by music. The training can be continued with stall bars, benches, bars, ladders, a springboard, therapeutic balls, or tilting boards.

It is important that the exercises always have a corrective effect and that coordination of muscles is emphasized during training of tone and strength. The basic principles of postural training are repeated in a little play at the end of the session. Motivation and ambition must be stimulated in the children.

Foot exercises belong in every posture training session to create a good base for the upright position. Each postural exercise is finished in this position. Visual observation in the mirror helps the child to understand the correction.

The child and his or her parents (or family members) should also be instructed in the child's home exercise program. This may include suggestions for modifying activities of daily living. The home program should be monitored at regular intervals.

Whenever possible reading and learning should be done in a prone position (with a supporting pillow in severe lordosis); writing should be in a chair with back support and on a sufficiently high and possibly tilted table.

The following sports are suggested:

- Swimming: This is of fundamental importance and should be learned.

Postural Weakness and Malpositions

- Ball games: In volleyball and basketball, total extension is constantly required and a possible increase of lordosis is counteracted by intensive use of the arms.
- Floor gymnastics: A selection of exercises is presented below.

Exercise Examples. The following exercise examples emphasize the particular muscle mentioned, but other muscles are also involved.

Exercises for the Back Muscles

- In quadriped: The left arm and the right leg support the body on the mat; the right elbow and left knee touch each other beneath the stomach and are extended diagonally. The exercise is intensified by rotation, extended time, and accelerated speed (Fig. 10–10).
- Dynamically concentric and eccentric work, especially with the extensors of the back (Fig. 10–11). Sitting on the heels: the forehead touches the floor,

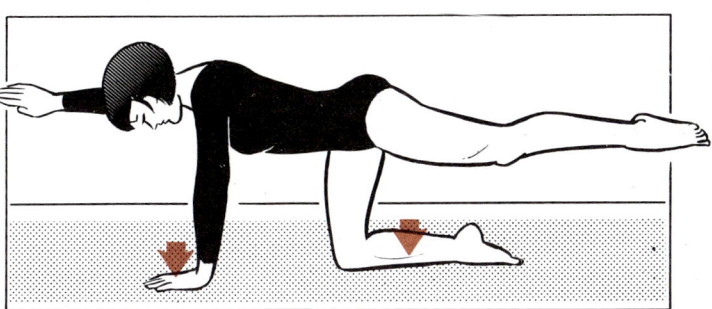

Fig. 10–10 In quadriped—static work of the back muscles.

Fig. 10–11 Dynamically concentric and eccentric work of the back extensors.

hands are folded behind the head, upper body and head are raised until an upright extended position of the spine is attained and are then lowered. The exercise is done in slow motion and can be modified by different positions of the arms, lateral flexion, and rotation during the extension.
- Balance training with partner: In kneeling, throwing of a ball by moving the trunk forward increases the tone of the back muscles.

Exercises for the Abdominal Muscles

- Supine position, legs angled, and feet on the floor; knees are pulled up to the torso and then the legs are extended straight up. The legs—closely parallel to each other—are moved to the right and left sides, forward and backward, only to the point where the back remains flat on the floor.
- Exercises initiated by the upper body tone back muscles and train balance (Fig. 10–12): Sitting position with extended legs; a rod is held with both hands in front of the body, moving both legs behind each other across the rod. The thighs are placed on the rod and the body is laid back down on the floor. The knee joints are alternately bent and stretched.
- Balance training in kneeling (Fig. 10–13): The trunk is tilted back by increased flexion of the knee joints and increased tone of the back muscles. Back and hips are not bent.

Coordination and Reaction Exercises

- Exercising on the balance beam: From simple walking to special steps on tiptoe, moving one foot behind the other with different length of stride and

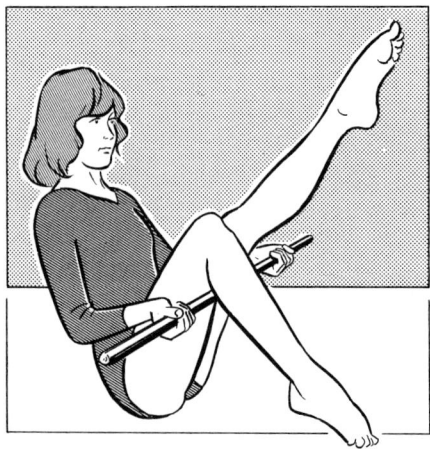

Fig. 10–12 Exercising the abdominal muscles and maintaining equilibrium.

Postural Weakness and Malpositions 101

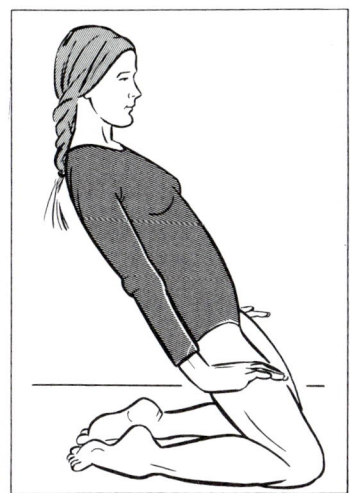

Fig. 10–13 Maintaining equilibrium in a kneeling position.

increased speed. A ring is worn on top of the head to emphasize maintaining of the upright position.

- Balancing exercises on a tilt board (Fig. 10–14): Sitting Indian-style, group members sit behind one another. One member rocks the board, while the

Fig. 10–14 Balancing on a tilt board.

others keep their upright position with the head as high as possible. This exercise can also be done with a disk or ring on the head.
- Balancing on a therapeutic ball (Fig. 10–15), while alternating flexion and extension of the spine. Initial position: sitting on the heels, and then rolling the stomach across the ball, while the hands move forward on the floor; rolling until the thigh/knee is on the ball; moving the ball beneath the trunk by flexion of the knees and hips and then moving the ball back into the initial position by extension of the legs. The hands remain tightly on the floor.

Special Exercises for a Flat Back

- Klapp's crawling (walking on all fours to mobilize the spine, especially in the lateral direction; Fig. 10–16): Swinging motions are performed in a crosswise gait or ambling.

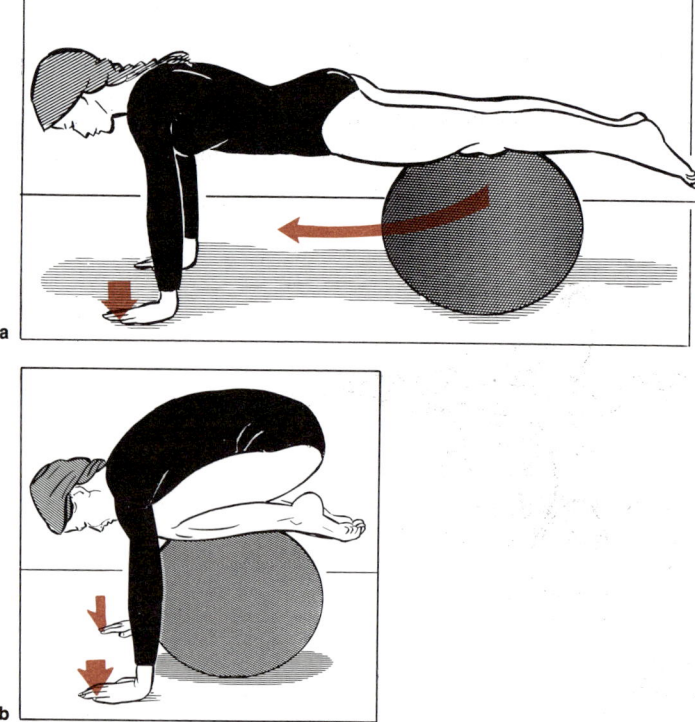

Fig. 10–15 Exercises for extension/flexion of the spine.

Postural Weakness and Malpositions 103

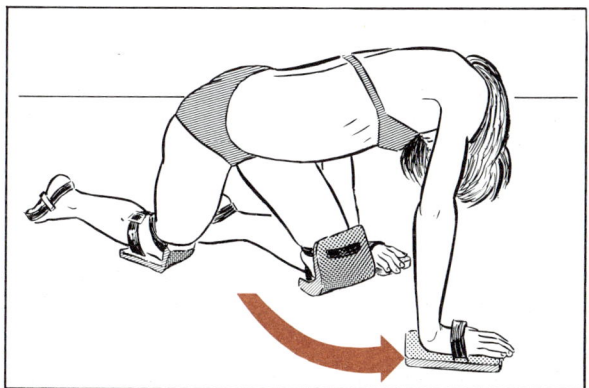

Fig. 10–16 Walking in quadriped according to Klapp.

- PNF trunk pattern to mobilize and correct the shape: Scapula and pelvic pattern technique ''slow return'' for mobilization. Pelvic pattern of flexion, abduction, external rotation, and scapula pattern of elevation, abduction for correction. The exercises are done on both sides.
- ''Frog'' position (Klein-Vogelbach) to train the abdominal muscles (Fig. 10–17): Standing on tiptoe, arms and legs extended diagonally in

Fig. 10–17 ''Frog position''—final position.

external rotation. Course of the movement: While the arms are being moved in a classic PNF pattern, elbows are touching each other in front of the umbilicus; the legs are slightly flexed at the hips and knees; the heels are tightly pushed against the floor. The movements continue along the thoracic spine for kyphosis and along the lumbar spine for lordosis.

Special Exercises for Kyphosis/Lordosis

- Klapp's crawling, "deep crawling and pulling through," to mobilize the spine and correct the shape in the final position; continuing crawling, emphasizing the deep phase.
- Correction on stall bars (Fig. 10–18): Sitting Indian-style with the back against the stall bars (compensating lordosis), arms extended in an oblique upward direction, catching one bar. The back is pushed away from the stall bars with adduction of the scapulae (compensating kyphosis by stretching the pectoral muscles).
- "Classic frog" (Klein-Vogelbach), training the abdominal muscles (Fig. 10–19): Standing on tiptoe, legs parallel and closed, arms in upward extension and internal rotation. Right elbow and left knee touch each other at the umbilical level. Both extremities are in external rotation, correcting the

Fig. 10–18 Correcting the kyphosis/lordosis on the stall bars.

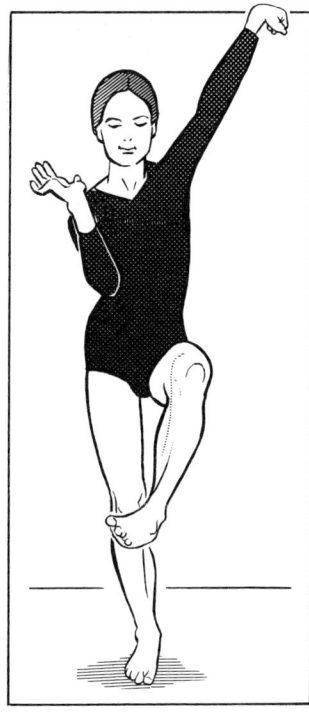

Fig. 10–19 "Classic frog"—final position.

spinal position. The other extremities maintain the tone. The exercise is done at a quick pace, since a slow motion would require considerable balance.

DEFORMITIES

The complex development of the spine is the reason for its frequent deformities, which are usually found at the transition area from cervical to thoracic spine and from lumbar spine to sacrum.

Congenital blocks are found exclusively on the vertebral bodies or the related arches and must be distinguished from blocked vertebrae caused by inflammative processes. Minor cranial or caudal deviations are usually not important. The developmental disturbances range from harmless irregularities of the vertebrae shape to severe deformities, which are combined with neurologic deficits.

Transitional Vertebrae

A deviation of the transition in the atlas–axis area is called atlas assimilation, which is a connection of the atlas to the skull. This condition may produce

106 Diseases of the Spine and Trunk

limitations of mobility and neurologic symptoms, but it can also remain clinically normal.

At the cervical–thoracic transition a "cervical" rib is a common deformity. It can be formed as an enlarged articular process, as a "silent" rib, or as a complete rib with an articular connection to the sternum. Overlapping with the anterior edge of the scalene muscles can cause painful complications and require surgical intervention. A similar condition is the scalenus syndrome, in which nerves and vessels are compressed by changes at the insertion and tension of the scalene muscles.

The dorsolumbar and lumbosacral transitional vertebrae are formed unilaterally or bilaterally. Usually they do not cause problems; however, they may indicate a congenital tendency to developmental disturbances. They are a potential source of problems if they are accompanied by abnormalities of development. Transitional lumbosacral vertebrae are occasionally the reason for local complaints and irritations of the nerve roots. Usually the fifth lumbar vertebra is the first sacral vertebra; however, sometimes it can be the sixth lumbar vertebra. Conversely, the fifth lumbar vertebra can be partially or completely incorporated into the sacrum.

Torticollis

The most common form of torticollis is muscular torticollis, which is caused by shortening of the sternocleidomastoid muscle (Fig. 10–20). Congenital factors and disturbances of the blood circulation (brain trauma) are considered as causes of this condition. The muscle contour with induration and shortening, tilting of the head to the side of the shortening, and rotation of the head toward the opposite side are typical clinical symptoms of muscular torticollis. In the severe form (and in the osseous form) the skull is asymmetric; this is called facial scoliosis.

Osseous torticollis is caused by a true asymmetric deformity. Fusion of several vertebrae (Klippel–Feil syndrome) results in an osseously fixated deformity of the

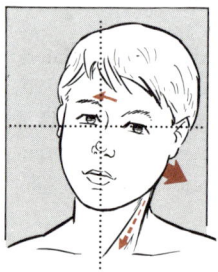

Fig. 10–20 Muscular torticollis. Shortening of the left sternocleidomastoid muscle causes a rotation of the head to the right and a tilt to the left.

cervical spine, affecting the statics of the entire spine. The clinical picture of the Klippel–Feil syndrome reveals, in addition to the torticollis, a short neck and a deformity and elevation of the scapula which may resemble Sprengel's deformity. Sprengel's deformity is a congenital elevation of the scapula, which is combined with spinal deformities and abnormal formation of the ribs.

Torticollis spasticus is based on an infant cerebral palsy with asymmetric muscle contractures.

A torticollis may also be related to a central disturbance, which must be diagnosed correctly for therapeutic purposes. In an otogenic or ocular torticollis, ear or eye specialists must be consulted.

So-called rheumatic or reflectoric torticollis is caused by an abrupt motion of the head and is explained by irregularities of the joints of the vertebral arch. The condition responds well to conservative treatment (see under cervical syndrome).

Radiographic examination is important for verifying or excluding osseous deformation.

Muscular torticollis is treated with exercises and the application of a corrective cast. In surgical intervention the shortened and indurated sternocleidomastoid muscle is incised at its insertion and then reinserted in an overcorrected position. This is followed by physical therapy.

Physical Therapy

Evaluation Results

The lateral head tilt is the most significant sign. The head is bent toward the affected side but rotated toward the opposite side. Frequently, the cervical lordosis is increased. Skull and face can be asymmetric. The entire spine must be examined, since the lateral flexion may continue to the thoracic spine.

The sternocleidomastoid muscle protrudes as a cordlike formation and can be palpated easily. In small infants it feels more like a nodular induration.

The mobility of the head and the cervical spine is examined passively, to determine the range of motion and stretching ability of the shortened muscle. The range of motion toward the opposite side is limited or completely eliminated.

Active examination, depending on the child's age, determines the ability for correction and the feeling for posture and movement.

Goals of Therapy

- Stretch the contracted sternocleidomastoid muscle.
- Correct the malposition.
- Restore the mobility of the head and the cervical spine in all possible directions.

- Retrain a new posture and movement pattern, aimed at a symmetric position of the head and body.
- Instruct the parents.

Techniques

Conservative Treatment (Infants). The position of the infant is part of the treatment. The head is placed between sandbags in a normal middle or overcorrected position. In a supine position the back of the head is placed in a foam ring. In side lying position the corrections are intensified by elevating or lowering the head against the trunk in addition to rotation.

- The child lies on the normal side with pillow supporting the shoulder girdle and thorax. The head is brought into a lateral flexion and turned into the corrected position by the child (Fig. 10–21).
- The child lies on the affected side, the back of the head supported by a wedge pillow, and corrects the position of the head in lateral flexion and rotation (Fig. 10–22).

A persistent malposition can only be corrected by use of an open cast that includes the shoulder girdle and thorax.

In all positions the child must be watched carefully by persons close to him or her. Another approach must be found if the child tries to get out of the forced position by a contralateral muscle contraction.

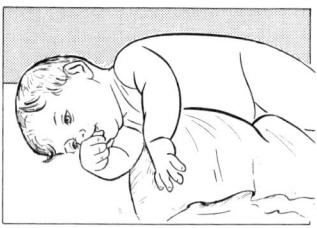

Fig. 10–21 Corrective position on the normal side.

Fig. 10–22 Corrective position on the affected side.

A nodular thickening of the sternocleidomastoid muscle can be softened somewhat by vibrating with one or two fingertips, and then stretching the muscle carefully under fixation of the shoulder. The child's head is moved first laterally to the opposite side and then in rotation, in an attempt to combine those components with flexion of the cervical spine (Fig. 10–23).

Arm and trunk movements (according to Neumann–Neurode gymnastics for infants) are added; this is symmetric training to support development and recognition of the body positioning. The child learns to know his or her body by a guided stroking and touching, especially of the face. Attention is focused on any asymmetries that must be corrected. The movements of the head are stimulated by visual and auditory stimuli. The corrective movements and positions are built into the general moving pattern.

Postoperative Treatment. Basically, the treatment of the older child is similar to that described earlier. Maintaining and stabilizing the position of the head is the main goal, since the malposition has already been corrected surgically.

After the postoperative cast treatment in an overcorrection, the child must learn a new posture and movement pattern. Movements of the head and cervical spine are exercised as well as the symmetry of the position of head and body. This can be achieved by training the righting and postural reflexes on the tilt board and by using a ball or orthopedic pillow.

Position and movement should be exercised in front of a mirror, and the exercises should be modified with rods, balls, and head plates. Because the older child's eye focus has been deviated for years, the focus must be coordinated again with the position of the head.

Exercise Examples

Infant:

- Movements of the head with the help of another person, child in supine position, the helper holding the shoulders: The therapist holds the head from

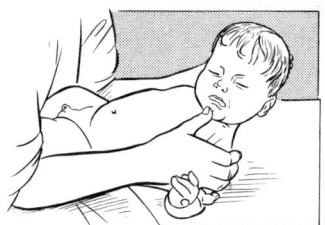

Fig. 10–23 Stretching the sternocleidomastoid muscle.

above with a hand on each side (the ears must not be pressed). The head is moved into corrected and overcorrected positions under careful traction, stretching the contracted muscles.

- Turning from a prone position with an active correction of the rotation (Fig. 10–24): With the infant in a prone position, the arm on the affected side is placed in extension and external rotation, which causes continuing rotatory movements on shoulders and spine; the child lifts and turns the head and thus actively corrects its position.
- Active correction in a supported prone position: The child is held beneath the lower legs and thorax in a prone position. A reflex tension of the correcting muscles and a correcting movement of the child's head is initiated by turning in side lying, supported by manual stimulation of the erector muscles on the same side and by visual stimuli.

Education of the parents creates additional opportunities to support an active correction of the malposition by proper positioning of the crib, during feeding and during handling and by placing toys across or around the crib.

Older Child:

- Adjusting the symmetry: With the child squatting in front of the mirror, the head is moved in a normal (middle) position under visual control and is held against the therapist's manual resistance.
- Active exercises against resistance to achieve overcorrection (head pattern with modified rotatory component): The child is in a supine position. The therapist holds the back of the head with one hand, while the other hand leads the chin. The head is pulled actively against the resistance from the malposition into flexion, followed by lateral flexion toward the normal side and rotation toward the affected side. The weight of the head acts as an additional resistance.

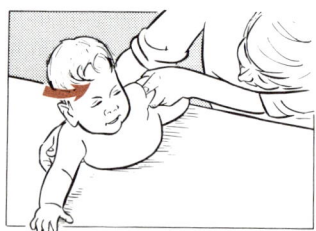

Fig. 10–24 Turning with active correction.

Deformities 111

- Sitting on the therapeutic ball and rolling in front of the mirror: Sitting with spread legs, feet on the floor, the therapist sits on the ball too, if working with younger children, and holds the child around the pelvis. The therapist rolls the ball in different directions to facilitate postural reactions according to the position of the head. The child can also experience the exercise by visual control. The corrected position must always be emphasized.

Thoracic Deformities

Thoracic deformities are congenital and can be combined with developmental disturbances of the spine, such as congenitally blocked vertebrae and subsequent scoliosis or congenital muscular defects. The most common forms are funnel chest and keeled chest (chicken breast). Bell-shaped chest (Fig. 10–25) is caused by an upward bending of the ribs.

Funnel chest (Fig. 10–26) is due to a mainly endogenous inhibition deformity; rachitis (rickets) is thought to contribute to the deformity as an exogenous factor. Pressure, for example, in a constantly bent position, can cause a deformity, especially in the presence of an endogenous precondition (pathological softness of the cartilaginous bony components of the thorax).

The appearance is characterized by a funnel-shaped depression of the anterior thoracic wall in the caudal or middle part of the sternum and the adjacent part of the ribs. The caudal part of the sternum is bent convexly and ventrally. The funnel can be symmetric, depressed flatly or deeply; the depth of the depression decreases the sagittal diameter of the thorax and, in severe deformities, can interfere with the function of the internal thoracic organs. Combined with funnel chest are developmental abnormalities of the spine, such as kyphosis/scoliosis and a flat back,

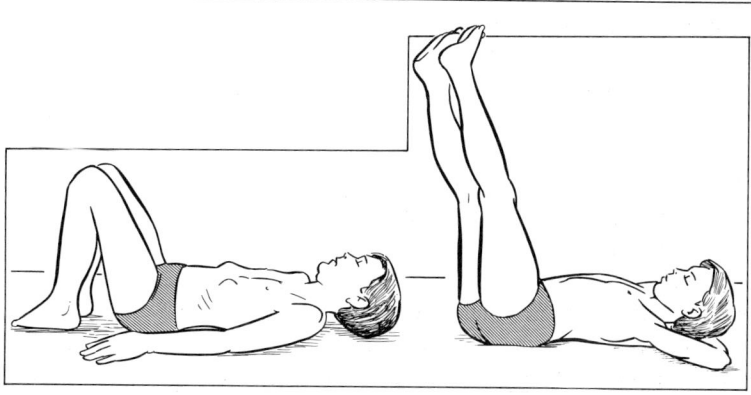

Fig. 10–25 Bell-shaped thorax owing to upward bending of the ribs.

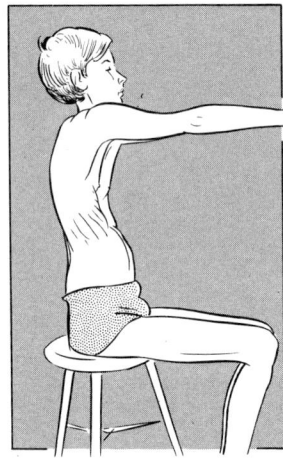

Fig. 10–26 Funnel-shaped thorax.

which can resemble kyphosis in a sitting position. The lumbar lordosis is eliminated; the posture is weak with protracted shoulders and bulging abdomen.

Hypotonic abdominal muscles and tension in the intercostal spaces can be palpated. Respiratory function and vital capacity can be restricted. The respiration is paradoxical in that the sternum is pulled inside even more during inspiration and only the flanks widen. Abdominal breathing occurs if the thoracic movements are severely restricted. The general condition of a mostly leptosomatic patient can also be affected by circulatory stress. The patient describes occasional respiratory troubles, heart pain, and the feeling of depression.

Funnel chest is usually treated conservatively. Besides physical therapy, an attempt with prone position and later with bandages can be considered at a very young age. The indication for surgery depends on possible circulatory restrictions. The mental status must also be evaluated; in particular, girls may overemphasize the deformity. In an operation the sternum is split, the ribs along the edges of the funnel are osteotomized in a wedge, and the funnel is elevated and finally stabilized.

Keeled chest (Fig. 10–27) results from rickets and is also observed in congenital developmental disturbances of the skeleton. Sometimes a small uterus is blamed for the condition.

In a rachitic keeled chest the protrusion of the sternum is frequently combined with an upward bending of the ribs in the area of the thoracic aperture (bell-shaped thorax). The depression above the bend is called Harrison's groove. The border between cartilage and bone on the ribs is visible and palpable during the acute stage of rickets (rachitic beads).

Deformities 113

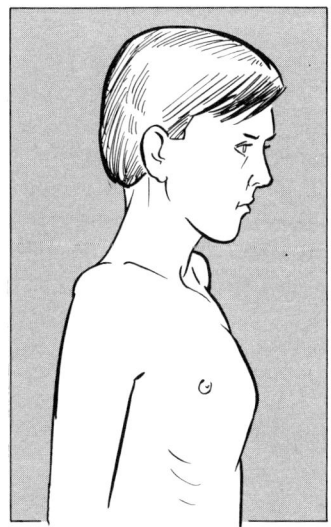

Fig. 10–27 Keel-shaped chest.

Treatment of the underlying disease is most important in a rachitic thorax deformity, and the prognosis is favorable in early childhood. Besides antirachitic treatment, physical therapy is indicated for bell-shaped and funnel chest. In addition, an open cast and orthoses are used at night for a still soft and pliable thorax.

Physical Therapy for Funnel Chest

Goals of Therapy

Conservative and Preoperative Treatment

- Mobilize the thorax.
- Change the respiratory technique with widening of the thoracic space.
- Increase effective cough through exercise.
- Train posture.
- Exercise muscles under load.

Postoperative Treatment

- Maintain the corrections and gradually intensify all exercises.

Techniques

Preoperative and postoperative physical therapy must be scheduled twice a day. At first, mobility of the ribs is trained, stretching and turning with movements of the spine. The abdominal muscles are trained as activators for the movements of the ribs. The posture is trained in different positions, if necessary including the pectoral muscles. Respiratory exercises are performed in between. A corrective respiratory technique must be learned until it can be done automatically. From the physiologic standpoint it is abnormal, but it affects the thorax favorably. Panting and vocal exhaling are used to assist coughing. Therapy must be started early and continued over a long period in order to be successful.

Exercise Examples

- Corrective respiration in supine position: The patient inhales against a resistance on the ventrolateral thorax to elevate and spread the ribs. In addition, the patient tries to press the sternum upward. The correction is maintained during exhalation. Whistling during exhalation augments the function.
- Exercising the abdominal muscles with correction (Fig. 10–28): Supine position; all four extremities are brought together across the stomach with flexion of the elbows and knees, the sternum pressed outward. The exercise can be combined with corrective respiration (see preceding exercise).
- Bilateral arm pattern in supine position: Both arms are placed in flexion, abduction, and external rotation. The patient tries to pull the arms in the opposite movement against resistance applied by the therapist to stop any motion, but the pectoral muscles are elevated along with the ribs and sternum.
- Exercising the trunk muscles with correction (Fig. 10–29): Supine position, angulated legs, feet on the floor; elevating to a rocking position, inhaling and elevating the sternum.

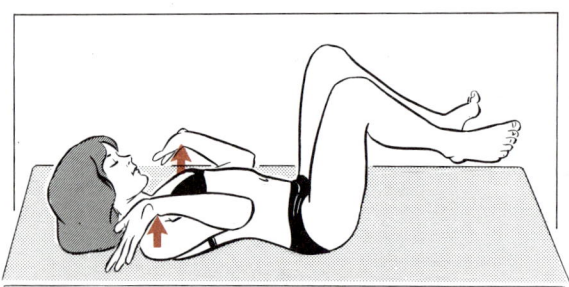

Fig. 10–28 Training the abdominal muscles with correction.

Deformities 115

Fig. 10–29 Training the trunk muscles with correction.

- Toning the trunk muscles with correction on the stall bars: Hanging on the stall bars with the back against the bars, hands holding the bars a wide distance apart (stretching the pectoral muscles); knees are pulled up toward the stomach, supplying additional tension as in a pull-up.

Spondylolysis and Spondylolisthesis (Sliding Vertebra)

Origin. Congenital fissure of the vertebral arch. Spondylolysis of the lower lumbar spine is observed in approximately 4.5 percent of the population, without causing clinical symptoms. It can also be caused by trauma, such as frequent maximum hyperlordosis (high diving, athletic gymnastics).

This mostly congenital fissure around the roots of the arch can initiate a slipping of the vertebral body in an anterior direction (spondylolisthesis means slipping vertebra). A pseudospondylolisthesis is a process in which the slipping is not caused by an interruption of the vertebral arches, but by a progressive osteochondrosis.

The degree of dislocation caused by the slipping depends also on the surrounding soft tissue, especially the muscles. The gliding usually starts between the 12th year and the completion of growth, and it is mostly observed between the fifth lumbar vertebra and the sacrum or between the fourth and fifth lumbar vertebrae.

Symptoms. Spondylolysis does not usually cause any symptoms and is frequently diagnosed accidentally. Spondylolisthesis causes pain around the sacral area, which radiates to the buttocks and the legs. The symptoms often become evident later in life, when the muscles are less sufficient. The patient complains of fatigue and stiffness of the lower back. Clinically, increased lumbar lordosis is most prominent. A moderate dent or impression can be palpated above a protruding spinous process, which is sensitive to pressure. The lumbodorsal groove is deepened because of the direction of the slipping. Severe slipping can cause neurologic deficits. Radiographically, a supporting console along the caudal vertebral body or the sacrum can be diagnosed.

Treatment. Conservative therapy consists mainly of exercises to strengthen the muscles. In addition to sports (swimming), the application of a brace can be considered. With operative treatment, the slipping vertebra is stabilized by spondylodesis. In accompanying neurologic deficits the spondylodesis is combined with evacuation of the disk. Physical therapy management is discussed later in this chapter under spondylodesis.

Physical Therapy

Evaluation Results

The following symptoms are typical:

- Pronounced flexion of the pelvis
- Apparently increased lordosis
- Ridge or bend within the lordosis
- Protruding stomach.

The muscle tone of the back extensors is often increased; the erector spinae muscle protrudes like a rope in the lumbar area; the abdominal muscles are flaccid. The lumbar spine does not show a continuing curvature and shows no kyphosis, possibly owing to contracture of the back extensors. In extension there is also not an even curve, but there is often a painful bending in the area of the lumbar spine.

Goals of Therapy

- Decrease muscle spasm.
- Correct the position of the pelvis.
- Train posture and trunk movements.
- Support activities of daily living skills.

Techniques

- Decrease tensed musculature and improve circulation by electrotherapy, hydrotherapy, and massage techniques.
- Correct the position of the pelvis with exercises for pelvic–lumbar movements, emphasizing extension of the pelvis.

- Perform PNF pelvic pattern (emphasis again on the pelvis). For stabilization these exercises are based on the "rhythmic stabilization" technique. All components of the abdominal muscles must be trained both isotonically and isometrically.

- Any exercises favoring lordosis must be avoided. The position of the pelvis is trained in preparation for the quadriped position, again working with rhythmic stabilization.

- In an upright position before a mirror, the patient must learn to stabilize the corrected position of the pelvis. This is especially necessary when bending down and while carrying weight, during which the patient must learn how to maintain stabilized extension of the spine.

Swimming with the backstroke is recommended, since the tendency toward lordosis is less than when the breaststroke is used; at the same time, the crawling motion of the legs is good exercise for the abdominal muscles.

Exercise Examples

- Training the oblique abdominal muscles and correcting the position of the pelvis: Side lying, PNF pelvis pattern of extension, abduction, and internal rotation; the technique used is "repeated contraction."

- Stabilizing the pelvis (Fig. 10–30): Side lying, PNF pelvic pattern keeping the pelvis in neutral; the technique used is "rhythmic stabilization."

- Exercising the abdominal muscles with contralateral tension of the back muscles (Fig. 10–31): Supine position. The extremities are placed along the diagonals of the body; right elbow and left knee are pulled toward each other in front of the body, while the other arm and leg remain tightly on the floor.

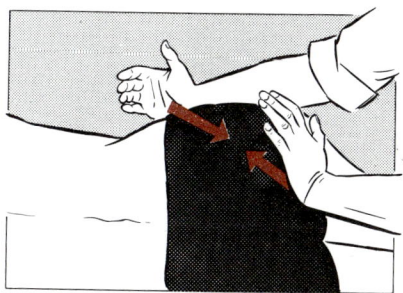

Fig. 10–30 PNF pelvic pattern using a "rhythmic stabilization" technique.

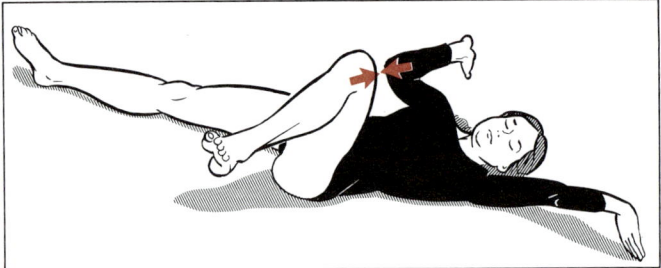

Fig. 10–31 Exercising the abdominal muscles with contralateral tension of the back muscles.

- Stabilizing the trunk (Fig. 10–32): Quadriped position, head in the direction of the spine, pelvis in neutral position; the therapist's manual stimulation on the pelvis and thorax/shoulder girdle or head in flexion/extension, lateral flexion, and rotation results in isometric contraction of the trunk musculature.

Vertebral Fissures

Vertebral fissures are disturbances of the development of the notochord (chorda dorsalis) that can lead to various degrees of vertebral deformity. There are frontal or sagittal vertebral fissures or wedged half vertebrae that cause subsequent bending and deformities of the spine.

Fissures in the first and second cervical vertebrae can cause problems owing to an open posterior arch of the atlas or an interruption of the connection of the dens

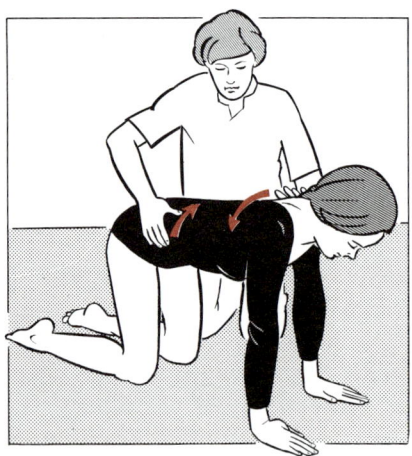

Fig. 10–32 Stabilization of the quadriped position.

Deformities 119

with the axis (epistropheus). Fissures within the upper cervical segment and on the apophyses of joints and spinous processes are sometimes misinterpreted as fractures or a sequel thereof.

Frontal fissures of the vertebral body (Fig. 10–33) must be differentiated from other pathological conditions and must be treated.

Dorsal fissures of the lower lumbar segment result in spina bifida. This is often accompanied by abnormal growth of hair in this area (Fig. 10–34). The occasional pain felt by the patient is due to the change in position and shape of the vertebral joints rather than to the incomplete closure of the arch.

Extensive dorsal fissures can be accompanied by a malformation of the spinal cord and its membranes; they are called meningoceles, or myelomeningoceles if

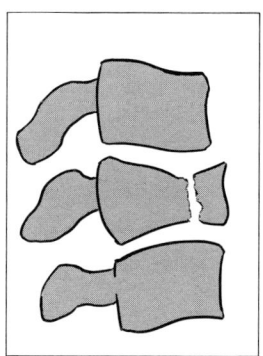

Fig. 10–33 Frontal fissure of the vertebral body.

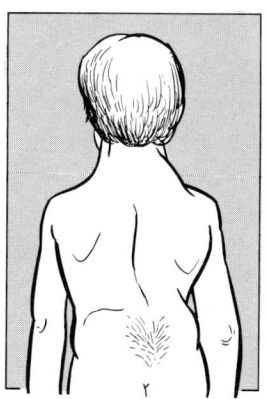

Fig. 10–34 Hair growth across the spina bifida with accompanying scoliosis.

the spinal cord is involved. These deformities result in paralysis of the lower extremities, bladder, and colon.

SPINAL CHANGES IN SYSTEMIC DISEASES

Systemic diseases of the skeleton are either congenital or develop during the growth period when there is a congenital disposition. They cause typical lesions of the spine, which vary depending on the localization and the impact on growth. Clinically important are achondroplasia (formerly called chondrodystrophy), mucopolysaccharidosis, osteogenesis imperfecta, and cleidocranial dysostosis.

Achondroplasia

In achondroplasia the cartilaginous growth of the epiphyses is disturbed. The enchondral ossification is affected, which interferes especially with the growth of the long bones and produces the typical appearance of dwarfism (Fig. 10–35). The perichondral ossification (thickness) and development of the remaining bones are basically normal.

The vertebral bodies are small with lower arches. The subsequently narrow spinal canal (spinal stenosis), additional scolioses, and increased kyphoses at the transition of the thoracic to the lumbar spine can cause irritation of the nerve roots with persistent discomfort (recurrent lumbar syndrome) (see also Chapter 2).

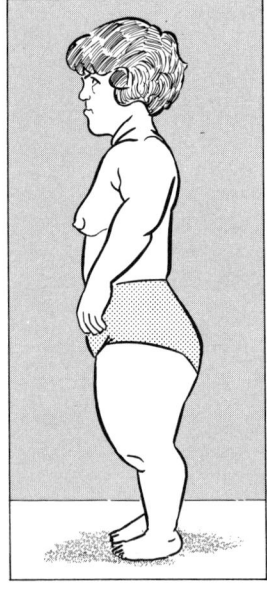

Fig. 10–35 Achondroplasia.

Mucopolysaccharidosis

Hereditary disturbance of the mucopolysaccharide metabolism is combined with pronounced skeletal changes. Several forms of this disease are distinguished. Among them, two forms are important with respect to the spine: gargoylism (Hurler-Pfaundler syndrome) and osteochorndrodystrophy (Morquio-Brailsford disease). Both conditions cause dwarfism and disproportional growth, such as bending of the spine and deformities of the pelvis and thorax (see also Chapter 2).

Osteogenesis Imperfecta (Brittle Bone Disease)

Insufficient diaphyseal/apophyseal bone formation results in the development of long thin bones that fracture easily. The early type of osteogenesis imperfecta (recessively hereditary) causes multiple intrauterine fractures and frequently stillbirths. The late type (dominantly hereditary) becomes obvious in young children because of brittle bones. After puberty the tendency to fractures decreases. Fractures of the vertebral bodies result in flat vertebrae and the development of a kyphoscoliosis (see also Chapter 2).

Treatment consists of correct stabilization of the fracture and possibly corrective osteotomy with accompanying physical therapy. Additional devices might be necessary.

Cleidocranial Dysostosis

Cleidocranial dysostosis is a disturbance of the development of flat bones, especially in the area of the scapulae. Partial defects or lack of clavicles results in abnormal mobility of the shoulder girdle. These defects are frequently combined with vertebral deformities (scoliosis, spina bifida) and deformities of the thorax (funnel chest). Dwarfism and a short neck with restricted mobility of the cervical spine are typical signs. In addition, paralysis and intelligence deficits are sometimes observed.

Marfan's Syndrome (Arachnodactyly)

Marfan's syndrome is caused by a hereditary disturbance of the mesenchyme. The most characteristic sign is spiderlike fingers. Fingers and toes are abnormally long, the muscles are hypotonic, and the articular ligaments are loose with hyperextension of the joints until there is complete instability. Finally, bending of the spine and thoracic deformities occur. The changes in the vertebral bodies are similar to those in juvenile kyphosis (see also Chapter 2).

122 DISEASES OF THE SPINE AND TRUNK

Marble Bone Disease

Marble bone disease (osteopetrosis or Albers–Schoenberg disease) results from decreased osteoclastic activity and causes calcification of the skeleton, including the spine (Fig. 10–36). Spontaneous fractures can occur, which heal poorly.

Physical Therapy

Physical therapy of the spine in a systemic disease is oriented toward the underlying disease and its symptoms.

ASEPTIC BONE NECROSES OF THE SPINE

For more information, see Chapter 6.

Juvenile Kyphoses

Origin. Juvenile kyphosis, also called kyphosis of adolescents, Scheuermann's disease, or juvenile osteochondrosis, is frequently seen during the growth period. It is an aseptic bone necrosis caused by various factors that are not yet fully understood. Lindemann emphasized a hereditary disturbance of the enchondral growth; in 25 percent of the affected juvenile patients dominant heritability has been observed. Hormonal imbalance is also a contributing factor; frequently, small gonads are associated with the disease. Schmorl assumed that the nodules (named after him) caused the disease.

According to recent studies, the process starts on the cartilaginous plate on the upper and under surfaces of the vertebral body, which do not withstand weight-

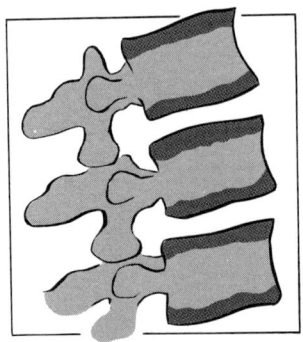

Fig. 10–36 Marble bone disease of the spine.

Aseptic Bone Necroses of the Spine 123

bearing stress. They exhibit preformed gaps, or disturbances in the fiber system. Around these areas growth is inhibited. The disk can penetrate through those gaps into the vertebral body.

The so-called Schmorl's nodules start to form. The disease is characterized by irregular vertebral end plates. The spinal kyphosis (Fig. 10–37) is due to the anterior flattening and wedge shape of the vertebral bodies. The intervertebral tissue becomes less elastic and loses its articular function, which explains the rigidity of the affected spinal segment. The disease, based on disposition, can be worsened by exogenous factors. The persistent kyphotic position of the spine results in a mechanical overstress and pressure atrophy of the ventral portions of the vertebral bodies.

Vigorous physical therapy can counteract the increasing kyphotic curve. Unfortunately, the opportunity for early successful therapy is often missed, since the disease causes discomfort in only some patients in the early stage.

Symptoms. The symptoms of Scheuermann's disease depend on the localization and stage of the pathological process. The first stage starts before age 10 with a functional disturbance (weak posture and kypholordosis of the spine). There is no pain and mobility is not essentially restricted.

The second stage, or florid stage, occurs between ages 12 and 18 and within 6 to 9 months results in a rigid kyphosis, owing to the transformation of the disks. Some patients complain about pain in the affected area caused by the overstressed

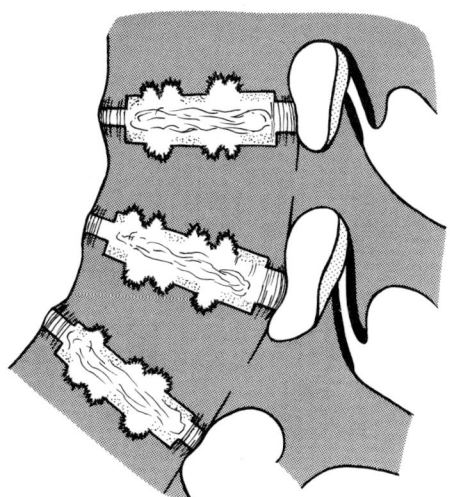

Fig. 10–37 Schematic drawing of a radiograph in Scheuermann's disease (from W. Heipertz, E. Schmitt: Wirbelsäulenerkrankungen—Diagnostik und Therapie, 2. Aufl. Springer, Berlin 1984).

muscles, fibrous tissue, ligaments, and capsules of the joints (arch), which finally leads to circulatory disturbances.

The third stage (end stage) occurs after age 18 and is characterized by a rigid kyphosis of the thoracic spine. There is also a lumbar kyphosis with corresponding symptoms. The rigid kyphosis changes the entire status of the spine and forces the cervical and lumbar spinal segments into a compensating lordosis—insofar as they are not included in the kyphotic curve. The malposition and functional overstress accelerate the wear of the intervertebral structures and the small vertebral joints and overload the muscles. The end stage is therefore characterized by myostatic problems, cervical syndrome, chronic lumbar syndrome, and myalgic syndrome. The rigid part of the spine is usually pain-free.

Treatment. Juvenile kyphosis is treated by postural training. Because the patients are not bothered by pain and the clinical picture seems only to suggest weak posture, there does not seem to be a convincing need for treatment. However, the patient must be instructed in an intensive and continuous exercise program over a long period to prevent late complications and problems later.

During the florid stage of Scheuermann's disease temporary immobilization may be required. Besides positioning and corrective casts, the application of supporting braces may be considered. A physical therapy program and swimming are also recommended. A severe kyphosis can be corrected surgically. First the kyphosis is reduced and then the correction is stabilized by a dorsal spondylosyndesis.

The treatment of juvenile kyphosis in the final stage depends on the symptoms. The syndromes, especially the myalgic syndrome, are treated and the muscles strengthened.

Physical Therapy

Prior to the initiation of therapy the status of posture and movement is assessed. Usually the spine is curved in a kyphosis in classical Scheuermann's disease, but it can also be flat or even without a major deviation. Since the mobility of the affected segments is decreased or eliminated, the kyphosis cannot be overcome by extension. The shoulder girdle is protracted, and in many cases the pectoral muscle is shortened. The respiratory movements of the thorax may be limited. In a kyphotic position the back extensors are hard and tensed.

Goals of Therapy

- Mobilize and correct the spine.
- Obtain extension of the spine.
- Strengthen back musculature.

- Promote good posture.
- Prevent early deterioration and premature wear.

Techniques

Heat is indicated if the patient is in pain; it relaxes the muscles and improves the (local) blood circulation. Electrotherapy, massage, and hydrotherapy are recommended. The exercise program is similar to a program for malpositions. Mobilization of one or all of the affected spinal segments is carefully initiated with active muscle work contraction in order to improve the extension of the spine. Some of Klapp's crawling exercises that favor the mobilization, extension, and muscle work (deep crawling, pulling trunk and extremities through, or walking on all fours) are suitable. Various initial positions are chosen according to the spinal segment involved.

Exercises for the abdominal muscles and postural exercises in various positions, including the upright position in front of the mirror, are daily routine. If necessary, exercises must be added to stretch the pectoral muscle. In swimming, the patient must find the best position; in most cases a combination of all styles is most effective for adolescents and provides general training. Any special correction can be pursued during the exercise treatment. Sports that stress the spine, such as jumping and weight lifting, should be avoided, especially during the florid stage.

Exercise Examples

- Rotation exercise from Klapp's crawling exercises: The sliding position improves the extension of the spinal kyphosis; the rotation, initiated over the arm, intensifies it. The exercises are done symmetrically.
- Active correction of the kyphotic segments (Fig. 10–38): In riding position on the (kyphosis) bench, upper body and head are shifted forward; the hands are folded cross the buttocks and pulled caudally with depression and abduction of the scapulae. The patient must elevate the head and upper body with active extension of the cervical spine until the kyphotic segment is included in the extension. The active extension of the cervical spine results in stabilization of the thoracic spine in extension.
- Extension and rotation on the therapeutic ball (Fig. 10–39): The patient rolls with his or her stomach across the ball to the pelvic level; the legs are elevated diagonally upward and the arms are extended forward and downward, forming an oblique plane. While rolling the ball sidewise the patient lifts one arm, turning it across the shoulder diagonally upward and following the hand with his or her eyes. This exercise requires intensive balancing.
- Stretching the pectorals: While in the supine position, the PNF arm pattern of flexion, abduction, external rotation is used unilaterally or bilaterally.

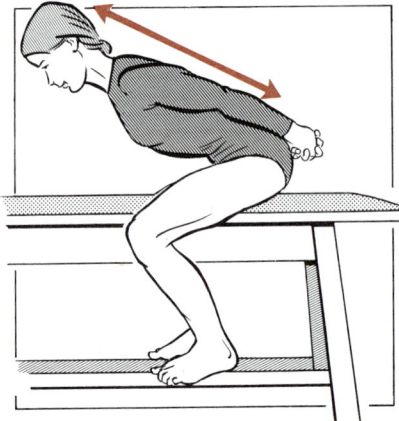

Fig. 10–38 Active correction of the kyphosis.

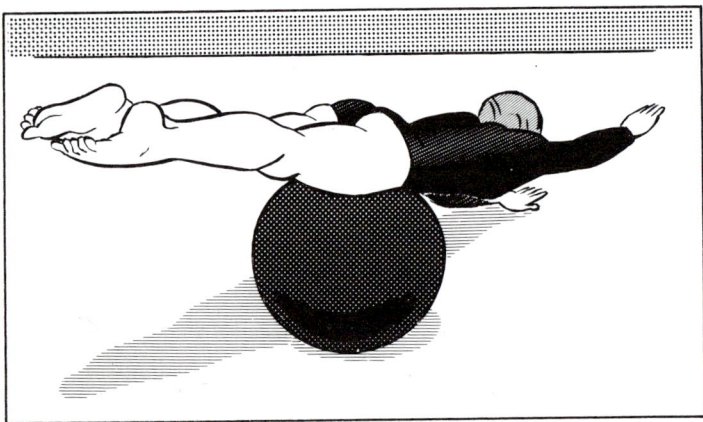

Fig. 10–39 Active correction on the ball.

Vertebra Plana

Besides juvenile kyphosis (Scheuermann's disease), vertebra plana (flat vertebrae) is also characterized as juvenile osteochondrosis. This is a growth disturbance that occurs at an early age and results in flat vertebrae (Fig. 10–40). The ossification of one or more vertebral bodies is disturbed, causing weak posture. Affected children complain about back pain, which sometimes requires a long period of rest. During the regenerative stage the muscles are strengthened and function is restored.

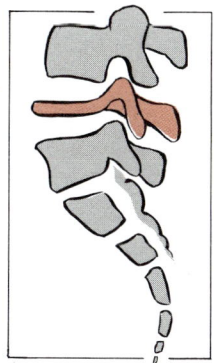

Fig. 10–40 Flat vertebra (vertebra plana).

The flat vertebrae must be differentiated from similar conditions in adults after trauma, osteoporosis, or inflammation of the spine, which can cause similar deformities.

"Fatigue Man's" Disease

This disease is caused by an insidious fracture of the spinous process of the sixth or seventh cervical vertebra owing to an aseptic necrosis of the spinous processes. The necroses are caused by overload on the spinous processes in the lower segment of the cervical spine (for example, by intermittent strong traction in unusually strong labor). The fracture occurs in the areas of necrotic tissue changes. There is no therapeutic intervention other than care and rest.

SCOLIOSIS

Scolioses are rigid lateral deviations of the spine in combination with torsion and rotation (Fig. 10–41). The torsion is a rotation of the spine itself that causes asymmetry of the vertebrae. The rotation is a turning of the vertebrae against one another. The deformation of the vertebral body is caused by impact on the growing tissue.

Torsion and rotation result in thoracic deformities by pulling the ribs into abnormal positions. Posterior curvature of the ribs occurs on the convex side of the scoliosis. The thorax is drawn out frontally on the concave side. The curvature of the ribs mimics a kyphosis, but the course of the spine in a scoliosis is rather steep. In the lumbar segment the outward rotation of the transverse processes causes a lumbar hump. Lateral deviations are prominent within the row of spinous processes, which can run in simple or multiple bendings. In severe torsion and lateral

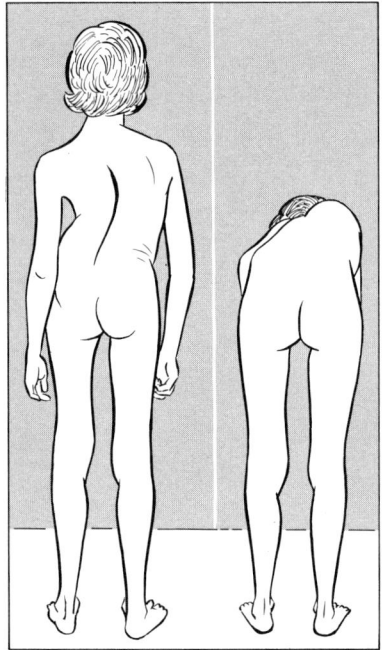

Fig. 10–41 Scoliosis with costal hump on the right side.

deviation one vertebral body can slip away laterally from the neighboring vertebrae (rotatory slipping). These must be differentiated from true structural scolioses, in which rotation and torsion are missing, for example, "sciatic scoliosis" in chronic sciatica. The varying etiology and prognosis of scolioses suggest the following classification:

- Idiopathic scoliosis
- Osteochondropathic scoliosis (deformity, traumatic sequel, neurofibromatosis)
- Neuropathic scoliosis (paralytic scoliosis after poliomyelitis, in infant cerebral palsy)
- Myopathic scoliosis
- Fibropathic scoliosis (scarry scoliosis).

Ninety percent of scolioses are idiopathic; their origin is unknown. Girls are affected in a 4:1 ratio over boys. A primary hereditary disturbance of the muscular balance or the metabolism may be important. Mechanical factors—including malposition—can be considered as predisposing and initiating momentum.

The majority of idiopathic scolioses are diagnosed at age 10 to 12 years. The scoliosis is progressive, especially during growth episodes (Fig. 10–42), but it can also worsen in later life. Progressive stages are observed during accelerated osteochondrosis, pregnancy, menopause, and osteoporosis.

Scoliosis limits spine mobility. Adolescents do not often complain about pain. In adults pain is due mainly to muscular insufficiency, but also to intercostal neuralgia, to collision of the last rib with the iliac crest, or to secondary degenerative changes of the disks and small vertebral joints. The pulmonary capacity is limited in severer scoliosis.

The extent of scoliosis is estimated according to the degree of curvature in the radiograph. The measurement is made following Cobb's technique (Fig. 10–43): A scoliosis is mild below 40°, moderate between 40° and 60°, severe between 60° and 80°, and very severe above 80°. The prognosis depends on the degree and localization of the scoliosis and the age of the patient at the onset of the disease. The course is essentially influenced by the strength of the spinal growth. Scolioses that are diagnosed early respond better to therapy.

The frequent idiopathic scoliosis of adolescents is differentiated from the juvenile form (ages 4 to 9 years) and infant scoliosis (ages 3 to 5). Connections between early infant scoliosis and scoliosis between ages 3 and 5 are possible but not proved. Malignant forms involving short primary curvatures, which are difficult to correct, and severe rotation cause complete stiffness even before age 10 and have an unfavorable prognosis.

Deformity scolioses are combined with abnormally shaped vertebrae; they usually do not develop as progressively as idiopathic scolioses. Asymmetric abnormal formations of the axial spine (half, split, or butterfly vertebrae, Klippel-Feil syndrome, synostoses of the ribs, etc.) cause scoliosis, which affects the overall status only in some cases.

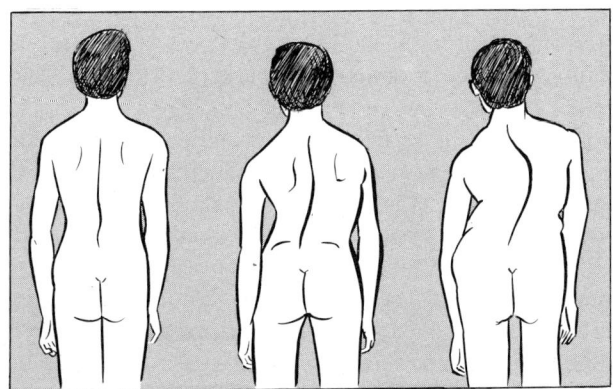

Fig. 10–42 Progressive scoliosis (right convex)

130 Diseases of the Spine and Trunk

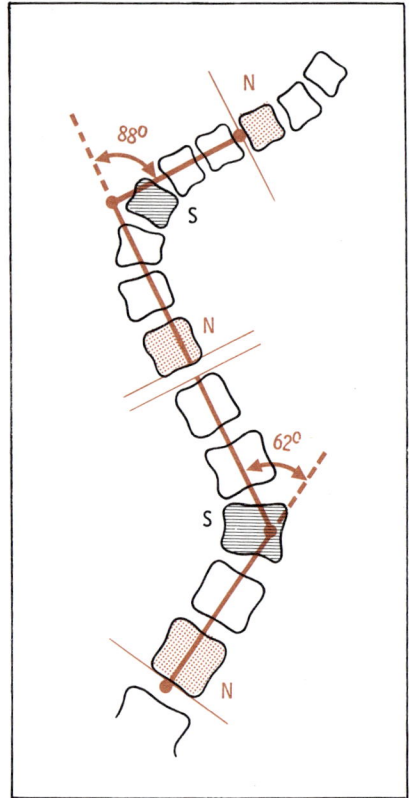

Fig. 10–43 Measuring the scoliosis according to Cobb. The perpendicular line is drawn on the upper plate of the neutral vertebra (**N**), and the angle is measured, which is formed by both perpendicular lines. (**S**) Apical vertebra.

Neuropathic scoliosis (paralytic necrosis) develops progressively, especially as a sequel to poliomyelitis. Asymmetric paralysis of the back, abdominal, and pelvic muscles are responsible for the progressive scoliosis.

Scoliosis with osteopathic necroses, especially in a neurofibromatosis (Recklinghausen's disease) has a grave prognosis. The bones are soft and the mesodermal formation of the spine is insufficient owing to endocrinologic dysfunctions. The scoliosis is combined with a strong kyphosis and may cause paralysis during puberty. Frequently a ventral spondylosyndesis is required. Posttraumatic scolioses are observed after fractures and subluxations. The destructive scoliosis that occurs after inflammations and tumors is characterized by the formation of extreme kyphoses (gibbus) and the involvement of other organs, especially the spinal cord. Scar scolioses are due to extensive surgical manipulations (thoracoplasty) and burns.

The medical treatment is based on the origin, localization, and course of the scoliosis. Myopathic and neuropathic scoliosis is treated in the same way as idiopathic scoliosis; however, the more progressive course of the neuropathic scoliosis must be considered. In addition to physical therapy, the application of corrective casts or braces may be considered. Swimming is recommended. Maintaining a prone position for several hours daily and using a flat, firm mattress help to reduce stress on the spine.

Exercises must be done daily at home. Children of school age should participate in special exercise lessons.

The course of the disease is controlled by regular clinical and radiographic examinations. A critical stage occurs between ages 8 and 10 and during puberty. Progressive worsening and an angle of more than 50° according to Cobb's measuring technique suggest a spondylosyndesis. The period before puberty is a favorable time for surgery. It may also be indicated later under certain conditions.

Physical Therapy

Even after decades of research and the development of numerous special techniques, the success of physical therapy in the treatment of scoliosis is still limited. No exercise regimen, even if it is excellent, results in healing. However, the progression of a scoliosis can be counteracted and the period of adolescence can be influenced favorably.

The necessity for and purpose of regular exercises must be pointed out again and again to both younger and older patients. The patient must understand the relation between exercise and muscle training, upright position and respiration, and possible influence on their growth pattern. More than in cases of weak posture, children and adolescents must be motivated to carry out an exercise program for years and the parents must be included in the therapeutic program.

The therapeutic schedule is classified according to the medical treatment, the degree of the deformity, and the stage of development:

- Conservative treatment without additional aids
- Treatment in braces
- Preoperative treatment
- Postoperative early and late treatment (weaning from the braces).

Conservative Treatment without Additional Aids

Evaluation Results

In conservative treatment a detailed assessment of posture and movement is made, which includes the following aspects:

- The patient is observed in a standing position and his or her ability to balance and compensate in erect standing is evaluated.
- The patient is observed bilaterally in the sagittal plane. A lumbar curvature makes the spine appear as a flat back from the convex side, but in a thoracic curvature the costal hump resembles lordosis/kyphosis of the spine. The position of the pelvis and its effect on the spine are therefore important.
- In the transverse plane, deviations in the pelvic and shoulder areas are most prominent. All levels must be checked and deviations must be assessed.
- Documenting by sketches simplifies the evaluation procedure and visually records the deviations. The sketches also serve as a reference during the treatment period.
- Forward bending of the trunk followed by straightening to an upright position reveals the extent of rigidity, lateral flexion, and rotation. In a standing position lateral flexion to both sides makes the fixation of the curve obvious. The evaluation is completed by having the patient stand on one leg and demonstrate the ability to balance.
- Passive stretching is checked by traction on the head in a sitting position. Active extension reveals strength and postural awareness.
- It is important to check for extension of the hip joints, using the Thomas test.
- Vital capacity and chest expansion measurements must be done to determine thoracic mobility, pulmonary function, and pulmonary effectiveness. The direction and rhythm of respiration must also be observed. The muscle tone of the different back musculature must be palpated, together with the tone of the abdominal muscles.

Goals of Therapy

- Avoid further progression.
- Influence spinal mobility toward extension.
- Elongate contracted muscles.
- Correct the curvature within possible limits.
- Strengthen trunk muscles.
- Create a strong spine.
- Improve both respiratory and circulatory status.
- Retrain in symmetrical dynamic moving patterns.
- Promote favorable daily habits.
- Educate the patient about his or her spine, the necessity for regular treatment, and motivation to take the initiative.

Therapy

Before the exercises a short and intensive massage is recommended.

The exercise program for a scoliosis is based on functional aspects and should be designed according to the individual needs of the patient, using every available exercise. The exercise program depends on the patient's endurance, strength, age, and the severity of the scoliosis; an individual's program might be developed from any number of the following exercises:

1. Crawling according to Klapp: These exercises are done in quadriped, in a sliding position, and on both knees. The spine is placed in a favorable position (except for the position on both knees), supported by the extremities, and can be exercised in two or three dimensions. The four goals are extension, mobilization, correction, and strengthening. In different positions each spinal segment is exercised in a special way; the exercises also support lordotic and kyphotic curves. The exercises are most effective when done in a series. Although they are strenuous, they can also be pleasant. The muscles on the concave and the convex sides and the muscles of the arms and legs are involved in the workout.
2. Exercises according to Niederhoeffer: These exercises mainly stress the back muscles on the concave side. Arms and legs are used as a fixed point, toward which the spine is pulled by active muscle contraction. The convex curvature can be flattened; however, a decrease in the rotation by muscle contraction on the spinous processes is impossible. The patient experiences a widening of the thorax owing to the exercises and can use the new sense of muscle tone to correct his or her posture along the perpendicular line.
3. Exercises according to Gocht-Gessner: These exercises favor strengthening of the muscles on the convex side and extension of the muscles on the concave side. They help to correct and stretch the spine. The exercises are built up initially from a prone to an upright position.
4. Exercises according to Scharll: These exercises improve posture symmetrically. As the patient exercises he or she uses kinesthetic awareness to obtain a symmetrical position or to localize a certain point on the body. Posture is improved by repositioning the twisted shoulder girdle in a frontal plane above the pelvis. The rotation is not limited to the spine, but includes entire moving patterns, which can be learned systematically. The patient is instructed to move symmetrically and to extend the spine by rotatory exercise patterns. The training of the ventral trunk muscles is especially important.
5. Exercises according to Lehnert-Schroth: These exercises are based on the theory that the single segments of the curvature have shifted against one another en bloc, causing muscle imbalance, and must be realigned into a

perpendicular line by correcting the pelvic position. The thoracic shape is also improved by a special breathing technique. The correction gained during an exercise is maintained by muscle tone, which helps to convey the sense of straight posture. A variety of exercises with or without additional equipment is available.
6. Exercises based on PNF: Pelvic or scapular patterns, single or in combination, can correct the malposition to an extent as well as strengthen the muscles involved. The scoliosis can be influenced in its three dimensions, since the exercises include three dimensions. These exercises are possible only with a therapist's assistance, since they require manual contact.
7. Training the trunk muscles according to the "functional movements" of Klein-Vogelbach, by using the frog positions, quadriped, and the therapeutic ball: These exercises help the patient with a lordosis to mobilize and correct the spine by muscle contraction work. They are modified according to the patient's endurance and condition, are based on righting reactions or conscious conception, and are a favorable prerequisite for a free perpendicular posture.
8. Pushing exercises according to Brunkow: Pushing exercises using all four extremities increase the tone of the entire body. In a scoliosis a sense of postural symmetry is learned. In addition, even weight bearing on both legs is learned by challenges in the standing position.
9. Orthopedic gymnastics in small groups: Stretching, respiratory exercises, and exercises with equipment, sometimes in the form of a game, often enrich rigid exercise schedules and can be designed as a useful modification.

The following section outlines an exercise program that lasts for 30 to 45 minutes. A number of the methods mentioned earlier are used. A critical evaluation is necessary, however, to adjust the exercises to individual needs.

- Start in a lying position, stretching the arm and leg on the concave side. An abduction position of the extremities must be attained in order to influence the entire lateral curvature, starting at the apical point. Respiratory exercises are scheduled in between. Hand contact by the therapist on the concave side can add resistance.
- In a supine position, exercises for the abdominal muscles are done. Respiratory exercises are added to improve rib mobility.
- Exercises according to Scharll and Niederhoeffer are done in the lying position. While in quadriped, the patient exercises according to Klapp, Klein-Vogelbach, and Scharll, to achieve symmetry.
- Additional muscle strengthening exercises according to Lehnert-Schroth are scheduled at the stall bars or ladder, between perpendicular rods or bars, in an Indian or a standing position.

- Postural correction by muscle contraction is achieved through exercises with a therapeutic ball or tilt board.
- Posture while standing is corrected under visual control in front of a mirror. Posture is trained in standing, but control is also learned through playful exercises.
- In a scoliosis program, as well as in general exercises, good posture is based on good support, i.e., healthy feet. Exercises for the feet must be included in the program and symmetrical weight bearing must be emphasized.
- Exercises in quadriped and in standing can be done in small groups, using individualized instruction. Speed and competition stimulate circulation and endurance and support motivation.

Exercise Examples

- PNF: Pelvic and scapular patterns are used to correct a right thorax/left lumbar convex scoliosis (Fig. 10–44); in left side lying against resistance the pelvic pattern of flexion, adduction, external rotation and the scapular pattern of depression and adduction are used. (Note: No general rotation of the upper extremity is used.)
- Klapp's crawling exercise: Step and push for correction and strengthening: During crawling the left arm and the right leg are moved in a swinging motion into a transverse plane. Then the height of the moving extremities is adjusted and abduction and rotation components are added to their fullest extent.
- Exercises with the therapeutic ball for correction and strengthening by use of equilibrium reactions (Fig. 10–45): The patient is prone over the ball, supported by the toes on the ground or by the therapist's hand on the pelvis. Equilibrium reactions can be achieved by muscle contraction, by rolling in a

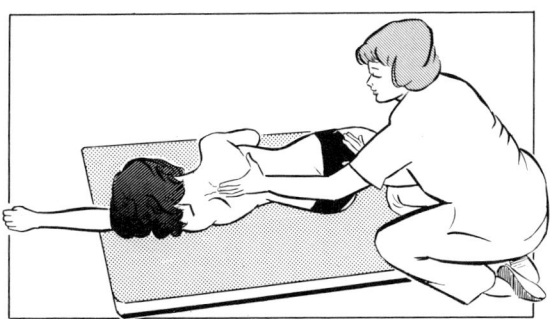

Fig. 10–44 PNF—pelvic and shoulder pattern.

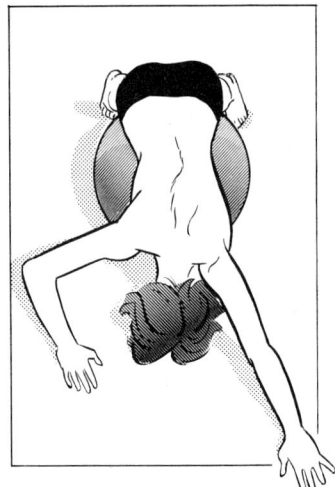

Fig. 10–45 Correction on the ball.

---

certain direction, or by maintaining balance. These exercises should be done symmetrically in cases of mild scoliosis.

- Frog position on the stall bars (Fig. 10–46): The patient hangs in an asymmetric position with the face toward the stall bars for correction. The arm and leg on the convex side are flexed, and the leg is placed in external rotation. The leg on the concave side is extended downward. The patient is asked to pull up to increase tone within this corrective position.

- Corrective exercise standing in front of the mirror: The patient tries to achieve a symmetrical position; the pelvis is placed above the feet, and the depressed side of the thorax is placed above the pelvis with rotation of the shoulder girdle. The therapist facilitates the shoulder girdle and pelvis manually. After the training the patient should obtain these positions independently with closed eyes or spontaneously with light rotatory motions. Dynamic moving patterns are added, since many exercises are only done statically. A child can run, walk, and move the arms in the same rhythm, controlling the trunk. The even rhythm must be checked both visually and auditorally.

- Training in the therapeutic pool: Swimming as a general exercise is important for a patient with scoliosis. The style can be modified by training the legs while holding on to a float, or working with one arm, supporting the other arm with the float. The arms can be moved symmetrically; however, the correcting effect has not been proved.

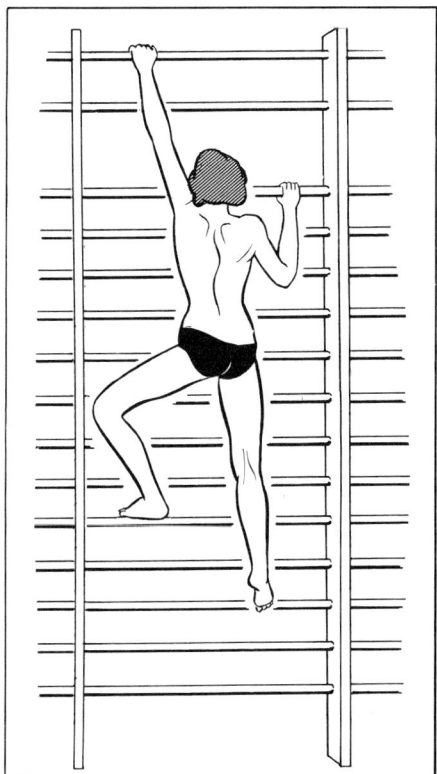

Fig. 10-46 Correction on the stall bars.

Treatment in Braces

Goals of Therapy

- Support the growth of active extension of the spine.
- Provide temporary preoperative support.
- Strengthen trunk musculature.
- Decrease trunk asymmetry.
- Improve extension of the spine.
- Maintain and promote a sense of active extension of the spine without a brace.
- Maintain or improve lung function.
- Provide psychological support of the patient through the long period of living with an immobilization device.

Therapy

The possibilities for therapy are limited because of the need for permanent immobilization. The therapist with imagination and understanding can design a schedule for young patients that provides stimulation and motivation for the years of stressful treatment.

Static exercises are designed for different initial positions. An upright position can be approached relatively early. Because the spine is supported, extension in a sitting or standing position is reasonable and the often required correction of the pelvic position is easier. The static work should be varied. Thus, the back muscles can be trained by working with the extremities. The exercises must be scheduled as a continued standard program and may be made more interesting and entertaining by adding equipment, such as a ball, a rod, a balance beam, or a tilt board. Corrective respiratory exercises are done in between. The feet should always be included in the program.

When the scoliosis is progressive, braces are necessary for external support. Corrective therapy includes extension and derotation. The derotation forces in a scoliosis are stronger than the extension forces when correcting a radiologically measurable lateral bend up to 50° (Cobb), and derotation braces are increasingly used (Stagnara, Boston, Chêneau, et al.) (Fig. 10–47). High scolioses with an apical point above T6 do not offer enough effective space for derotation braces and are more effectively treated with use of a Milwaukee brace. Recently, Boston and Chêneau braces have also been used. Boston braces are used especially in lumbar scolioses, whereas Chêneau braces are better applied in thoracic deviations and double-curved thoracic and lumbar scolioses. The braces have an immediate

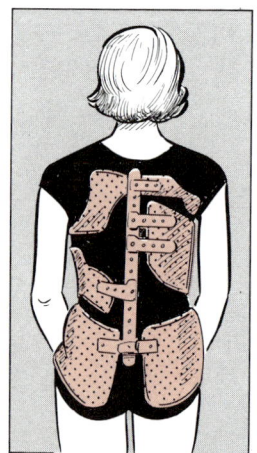 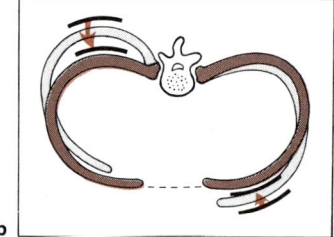

Fig. 10–47 a: Derotation braces; **b:** Derotation principle, demonstrated on the thoracic spine.

correcting effect on the spine and provide a favorable initial position for the therapy program, which includes exercising with and without the brace.

Exercise Examples

- Extension while sitting on a stool (Fig. 10–48): The patient sits bearing weight evenly on both buttocks. The pelvic correction is usually directed toward the direction of the extension; the trunk is extended out of the brace, reinforced by the therapist's manual pressure or by balancing an object on the patient's head.
- Extension while standing in front of a mirror: The patient stands on the floor with weight evenly distributed to both feet. The trunk is extended, with a widening of the thorax on the concave side. The therapist's hand supports the concave side or the patient is asked to pull away from the convex side.
- Balance training on the tilt board (Fig. 10–49): The patient shifts his or her weight in all directions while standing on the tilt board and tries to keep his or her balance. Use of the stall bars for support is allowed as long as the patient needs them to feel comfortable.
- Pushing exercise (Brunkow), alternating half-kneeling position and standing position: The patient comes to a standing position by pushing with the arms in internal rotation and pushing the wrists diagonally against the floor. During the return movement into the half-kneeling position, the arms push forward and upward.

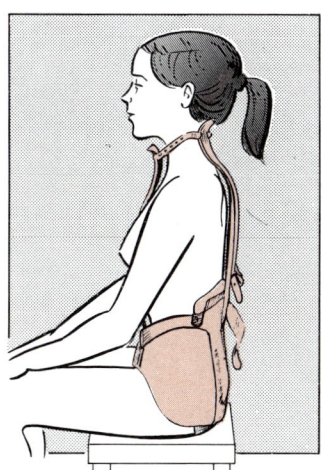

Fig. 10–48 Extension in a Milwaukee brace.

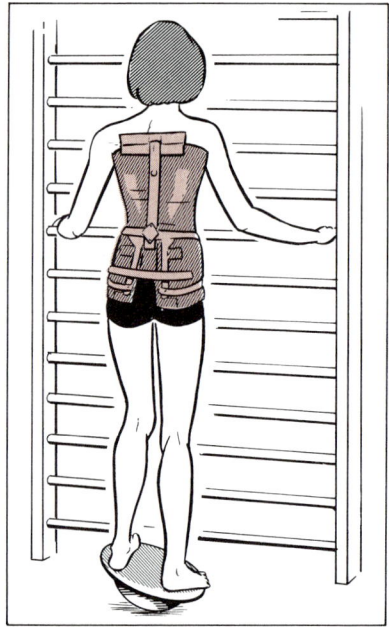

Fig. 10–49 Balance training on the tilt board.

Slow exercises provide an intensive isotonic workout of the trunk musculature and promote extension of the spine.

Exercises To Be Done While in a Brace

- Stretching the iliopsoas to prepare for pelvic extension while in supine position on the edge of a bench or while lying on side
- Active pelvic extension in all positions with and without the braces
- Active extension of the cervical spine
- Respiratory exercises

Preoperative Treatment

Goals of Therapy

- Prepare patient for surgery and help to achieve a favorable result.
- Promote muscle relaxation.
- Mobilize the spine as much as possible.

- Improve vital capacity.
- Maintain lower-extremity muscle strength.

Therapy

- Klapp's crawling exercises
- Mobilization and relaxation in quadriped: Arms and legs may not be elevated from the floor. Therefore, the patient has to slide along the floor.
- Stretching exercises are performed in prone, side lying, or supine position.
- Lower-extremity strength is maintained by use of PNF pattern; resistance is controlled to prevent increased tension of the back musculature.
- When the patient starts sitting up in a wheelchair, respiratory and extremity-strengthening exercises can also be done. The spine is extended rather than mobilized in lateral movements.

Exercise Examples

- Stretching and relaxation exercises are done in a prone position to improve mobilization: support kyphotic position by pillows. Arms are placed beside the head in forward extension; alternately stretch arms and legs, individually, on the same side, and diagonally.
- Twisting and winding during Klapp's crawling: The hands slide along the floor and the trunk remains close to the floor, swinging gently from side to side.
- Mobilization in slings (Fig. 10–50): The upper body hangs in a prone position, with the head touching the lower arms, which are placed in cuffs.

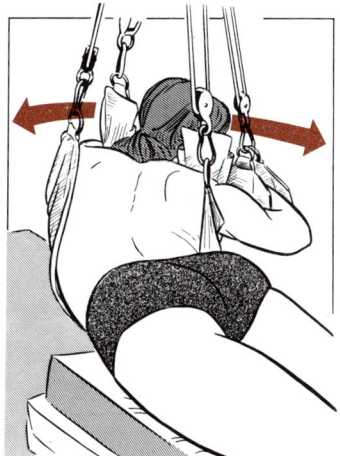

Fig. 10–50 Mobilization in slings.

The body swings from side to side, passively being pushed by another person and actively/passively under self-mobilization. The mobilizing effect is better if the patient swings to both sides and into the direction of the malposition.

- Exercises for patients with halo extension, sitting in a wheelchair (Fig. 10–51): On the concave side the buttock is tightly pushed down against the seat, and the arm on the same side is stretched toward the extension bar. The side of the trunk touches the arm rest of the wheelchair. This exercise is combined with respiration.

Postoperative Treatment after Spondylosyndesis

Early Phase Immediately after Surgery:

Goals of Therapy

- Improve the patient's reduced general condition.
- Help the patient get used to the cast, both physically and mentally.

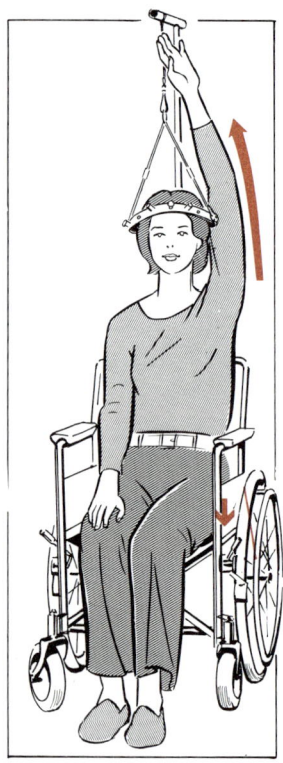

Fig. 10–51 Extension in halo immobilization.

Therapy

- Respiratory exercises and use of incentive spirometry
- Strengthening of lower-extremity musculature with use of PNF patterns that avoid any further movement toward the pelvis and the spine
- Exercising a new movement pattern with the trunk stabilized by the cast: for example, changing between supine and prone positions, standing and balance training, standing and walking.

Late Phase after Stabilization in a Brace:

Goals of Therapy

- Assist patient in transition away from the brace.
- Strengthen all four extremities while maintaining a rigid spine.
- Train in activities of daily living skills.
- Provide information/education on daily routine and sport activities.

Therapy

- After the stabilization phase by external support (cast or braces) the patient must learn again how to move around with a rigid spine but without any support. He or she is trained from a lying position and progresses to a standing position.
- The trunk muscles must be exercised isometrically, but the shoulder girdle is exercised actively. The PNF trunk pattern is useful again, in which the pelvic pattern with rhythmic stabilization can be combined with the scapula pattern with slow return.
- The abdominal muscles are strengthened in the supine position.
- The quadriped position is suitable for various exercises of the extremities and will improve the tone and strength of the back muscles. Balance in standing is trained in various positions, with use of additional equipment, such as a ball, which improves skill, speed, and reaction time.
- Respiratory exercises with emphasis on the thoracic component and restoration of costal mobility are frequently scheduled in between.

Swimming is recommended and, later, sports that the patient likes and is able to handle without stressing the spine too much, such as ball games, running, and gymnastics are allowed with certain limitations. Exercises such as jumping are not recommended because of the comminuting effect on the spine. The patient's exercises must be selected individually.

Infant Scoliosis

In infant scoliosis the spine is fixed in a lateral curvature, which is considered to be a contracture of the autochthonous trunk muscle in an infant. The reason is most likely not an asymmetric position of the infant, but rather a disturbance in the area of the intervertebral disks and the enchondral growth plates. The contracture position is frequently combined with different reflexes on both sides, which has led to the conclusion that disturbances of the motor development and different maturation patterns on the two sides contribute to the deformity.

Positioned radiographs are necessary for a diagnosis, especially for differentiation from a nonfixed malposition (Fig. 10–52). Infant scoliosis is shaped like a C and does not reveal any anatomical change that is different from a deformation scoliosis. Clinically most prominent is the unilateral flattening of one side of the back and the costal hump on the other side, frequently combined with pelvic asymmetry.

Infant scoliosis can be helped by special positioning (Fig. 10–53) and with physical therapy, which is different from that in other types of scoliosis. The mild torticollis that is frequently seen in infant scoliosis regresses during the first year with physical therapy.

Physical Therapy

The therapy must be adapted to the child's age and maturity. The exercises should be a pleasure for the young patient. Certain favorite exercises should be determined and fit into the schedule. Strenuous exercises should be alternated with

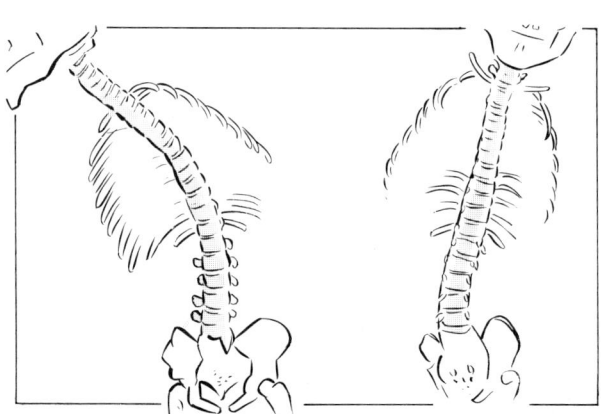

Fig. 10–52 Positioned radiographs confirm scoliosis with a rigid curvature of the lower thoracic spine.

Scoliosis 145

Fig. 10–53 Position in overcorrection (left convex infant scoliosis).

easy ones. However, treatment must be carried out vigorously to achieve a complete symmetry of posture and movements.

Exercises are scheduled daily during hospitalization and two or three times weekly as an outpatient. The intervals between physical therapy sessions may be longer if the parents are involved, so that in an ideal situation the child needs to be brought in only every 1 to 2 weeks. The exercises can be controlled, corrected, and, if necessary, modified. The parents must exercise the child daily. The time for the exercises is increased from a few minutes to a half-hour daily.

Evaluation Results

The examination includes supine and prone positions, sitting, and possibly hanging upside down.

- A distinct sign of infant scoliosis is a lateral deviation of the trunk and head, sometimes also with a lateral direction of the eyes. In a prone position the sides of the thorax are shaped differently: the convex side is narrow, the concave side is wide and flat. The spine is flexed in a wide lateral curvature. The pelvis and sometimes the skin folds of the thighs are asymmetric.
- The baby is held in a sitting position, bent slightly forward. Observing the spine from the head down, the curvature and rotation of the costal hump become obvious (Fig. 10–54). In an upside-down position the baby will try to pull up asymmetrically.

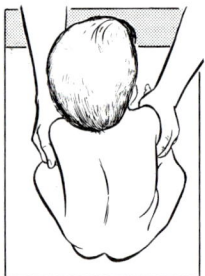

Fig. 10–54 Evaluation of spinal curvature in sitting position.

- Palpation reveals a hypertonus of the muscles on the concave side.
- Spinal mobility is checked. The mobility is restricted in flexion/extension and lateral flexion to the concave side (Fig. 10–55).
- The baby's general motor development and reflexes must be checked. Both can be delayed and different from side to side.

Additional results may be torticollis and asymmetry of the face and skull, restricted abduction of the hip joints, and foot deformities.

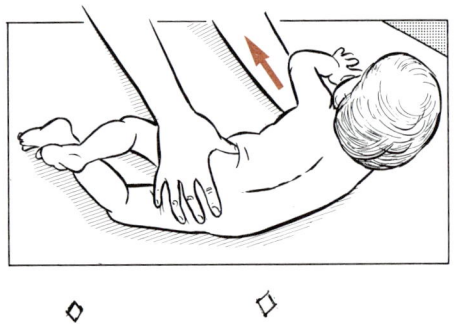

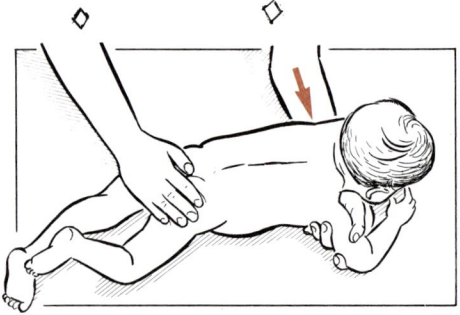

Fig. 10–55 Checking lateral flexion: **a:** free lateral flexion; **b:** restricted lateral flexion.

Scoliosis

Goals of Therapy

- Correct the malposition by training the muscles on the convex side and stretching the muscles on the concave side.
- Promote extension of the spine.
- Strengthen all trunk and extremity musculature.
- Facilitate physiologic symmetrical moving patterns according to the child's maturity.
- Instruct the parents in the child's program.

Therapy

Therapy is adapted to the child's age and developmental stage but should include the following aspects:

- Position: The physician will apply a bivalved cast or bandage for correction during the night. In severe deformities this support must also be used during the day, at least for a few hours. The child should rest in a prone position as much as possible. Active children must be strapped down around the pelvis (Fig. 10–56).
- Position of the crib: The child must lie with the concave side toward the wall, so that optic stimulation, such as light or toys, will cause him or her to get up over the convex side.
- Carrying the child (Fig. 10–57): The child is carried either in a prone position, resting on the iliac crest of the carrying person, or on his or her side with the convex side up, as long as the child gets up well on the side. If the child can prop himself or herself up well enough, he or she can be carried around sitting

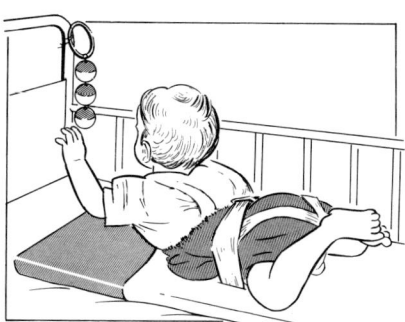

Fig. 10–56 Position of the bed for a right convex scoliosis.

148 Diseases of the Spine and Trunk

Fig. 10–57 Carrying the child: **a:** in prone position; **b:** in a riding position.

on the iliac crest, with the back toward the carrying person. The usual carrying position with the child resting on the arm should be avoided.

- As soon as the child has progressed sufficiently, he or she should play daily for a longer period on a scooter board (Fig. 10–58).
- The exercises consist of active training and facilitation of moving patterns according to the child's age: Active exercises are facilitated by the therapist with tactile, optic, and acoustic stimulation. The resistance is mainly provided by the weight of the entire body or parts of it. Facilitation is preferably done on the therapist's lap or on a ball or pillow. Movements of the head, arms, or legs cause a lateral flexion and rotation of the spine, thus correcting the malposition and activating the muscles. At first the exercises should be asymmetric, but with improving conditions they should include both sides equally. The child can rest while the back muscles are being massaged.
- Instructing the parents or other persons close to the child: Such persons must be familiar with the treatment in order to support and continue the exercises at home. Handling the child must also be learned, in order to observe the corrective influence of movements during changing, dressing, feeding, or

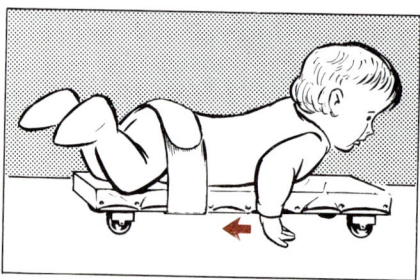

Fig. 10–58 Scooter board.

Scoliosis

playing. The child should never be carried in a bag or holder on a person's body. This will be allowed only when the child is able to maintain an upright position.

Exercise Examples

If the child is placed in a position, he or she should be picked up approximately 30 minutes before the exercises to be able to move freely.

- Moving from the side into an upright position (Fig. 10–59): The child lies on the concave side, with one of the therapist's hands placed under the concave side and the other hand touching the upper iliac crest. Both hands transmit a stretching stimulus on the muscles of the convex side, which reacts with contraction. The head and the shoulder girdle are elevated laterally.
- "Frog" from prone position (Fig. 10–60): The therapist fixes the pelvis with the arm and leg on the convex side in a frog position. The child tries to reach objects before and above him with the arm on the concave side.
- Lateral flexion (Fig. 10–61): In an upside-down position, with the therapist's hands tightly around his or her lower legs, the child hangs into the curvature. The child is encouraged to pull himself or herself up to a squatting position over the muscles on the convex side, supported on pelvis or thorax.

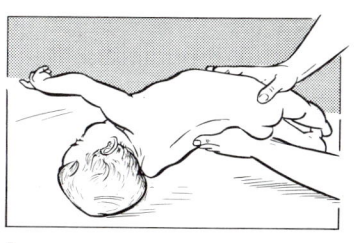
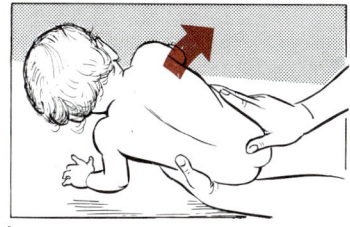

a **b**

Fig. 10–59 Getting up from the side.

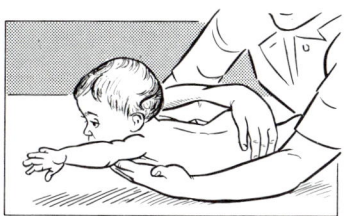

Fig. 10–60 "Frog" from prone position.

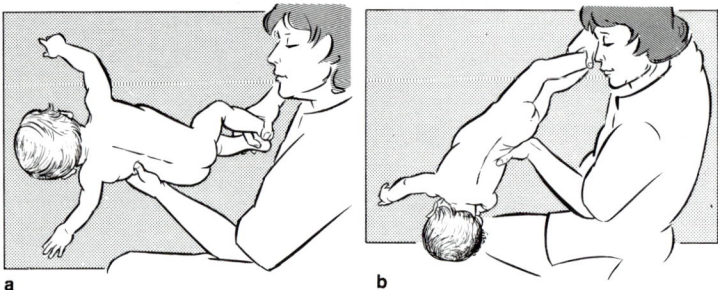

Fig. 10–61 Lateral flexion.

- Prone position on the therapeutic ball (Fig. 10–62): The child is held by the lower legs or possibly the pelvis, fixed, and shifted into a lateral upside-down position. Reflexes cause elevation and rotation.

DEGENERATIVE DISEASES OF THE SPINE

The spine is affected by degenerative processes at a relatively early age. Arthroses of the vertebral joints (spondylosis deformans) and the small vertebral joints (spondylarthrosis deformans) are exceeded in frequency only by arthrosis of the knee joint. Disposition, unphysiologic stress, and the lack of regenerative ability of the discoid tissue are blamed for this condition. Age-related wear of the spine results in a generally decreased quality of the axial spine. This affects bones, soft tissue, and joints and is usually limited to one segment. Endogenous and exogenous factors are thought to cause premature wear, exceeding that of the physiologic aging processes. Prenatal developmental disturbances may have remained in the discoid tissue, resulting in a constitutional weakness. In particu-

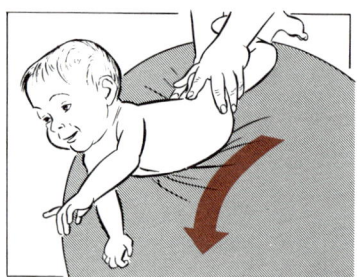

Fig. 10–62 Correction on the therapeutic ball.

lar, static and mechanic conditions (after juvenile kyphosis) are considered. The predominantly static stress on the spine is due to one's lifestyle, vibrations, and unphysiologic movements. Lack of exercise accelerates the wear process.

Spondylosis and Spondylarthrosis

Origin. The lower segments of the cervical and lumbar spine are mainly affected by spondylosis and spondylarthrosis. The wear processes match similar processes in other body joints. Increasing cartilaginous degeneration causes sclerosis of the subchondral area and the formation of marginal ridges or arthrotic processes (Fig. 10–63). An additional transformation in the area of the uncinate process occurs on the cervical vertebrae.

Symptoms. The cervical vertebral foramina are narrowed by this so-called uncovertebral arthrosis, followed by a possible compression of vessels and nerve roots (cervical syndrome). The degeneration of the thoracic spine may occasionally result in radiating pains (intercostal neuralgia), which must be differentiated from angina pectoris. After a ''wrong'' movement a rigid malposition may develop by blockage of the vertebral joints.

The lower segment of the lumbar spine is especially affected by spondylosis and spondylarthrosis deformans. The wear may be accompanied by various symptoms (lumbar syndrome, loosening syndrome).

A special senile ankylosing hyperostosis must be differentiated from the age- and constitution-related wear mentioned earlier. Forrestier's disease is characterized by overgrowing bone formation on the lumbar and thoracic vertebrae, which causes an ankylosis. Patients with diabetes mellitus are affected most often.

Baastrup's disease is characterized by a diminished distance between the neighboring spinous processes of the lumbar segment in combination with a

---

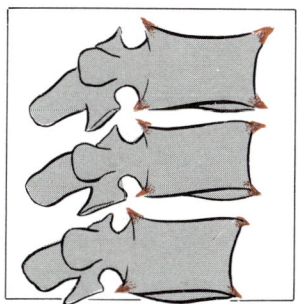

Fig. 10–63 Spondylosis deformans with elongation of the anterior and posterior vertebral edges. The upper intervertebral space is narrowed and the lower space is moderately shifted.

lordosis. The disease is classified as a periostosis, and radiography reveals areas of subperiosteal sclerosis. The symptoms are similar to those of spondylarthrosis and respond mostly to conservative therapy. Otherwise, a partial resection of spinous processes must be considered.

Degenerative changes of the spine can also be caused or worsened by a trauma. The conclusion about a traumatic origin is justified only in the presence of an adequate injury and the evidence of arthrotic changes in the traumatized area.

Treatment. The origin of the degenerative changes cannot be influenced therapeutically. Most important is the prevention of premature wear owing to the influence of one's lifestyle and lack of exercise. Therapy is matched to individual symptoms, including the syndrome of loosening. The pain caused by loosening in one segment must be differentiated from the discomfort owing to a lumbar syndrome. They are the result of diminished intervertebral space and reduced muscle tone. Loosening can also develop adjacent to a segment that is changed by osteochondrosis. Therapy is aimed at creating a compensatory muscular support of the affected segment. Occasionally, supporting braces or an operative spondylosyndesis may be required.

Chondrosis

Origin. The aging of intervertebral tissue, chondrosis intervertebralis, is mainly characterized by tears. The fibrous ring may rupture and give way to the gelatinous nucleus. This type of degeneration generally progresses gradually over a lifetime. It is therefore called "physiologic," considering the age.

The chondrosis can be diagnosed only by indirect symptoms, since the early stage cannot be verified radiographically. Later, the intervertebral space is diminished. During an osteochondrosis the intervertebral disk undergoes gradual degradation. The decrease in height is accompanied by a sclerotic bone reaction of the end plate of the vertebral body (Fig. 10–64). The vertebrae can be shifted against one another, causing a pseudospondylolisthesis in which the nerves are compressed by the narrow vertebral foramina.

Symptoms. The dislocation or protrusion of the discoid tissue, dorsally or dorsolaterally, transmits pressure to the spinal cord or the nerve roots, causing characteristic deficits: cervical syndrome, lumbar syndrome, and sciatica. (See discussion in those specific sections later in this chapter.)

Treatment. The treatment of the discomfort—without distinct neurologic symptoms—mainly consists of heat and exercises, which improve the circulation and muscle strength. Even though the disease cannot be cured, patients can get some relief from the permanent discomfort and pain and sometimes even a complete temporary elimination of the symptoms. The physician and the therapist

Degenerative Diseases of the Spine 153

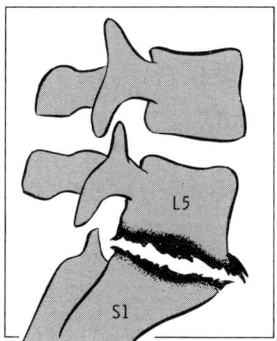

Fig. 10–64 Splitting of the lumbosacral intervertebral space. Osteochondrosis and spondylosis deformans.

must also help the patient to deal with the problems, which are often based only on age-related processes. The patient must learn that constant cooperation can improve his or her well-being, that good and bad periods can alternate, and that therapeutic sessions are indicated at regular intervals. In this way the chronic discomfort can often be prevented from worsening for several years.

Physical Therapy

Examination Result

The patient may exhibit different postures but generally appears rather tense. In the lumbar area the erector spinae muscle is prominent and increases the lordotic curvature. This situation may become more exaggerated by flaccid abdominal muscles and an increased flexion of the pelvis. The tone of the back muscles is increased.

Spinal mobility is restricted generally or in certain segments. Movements such as bending are troublesome and are done in a false pattern.

The patient feels depressed by the permanent discomfort which takes the form of initial, resting, or weight-bearing pain that is increased by an unphysiologic moving patterns.

Goals of Therapy

- Decrease muscle spasms.
- Mobilize the spine.
- Strengthen trunk musculature to provide muscular stability.
- Educate in favorable movement patterns (proper body mechanics).
- Motivate patient to adhere to an independent exercise program.

154 Diseases of the Spine and Trunk

Therapy

- Electrotherapy is used to decrease muscle spasm, which is always combined with decreased blood circulation. Manual massage or hydromassage provides additional relief of the muscle spasm.
- The type of complaint determines the mobilizing or stabilizing character of the treatment. The exercise program is adjusted by the evaluation results and reaction of the patient. In most cases the patient must first learn the sense of tension and relaxation and of the mobility of the lumbar spine.

In both sitting and standing positions the spine is prepared for the postures needed during daily life.

SPINAL SYNDROME

Cervical Syndrome

Origin. Degenerations of the cervical spine are the reason for the complaint called cervical syndrome, or shoulder-arm syndrome if the upper extremities are also involved. The neck, shoulder, and shoulder-arm area are affected by pain. Mobility is restricted around the cervical spine, and the shoulder joints in the shoulders and arms are involved. Neurologic deficits occur, depending on the severity.

Symptoms. Clinically, the situation must be differentiated from a stiff shoulder after injury, inflammation, tumor, congenital deformities, and metabolic disturbances.

The special symptoms of cervical syndrome are based on the structure and function of the cervical spine. In contrast to the lumbar syndrome, the degenerative processes of the cervical spine are due less to degeneration of the intervertebral disks than to narrowing of the intervertebral foramina, caused by hypertrophic marginal ridges of the uncovertebral processes. Uncovertebral arthroses are related to intervertebral osteochondrosis and can be verified radiographically. However, the radiographic result may be of little help, even in a strong cervical syndrome.

Diagnosis and therapy must be based on the complaints and the results of the clinical evaluation. Frequently, the patients complain of headaches and sometimes of nausea and visual disturbances. Pains radiate from the lower cervical spine into the arms and hands, followed by hypoesthesia or hyperesthesia and later by muscle atrophy as a sign of neurologic damage. This can be used to estimate the level of the cervical disturbance.

The close relation of the vertebral artery to the spine is responsible for the vascular involvement by irritation of the vascular walls and partial constriction of the vascular lumen. They mask the neurogenic disturbances, owing to the uncovertebral arthrosis and the arthrotic changes of the small vertebral joints with smaller intervertebral foramina. Patients often have a labile constitution.

Treatment. Treatment is based on the etiology and must be adapted to the symptoms. There is no therapy for the underlying degeneration, other than surgery in a few cases (enlargement of one intervertebral foramen or blockage of one segment under extension, spondylosyndesis according to Cloward). The conservative treatment deals with the resulting disturbances, such as hardened muscles, myogelosis, neuralgia, and restricted mobility. Acute symptoms require temporary immobilization (bandage or collar) and antiinflammatory and relaxing medication. Mild extension, and in some cases manual decompression of nerve roots, may be considered, especially in the subacute stage.

Physical Therapy

The diagnosis of cervical syndrome indicates a combination of symptoms; they may all occur at the same time or one may be prevalent. Therapy for chronic syndromes must be focused on the main complaints. Physical therapy, including hydrotherapy and electrotherapy, is important for such patients. The therapeutic schedule must be designed accordingly and is frequently oriented toward the patient's information and reactions.

Evaluation Results

Information about the patient must first be noted. This may include the following:

- *Cervical spine:* Pain, stiffness, tension, restricted mobility (realized first when looking backward in a car), instability
- *Head:* Headaches, nausea
- *Arms:* Radiating pains in one or both arms; sensations such as tingling, numbness, decreased strength; signs of epicondylitis

Inspection may reveal the following:

- Tension around head and shoulders
- More prominent muscle contours (upper edge of the trapezius and sternocleidomastoid muscles) may be unilateral
- Elevated shoulder
- A relatively straight, but frequently also a lordotically bent, cervical spine

The hardened edges of the trapezius and rhomboid muscles can be palpated.

The function of the cervical spine must be checked in all three dimensions. The lateral flexion and rotation are limited most (unilaterally and bilaterally). Retraction of the atlanto-occipital joint (pulling the chin back) is often impossible, especially in cervical lordosis.

The patient is reluctant to move in the requested way because of his or her unstable cervical spine and loose segments. The entire posture must be assessed, since this is the deciding position of the cervical spine and the head.

Goals of Therapy

The following goals of therapy are directed at relieving pain:

- Achieve relaxation of muscle spasm.
- Improve circulation in the shoulder-arm area.
- Reduce stress on the cervical spine.
- Improve mobility of the cervical spine.
- Achieve muscle balance in the cervical spine and thoracic area.
- Achieve postural realignment.
- Give advice concerning activities of daily living and work.

Therapy

The treatment is adjusted to the individual symptoms. Stress reduction is always important. Exercises must be done in a perpendicular line to improve relaxation or stability in a sitting position under visual control in front of a mirror.

- The exercises are preceded by the application of heat and electrotherapy to alleviate the pain, tension, and lack of circulation, which are all interdependent. Electrotherapy has proved successful for treating severely tensed muscles of the neck and shoulder girdle. Ultrasound is also useful, as are whirlpool baths.
- Stress reduction of the cervical spine in a younger patient can be accomplished by cervical traction. A halter sling should be placed on the patient's occiput with a traction force applied to the cervical spine that is in a mildly kyphotic position while the patient is supine. The period of traction is increased from 3 to 15 minutes. After this, exercises are scheduled.
- The muscles in spasm are relaxed by massage. Patients with headaches or nausea react well to connective-tissue massage.

The therapy schedule for patients with severe tension and limited mobility is as follows:

- Manual traction in longitudinal direction in a 10-second interval with paravertebral pulling (Fig. 10–65), possibly placing the head in a sling
- Effleurage between the transverse processes during lateral flexion
- Relaxation techniques for the trapezius and levator scapulae muscles
- Training active extension of the cervical spine by retraction
- Training isolated movements of the head under traction
- PNF: head pattern of flexion, lateral flexion, and rotation following active extension of the cervical spine by retraction.

Side Lying Position:

- PNF pattern for the scapula, using the "slow return" technique
- Relaxation technique for the muscles (described earlier).

Sitting Position:

- Manual traction for the upper and lower cervical spine
- Training active extension (described earlier). This exercise should become a daily routine.
- Intensification of extension by resistance dorsally within the single segments
- Relaxation exercises for shoulder girdle and, if necessary, arm exercises scheduled in between.

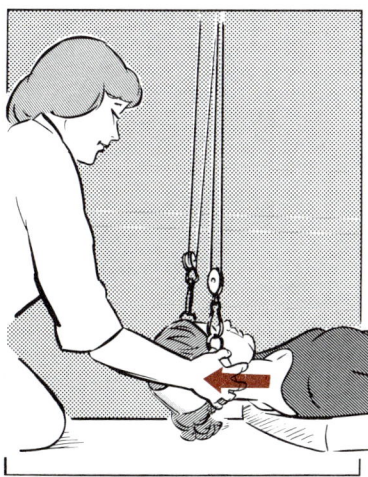

Fig. 10–65 Manual traction in longitudinal direction.

158 DISEASES OF THE SPINE AND TRUNK

Sitting and Standing:

- Correction of the entire posture
- Supported position in both sitting and standing.

If the arm is affected, it is placed in a sling in side lying position, to exercise movements of the scapula and shoulder under reduced weight (Fig. 10–66).

Some patients react favorably to cold packs and exercise with an ice pack around their necks.

Thoracic Syndrome

Origin. Degenerative changes of the thoracic spine segments and, occasionally, arthroses of the costotransverse joints result in thoracic syndrome.

Symptoms. The main symptom is pain along the ribs (intercostal neuralgia), which must be differentiated from angina pectoris and painful diseases of liver and gallbladder. Destructive processes, such as tumors, inflammations, or osteopathy, must be excluded by careful examination, since they could cause similar symptoms. Sometimes a blockage occurs, as in the cervical spine.

Therapy. The treatment is similar to that for a cervical syndrome: antiinflammatory medication, muscle relaxation, and, possibly, manual techniques. Intramuscular or paravertebral injections are commonly used.

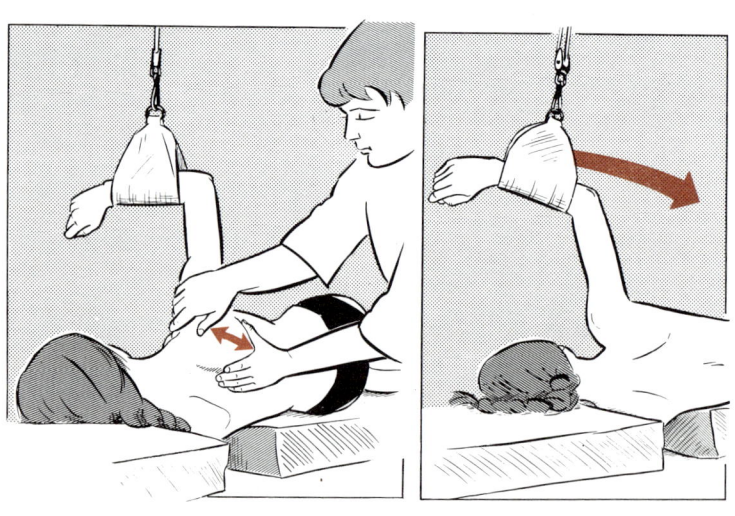

Fig. 10–66 Arm placed in a sling: **a:** scapular pattern; **b:** active swinging.

Lumbar Syndrome

Origin. The lumbar syndrome is characterized by pain around the sacral area. Sometimes it can occur suddenly. If the pains radiate into the legs (mostly unilaterally), it is called sciatica. In both cases pain is caused by degeneration of the lumbar spine and must be differentiated diagnostically from urologic, gynecologic, or psychological problems.

Symptoms. The complaints and evaluation results in lumbar syndrome depend on the type and location of the wear process and the resulting irritation of the nerve roots. Most often the intervertebral disks between the fourth and fifth lumbar vertebrae and between the fifth vertebra and the sacrum are diseased. Tears and gaps in the posterior part of the fibrous ring allow a dislocation of the nucleus pulposus. The nucleus protrudes into the vertebral canal. Extensive tears result in a prolapse of discoid tissue. Sometimes a sequester develops that must be removed surgically. Most often, the location of the prolapse is lateral due to the presence of the strong dorsal ligament. The displaced tissue causes pressure on the surrounding tissue, which results in persistent and recurrent discomfort involving the sympathetic nerve fibers.

The clinical picture in lumbar syndrome is characterized by hardening of the lumbar muscles, restricted motion, and stiff position of the lumbar spine. The pain increases with coughing or sneezing, and pain can be initiated by palpating the area of the affected segment. Lasègue's sign (straight leg raise test) is frequently positive. Besides differences in reflexes, sensory deficits and paralysis may develop. Sensory deficits along the outside of the thigh and the calf to the dorsum and the lateral edge of the foot are typical of disk prolapse at the lumbosacral space. The rare medial prolapse causes pain radiating into both legs and sensory deficits, which can be combined with disturbances of the urinary bladder and colon function. Careful differentiation from tumor and inflammation is required in case of bilateral neural deficits.

Radiographic evaluation often confirms the result by showing flattening of the lumbar lordosis or kyphosis (Fig. 10–67) and a lateral bend of the lumbar spine (Fig. 10–68). In advanced chondroses the affected intervertebral space is often narrower; however, it may appear wider in an early stage, owing to edematous tissue. An advanced osteochondrosis with severely narrowed intervertebral space and arthrotic enlargement of the vertebral edges often indicates a completed pathological process and may not be responsible for other problems (Fig. 10–69).

Not only are lumbar and sciatic syndromes based on chondroses or osteochondroses, but also problems caused by loosening and, in extreme cases, even pseudospondylolisthesis (see section on spondylosis and spondylolisthesis earlier in this chapter).

A special symptom is coccyalgia, and frequently a psychological component is predominant. Female patients in particular complain about pains radiating from

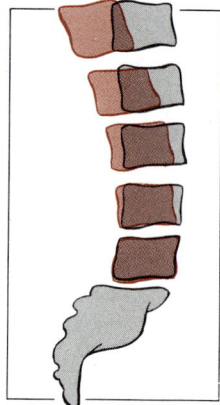

Fig. 10–67 Flattening of the physiologic lumbar lordosis—straight position.

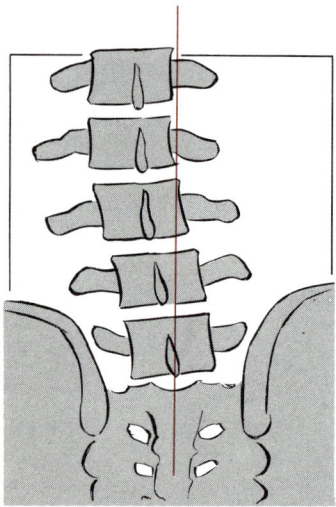

Fig. 10–68 Stiff posture in a lateral bend of the lumbar spine owing to irritation of the nerve roots.

the inguinal area to the sacrum. Sitting on a hard seat intensifies the pain, and the sacral area is sensitive to pressure. Sometimes the function of the colon is disturbed.

The radiograph is often not characteristic; however, occasionally a traumatic rotation or a congenitally abnormal position of the sacrum can be diagnosed.

Spinal Syndrome   161

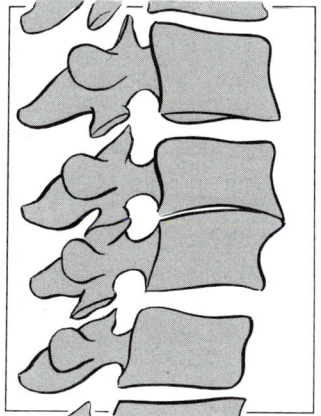

Fig. 10–69 Narrowing of the intervertebral space in the area of an old chondrosis with fixation of this segment.

Treatment. Therapeutic techniques vary, depending on the symptoms. Physical therapy can be combined with medication and injections, electrotherapy, acupuncture, psychotherapy, and sometimes resection of the sacrum.

The treatment of the lumbar syndrome is mainly conservative. An immediate indication for surgery is a medial prolapse with bilateral neurologic deficits (disturbances of urinary bladder and colon function), and in a prolapse or sequester with unilateral symptoms, as soon as paralysis starts to develop (Fig. 10–70). Acute complaints frequently improve with therapy. The lumbar spine is directed into a kyphosis by special positioning, and the intervertebral foramina are enlarged; in addition, antiinflammatory and sedating medication is given. Careful

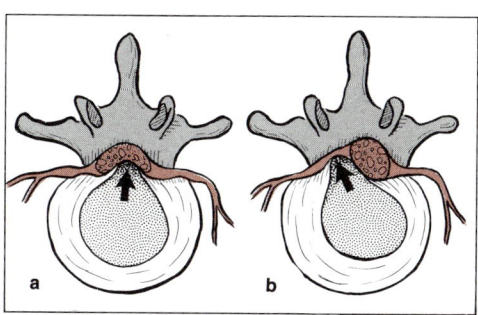

Fig. 10–70 Medial prolapse of the nucleus pulposus. In **a:** causing pressure on the spinal cord; **b:** dorsal-lateral prolapse with pressure on the nerve roots.

physical therapy, e.g., with hot packs and then gentle extension exercises, is scheduled to provide for more muscle relaxation.

As soon as the acute problems have subsided, intensive muscle training is important to build up effective muscle support for the affected segments and to counteract recurrent problems. During the subacute and chronic stage, use of a corset has proved successful (Fig. 10–71); however, with prolonged use it must not initiate muscle atrophy.

Disk surgery (removing the prolapse or sequester and evacuating the intervertebral space) is indicated if the conservative treatment fails and, especially, if the neural deficits worsen and myelography or tomography confirms the diagnosis (Fig. 10–72). Intensive muscle-strengthening exercises are mandatory postoperatively.

In cases of chronic discomfort without prolapse, especially with loosening symptoms but also in old or debilitated patients who cannot withstand surgery, the application of orthoses (special corsets) is helpful.

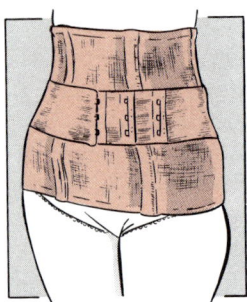

Fig. 10–71 Elastic corset in addition to physical therapy in conservative and postoperative treatment.

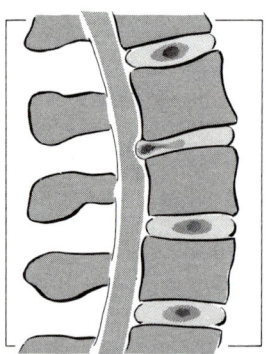

Fig. 10–72 Protrusion of the disk with displacement of the intervertebral tissue toward the spinal canal.

Spinal Syndrome

Physical Therapy

Therapy of acute and subacute lumbar syndrome must take into account the severe pain complaint by the patient.

Conservative Treatment:

Evaluation Results

The posture is stiff and tensed and the range of motion severely restricted. The trunk is drawn to one side, the thorax is shifted laterally against the pelvis, and the lumbar spine has an additional kyphotic curvature. Even weight bearing on both legs and overextension of the hip joints are often impossible. The back muscles, especially in the lumbar area, are hard and tensed.

In sciatica the sensory and motor function of the legs must be examined. There can be differences in sensory function in comparison to the normal side and motor deficits, especially in the quadriceps muscle and in the dorsiflexion of the foot. The stretching ability of the dorsal leg muscles is decreased, and stretching these muscles is frequently painful.

Goals of Therapy

- Promote muscle and general body relaxation.
- Mobilize the spine and restore movement.
- Strengthen back musculature.
- Promote optimal segmental movement.
- Avoid recidivism by counseling the patient concerning daily routines and work.
- Educate the patient in correct posture while lying down and in sitting and standing positions.

Therapy

It must be decided whether to attempt pain relief and muscle relaxation by the use of cold or heat. Cold packs are placed on the tensed back muscles during physical therapy. The duration of the application depends on the patient's tolerance. At first the patient is placed in a supine position, to provide the conditions for relaxation. The head, arms, and legs are supported accordingly. The lumbar spine is mobilized in a lateral flexion in a non-weight-bearing condition, followed by isometric exercises for the abdominal muscles. Arms and legs are used as levers, individually or together diagonally. Turning en bloc is exercised to reach the side lying position. Next the lumbar spine is mobilized in flexion/extension under non-weight-bearing conditions, followed by a rhythmic stabilization of the pelvis over the pelvic scapular pattern.

The exercises can be done under cold packs. A pelvic pattern combined with the "slow return" technique is added if the condition is improving. Emphasis is placed on the extension pattern. Exercises in quadriped are the next step, building up a perpendicular direction (static and dynamic). Movements that are part of a daily routine (e.g., bending down) are practiced. These exercises are matched to the individual's stage of recovery in order to avoid recidivism.

An individualized program of home exercises is designed.

Treatment After Disk Surgery

Evaluation Results

After surgery the evaluation is restricted to the patient's general status and function of the extremities, since the patient will be in supine position for the first treatment and should not be turned. The trunk may still exhibit a lateral tilt caused by the preoperative condition.

The range of motion of the extremities is tested actively and passively. Hip flexion is allowed only with knee flexion and then only to 90°. Extension is allowed only to 0°, to avoid continuing motion of the pelvis and the lumbar spine.

The muscles are tested for their strength, especially the dorsiflexion of the foot and the quadriceps muscles. The tension of the trunk muscles is tested. The patient's statements about pain sensitivity are recorded.

Goals of Therapy

- Prevent pneumonia and thrombosis.
- Strengthen trunk musculature.
- Provide muscular support to the spine.
- Strengthen the lower-extremity musculature.
- Strengthen weakened lower-extremity musculature.
- Promote well-coordinated daily living skill movement patterns.

Therapy

After 2 days of pneumonia and thrombosis prophylaxis, during which the upper extremities and the foot muscles are exercised actively and the leg muscles isometrically, the actual therapy is started with isometric exercises of the trunk muscles in a supine position. The abdominal muscles are trained while the hips and knees are in flexion because long lever arms during exercise sessions must be avoided.

Exercises to improve the tone of the abdominal and back muscles can be combined with training of the leg muscles by using lower-extremity PNF patterns. Resistance is increased during the course of the exercises, and a holding pattern is added to the end of the motion.

Repeated stretch, repeated contraction, and rhythmic stabilization are PNF techniques used for weak muscles of the lower extremities.

During the next therapy session the patient turns en bloc into a prone position. A prepared pillow prevents lordosis. This position should be maintained for 30 to 60 minutes to reduce stress on the back. Application of ice may be provided during prone lying.

Next the patient must learn to push up with a stiff back from a prone into a quadriped position. At first some patients feel nauseated, but this feeling gradually subsides with exercise. In this position the patient is stabilized by manual stimulation, especially in lateral flexion and rotation.

During the following exercises this position is preferred so that the area of surgery remains stable (the therapist's arm may support the patient under the stomach at the umbilical level if necessary).

On postoperative days 10 through 14 the patient gets up for the first time. Despite the daily training, circulation may be unstable. Support hose for the lower extremities and appropriate medication are necessary.

During the following treatment sessions, ambulation is practiced without support and trunk exercises are continued. It is important, again, to emphasize positional changes. The patient must learn to change from supine to sitting position and back by using side lying. Flexion exercises are eventually added. To improve postural stability, sitting postures are practiced on the therapeutic ball.

Exercise Examples

Isometric Muscle Contraction. Supine position with flexed knees and feet on the floor:

- The heels are pushed against the floor with dorsiflexion of the feet. The patient maintains this position against the therapist's pressure.
- The patient holds one arm in the position of extension, adduction, internal rotation against the therapist's pressure (Fig. 10–73).
- Both arms are extended toward the ceiling; rhythmic stabilization of both arms by the therapist in the diagonal direction, both unilaterally and bilaterally (Fig. 10–74).
- Bilateral scapular pattern in combination with exercise 1 (Fig. 10–75).
- Combination of exercises 1 and 2, 1 and 3.

In all exercises the tone of the trunk muscles increases as the extremity musculature contracts.

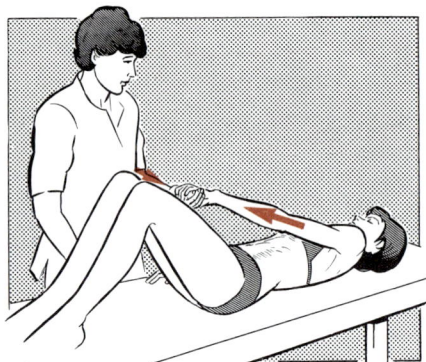

Fig. 10–73 Tension of the abdominal muscles over isometric arm pattern.

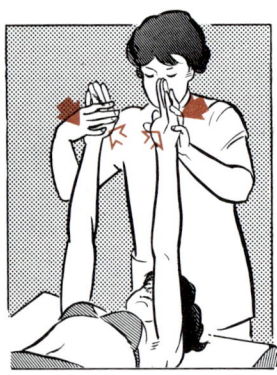

Fig. 10–74 Rhythmic stabilization PNF pattern.

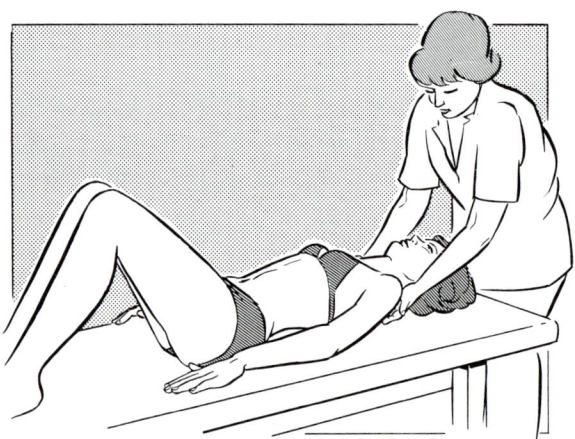

Fig. 10–75 Bilateral scapular pattern.

- Changing between supine position and side lying (Fig. 10–76). Turning en bloc into right side lying: Lower extremities flexed, right hand under the head, left arm pushing in the diagonal direction against the hand of the therapist, who is also supporting the pelvis. Patient then turns back into the supine position, using the opposite arm pattern, and the therapist supports the legs.

Side lying:

- PNF pelvic pattern with use of rhythmic stabilization technique.
- PNF pelvic and scapular patterns with the use of rhythmic stabilization technique.
- Turning en bloc into the prone position.
- Pushing up into the quadriped position; therapist may need to support the pelvis.
- Rhythmic stabilization of shoulder and pelvic girdle.
- Changing between side lying and sitting on the edge of the bench; from side lying the legs are brought up en bloc: While the upper body is brought up the arms are swung over the edge of the bench to the floor. Support: The patient puts his or her arm around the therapist's shoulder.
- Sitting on the edge of the bench: Patient shifts weight laterally by alternated pushing of the arms against the therapist's contact hand.
- Sitting on a stool: With the lower extremities in abduction, the patient shifts the trunk forward by flexing the pelvis at the hip joints. For added stability, rotation can be incorporated into this exercise.

Unassisted Exercises for the Patient. Isometric and active exercises such as turning en bloc, sitting up and lying down over the side, and bending down with stabilized spine, are all mandatory for patients with spinal problems.

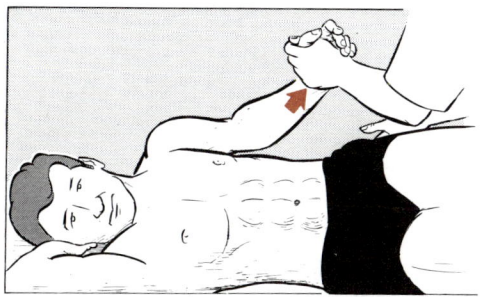

Fig. 10–76 Turning into side lying en bloc.

168   DISEASES OF THE SPINE AND TRUNK

Supine position:

- Weightless mobilization of the lumbar spine: The patient shifts the lumbar spine alternately, first cranially and then caudally; the range of motion is decreased and the speed increased, causing a mobilization of the single segments of the lumbar spine in lateral flexion.
- Bilateral extremity pattern: Upper and lower extremities are placed in the body diagonals; right arm and left leg are brought together above the umbilicus in elbow and knee flexion while the remaining extremities are pressed against the floor.

Side lying:

- Training flexion/extension of the cervical and lumbar spine by flexion/extension of the extremities of the upper side. Abduction/adduction and rotation can be added using PNF patterns (Fig. 10–77).
- Pushing: The hand of the upper arm pushes against the floor of the sternum, with the upper leg pushing in the direction of extension.

Quadriped:

- Weightless mobilization of single spinal segments; the extremities push into the floor; the head remains in a line extended from the spine.
- Flexion/extension of the entire spine over arm and leg movements (Fig. 10–78).
- Pushing all four extremities into the floor, try to move knees and hands toward each other and away from each other (Fig. 10–79).

Sitting on the therapeutic ball (Fig. 10–80):

- Mobilization of the lumbar spine into flexion/extension and lateral flexion, rolling the ball slowly, remaining sitting on the floor in an upright position.

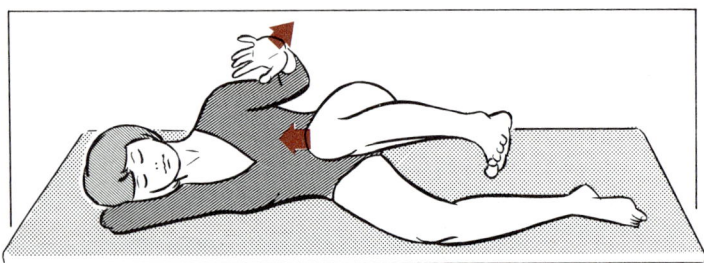

Fig. 10–77 Flexion and extension of the spine over the extremity in side lying.

Spinal Syndrome 169

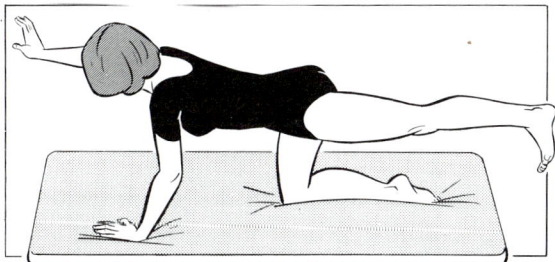

Fig. 10–78 Flexion and extension of the spine over the extremities in quadriped.

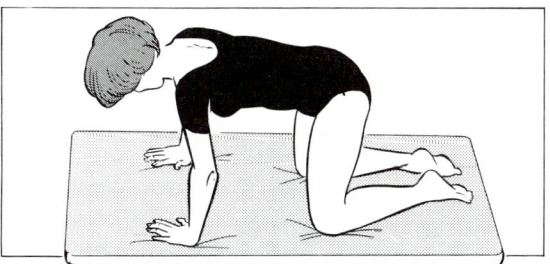

Fig. 10–79 Pushing exercise in quadriped.

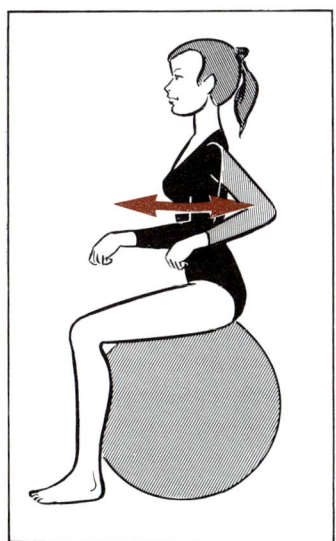

Fig. 10–80 Mobilizing the lumbar spine on the ball.

Variations:

> —Force transmission by the plantar flexion of the feet, and rhythmic arm movement (as in walking).
>
> —To increase the tone of the trunk musculature the arms are moved away abruptly from the trunk.

- Pushing exercises to change position between standing and squatting (Fig. 10–81): The position is changed with stabilized spine by pushing the arms in the opposite direction.
- Walking with imaginary resistance: The arms are moved opposite to the walking rhythm and pushed caudal/ventrally and caudal/dorsally.
- Rhythmic walking: At high walking speeds the patient is forced to stabilize the thoracic spine in free rotation, which makes economic use of the pelvis and lower-extremity musculature.

Exercising bending down with a stable spine:

Preparation on a stool:

- Sitting upright with slightly abducted legs, the patient palpates with two fingers of one hand the distance from umbilicus to symphysis and with two

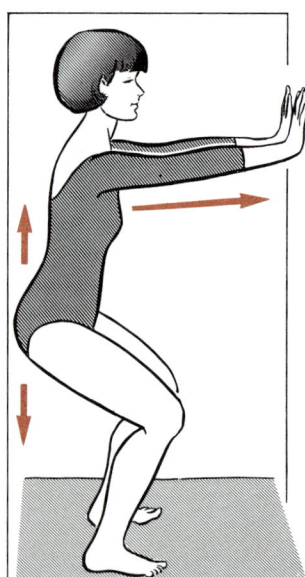

Fig. 10–81 Alternating position between standing and squatting combined with pushing.

fingers of the other hand the distance from umbilicus to tip of sternum. The patient "measures" the distance and maintains it and moves the trunk forward into flexion/extension of the pelvis at the hip joints and then back to the starting position.
- The exercise is repeated without palpating, holding the arms extended beside the trunk.
- The arms are flexed and moved quickly backward and forward, as in marching.
- During "marching" the buttocks are raised from the seat and the trunk is bent forward.

Preparation on a ball:

- Sitting in upright position with slightly abducted legs, rolling the ball under the buttocks both forward and backward; the distances between the symphysis, umbilicus, and tip of the sternum remain the same, causing the trunk to shift.

Standing:

- Legs in slight abduction, with the feet firmly on the floor, the patient performs "marching" with the arms.
- During "marching" flexion/extension of the legs with a backward and forward shifting of the upper and lower trunk is performed.

Small items are picked up only if the spine can be kept in extension during these exercises.

Exercise Examples in the Therapeutic Pool. Patients with spine problems usually enjoy the pool. The heat, buoyancy, and resistive qualities of water allow a greater range of motion without pain, or at least with greatly reduced discomfort. The exercises can be easily designed, starting with swimming movements, "bicycling," paddling with the legs, etc.

- On tiptoe, holding onto the edge of the pool: One leg is held stiffly and moved within small ranges of motion quickly back and forth and from side to side.
- Standing freely in the water: Both arms are held stiffly and moved quickly, alternating back and forth. *Modification:* To increase resistance lead with the edges of the palms or the inside of the palms.
- Jumping from the standing position, both arms striking backward against the water: During these exercises the trunk must not flex.

OSTEOPOROSIS

Origin. Osteoporosis develops when bone resorption exceeds bone formation. The bone is an active organ system and is continually undergoing remodeling. With increasing age the bone, like all tissues, shows involution (senile atrophy). This decrease of bone tissue (senile osteoporosis) is a compensative, physiologic process, which must be differentiated from osteoporotic disease.

Osteoporosis is pathomorphologically defined as a decrease of bone tissue. The quality of the remaining tissue is unchanged.

The ratio of bone resorption to bone formation is called the remodeling balance. It is positive during adolescence, when there is more bone formation. For a short period the balance is even; then it becomes negative. From the third decade of life on an increasing bone deficit is noted.

With increasing age the spongy bone and the cortex develop a negative remodeling balance. The spongy platelets and trabeculae become porous, resulting in a delicate mesh structure. At first the transverse and then the longitudinal trabeculae are decreased. Finally, only the frame structure of the vertebral bodies remains intact.

Symptoms. In a physiologic aging process bone resorption is counteracted by a contraregulation. However, if that mechanism is diseased, osteoporosis begins to develop; it is characterized by wedge-shaped vertebrae in the thoracic spine and fish-shaped vertebrae in the lumbar spine, with decreased weight-bearing ability of the spine itself as well as single vertebra. Finally, osteoporotic fractures can develop, causing sudden violent pain. Besides the so-called senile osteoporosis (or after menopause) there is a special form of juvenile transitory osteoporosis (fish-shaped vertebra disease, according to Lindemann), which results in the same radiologic and clinical symptoms but heals by itself after the onset of sexual maturity.

Osteoporosis can be a symptom of hormonal imbalance (deficit), as in hypogonadism or Cushing's disease. It can be caused by medication with cortisone or by disturbance of the vitamin function (lack of vitamin D) or disturbances of protein metabolism. Symptoms resembling those of osteoporosis can also be caused by loss of electrolytes (abuse of laxatives).

Treatment. In a secondary osteoporosis the cause must be eliminated. If a central regulatory disturbance cannot be found, the treatment is aimed at increasing the bone tissue through improved formation of new bone. The remodeling process is influenced by medication. Sodium fluoride has proved successful in stimulating the formation of new bone and development of fibrous bone tissue. Radiographically, new bone is added to old hypertrophically atrophic trabeculae and appears as sclerotic lines. Calcium, antibiotics, estrogens, calcitonin, and phosphates have not fulfilled therapeutic expectations.

During acute pain episodes analgesics are also given. In some cases it is necessary to apply braces to prevent severe deformities. Physical therapy is extremely important, since exercise stimulates osteoblastic activity. Muscle activity stimulates the osteoblasts indirectly by initiating electrical potentials, which stimulate more cells to build new bone. Activity strengthens atrophic muscles, and the spine is kept in better alignment.

Osteomalacia

Symptoms and radiographic results are similar to those in osteoporosis. The condition results from a decreased mineral content of the bone. The areas of trabecular formation are not sufficiently calcified, and this leads to wide osteoid seams. In adults osteomalacia is caused by D hypovitaminosis and is called starvation osteoporosis if it results from low-quality nutrition with too little fat, protein, or vitamins. It is treated with proper diet.

Histologically, osteomalacia is characterized by wide noncalcified osteoid seams on preexisting normal bony trabeculae. Radiographically, the vertebral structure appears softer and blurred in osteomalacia, whereas it is distinct in osteoporosis (Fig. 10–82). Combinations of both diseases can occur in old age.

Its occurrence is frequently found after stomach surgery or gallbladder resection. The result is similar to that found for starvation osteopathy caused by low-quality nutrition and lack of fat-soluble vitamins. The treatment consists of vitamin D and calcium supplements in combination with physical therapy as outlined for osteoporosis.

Hyperparathyroidism must be ruled out as a differential diagnosis in osteoporosis. It results primarily from the formation of an adenoma of the parathyroids as a generalized fibrous osteodystrophy (Recklinghausen's disease), secondarily

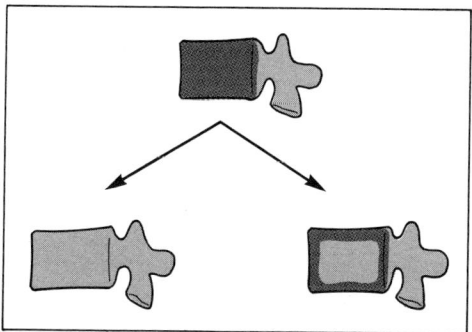

Fig. 10–82 Decreased calcium content in osteoporosis (left below) and osteomalacia "frame" structure (right above).

after impaired renal function (renal osteodystrophy), or tertiarily owing to the formation of a secondary hyperparathyroidism. The treatment is oriented toward the underlying disease. Adenomas of the parathyroids are removed surgically. Additional physical therapy is necessary.

Physical Therapy

Evaluation Results

The examination often cannot be complete, since the spine is immobilized or must stay immobilized in a supine position. The tone and strength of the muscles of the trunk and extremities are checked, and the mobility of the lower extremities is assessed. Any motion of the pelvis and spine must be strictly avoided. The true range of motion of shoulders and hips cannot be evaluated completely without risk to the spine. The patient's pain complaints must always be noted.

Goals of Therapy

- Maintain the status of respiratory and circulatory systems.
- Improve muscular stability of the spine in non-weight bearing, partial, and total weight bearing.
- Support the patient during the immobilization period.
- Teach activities of daily living skills with use of aids as needed.
- Provide a home exercise program.

Therapy

Patients are often placed in a bivalved cast for weeks, and this requires prophylactic treatment of pneumonia and thrombosis. At the beginning of therapy the patient is placed in a prone position with the cast, making sure he or she is comfortable and pain-free. Then the back muscles are massaged. Some patients benefit from application of ice and isometric muscle work. The superficial blood supply is improved and decubitus is prevented. In a supine position the back muscles are exercised isometrically or actively. Arms and legs must be trained to improve overall strength and coordination. Turning en bloc is practiced to prepare for use of a brace.

At first the patient must learn how to get in and out of the brace, depending on his or her individual ability. Frequently, the technique must be changed several times to facilitate this procedure. The patient may become discouraged when first handling the brace. He or she needs to exercise with the brace in positions matched to his or her age. In most cases the perpendicular position is most suitable. Changing positions is practiced. Need for additional aids is assessed.

SPONDYLITIS

Spondylitis, an inflammation of the vertebrae, can be acute, subacute, or chronic. Usually it is caused hematogenously, spreading from a primary focus. A specific spondylitis is caused by a specific pathogenic agent. The most frequent specific spondylitis is tuberculosis. During the course of other infectious diseases, such as abdominal typhus or scarlet fever, septic spondylitis can occur. Pathogenic cocci cause lesions of the intervertebral disks and small vertebral joints during spondylitis caused by *Brucella*. The cause of a luetic (syphilitic) spondylitis is unspecific. Mycoses and echinococcoses can also manifest themselves in the spine.

Specific Spondylitis

Origin. Tuberculosis is the most common form of a specific spondylitis. Until recently, it usually occurred during childhood or late adolescence. Whereas in the past the group up to age 20 was most susceptible, today the so-called senile tuberculosis is more prevalent and occurs in people aged 60 to 70. This type of spondylitis has a long latency period, especially in children, and the symptoms can be unspecific. Persistent pain in the lower area of the trunk, which increase under stress, must be checked for tuberculosis. The lesions are found most often in the vertebral body close to the end plates but can extend over several segments. A characteristic formation of a gibbus can be caused by insufficient treatment. The primary lesion of a vertebral tuberculosis is usually found in the lungs and the related bronchial lymph nodes and, less frequently, in the intestines.

Symptoms. Besides general symptoms (such as sweating at night and weakness or subfebrile temperatures), the spine is held in a locally stiff position, as a reflex reaction with the need for additional support during changes of position. Usually an abscess starts to develop that has a tendency to burst open spontaneously and spread the infection. Radiographs reveal a decreased calcium content in the affected spinal segments, a progressing deformation and destruction of the vertebral bodies with elimination of the intervertebral space (Fig. 10–83). Bone density is usually observed next to the healthy bone tissue. Round shaded areas indicate abscess formation in the soft tissue. As a differential diagnosis other conditions should be ruled out, including tumors or kyphoses owing to other reasons, such as flat vertebrae, and congenital fusion of vertebral bodies.

Treatment. Surgical evacuation might have to be considered. It accelerates the healing process, allows the local application of drugs, and prevents complications from rupture of an abscess. This will also confirm the diagnosis. Otherwise, the treatment is conservative with tuberculostatic medication over a period of 2 years. Immobilization in a cast prevents the development of significant malpositions.

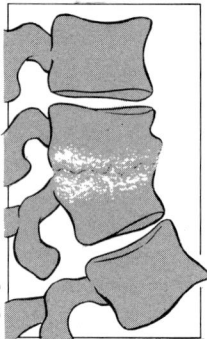

Fig. 10–83 Spondylitis tuberculosa.

After the consolidation of the affected spinal segment and the subsidence of the general symptoms, a brace is applied (Fig. 10–84) and the patient is mobilized. Physical therapy, especially isometric exercises to strengthen the muscles, is indicated and prepares the patient for a later period of weaning from the brace. The patient first gets up from a supine position by rolling from side lying to prone to quadriped and then to a standing position.

Favorable healing of a spondylitis tuberculosa occurs in a block formation and provides for sufficient stability. An operative fusion might be indicated to achieve final bony stability of the segment if the course of the healing is less favorable. The spondylosyndesis also provides for healing of the inflammation and prevention of deformities.

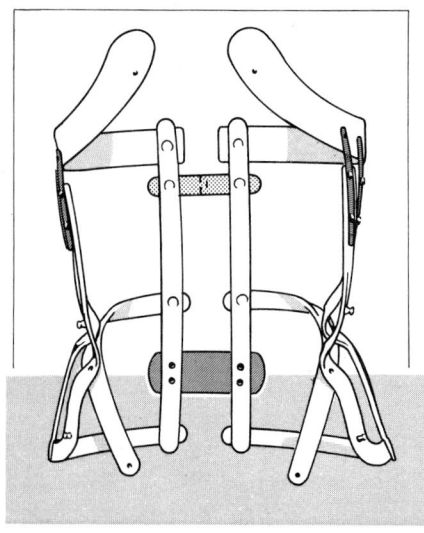

Fig. 10–84 Spinal brace.

Unspecific Spondylitis

Course and Symptoms. Unspecific spondylitis usually has a subacute or acute course, with severe inflammation, high fever, pain, and restricted function opposite to the specific spondylitis. The nerve roots may also be irritated. The motility of the spine is severely restricted; pain can be initiated above the spinous processes of the affected vertebrae. A few weeks after the onset of the disease, radiographs show various degrees of destruction of the vertebral bodies, initially without and later with a strong sclerotic seam (Fig. 10–85). Unspecific spondylitis may take years to heal.

Unspecific spondylitis is often accompanied by a subperiosteal abscess, which seldom ruptures. Sequester formation is also not usual. An abscess can develop in the medullary canal if the inflammative process progresses into the spinal canal. Meningitis can follow with all its subsequent complications and possibly death.

Considerable changes in the shape of the affected vertebral bodies and bending of the spine are also possible in unspecific spondylitis. The patient must be positioned appropriately to prevent these complications.

Treatment. The patient is immobilized after surgical evacuation. A sample of the diseased tissue is taken and cultured to determine the appropriate antibiotic treatment. Antibiotics are administered until the symptoms have subsided and bony consolidation takes place.

The physical therapy program addresses muscle strengthening during the period of immobilization in the brace (Fig. 10–86) and until the healing process is completed. This is indicated by a return to normal erythrocyte sedimentation rate. Surgical intervention in spondylosyndesis must be considered if the spine cannot be stabilized in the way described earlier.

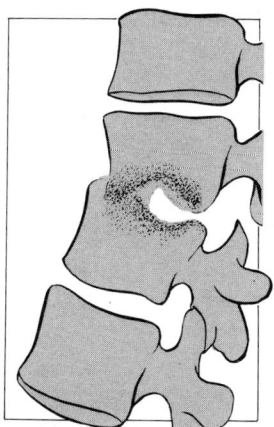

Fig. 10–85 Unspecific spondylitis.

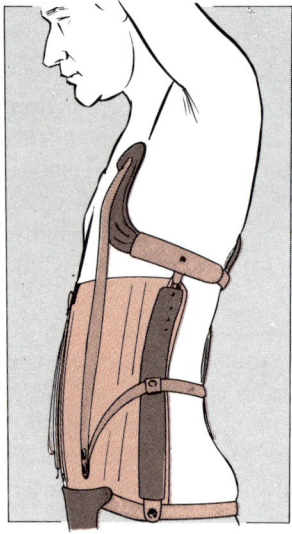

Fig. 10–86 Spondylitis brace.

ANKYLOSING SPONDYLITIS

Origin. Ankylosing spondylitis (Pierre–Marie–Strümpell–Bechterew's disease) is a rheumatoid disease that affects the connective tissue systemically in consecutive episodes. Patients with a leptosomic constitution are mainly affected. The inflammation usually starts at the iliosacral connection (ascending) and, less frequently, in the cervical spine (descending).

This spondylitis is characterized by an ossification tendency of the spine originating from the joints of the vertebral arches. After the atrophy of the articular cartilage and primary periarticular calcifications in the area of the articular capsule, a bony remodeling starts and the subsequent calcification of the disks leads to stiffness of the spine (Fig. 10–87). In Bechterew's disease this process is limited to the spine, whereas in the Strümpell–Pierre–Marie type the large joints of the extremities (hip, shoulder) are also involved. Onset of the disease usually occurs between ages 20 and 30, and men are affected more often than women.

The basic inflammative process is accompanied by disturbances of protein and mineral metabolism, which cause an osteoporosis of the vertebral bodies. Usually the erythrocyte sedimentation rate is accelerated, owing to a dysproteinemia. The temperature is subfebrile. The serologic result is usually negative. The reason is thought to be an infection or focal process (intoxication), similar to chronic rheumatism of the joints. However, a hormonal imbalance is also under present consideration. There also appears to be an inherited disposition (see also Chapter 9).

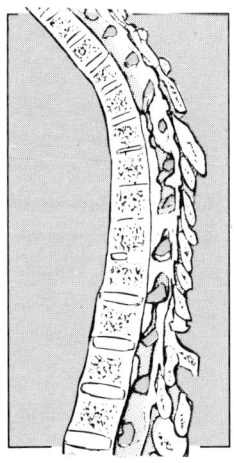

Fig. 10–87 Ankylosing spondylitis with a bamboo-shaped spine.

Symptoms. The course of the disease varies. There are extremely painful cases, in which increasing and stiffening kyphosis is typical. Pain in the heels and knee and hip joints may precede the complications of the spine. An early warning sign is a restriction of respiratory movements, owing to the involvement of the costal joints. Patients complain of an increasingly stiff and painful back (pain at night), weakness, fatigue, nocturnal sweating, pain radiating to the sternum, pain around the iliosacral area, persistent lumbar pain, and pulsating pain during spinal movements. The disease runs its course gradually. In many cases the spine eventually becomes rigid in a widely curved kyphosis (Fig. 10–88). Differential diagnosis of the following diseases must be ruled out: myostatic spinal problems, lumbalgias, inflammations, chronic rheumatism, and Reiter's syndrome.

Treatment. Physical therapy must counteract the increasing kyphosis and maintain sufficient pulmonary function. Also, during the typical painful episodes, analgesics and antirheumatic medication are indicated. Radium isotopes with a short half-life are injected intravenously. They are mainly deposited in the bone, where they inhibit osteoblastic activity. Radiation and cortisone therapy are also common. Osteotomies to straighten the spine must be considered when the kyphosis is so severe that the patient is unable to raise the head to a horizontal position. Early endoprosthetic replacement is indicated if the hip joints are also involved.

Physical Therapy

Ankylosing spondylitis is commonly diagnosed during its early stage. Results of treatment and physical therapy vary. The early phase of treatment is mainly

180   DISEASES OF THE SPINE AND TRUNK

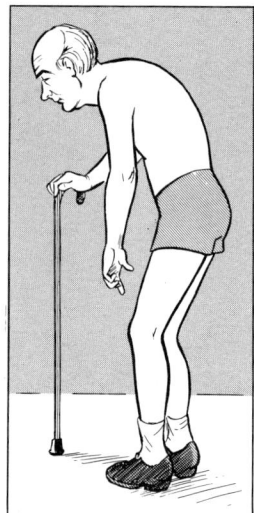

Fig. 10–88 Typical kyphosis with the stiff spine in ankylosing spondylitis.

prophylactic. A patient who has had problems for years, however, must be treated symptomatically.

Although patients with ankylosing spondylitis generally have a positive attitude toward physical therapy, the therapist still needs to motivate the patient during the years of therapy. The program should be attractive, especially since the course of the disease is progressive and the patients' activities have to gradually be cut down.

Evaluation Results

A thorough examination must consider minor symptoms during the early phase. Watching the patient changing clothes gives an indication of his or her ability to move. In an advanced stage the patient's daily living skills will be restricted.

Posture and movements are assessed as follows:

- The entire spine must be evaluated, including respiratory function and costal mobility.
- All proximal, and possibly medial and distal, joints of the extremities must be checked.

During the evaluation note the tone, strength, and stretching ability of the muscles. The following parameters are measured:

- Spinal mobility
  —Distance: Finger to floor in centimeters forward and laterally
- Schober sign in centimeters or inches (see pg. 93)
- Ott sign in centimeters or inches (see pg. 94)
- Cervical spine mobility
  —Distance: Chin to sternal notch in centimeters (or inches)
- Respiratory function
  —Respiratory measurements
  —Vital capacity
  —Respiration frequency and depth during stress
- Range of motion of affected extremities
- Gait evaluation with observation of spinal and hip mobility
- Activities of daily living skills (combing hair, putting on socks, etc.)

All motions can be restricted slightly or severely. The spine of a patient with a longstanding disease is stiff and respiration is typically abdominal. The rigid thorax can cause cardiac insufficiency. The mobility of shoulders and hips can be impaired considerably. The patient can only ambulate with crutches and suffers from frequent and persistent pain. The patient's endurance is minimal.

Goals of Therapy

- Maintain the mobility of the spine, ribs, and extremity joints.
- Mobilize the thoracic spine.
- Improve vital capacity.
- Improve spinal and extremity range of motion.
- Maintain spinal extension ability.
- Improve cardiopulmonary endurance, especially in younger patients.
- Provide aids for activities of daily living.

Therapy

Therapy is oriented toward the aspects mentioned above, regardless of the stage of the disease. The importance of the individual aspects varies, depending on the stage and severity of the symptoms.

- Application of ice or hot packs: The therapist decides after a trial period which method is best for the individual patient.
- Mobilizing the thorax and improving respiration by

    —connective tissue massage of the entire thorax.
    —stretching and positioning in extension, using the supine, side lying, and, if possible, prone positions.
    —respiratory exercises in all positions.
    —respiratory exercises sitting on a stool.

- Training spinal motility in all possible positions: In quadriped, sitting on a stool, or on the therapeutic ball.
- Exercises for the abdominal and trunk muscles in non-weight-bearing positions.
- Manual mobilization of joints of the extremities. The range of motion achieved is exercised and maintained by PNF patterns.
- During hydrotherapy the patients exercise alone or in groups, moving the extremities toward the thorax and spine. Hydrotherapy is also used as endurance training, since the hydrostatic pressure and temperature stress the heart and circulation. Cardiac activity is additionally challenged by increasing speed during the exercises.
- *Group therapy:* Several patients should be treated together for an extended period, as long as the stage of the disease allows it. Exercises can be chosen that make the program more attractive, such as exercises with a partner, games, and using hand equipment. Patients often enjoy group activity. Sessions should be scheduled twice a week and should last for 30 to 40 minutes. For all types of treatment it is important to remember that the more the patient is affected and the older he or she is, the more the program has to be modified.

Exercise Examples

- Extension position and manual stimulation of respiration (Fig. 10–89): In side lying position with the legs flexed, the upper arm is placed across the head. It must be decided whether the head should be placed on a cushion, since lateral flexion of the cervical spine can be favorable for the extension and stretching position. The patient's respiration is deepened by manual stimulation.
- Side lying position with rotation to relax tension (Fig. 10–90): Supine position; the arms rest loosely beside the head; one leg is placed in a flexed position across the other, resulting in an intensive rotation of one side of the trunk-thorax. Some supporting cushion is necessary, but only a minimum. Position stimulates deepened respiration.

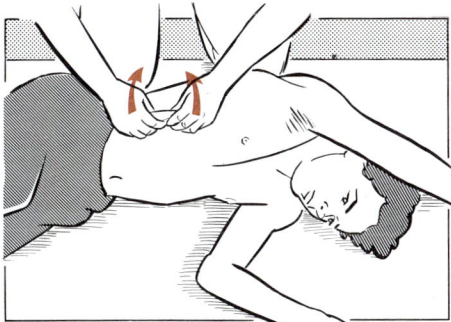

Fig. 10–89 Stretching with respiratory stimulation.

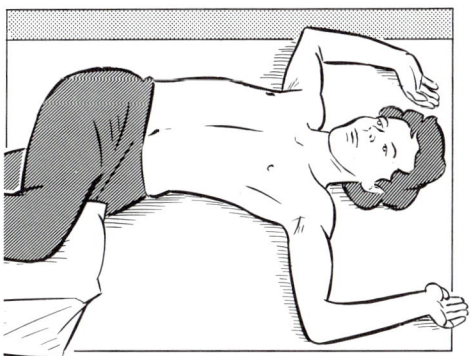

Fig. 10–90 Side lying with rotation.

- Bending and rotating the trunk while sitting on a stool (Fig. 10–91): Sitting on a stool; right arm is behind the head. Right elbow is then extended and rotated back beyond the initial position, against the therapist's manual resistance.

- Mobilization exercises on the stool: Sitting on a stool, feet securely on the floor. Swinging the arms, continuing the motion toward the spine, for instance, swinging the arms upward in combination with extension of the spine. Ideal use: lordosis, swinging backward toward kyphosis.

- Mobilization in lateral flexion on the therapeutic ball (Fig. 10–92): In a riding position on the ball, facing the stall bars, holding onto a bar above the head, the patient rolls on the ball to the sides, trying to maintain his or her position on the ball.

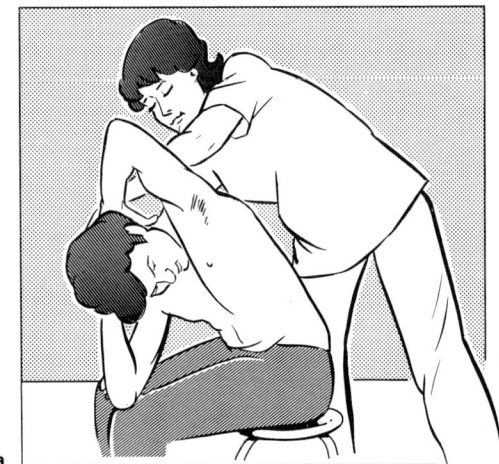

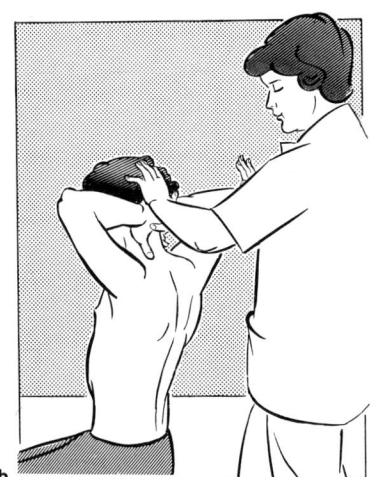

Fig. 10–91 Bending and rotating the trunk while sitting on a stool.

SPINAL TUMORS

Primary tumors of the spine are uncommon but impact on the function of the axial spine. The tumors may be benign or malignant. The most common type of spinal tumors are metastases, or secondary tumors.

The symptoms of spinal tumors are unspecific, which makes it difficult to distinguish them from degenerative or inflammative spinal diseases. Pain that is

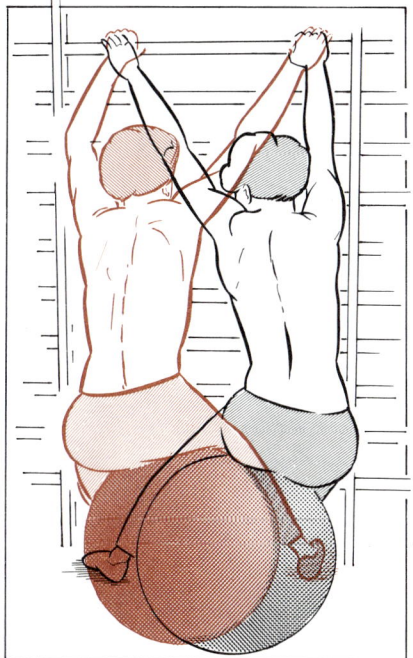

Fig. 10–92 Mobilization in lateral flexion while sitting on the therapeutic ball.

unresponsive to therapy and neurologic deficits based on a pathologic fracture may suggest a tumor. Malignant tumors also cause an elevated erythrocyte sedimentation rate and other characteristic laboratory results.

Radiography reveals structural changes of the vertebral bodies. The disks remain intact for a long time, in contrast to inflammations, during which they become narrower within a short time. In tumors as well as inflammations there is a scintigraphic concentration. A correct diagnosis can be made only with a tissue biopsy and histopathologic evaluation.

Primary Spinal Tumors

Primary spinal tumors usually occur from age 40 on and are found in all types of tissues.

Benign and malignant tumors seldom originate from cartilaginous tissue; more often they are formed in bone tissue. Benign primary tumors are mainly osteomas on the vertebral arch or the spinous process. Pain and interference with spinal stability can develop as the tumor grows. Such tumors require surgical removal.

Osteoid osteomas are tumorlike formations on the spinous processes that usually cause nocturnal pain, and therefore require surgery, and are usually benign.

In multiple cartilaginous exostoses, osteochondromas can also be found on the spine. They cause neurologic deficits by compressing the spinal cord and the nerve roots. They can also result in spinal bending.

Benign osteoblastomas mainly affect the vertebral arches and the processes. They can cause irritation of the nerve roots, which is also true for giant cell tumors and the uncommon aneurysmatic bone cysts.

The most common primary tumors of the spine are hemangiomas, which occur in the elderly. They cause a coarseness to the structure of the bony trabeculae owing to the blood-filled spaces of the mostly cavernous angioma. Often they are discovered accidentally. Large hemangiomas cause pain and seldom penetrate into the spinal canal. Usually the hemangioma vertebra is stable, and only with additional osteoporosis is there increased risk of fracture. Patients under such risk need a brace or an operative spondylosyndesis.

Malignant osteosarcomas of the spine of either the osteoblastic or osteolytic type are uncommon. The chondroma, as a persistent remnant of the dorsal cord, is a typical spinal tumor and is usually located between the cervical spine and the head and the lumbar spine and the sacrum. The course can be benign or malignant, and no effective therapy is known.

Benign and malignant soft tissue tumors, which can be located on the spine, are fibroma and fibrosarcoma, lipoma and liposarcoma, myxoma and myxosarcoma.

A common malignant tumor is the plasma cell myeloma, which can occur singly or multiply, causing a monoclonal gammopathy. This tumor is mostly found in men over age 40. The unspecific symptoms are often misinterpreted as rheumatism or lumbago. Pathologic fractures of the spine can occur. Osteoporosis must be ruled out, as well as leukemia, during which the vertebral bodies can be deformed with the decrease of calcium content.

The spine is frequently also affected in lymphogranuloma. Osteolysis causes spontaneous fractures and gibbus formation, and sometimes also osteosclerotic foci. Other malignant tumors are the reticulosarcoma and the Ewing sarcoma, both of which are far more uncommon on the spine than on the long bones.

The eosinophilic granuloma, a tumorlike process of histiocytosis, is mainly found in children. The process decreases the stability of the vertebral bodies and leads to deformities called vertebra plana (Fig. 10–93). The course is usually benign. A vertebral reposition has occasionally been observed. Radiation causes a focal sclerosis.

Secondary Tumors

Metastases in the spine can originate from all malignant tumors. Most frequently the metastases are disseminated from a carcinoma of the prostate, breast,

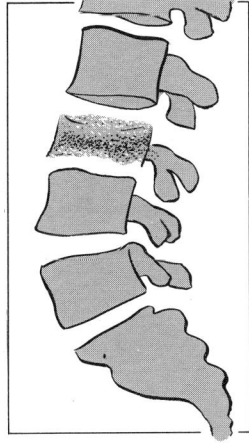

Fig. 10–93 Deformation of the vertebral bodies owing to a tumor.

or kidney, followed by malignomas of the bronchi and the thyroid. The secondary tumors of the spine cause pain, spontaneous fractures, and paralysis. Some metastases remain silent for a long time.

Bony tumor metastases are classified into purely osteolytic types (circumscribed destruction without bony reaction), a cystlike bone destruction with formation of a surrounding bone capsule, a purely osteoblastic type (with incorporation of calcified bone), and, finally, partly osteoblastic, partly osteolytic metastases.

Treatment

Treatment must consider localization, extent, and, in case of metastases, the type of the primary tumor, choosing cytostatics, hormones, or radiation. A brace may be necessary to support the spine, reduce pain, and prevent pathologic fractures. In cases of paralysis the spinal cord must be decompressed and the spine supported. Besides the tumor evacuation or removal of the metastases and filling with autologous bone, the spine is straightened and fixed with Harrington rods and bone cement. These techniques may eliminate the use of a brace, which is often troublesome to the patient.

Physical Therapy

The accompanying and subsequent physical therapy program is oriented toward local treatment. Pneumonia and thrombosis prophylaxis are always obligatory, and at a given time isometric exercise training is done to stabilize the trunk. For exercise suggestions see the section on isometric muscle contraction exercises earlier in the chapter; specific exercises will depend on the basic treatment and the course of the disease.

Chapter 11

Upper Extremities

H. Cotta, W. Puhl, and G. Koester

SHOULDER

EVALUATION RESULTS IN PHYSICAL THERAPY

The evaluation includes the shoulder girdle and the cervical and thoracic spine. It should be done in the following sequence: First, the cervical and thoracic spine is evaluated and then the scapula and clavicle, elbow, hand, and fingers. Finally, the shoulder joint is examined while the patient is in a standing or sitting position, and the ability to move the joint actively should be observed:

- Forward flexion and abduction bilaterally (Fig. 11–1a and b)
- Touching the back of the head bilaterally (Fig. 11–1c)
- Touching the sacrum bilaterally (apron string) (Fig. 11–1d)
- Crosswise grip behind the back, alternating both sides; compare the distance between the fingertips (Fig. 11–1e and f).

Simultaneous movement of both scapulae and deviating motions of the trunk are observed. Pain and restricted mobility are localized and assessed during the evaluation of the joint.

Through examination of painful and/or restricted motion (active, passive, and against resistance) is done. All results are compared with the opposite side or with normal values.

Complete range-of-motion measurements of the shoulder are recorded (Fig. 11–2a through f). The circumference of the upper arm (comparing both sides) is measured 15 cm above the ulnar epicondyle.

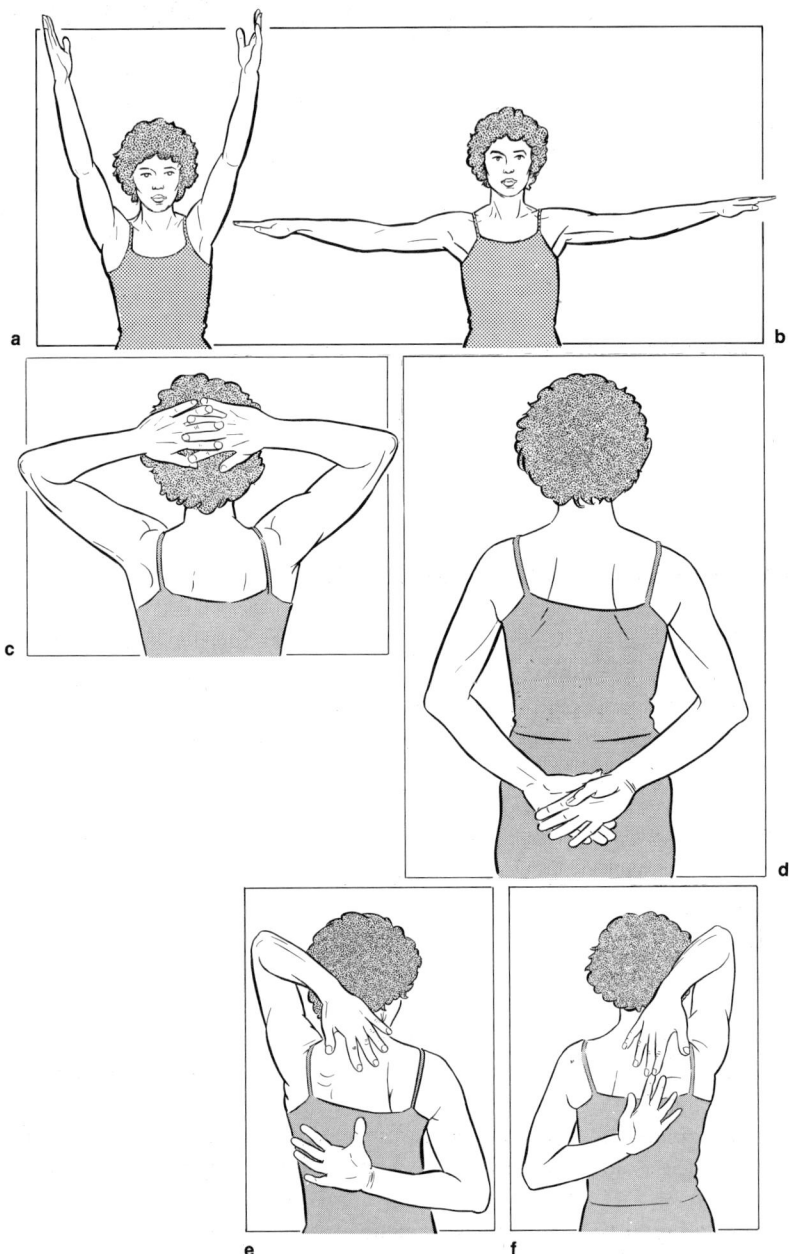

Fig. 11–1 Evaluation of active shoulder mobility.

Shoulder/Evaluation Results in Physical Therapy   191

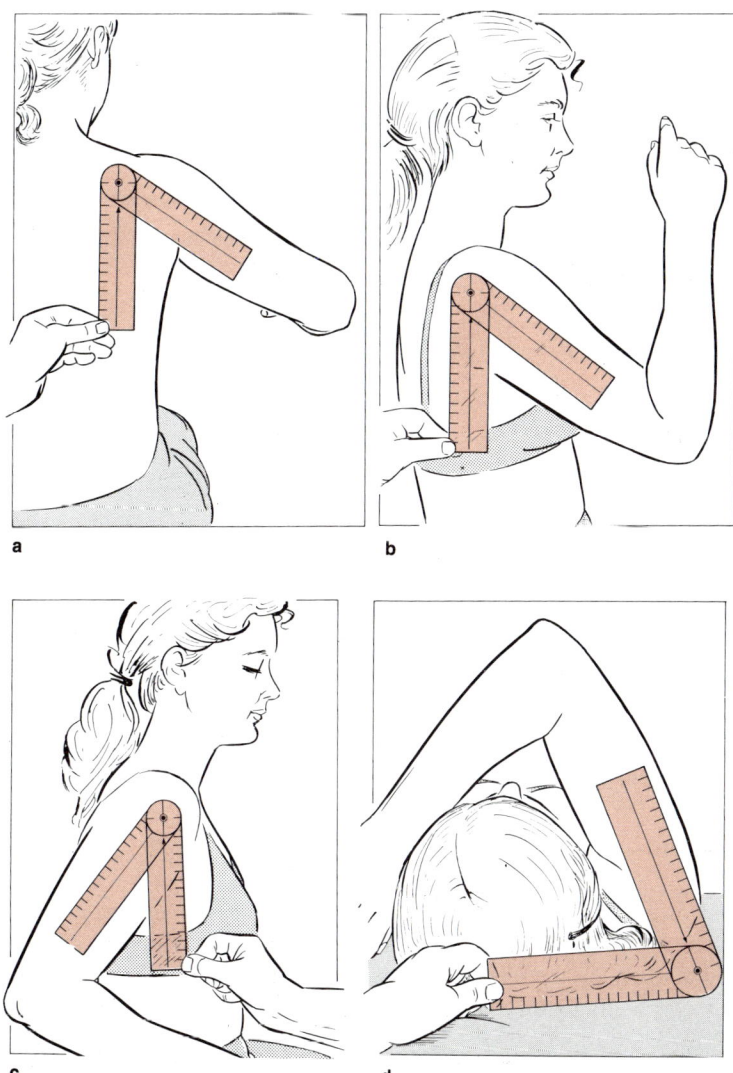

Fig. 11–2 Range-of-motion measurements of the shoulder.

Note if a painful arc (according to Cyriax) exists: During active and passive motion of the shoulder, pain may occur in midrange (pain starts at approximately 80° of abduction and subsides at about 120°; movements are pain-free above and below those measurements). The reason for the presence of a painful arc is the

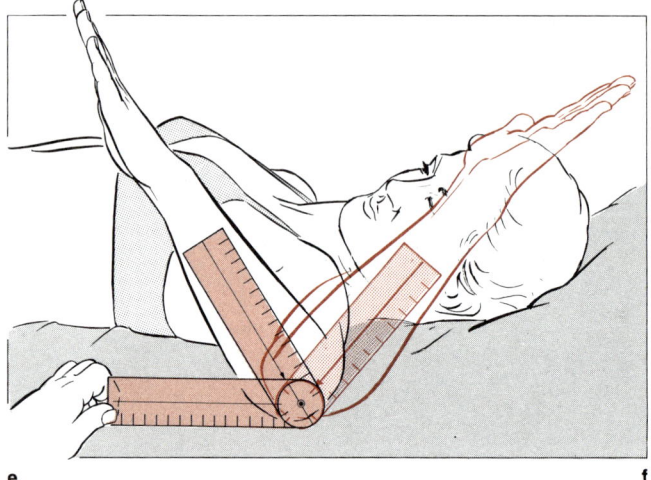

Fig. 11–2 continued

presence of soft-tissue compression between the greater tubercle of the humerus and the acromion. This may be due to a subacromial bursa.

Differentiated resistance tests and palpation will reveal the cause of a painful arc.

CLINICAL SYMPTOMS

Scalenus Syndrome

Origin. Narrowing of the "scalenus gap" causes compression of the brachial plexus, which results in neurovascular disturbances in the arm. The compression can be caused actively by the changing tone of the anterior or middle scalene muscle but also passively by the changing position or size of the muscle.

Symptoms. Pressure on the brachial plexus results in paralysis. Initially, sensory deficits occur, followed by motor deficits in the distribution of the ulnar nerve. Compressive damage and subsequent circulatory disturbances of the subclavian artery cause intermittent ischemic spasms and pain in the fingers until cyanosis and metabolic disturbances occur.

Treatment. For occasional pain, nerve blocks with injections of Novocain and temporary immobilization are used. For chronic problems, surgical widening of the scalenus gap by dissection of the anterior scalene muscle at the insertion point is done.

Arthrosis Deformans of the Shoulder Joint

Origin. See Chapter 7.

Symptoms. Pain during shoulder motions, especially when moving the arm backward and to the side. A delicate grinding of the cartilage or even loud crepitation is possible. The pain increases when the patient lies on the shoulder. Limited range of motion is caused primarily by changes within the periarticular soft tissue. Pain-related contractures can occur, as in a stiff shoulder.

Radiographic Findings. Typical signs of arthrosis; additional calcium deposits can be found in the soft tissue, indicating a subsequent periarthritis.

Differential Diagnosis. Humeroscapular periarthritis, inflammation, tumor.

Treatment. See section on arthrosis in Chapter 7. In severe conditions, resistant to therapy and resulting in pain, adduction contracture, and instability, an arthrosyndesis of the shoulder may be performed; in some patients an endoprosthetic replacement may be necessary.

Periarthropathia Humeroscapularis (PHS)

The term includes the four types described below.

Origin. Mainly degenerative changes of the periarticular tissue, tendon sheaths, and bursae can cause deposition of calcium, inflammation, adhesions, and shrinking, which in turn result in pain and restricted mobility (Fig. 11–3). Circulatory and metabolic disturbances are also contributing factors.

Symptoms. Four courses of the disease are distinguished clinically:

Simple Periarthritis: Pain during rotation and abduction. Nocturnal pain, if lying on the affected side. Increased pain radiating into the upper arm under mechanical stress. Active mobility is mostly restricted. A supraspinous and a biceps syndrome can be differentiated.

- Supraspinous syndrome: Maximum pain at the insertion of the supraspinous tendon, pain during lateral elevation of the arm between 60° and 80°. Pain is increased during upward rotation and abduction against resistance.
- Biceps syndrome: Pain is localized in the anterior shoulder area and is initiated or increased with tension of the biceps. Pain is present along the intertubercular sulcus; crepitation may also be palpated.

Acute shoulder stiffness: Sudden, severe pain, sometimes radiating into the fingertips. The entire shoulder is painful to pressure and often red and hot.

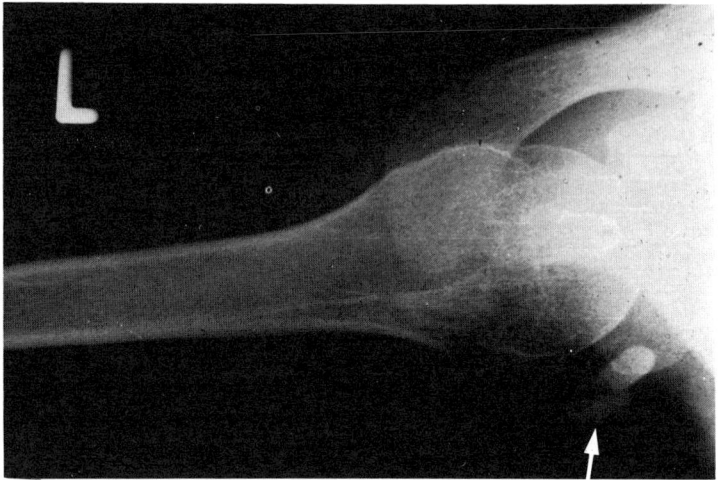

Fig. 11-3 Periarthritis humeroscapularis. Periarticular calcifications (from H. Cotta: Orthopädie, 4. Aufl., Thieme, Stuttgart, 1984).

Evaluation is often impossible because of severe pain. The origin is an acute inflammation around calcified tendons, or bursitis.

Pseudoparalytic shoulder stiffness (ruptured rotator cuff): The passively abducted arm cannot be actively held in this position. The shoulder can be moved passively without restrictions. There are no neurologic deficits. Symptoms occur suddenly after a major impact or overstressing of the shoulder. The most common reason is a rupture of the supraspinous tendon, which does not cause external changes. However, rupture of the long biceps tendon causes a soft round bulging of the long head of the biceps on the upper arm with little loss of function.

Ankylosing shoulder stiffness: Actively and passively restricted range of motion by fibrous adhesions and shrinking of the periarticular soft tissue. This is frequently caused by an extended period of immobilization during a disease or trauma to the arm and shoulder.

Radiographic Findings. Frequent calcifications, which can also be found accidentally, especially around the tendinous insertions.

Treatment. Acute shoulder stiffness: Immobilization in abduction splint or an abduction pillow; antiinflammatory and analgesic medication, if necessary. Extremely painful areas can be infiltrated with local anesthetics. Use of electrotherapy and ice application is indicated. Radiation of the inflammation is done in persistent cases. Surgical removal of calcified deposits is seldom done.

Pseudoparalytic form: suture of the supraspinous tendon is necessary. In persistent shoulder stiffness: passive mobilization under general anesthesia may be considered. For details of the treatment of a stiff shoulder, see physical therapy section.

Recurrent (Habitual) Dislocation of the Shoulder

Origin. The origins are:

- Constitutionally: Dysplasia (flat socket, humerus valgus) or weakness of muscles, capsule, or tendon
- Recurrent dislocation of the shoulder joint after a primary traumatic dislocation with a torn lower glenoid rim, followed by insufficient immobilization of the reduced joint. After a while, recurrent shoulder dislocation can no longer be distinguished from repeated dislocation.

Symptoms. The humeral head can be dislocated in a posterior, anterior, or downward direction. Anterior dislocation is by far most common. The humeral head is positioned ventrally to the subcoracoid process.

Recurrent dislocation occurs during daily routine, especially during a combination of abduction and external rotation. The humeral head slides out of the socket in an anterior or downward direction. Often the head can be reduced as easily, even without medical assistance—the same way it dislocates. Therefore, the actual recurrent dislocation is seldom seen by a physician as is a traumatic dislocation.

Radiographic Findings. During dislocation the humeral head is outside the socket. The socket is frequently flattened and too small. The size of the head is disproportionate to the size of the socket. There is accompanying bone lesion after previous dislocations (impression of the humeral head, separation of the major tubercle, edge of the socket is torn).

Treatment. Conservative therapy is not promising. Sufficient scarring can be expected in young patients after the first or second dislocation, if the shoulder is properly immobilized for at least 3 weeks. In some patients scar formation, combined with muscle stability, prevents another dislocation.

Surgery is more common. It improves the use of the arm, restores reliability and stability, and reduces the risk of early arthrosis owing to recurrent dislocation. A variety of surgical techniques for preventing recurrent dislocation are known:

- Plastic surgery of tendon and fascia and reinsertion of the subscapular muscle on the capsule of the shoulder joint with strong internal rotation of the joint creates tighter containment within the soft tissue.

- The lower edge of the socket is elevated by implantation of a bone chip into the lower posterior edge of the shoulder socket, creating a better support for the humeral head. The direction of the dislocation is blocked by scarring at the same time (Lange).
- A rotation osteotomy below the humeral head provides for improved articulation of the surfaces and safety of the joint function.

PHYSICAL THERAPY

Painful Shoulder Stiffness

The treatment described for a stiff shoulder also applies to conditions that are characterized by a limited range of motion in the shoulder joint.

Evaluation Results

Pain to different degrees:

- The pain is most relevant; movement is careful, sparing the shoulder area, but not actually restricted.
- Pain and limited range of motion are equal.
- The pain is minor but the restricted range of motion is prevalent.

Pain in different locations:

- Mainly around the deltoid muscle and its insertion, also radiating into the radial area of the arm to the fingers
- Typical painful points at the tendinous insertions
- Painful movements, such as a painful arc

Information about the pain indicates the localization and the type of lesion:

- Stillness of the arm
- Deviating movement or malposition of the upper body
- Muscle tension in the area of the shoulder girdle, arm, neck, and back
- Hypermobility or hypomobility of the scapula; elevated scapula
- Restricted mobility of the clavicular joints
- Restricted mobility in the area of the shoulder girdle, especially the deltoid muscle

- Restricted ability to perform daily activities as well as professional and sports activity
- Restriction of the fine motor activities of the hand.

Goals of Therapy

- End the cycle of disuse, muscle insufficiency, restricted range of motion, pain, etc. Pain relief is therefore the most important issue. Treatment should not increase pain in any way.
- Relax muscle spasms.
- Mobilize the cervical and thoracic spine with training of posture and movement.
- Stabilize or mobilize the scapula.
- Mobilize the clavicular joints.
- Mobilize the shoulder joint.
- Strengthen muscles.
- Retrain activity of daily living skills.
- Provide a home exercise program and suggestions for sports activities.

Lubrication of the Joint and Blood Supply to the Shoulder Joint and the Periarticuar Tissue. Synovial fluid accumulates in the lower recesses of the joint capsule and the upper part of the capsule has little or no fluid if the arm is elevated laterally and externally rotated. The blood supply to the capsule is least with the arm hanging down in adduction. The mostly stressed superior portion of the joint capsule is best supplied with synovial fluid and blood if the arm hangs down in slight abduction.

The tendons of the rotator cuff are affected, mostly the tendon of the supraspinous muscle. Permanent stress in unfavorable positions can be disadvantageous, as in continuously working with the arms elevated above the head, throwing balls as in sports, or carrying heavy items with the arms hanging.

Summary

- Little or no joint lubrication in the upper part of the capsule if the arms are elevated in abduction and external rotation.
- Insufficient blood supply for the rotator cuff if the arm is in weight-bearing position, hanging down in adduction, and in extreme adduction.
- Sufficient lubrication and blood supply to the endangered area during exercises in slight abduction, for instance, pendular exercises. Such exercises

should frequently be included in the therapy program and should be recommended for use in a home program.

Pain Relief Therapy

- Supported position; resting the shoulder joint without pain or with as little discomfort as possible. Position the arm with the shoulder joint in a resting position:

  —Shoulder joint: 55° abduction, 30° horizontal adduction, 0° rotation

  —Elbow joint: 90° flexion, 10° pronation

  —Hand and finger joints: functional position or with free mobility.

- The upper arm is supported up to the armpit. The position must be stable; it provides for relaxation and is the initial position for exercise, which can be applied in slings or in water by using floats.

  An adjustable abduction splint (Fig. 11–4) can also be worn for hours or the entire day, especially to support a weak deltoid muscle and to maintain the daily exercise results. The patient is instructed to exercise isometrically and abduct the arm actively from the splint. The splint is no longer necessary if the arm can be abducted forcefully enough from a 0 position to a horizontal line. The abduction is less on the pillow (Fig. 11–5).

- Moist heat application to improve local hyperemia and relax painful muscle tension, myogeloses, and hardening

- Relaxing muscle massage of the neck-shoulder area. Intensive local heat and massage may increase the pain.

Fig. 11–4 Adjustable abduction splint.

Shoulder/Physical Therapy 199

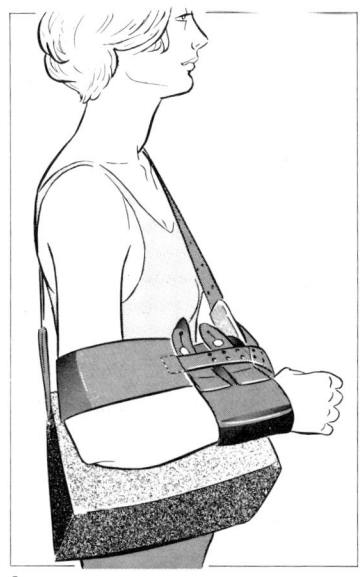

Fig. 11–5 Abduction on a pillow.

- Ice application and deep friction massage according to Cyriax for painful spots on the tendinous insertions. Ice application around the shoulder joint in combination with muscle work. The choice of heat or ice application depends on the patient's comfort.
- Electrotherapy and ultrasound
- Manual traction, degrees 1 and 2
- Suitable PNF techniques to improve the blood supply and relaxation, also over the contralateral side
- Pendular exercises within the pain-free range
- Persistent slight resistance during active motion
- Avoidance of sudden interruption of a motion or sudden change of direction.

Analgesic medication must also be given if the exercises alone do not relieve the pain sufficiently.

Effective pain relief can counteract shoulder stiffness that becomes resistant to therapy.

Mobilization

Together with the pain relief a mobilization of various degrees is achieved; tension and increased muscle tone are diminished. The mobilizing exercises are started on the cervical and thoracic spine. Recommended are exercises according to PNF for head, trunk, and scapulae and free exercises to straighten the spine from increased lordosis of the cervical spine and kyphosis of the thoracic spine (see section in Chapter 10 on physical therapy program for postural weakness and malpositions).

Clavicular Joints. In case of hypomobility, manual therapy techniques are used for the sternoclavicular and acromioclavicular joints.

Scapula. Manual mobilization is indicated only for an elevated scapula or a scapula tightly fixed to the thorax. Passive manual therapy is possible in each restricted direction. These provide some relaxation and comfort.

Less severe symptoms are alleviated with increased muscle work. In case of an elevated scapula owing to shortening of the trapezius and levator scapulae muscles, muscle are stretched by massage transverse to the fibers of the muscles, followed by specific stretching exercises with the therapist and by the patient alone.

Shoulder Joint. Manual therapy traction and sliding, according to the restricted direction of the motion.

- PNF technique: hold-relax or contract-relax
- Specific muscle stretching, mainly for the pectoralis major
- Swinging exercises with weight (1 lb) in a slight abduction
- Free exercises with or without equipment, such as club or ball (Figs. 11–6 through 11–8)
- Exercises on the stall bars for reversion of the fixed and mobile points. This principle can also be used in hydrotherapy.
- Position in slings to support the mobilizing exercises

Each exercise has to be controlled as much as possible in order to avoid compensating movements in the shoulder girdle and spine. They can occur especially during hydrotherapy and in incorrect use of PNF patterns and techniques.

As long as there is a restricted range of motion, the patient needs to learn how to distinguish between the movements of the shoulder joint and the movements of the scapula or the entire shoulder girdle.

Treatment After Mobilization of the Shoulder Joint Under Anesthesia. Position in bed: as much abduction as possible and elevation, 0 rotation, or external rotation. The arm, including hand and fingers, is well supported.

Day 1: Analgesic and antiinflammatory medication; active (supported) and passive movement and position changes several times daily; ice application

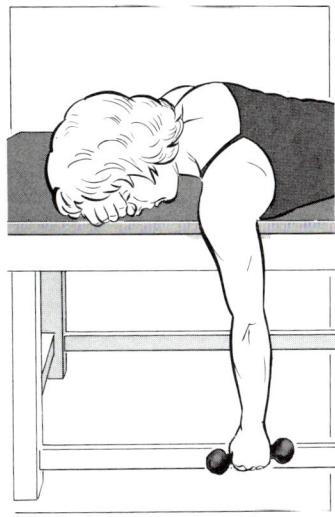

Fig. 11–6 Swinging exercises using dumbbells.

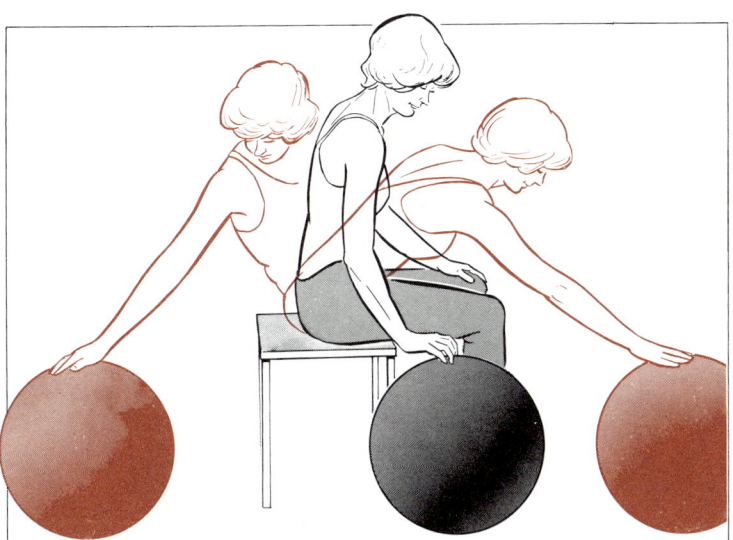

Fig. 11–7 Free exercises using the ball.

Day 2: Standing up with the arm placed in an abduction splint. The active exercise treatment is intensified. The patient is asked to elevate the arm from the splint. The splint is taken off during the treatment.

Day 4: Addition of hydrotherapy, gradually continuing with swimming, especially the backstroke. As soon as the arm can be elevated above the horizontal

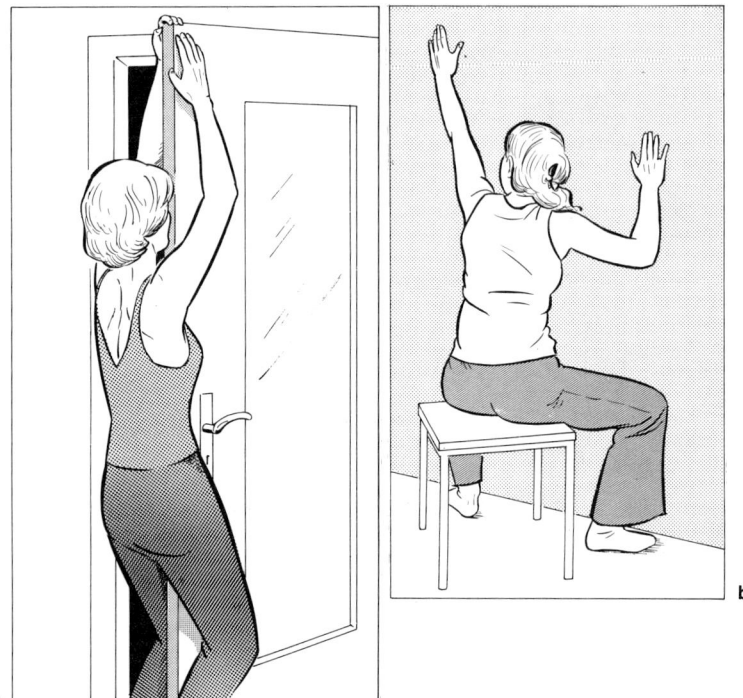

Fig. 11–8 Active elevation of the arm.

line with enough strength, the splint is taken off and the treatment is continued on an outpatient basis.

The exercise treatment is continued as long as normal function is regained. Recidivism can occur if the treatment is stopped too early.

Muscle Strengthening

The increasing muscle strength stabilizes the newly achieved range of motion and helps to increase it.

Scapula. Active stabilization of the scapula is essential. "When we are moving the arm, we have to fixate the scapula and the socket at first, to achieve a favorable position for the motion" (Hoepke-Kantner). Frequently, the mobile scapula simulates a motion of the arm in the shoulder joint that does not exist. In the long run these movements will cause an overstretching of the scapula muscles, especially the trapezius and the rhomboids, whereas the range of motion in the shoulder joint gradually decreases.

The following exercises are recommended:

- PNF pattern for the scapula
- Active fixation of the scapula during movements of the arm, which is placed in a sling

Shoulder Joint. Regaining muscle support of the joint by intensive training of the muscles of the rotator cuff and the deltoids.

The following exercises are recommended:

- Isometric contractions, initiated peripherally by muscles of the fingers and hand (Fig. 11-9)
- Active exercises against controlled resistance with active fixation of the joint, using a short and long lever arm
- PNF pattern in suitable techniques; stretch and approximation are not used in painful stages; choice of the best initial position and the use of bilateral and contralateral patterns
- Preparation and simultaneous application of ice to increase the muscle activity and pain relief during the exercises
- Free exercises with equipment, such as active pulling against resistance in slings or pulleys (Fig. 11-10), with light dumbbells, or the therapeutic ball (not throwing).

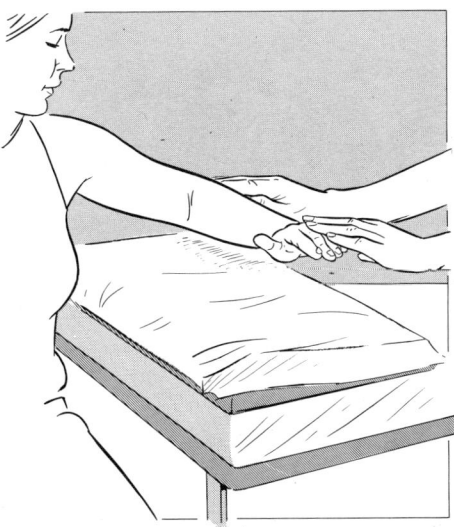

Fig. 11-9 Isometric contraction.

204 UPPER EXTREMITIES

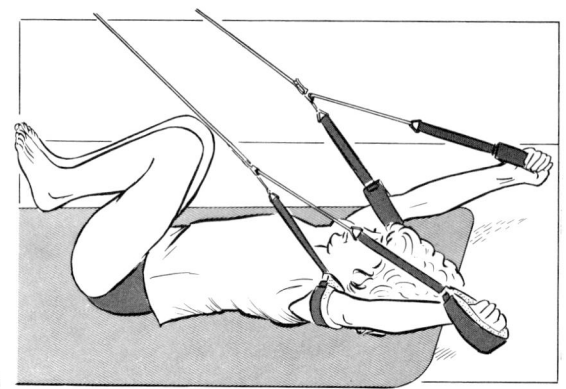

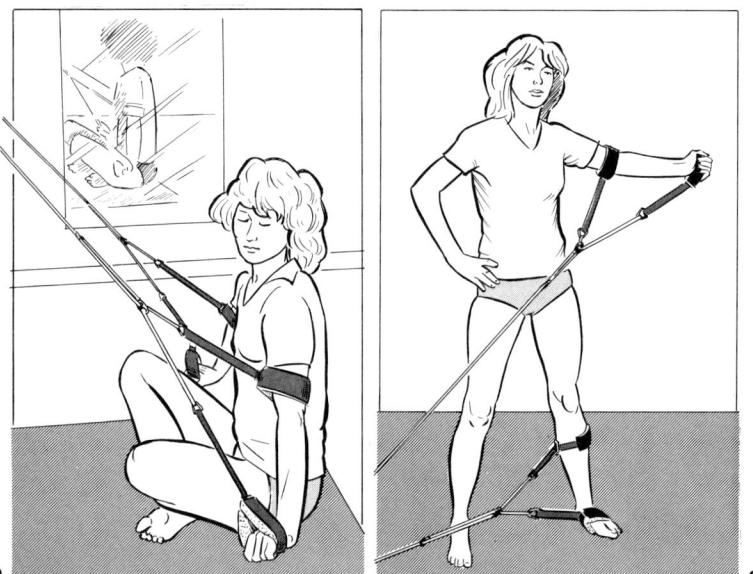

Fig. 11–10 Exercises with pulleys.

The example in Fig. 11–11 demonstrates training the posture, movement, and muscles under visual control in front of a mirror.

Hydrotherapy

Hydrotherapy exercises use the resistance of the water with quick and vigorous motions by working with floats.

Fig. 11–11 Visual control in front of the mirror.

Daily Routine and Skills

Exercises with a partner and games within the group improve the coordination of movements and endurance of the muscles by increasing attention, skills, and reaction speed. Along with the increased challenge, the use of the arm gradually becomes normal. Occupational therapy offers many possibilities by working with different materials and tools. Activity is gradually increased in preparation for the requirements of daily living skills and a job.

Home Exercises and Suggestions for Sports Activities

The patient must work constantly on his or her regained range of motion and strength with an individual home exercise program. Recommended sports include swimming (backstroke), water ball, bowling, gymnastics, and table tennis.

Recurrent Dislocation of the Shoulder

Evaluation Results

The evaluation is done only actively. Movements of the arm in the direction favorable for dislocation must be avoided; these are as follows:

- Anterior dislocation: abduction with external rotation, especially elevating the arm above the horizontal
- Posterior dislocation: adduction with internal rotation

The result is usually unspecific:

- No restricted range of motion
- Slight weakness of all muscles of the upper extremity and shoulder
- Possibly shortened or tensed pectoral muscle
- Risk of dislocation owing to the movements (listed earlier); possibility of voluntary dislocation
- Fear of moving after repeated dislocations

Goals of Therapy

- Strengthen muscles, especially the rotator cuff. Muscles reinforcing the capsule of the shoulder joint that can be overstretched or injured owing to dislocation of the shoulder are as follows:
    Anterior Part of the Capsule (Luxatio Anterior):
    —Subscapular muscle, an internal rotator
    —Biceps muscle, a flexor
    Posterior Part of the Capsule (Luxatio Posterior):
    —Supraspinous muscle, an external rotator
    —Infraspinous muscle, an external rotator
    —Teres minor muscle, an external rotator
    —Triceps muscle, an extensor
- Decrease muscle spasm of the pectoral muscle. A severely tensed or shortened pectoral can favor dislocation as soon as the arm is elevated above the horizontal, especially if the remaining muscles are insufficient.
- Restore activity of daily living skills/daily routine.
- Provide/teach a home exercise program.
- Provide counseling about sports activity.

Therapy

Anterior dislocation is the most common form and is therefore described here. Treatment of posterior dislocations can be modified accordingly.

Therapy for muscle strengthening includes the following:

- Isometric and active training for the deltoid muscle, especially the anterior and medial portions

After 5 weeks: Splint is replaced by a pillow.

After 6 weeks: Exercises for external rotation are started, but movements prone to dislocation are avoided. A slight restriction in external rotation is recommended permanently for the protection of the joint after surgery.

Arthrodesis of the Shoulder

Preoperative Treatment

A prerequisite is normal or sufficient function of the hand and fingers, or the possibility of regaining it. The elbow should be functional, at least in one direction, into flexion or extension. Excellent function of the following muscles is also necessary: trapezius, levator scapulae, pectoralis major and minor, rhomboids, and serratus anterior. A dynamic splint can be applied.

Another prerequisite is free mobility of the sternoclavicular joint and, subsequently the scapula after surgery.

Goals of Therapy

- Intensive strengthening of the muscles of the scapula.
- Correction of the malposition of the spine and trunk by training the back and abdominal muscles and improving posture.
- Generally prepare for the postoperative phase with respiratory exercises, etc.

The arthrosyndesis is done in the following position: 55° to 60° abduction, 30° horizontal abduction, 30° internal rotation. In this position the arm can actively be lifted with strong muscles slightly above the horizontal and approached toward the thorax up to 20°. The hand will reach the mouth. Rotation is eliminated. The hand cannot be moved behind the head or the back. The patient is informed of this outcome, as well as any absolute restrictions, preoperatively.

Postoperative Treatment

Position: Immobilization in a thorax-arm splint for about 16 weeks.

After day 1: Patient is standing up and moving the fingers on the affected side.

After 2 weeks: If wound is healed, the cast is changed and the patient is discharged from the hospital.

After 6 weeks: Radiographic control and the cast is changed again.

After 10 weeks: Radiographs are repeated and the cast is changed again.

After 14 weeks: Cast is removed, prior to repeated radiographic control. If the arthrosyndesis is consolidated sufficiently, the arm is placed in a splint in the arthrosyndesis position and physical therapy is started.

- Isometric and active training for the subscapular and biceps muscles (long head)
- Isometric static training for external-rotator muscles

At first the muscle training mainly consists of isometric contractions and controlled resistance with monoaxial movements, strictly avoiding the direction of movement that is favorable for dislocation.

Strengthening the subscapular muscle is most important. The patient exercises with slight abduction of the shoulder joint. The upper extremity is supported, and controlled relaxation of the pectoral muscle is achieved and restricted only to this muscle.

Exercises in a PNF pattern are less suitable. They initiate movements into the direction prone to dislocate and include the pectoral muscle in the strengthening training, which also favors a tendency to dislocate. PNF techniques are justified only if used carefully, avoiding any exaggerated motion, stretching, or pulling.

- Vibrations, soft kneading, and relaxation exercises are used for the pectoral and trapezius muscles.
- As strength increases, consecutive movements and free exercises are added.
- Sports that stress the arm, especially all sorts of ball games, skiing, and swimming, are not recommended, since they also cause movements that trigger dislocation. Physician should be consulted for individual recommendations.

Postoperative Treatment

Surgery According to Lange

Position: Thorax-arm-abduction cast; shoulder position: 60° abduction, 30° horizontal abduction, 30° internal rotation

After day 1: Patient gets out of the bed.

After 10 days: Patient discharged from the hospital.

After 3 weeks: Arm portion of cast is bivalved.

Exercises are started as described. Active exercises are done against resistance for the hand and elbow. If necessary, manual therapy is done. Active abduction and flexion out of the bivalved cast are encouraged as well as active internal rotation and isometric exercises for all muscle groups, including the external rotator muscles. Retroversion, horizontal abduction, external rotation, and all combinations thereof are prohibited.

After 4 weeks: Cast is removed with application of an abduction splint (airplane splint) which is taken off only for therapy. Intensive exercise is started. To protect the implanted bone chip, full abduction of the arm is not allowed. Use of hydrotherapy may be considered.

Evaluation Results After Cast Removal

- Limited range of motion in the joints of the hand and elbow
- Reduced strength of the muscles of the hand, elbow, and shoulder girdle
- Limited spinal mobility, tensed posture of the trunk.

Goals of Therapy

- Mobilize the hand, elbow, and possibly the scapula.
- Strengthen the muscles of the hand, elbow, and scapula.
- Retrain in activities of daily living skills.
- Promote normal posture and movement of the trunk.

Therapy

- Mobilization of hand and elbow accomplished by manual therapy techniques, with active exercises against resistance. The splint is taken off during treatment, and the arm is placed in an arthrosyndesis position on a pillow.
- Manual therapy and PNF techniques are recommended to mobilize the scapula and strengthen the muscles. In the beginning the therapist supports the arm to avoid any leverage on the arthrosyndesis.
- After another week, hydrotherapy is added. The splint is taken off if the arm no longer hurts and can actively be raised. An abduction pillow may be used for a short time.
- The muscle strengthening is intensified. The patient is quickly becoming used to the regained function, if everything goes well.
- After cast removal, treatment for 2 to 3 weeks in the hospital is sufficient, and usually continuing treatment afterward is not necessary. Use of the arm during daily routine is the best exercise.

Physical therapy should be continued only if the muscles were affected before surgery (partial paresis). Discomfort owing to malposition of the spine is treated with heat, massage, and exercises. Regular swimming helps to prevent problems.

ELBOW

EVALUATION RESULTS IN PHYSICAL THERAPY

The elbow is flexed and stretched in a hinge joint between the ulna and trochlea humeri. The joint of the small radial head (together with the distal radioulnar joint) makes pronation and supination of the forearm possible. In extension, rotation of the forearm can hardly be separated from rotation of the shoulder joint. Restricted mobility might be missed because of this fact. The elbow joint is an important joint. The function of the hand is essentially hampered if the elbow joint function is restricted or eliminated.

Measurements

Range-of-motion measurements are recorded for flexion/extension (Fig. 11–12a) and supination/pronation (Fig. 11–12b). Circumferences are as follows:

- Elbow joint: Across epicondyles and olecranon in a neutral position of the joint
- Upper arm: 15 cm above the ulnar epicondyle
- Lower arm: 10 cm below the ulnar epicondyle

CLINICAL SYMPTOMS

Osteochondritis Dissecans (Free Joint Bodies)

For more information, see Chapter 6, Aseptic Bone Necroses.

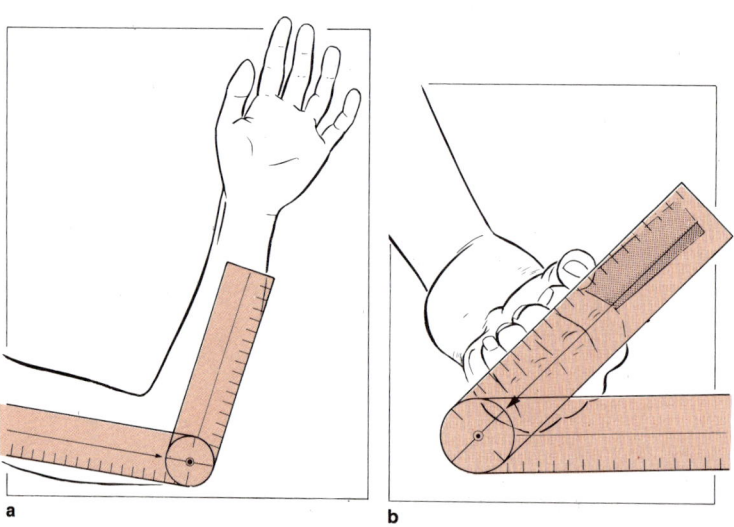

Fig. 11–12 Elbow and forearm range-of-motion measurements.

Arthritis

Origin. Affected in chronic polyarthritis in 50 percent of the cases, seldom as a monarthritis by infection.

Symptoms. Pain, swelling, insufficient extension, characteristic radiographic and laboratory results

Treatment. Treatment of the basic disease and the contractures if they are painful or unstable includes the following:

- Synovectomy
- Resection of the radial head
- Resection arthroplasty
- Total endoprosthetic replacement

Epicondylitis (Epicondylopathia Humeri, Tennis Elbow)

Origin. Insertion tendopathy on the humeral epicondyles. The radial form, affecting the origin of the extensors to the hand and fingers (tennis elbow), occurs more often than the ulnar form, in which not only the insertion tendopathy of the flexors contributes to the symptoms, but also the valgus stress of the elbow.

Symptoms. After repeated overstress, pain develops on the insertion of the tendons or on the ligamentous origin (pressure pain).

Treatment. During the acute stage, treatment consists of immobilization, perhaps in a cast, infiltration of a local anesthetic, possibly adding cortisone and physical therapy. If conservative therapy fails, the affected tendon is incised close to the insertion, and the epicondyle is circumcised for denervation.

PHYSICAL THERAPY

Epicondylitis

Evaluation Results

- Pressure pain, pain during moving, muscle-tendon pain during resistance and stretching test; must be localized correctly
- Tension, possibly swelling around the epicondyle
- Easy fatigue of the hand
- Weakened muscles owing to inactivity of the hand and arm.

All symptoms may be more or less pronounced.

Goals of Therapy

- Regain pain-free muscle contraction.
- Restore muscle strength and endurance.
- Prevent recidivism.

Conservative Therapy

Treatment can be started as a prophylaxis if a functional overstress is pending, as in special sports, playing musical instruments, or special activities (typing). It is recommended that the arm muscles be built up, especially the extensors of the hand and fingers, in strengthening and endurance training. The following treatment schedule should be applied if the signs of disease are already obvious:

- Pain is relieved with electrotherapy. Ice application, friction massage, and relaxation techniques are used for arms and shoulder girdle.
- After the pain subsides, the affected muscles are stretched and worked against resistance. Training starts on the trunk and shoulder girdle according to PNF techniques and is gradually built up.
- If the pain does not recur, the hand is used systematically in various skills and daily routine in occupational therapy.
- A training program to prevent recidivism is designed. Advice is given for sports activities and correction of false techniques.

Immobilization. The elbow is immobilized in a cast bandage or bivalved cast for at least 2 weeks. After cast removal, the evaluation results show decreased elbow range of motion, muscle weakness of the hand and lower arm, and possibly pressure pain.

Therapy

- The elbow is mobilized without involving the muscles of hand and fingers.
- Hydrotherapy is used for the trunk, shoulder girdle, and arms.
- Active exercise of the affected muscles is started under ice application, and increased according to the result.
- Conscious relaxation of the affected muscles is practiced.
- Occupational therapy is gradually increased.

Postoperative Treatment

Hohmann Procedure
Position: Bivalved cast for the upper arm and hand in 90° flexion of the elbow, medium rotatory position, 15° to 20° extension of the hand
After 2 days: If wound is healed, patient is discharged from the hospital.
After 14 days: Stitches are removed and exercises started.

HAND

EVALUATION RESULTS IN PHYSICAL THERAPY

In orthopedics the therapist is confronted with only a few disorders of the hand, but with a variety of restorative surgeries after injuries and with mobilization and reactivation after the immobilization of the arm.

The therapist must understand the anatomy of the hand: the position of the single bones in relation to one another, the shape and constitution of the joints with capsules and ligaments, the sometimes complex muscle functions, and the sensory innervation.

According to Littler, the hand is divided into three mobile segments:

- *Segment I:* Thumb. Metacarpal I is independent of the fingers and can be opposed to them owing to the saddle joint and nine special muscles.
- *Segment II:* Index finger; it can be moved separately by seven muscles away from the remaining three fingers. Segments I and II form a functional unit for precise work, to a certain extent accompanied by the third finger.
- *Segment III:* Third to fifth fingers, including metacarpals III through V.

The three fingers work together because of their muscle connections, especially if a strong grip is necessary. For example, in an extension contracture of the third finger, the remaining fingers cannot be clenched in a fist. The three fingers are restricted in their function if one of them is injured.

The three mobile segments surround a stable central unit, consisting of the distal carpal bones, the second and third metacarpal bones, and the inserting muscles—the radial flexor and the long and short radial extensors.

The following exercises are based on the anatomical structures. The thumb and the index finger can be trained on their own in all functions. The third, fourth, and fifth fingers should always be considered in relation to one another. Further functional specialties are that the extensors of the hand and the flexors and adductors of the fingers work synergistically, as well as the flexors of the hand and the extensors and abductors of the fingers. This becomes obvious when the hand is clenched in a fist and then reopened (Fig. 11–13).

The muscle synergism is also important in planning muscle transpositions. For example, the flexors of the hand are a suitable replacement for the extensors of the fingers. The more important the function is, the easier the training of a new function for a transposed muscle.

An intensive preoperative treatment is necessary. The mobility of the joint must be maintained or regained and the muscle to be transposed must be strengthened on its own, since it will lose one or two grades of strength by the transposition.

The interosseous and lumbrical muscles are flexors and extensors at the same time. They connect the flexors and extensors of the fingers with their origin on the flexor digitorum profundus and their insertion on the dorsal aponeurosis.

The fingers can only be spread with extended metacarpophalangeal joints; if these joints are in complete flexion, the fingers cannot be spread actively or passively. This is partly due to the collateral ligaments. They are relaxed when the joints are in extension and allow spreading of the fingers; in flexion they are tensed and thus interfere with spreading of the fingers. The lateral stability of the metacarpophalangeal joints during flexion provides for the strong grip of a fist.

The metacarpophalangeal joints are immobilized in flexion of 80°. In immobilization in extension the flaccid collateral ligaments would shrink, become too short, and later interfere with flexion.

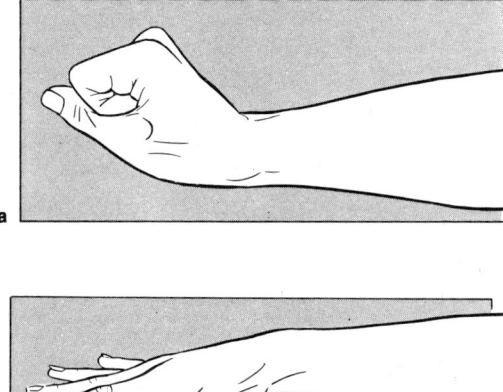

Fig. 11–13 Muscle synergism of the hand.

Hand/Evaluation Results in Physical Therapy   215

The ability to clench a fist depends on the free mobility of all joints and the strength of all flexors. The sliding ability of the flexor tendons, especially of the flexor digitorum profundus, is often at risk after surgery or injuries. It is important to maintain or restore this ability. Suitable exercises include: flexing end and middle joints with extended base joints (Fig. 11–14) to eliminate the extending function of the lumbrical muscles. Without the effect of the flexor digitorum profundus muscle (even temporarily) a so-called lumbrical grip develops (Fig. 11–15). In the long run it will endanger the sliding ability of the flexor tendons. Therefore, a functional splint is recommended.

Sensory Function

The delicate sensory ability of the hand is helpful for exercises. Thumb, index finger, and third finger are supplied with a delicate sensitivity by the median nerve. In case of a neurologic deficit the fourth and fifth fingers take over the touch function mediated by the ulnar nerve.

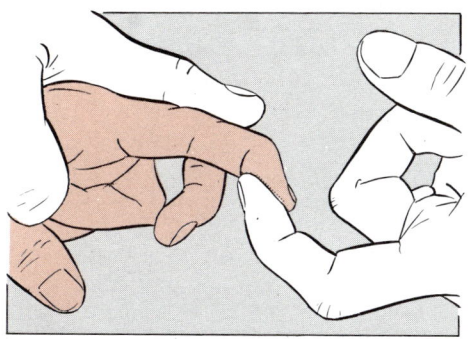

Fig. 11–14 Mobilizing the flexors of the fingers with the base joints fixed in extension.

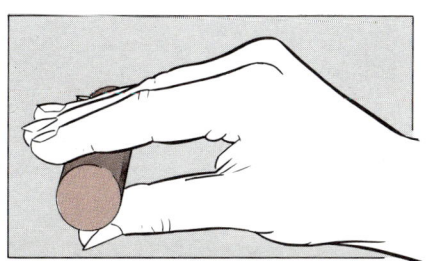

Fig. 11–15 So-called lumbrical grip.

216   Upper Extremities

The main goal in occupational therapy is training the sensory function, using materials of different consistency, surface, and shape. The fine motor coordination is also trained by feeling and touching without visual contact.

The two grip forms of the hand are pencil or precision grip (Fig. 11–16a and b) and claw or power grip (Fig. 11–16c and d).

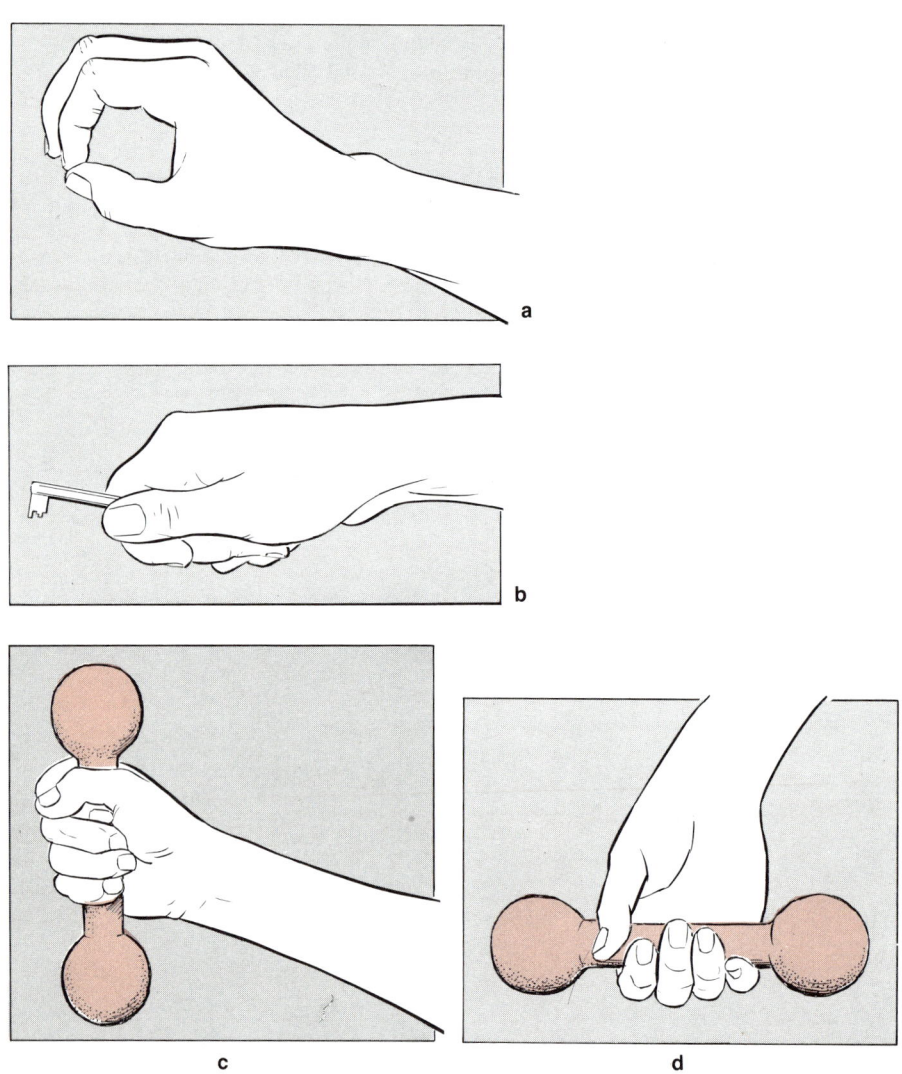

Fig. 11–16 a: Pencil grip; **b:** key grip; **c:** power grip; **d:** claw grip.

Hand/Evaluation Results in Physical Therapy 217

Replacing grip types to compensate for functional deficit varies according to the type of the lost normal function. Either the patient uses them spontaneously, or they must be learned consciously, or they are possible only after surgical correction, such as the transposition of muscles. They also play a role in loss of sensory function, such as the deficit of the median nerve. The hand is turned around during the grip and the radial nerve takes over the function. An example of compensation is the replacing pencil grip, between index and third fingers, in a squeezing grip (Fig. 11–17).

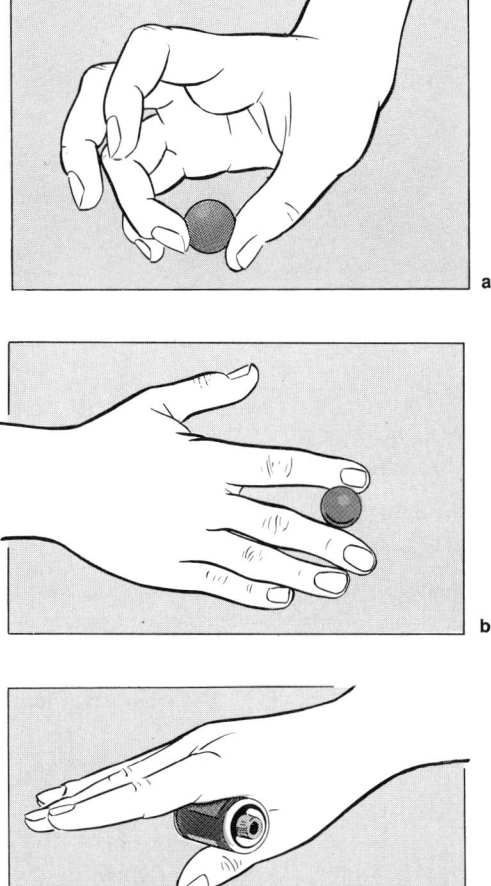

Fig. 11–17 a: Replacing pencil grip; **b:** between index and third fingers; **c:** pinching grip.

Single Evaluation Results

- Compare active and passive evaluation results.
- Measure range of motion.
- Assess sensation.
- Assess grip functions, activity of daily living skills, and functional tests in occupational therapy.
- Documentation, preferably photographic, of the functional ability at the beginning, during, and after completion of the treatment.

Measurement

Evaluate range of motion:

- *Wrist:* Flexion/extension, ulnar/radial deviation (Fig. 11–18)
- *Fingers:* Flexion/extension (Fig. 11–19).

The mobility of the fingers and thumb joints can also be measured with tape as follows:

- *Finger flexion:* The distance from the fingertip to the hollow of the hand and the distance from the fingertip to the distal fold of the hollow of the hand
- *Finger extension:* With the back of the hand lying flat on the table, the distance between fingernail and table surface
- *Thumb opposition:* The distance between the tip of the thumb and the fold in the flexion side of the metacarpophalangeal joint of the fifth finger; taken as an individual standard
- *Finger and thumb abduction:* Comparison of spreading of the inner surfaces of the healthy and the affected hand.

Circumferences:

- *Wrist:* Below the styloid process of the ulna
- *Middle hand:* Around the heads of the metacarpal bones except the thumb

Hand/Evaluation Results in Physical Therapy 219

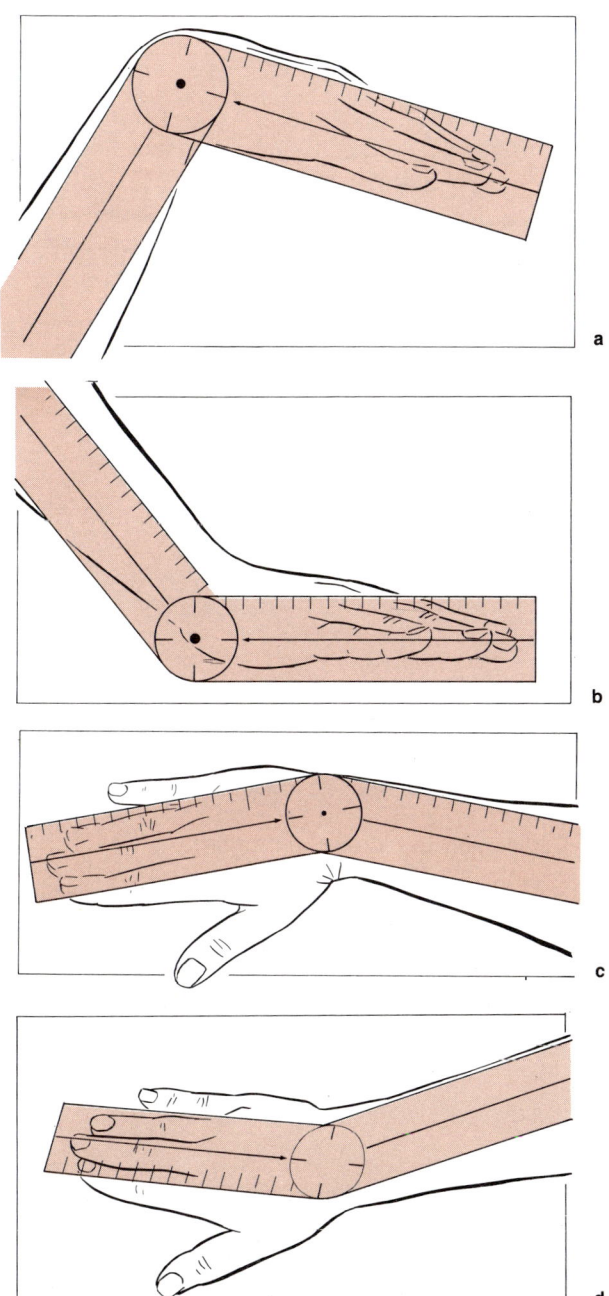

Fig. 11–18 Hand range-of-motion measurements.

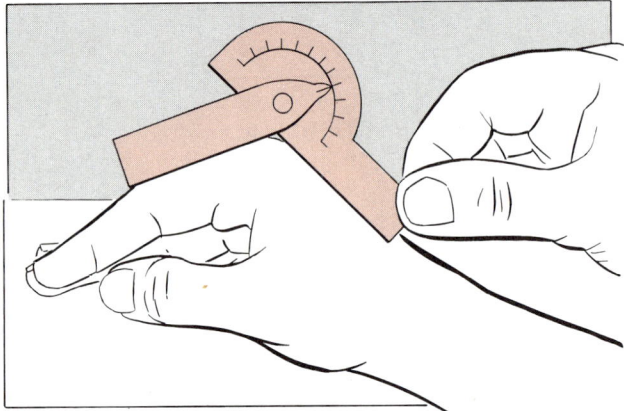

Fig. 11–19 Finger joint range-of-motion measurement.

CLINICAL SYMPTOMS

Arthrosis of the Wrist

Origin. Mostly a sequel to an accident (typical radial fracture) or secondary to a pseudoarthrosis of the navicular bone, osteomalacia of the lunar bone, etc.

Differential Diagnosis. Carpal tunnel syndrome, polyarthritis

Treatment. Decreasing stress, antiinflammatory and antirheumatic medication. *If the conservative treatment fails,* therapy consists of wrist denervation according to Wilhelm or arthrosyndesis with bone chip or osteosynthesis. For *arthrosis of the thumb, saddle joint,* the trapezium, with or without a piece of tendon in between, is removed.

Quervain's Disease (Tendovaginitis Stenosans of Quervain)

Origin. Chronic irritation and inflammation, possibly within an inflammative rheumatic disease

Symptoms. The first tendon cuff, through which the tendons of the thumb extensor and abductor run, is affected. Gradually increasing pain across the styloid (styloiditis), sometimes radiating into the periphery. Snapping tendons, inducing or increasing pain by abducting and extending the thumb against resistance.

Treatment. Immobilization, local injections; surgical splitting of the tendon sheath in case of resistance to therapy

Trigger Fingers

Origin. Changes within the tendon sheath of the finger flexors owing to stenosis, mostly at the level of the metacarpophalangeal joints (annular ligament) and swelling of the tendon by nodules

Symptoms. Abrupt snapping during movement; the nodules can be palpated. In pronounced cases the fingers are fixed in a position of flexion.

Treatment. Surgical splitting of the tendon sheath or the annular ligament

Dupuytren's Contracture

Origin. Transformation and thickening of the connective tissue in the palmar fascia, for unknown reasons

Symptoms. Occurs mostly in males around 40 years of age with nodular formations in the hollow of the hand, at first opposite the fourth finger. Several nodules merge into scarry strings, adhering to the skin. Usually there is no pain. Increasing impairment by progressing flexion contracture of one or several fingers occurs (Fig. 11–20). An analogous condition of the foot is called Ledderhose's disease.

Treatment. Regular, independent stretching; careful skin care. If contractures are already manifest, splints and cortisone injections will not be useful.

The treatment must be surgical, extirpating the diseased parts of the palmar fascia and the scar tissue, running deeper into the adjacent tissue. In advanced cases amputation of the fingers may be required. Recidivism cannot be completely prevented by radical removal of the palmar fascia.

PHYSICAL THERAPY

General Guidelines

Evaluation Results

Common symptoms of the hand that are responsive to therapy:

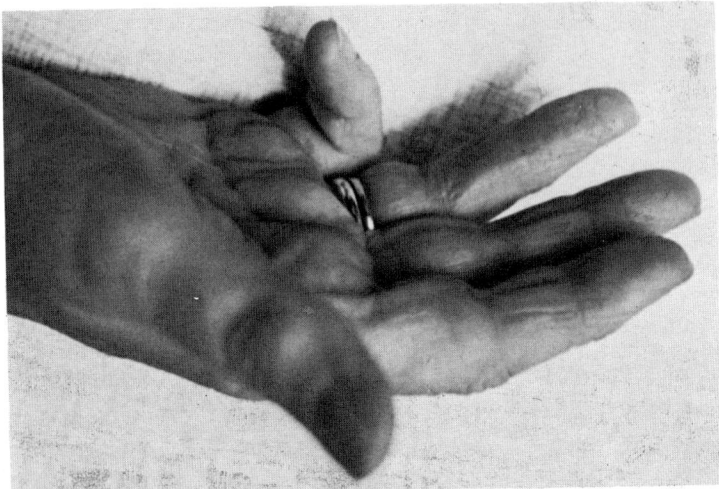

Fig. 11–20 Dupuytren's contracture (from H. Cotta: Orthopädie, 4. Aufl., Thieme, Stuttgart, 1984).

- Swelling
- Disturbed skin temperature
- Disturbed sensitivity
- Pain during movement and touch
- Muscle weakness
- Joint contractures for various reasons, such as muscle imbalance, shortening of tendons owing to adhesions or scar formation, shrinking of joint capsule and ligaments, skin scars, bone dystrophy
- Malpositions
- Functional deficits
- Replacement grips
- Reduced fine motor coordination

Goals of Therapy

Generally:

- Restore hand function by regaining the normal grip or learning replacement grips.

Specifically:

- Improve blood circulation.
- Decrease muscle spasm.
- Mobilize involved joints.
- Improve tendon gliding.
- Stretch shortened muscles.
- Strengthen weak muscles.
- Correct or eliminate malpositions and unwanted replacement functions.
- Improve activity of daily living skills and fine motor coordination.
- Provide additional aids as needed.
- Restore the mobility of the hand, arm, shoulder girdle, and spine.

Therapy

- Relieving pain: Controlled positioning, immobilization in splints, application of heat or ice, relaxation techniques, manual therapy
- Relieving the swelling: Elevated position, effleurage, isometric muscle contraction and active pumping motions, active movement of all free joints of the arm; exercises in elevated position
- Improving circulation: Active exercises, brushing arm and shoulder, electrotherapy
- Improving function: Manual therapy to stretch the joint capsule and ligaments; active treatment of the contracture to stretch shortened muscles and tendons; careful scar massage; active correction of malpositions, passively supported by splints.

In active exercises, single functions are worked on against increasing resistance, in PNF techniques and free exercises with or without equipment.

- For example: Exercising the finger flexion with a foam ball (Fig. 11–21) and paper (Fig. 11–22), isolated for base, middle, and end joints with the fixation board (Fig. 11–23), for the lumbrical muscles on the edge of the table (Fig. 11–24)
- Isolated exercises for extension of the fingers and hand against resistance (Fig. 11–25).
- Isolated exercises for finger abduction against resistance (Fig. 11–26)
- Exercising the fingers together for extension and abduction (Fig. 11–27)
- Combined exercises for hand and elbow (Fig. 11–28)
- Stabilizing the hand and arm in a strong grip (Fig. 11–29). Important directions for the motion are flexion of the fingers and the thumb and

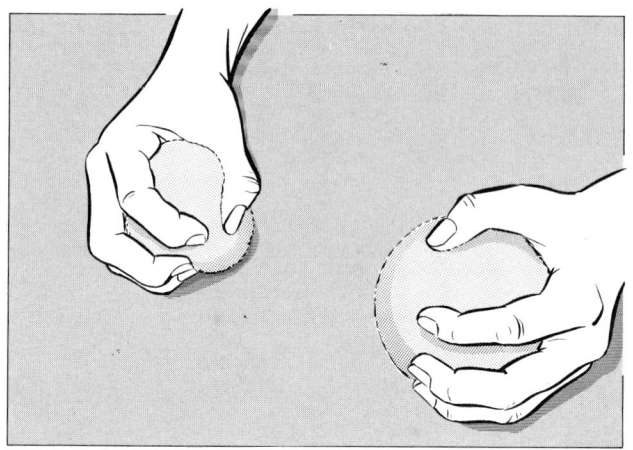

Fig. 11–21 Exercising with the foam ball.

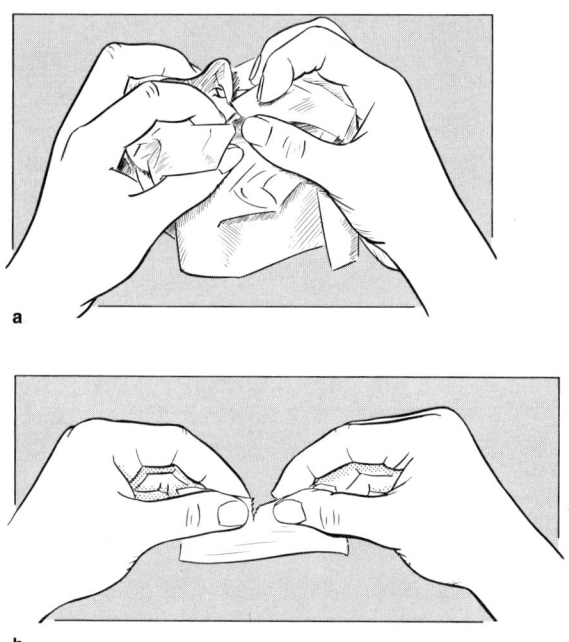

Fig. 11–22 Exercising with paper.

Hand/Physical Therapy 225

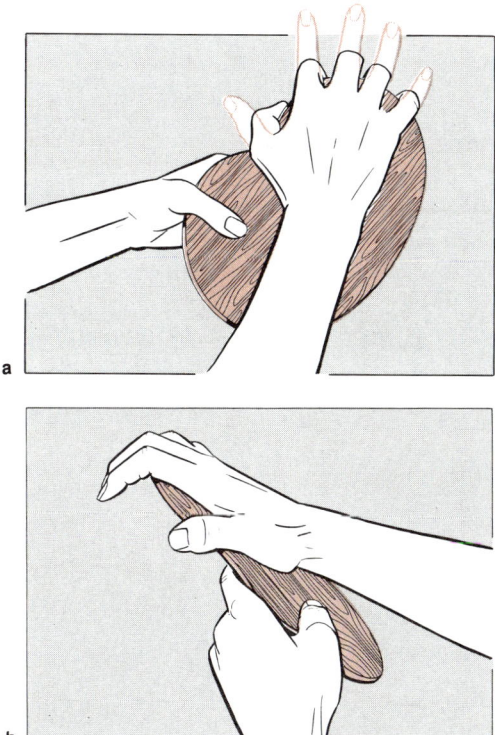

Fig. 11–23 Exercising with the fixation board for the hand.

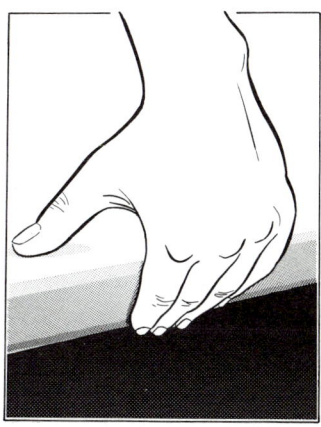

Fig. 11–24 Exercising on the edge of the table.

226 Upper Extremities

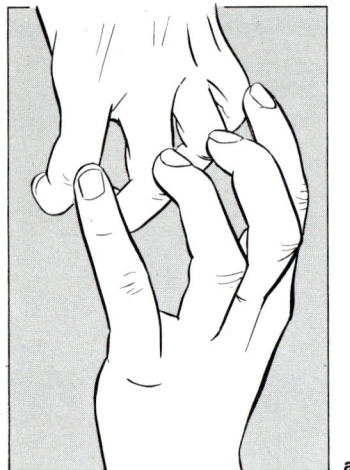

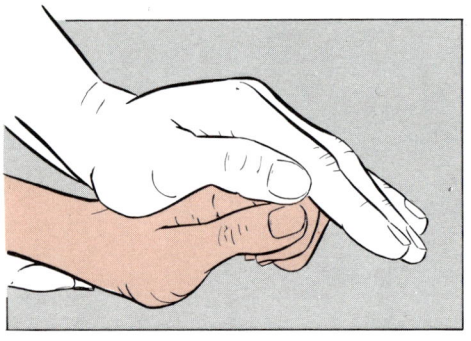

Fig. 11–25 Exercising extension of the fingers and hand against resistance.

opposition of the thumb and the little finger. Limitation of hand opening is easier to compensate than a missing strong clenching of the fist and fingertips. Passive opening of the fingers and the hand is temporarily possible with a splint.

Basic Principles of Technique and Intensity in Physical Therapy of the Hand

Consultation with the physician is especially important in the treatment of the hand, especially after surgery so that the therapist is informed about the surgical procedure and goals of treatment are established.

Hand/Physical Therapy 227

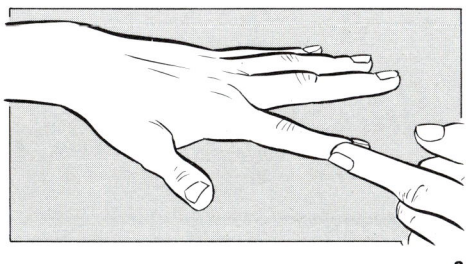

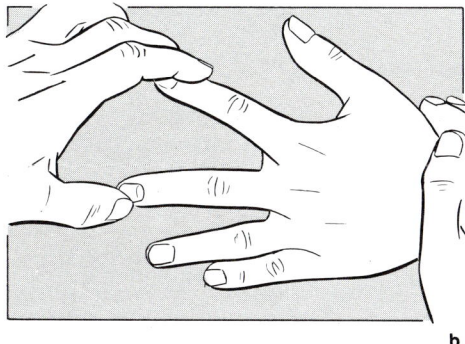

Fig. 11–26 Exercising finger abduction against resistance.

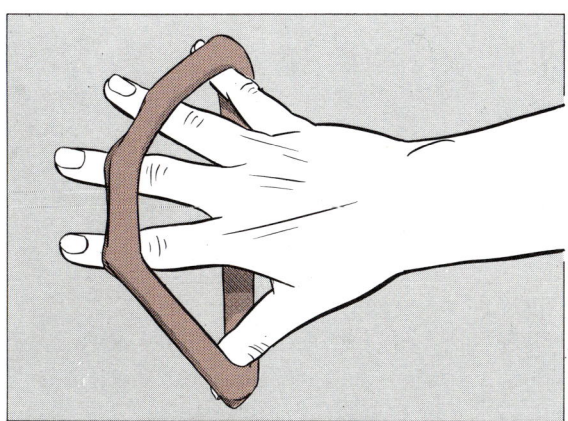

Fig. 11–27 Exercising extension and abduction of the fingers.

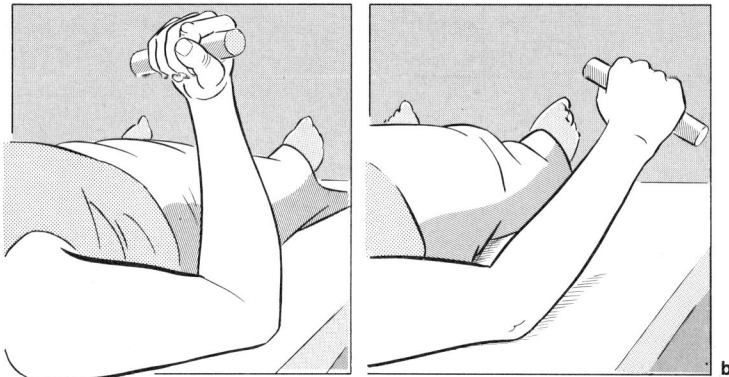

Fig. 11–28 Combined exercises for hand and elbow.

Fig. 11–29 Stabilizing hand and arm in a strong grip.

- The primary therapist should not be changed, if possible.
- Treatment sessions should be short and scheduled several times daily.
- All mobilization techniques are matched to the individual situation and applied carefully. Attention must be paid to any heat, swelling, and pain. Treatment is interrupted until such signs subside, or the treatment is aimed at the symptoms.

- During treatment the pain threshold may be exceeded briefly. After the treatment the pain should have subsided. Before the next treatment the hand should be pain-free.
- Active exercises are most important.
- Passive movements are initiated by manual therapy, if necessary. Thorough passive movements are indicated only in paralysis to prevent a contracture.
- All affected or nonimmobilized joints of the upper extremity are included in the treatment.
- The development of Sudeck's atrophy (dystrophy), to which the hand is especially prone, must be avoided. As a preventive measure, exercises for the shoulder girdle and spine and relaxing exercises for both arms are suitable, to distract from the diseased hand.
- Usually each therapy session should be started with exercises for the shoulder and elbow.
- Hydrotherapy can be useful for improving blood circulation, relieving pain, and mobilization. It may be contraindicated, however, if the hand starts to swell during or after the treatment, and it is always contraindicated if there is a tendency for swelling or overheating.
- Application of ice helps to decrease the pain. In combination with active exercises, it stimulates the blood circulation of the hand and its muscle function. Pain resulting from cold should not occur. Because the hand does not have much soft tissue, the pain threshold is reached quickly. Ice therapy is recommended only for a warm hand.
- Massage to relax hard muscles, especially in the area of the shoulder and neck, can facilitate the exercise treatment, but it is not applied in proximity to a joint on the hand. The loosening of scar tissue can be improved by special massage techniques.
- Additional electrotherapeutic techniques are used to treat paralysis, muscle weakness, and sensory deficits.
- Heat, cold, or electrotherapy must be used carefully in the presence of sensory deficits.
- Complete loss of sensory function requires permanent visual control during the exercises to avoid any kind of injury. Well-cushioned splints can be used if motor deficits exist.
- Splints for positioning and dynamic function (Fig. 11–30) must be matched to the evaluation results and adjusted or replaced accordingly.

The therapist must be sensitive and choose subtle treatment methods. He or she should communicate with the physician during each stage of therapy. Occupa-

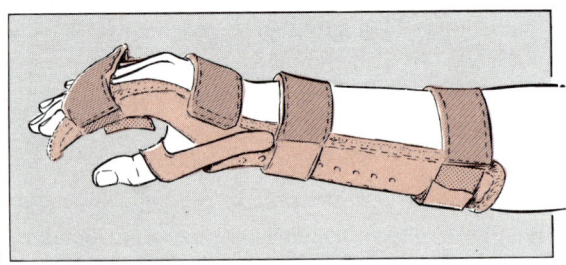
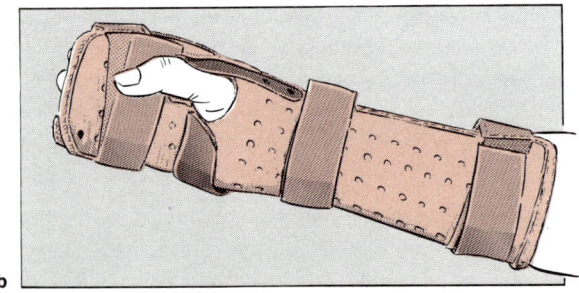

Fig. 11–30 Position of the hand in a splint.

tional therapy supports and completes physical therapy, especially in preparing the patient for the daily routine and his or her profession.

Position of the Hand during the Immobilization

- *Wrist:* 20° extension and 5° ulnar deviation
- *Distal finger joint:* 20° flexion
- *Middle finger joint:* 40° flexion
- *Proximal finger joint:* 60 to 80° flexion
- *Thumb:* Placed in middle opposition with extension of the proximal and distal segments

Position of the Affected Arm When Patient Is in Bed

If the hand has to be immobilized for a longer period, changing between the following positions is recommended:

- Shoulder joint, 70° to 90° abduction, 30° external rotation; elbow joint, 30° flexion
- Elbow joint, 0° flexion, 10° pronation

Arthroses of the Hand

Postoperative Treatment

Thumb Saddle Joint (Rhizarthrosis):

Removal of the trapezoid bone with or without interposed tendon: Lower arm is immobilized, including the thumb, in a bivalved cast; arm is elevated. Depending on the surgical technique, active exercise and occupational therapy is started 6 to 8 weeks after surgery.

Removal of the trapezoid bone with tendoplasty or endoprosthesis: Immobilization as above

After 2 weeks: Active exercises are started; mobility has improved spontaneously; strengthening and occupational therapy can be started.

Wrist:

Denervation of the wrist: Bandage

After 1 day: Active exercises are started under traction; occupational therapy is added.

Osteosynthesis with a plate (arthrosyndesis): Arm is bandaged and elevated in a splint.

After 1 day: Active exercise program for fingers, elbow, and shoulder is started.

After 2 weeks: Pronation and supination of the forearm are possible; occupational therapy is started.

After 6 weeks: Depending on radiographic findings, strengthening exercises for the hand and arm are begun.

Dupuytren Contracture

Exercise therapy may still be effective if the formation of nodules and scar cords in the palm is still minor and restriction of finger extension is still below 20°.

Goals of Therapy

- Increase joint mobility.
- Strengthen extensor muscle.

Therapy

- Techniques of manual therapy to mobilize the hand and finger joints
- Passive stretching

- Exercises against resistance for all finger extensors and abductors
- Exercises using PNF techniques
- Home program instruction

Postoperative Treatment

Fasciectomy (Aponeurectomy):

Position: Volar bivalved cast for the forearm with the wrist extended approximately 20°, elevation of the arm

After day 1: Patient stands up and performs active exercises for the elbow and shoulder.

After day 2: Drainage is removed, and active and passive movements for all finger joints are started. Patient moves and elevates the arm above the head. Occupational therapy is started.

After 2 weeks: The cast is taken off; exercise and occupational therapy are intensified. A splint, if necessary, is used. Treatment can be continued on an outpatient basis if there are no complications. Instructions are given for home exercises. Treatment is finished after sufficient function is regained.

Snapping Fingers

Postoperative Treatment

Resection of the annular ligament: Outpatient care; bandage
After day 1: Patient moves the finger. Usually physical therapy is not necessary.

Chapter 12

Lower Limbs

H. Cotta, W. Puhl, and G. Koester

HIP JOINT

EVALUATION RESULTS IN PHYSICAL THERAPY

Assessment of static and dynamic leg function, in its entirety or in single segments, is possible only by considering the combined function of the lumbar spine, pelvis, and leg.

Pelvis

The pelvis balances on the acetabula and the femoral heads and carries the spine. The active motion of the pelvis is the result of a combined effect of all the muscles that move the hip joint and the spine. Extension in the hip joint and flexion of the lumbar spine, together with a fixed lower limb, make pelvic extension possible, where flexion in the hip joints and extension of the lumbar spine result in pelvic flexion. Muscles that extend the pelvis are the lumbar extensors of the back, iliopsoas, spinal, and adductor longus muscles.

Pelvic extension and flexion must be examined in both a sitting and a standing position. In a sitting position it is easier to extend the pelvis, since the iliofemoral ligaments are relaxed.

Abduction in one hip joint and adduction in the other, in combination with lateral flexion of the lumbar spine, cause pelvic motion in the frontal plane, which becomes obvious in the rotated position of the pelvis.

Muscles for rotation position of the pelvis are abductors and adductors of the hip joint, longitudinal and oblique abdominal muscles, lumbar extensors of the back, quadratus lumborum, and latissimus dorsi. Such pelvic internal and external rotation can be observed in walking especially during weight bearing on the stance leg.

Malfunctions of the lumbar spine and hip joint become obvious in pelvic motions. The observation of pelvic motions and positions is an important part of the examination in physical therapy and subsequent treatment of the hip joint.

Hip Joint

The patient must be undressed sufficiently so that the movements of pelvis and spine can be observed and the true, isolated movement of the hip joint can be exactly measured.

Measuring Hip Flexion and Extension

The patient is in a supine position (Fig. 12–1). The position of the pelvis is examined and, if necessary, corrected. Both anterior superior iliac spines are marked with a pencil or fixated by an assistant (slight lumbar lordosis). The simultaneous pelvic movements are also observed.

Thomas Test. With free mobility of the joint it is possible to pull one leg with flexed knee toward the abdomen, while the other leg remains on the table in an extended position with the lumbar spine in a normal position. The flexed leg should also be rotated external to avoid lateral deviation of the lumbar spine (Fig. 12–2). If extension of the hip joint is not restricted, the other leg remains on the table. Full extension is examined in a prone position. Restricted motions become obvious by simultaneous pelvic motions in extension or flexion.

Measuring Hip Abduction and Adduction

A prerequisite is again the correct position of the pelvis (Fig. 12–3). Measure abduction and adduction of both legs at the same time, keeping the pelvis in a fixed

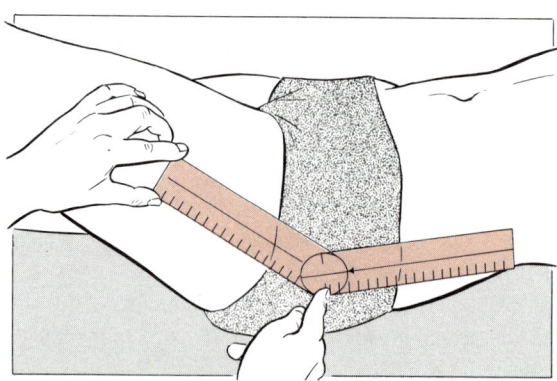

Fig. 12–1 Measuring hip flexion and extension.

Hip Joint/Evaluation Results in Physical Therapy 235

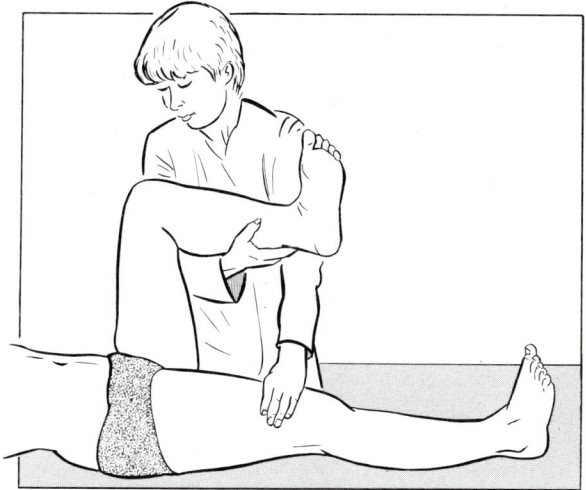

Fig. 12–2 Thomas test.

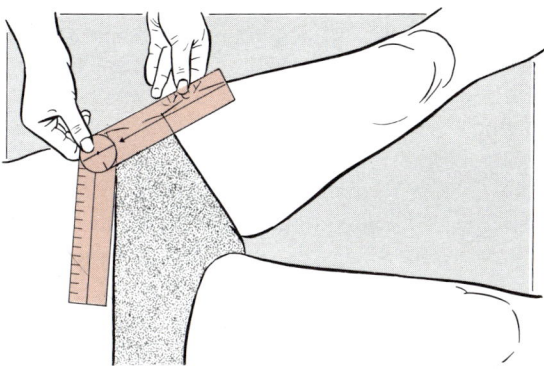

Fig. 12–3 Measuring hip abduction and adduction.

position. Abduction is greater with the hip joint in a flexed position than in an extended position, since the pubofemoral ligament is relaxed. Comparative measurements can be taken in both positions.

Measuring Hip Rotation

Measuring can be done according to one of three methods as follows:

- Supine position with limb in neutral position, if possible; both legs are evaluated with the pelvis in a fixed position to eliminate simultaneous pelvic motions.

- Supine position with hip and knee joints flexed to a right angle (Fig. 12–4); usually the values are twice as high due to the relaxation of the pubofemoral ligament.
- Prone position with hip joint in neutral position, if possible; knee joints are flexed at a right angle.

After evaluation of hip mobility the strength of all leg muscles (especially the hip muscles) is tested and compared to the other side. At the same time the muscles are checked for flexibility and possible shortening. In the area of the pelvis and leg, the following muscles have a tendency to shorten: quadratus lumborum, iliopsoas, tensor fasciae latae, rectus femoris, the adductors, the external rotators, the semitendinosus and membranosus muscles, biceps femoris, and triceps surae.

To measure muscle atrophy, the circumference of each thigh is compared (see section on atrophy of knee muscles later in this chapter).

Differences in Leg Length

The difference is visible by a tilted position of the pelvis. One method to measure for a leg length discrepancy is to take the measurements with the patient standing barefoot. If there is a true length difference and the hip joints are mobile. The pelvic position can be corrected by placing the shortened leg on a board of appropriate height. This measurement can be used to elevate the heel (up to 2 cm) or the shoe (2 to 4 cm).

Orthopedic shoes or surgery is necessary if the shortening of the leg is severer. Older patients in particular need time to get used to the correction of the length difference. If the condition has persisted for a long time, the heel or shoe should be elevated gradually.

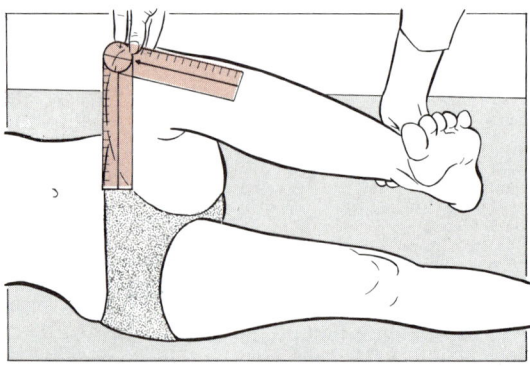

Fig. 12–4 Measuring hip rotation.

A difference in leg length is simulated by a pelvic tilt if the hip joint is contracted in a malposition. The abduction contraction of the hip joint results in an apparent shortening of the contralateral side, since the pelvis must be elevated on the normal side when the foot on the affected side touches the floor.

The situation is opposite in an adduction contracture of the hip. The pelvis must be elevated on the affected side in order for the foot to touch the floor. The unaffected leg appears to be too long. In those cases the position of the pelvis can only be equalized if the normal mobile joint can be put in the same position as the contracted joint. An adjustment of this length difference would not eliminate the malposition of the joint and spine and could even increase it. Leg length discrepancies caused by contractures cannot be compensated for by elevation of the shoe or heel. The same is true for contractures combined with leg length discrepancies.

Only approximate measurements of leg length differences can be made with a tape measure with the patient in a supine position. Exact measurement of leg length is possible by comparison of radiographs. The extent of the pelvic tilt is shown by a pelvic radiograph, taken with the patient in a standing position, possibly barefoot, with extended knees and even weight bearing on both legs. Because the difference is important only for walking, it is not necessary to examine the patient lying down.

Both abduction and adduction contracture of the hip joint and flexion contracture of the hip and knee joints can cause a functional difference in leg length and a pelvic tilt. Weak muscles can also lead to symptoms of a shortened leg, such as the Trendelenburg sign owing to a weakness or deficit in the gluteal muscles.

CLINICAL SYMPTOMS

Hip Dysplasia/Hip Dislocation (Congenital Dislocation of the Hip Joint, Luxatio Coxae Congenita)

Most common congenital skeletal disturbance, which includes disturbances in the development of the acetabulum (dysplasia) and the coxal part of the femur (steep position of the femoral neck with increased antetorsion: coxa valga antetorta) and ranges from an incongruity of the hip joint to subluxation and complete dislocation.

Two to 4 percent of the population are affected, among them 2 percent with dislocation. In the Federal Republic of Germany, out of 700,000 infants each year, 30,000 are affected by dysplasia and 14,000 by dislocation of the hip. True congenital teratological dislocation (also called prenatal dislocation) must be differentiated from so-called congenital dislocation of the hip. It is mostly combined with other congenital deformities.

Origin. The origin and extent of the disorder are dependent on exogenous and endogenous factors. Concerning the importance of endocrinologic factors there is a constant sex-linked male-female ratio which is 1:6; there is 40 percent bilateral occurrence and an epidemiological clustering of dislocations in some areas in West Germany.

The importance of exogenous, intrauterine factors (abnormal positions or space-taking processes) is not well known. Tight wrapping of infants, muscle pull, and static stress accelerate the progression from hip dysplasia to dislocation. At first by muscle pull, with the onset of standing and walking and additional static load, the steep coxal end of the femur, insufficiently supported by the dysplastic acetabulum, pushes against the cranial acetabular rim and grinds it down, creating a path for the dislocation, usually dorsocranially. According to the new position of the femoral head, a functionally insufficient secondary acetabulum starts to develop. The unfavorable position of the joint causes faulty growth and disturbances in the remodeling of the femoral head (Perthes' dislocation). During the cranial shift of the coxal part of the femur, the adductor and abductor muscles become insufficient.

Symptoms. Dysplasia of the hip cannot be easily recognized in a newborn child. However, the earlier treatment is started during the first year of life, the more successful it is.

Unreliable Signs:

- Past medical history or family history
- Restricted abduction (Fig. 12–5); decreased ability to abduct the leg in a right-angle flexion of the hip joint (normal: during the first month, 80° to 90°; during the second and third months, 60° to 65°).

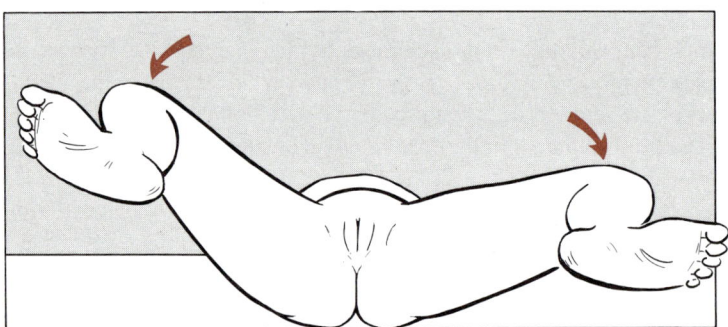

Fig. 12–5 Restricted abduction of the right hip joint.

- Less movement with the affected leg
- Difference in leg length: In case of dislocation the leg shortening is caused by the dislocation between the femur and the pelvis in the area of the thigh. In dysplasia of the hip the affected leg might show retarded growth. Looking directly across the knee joints, even minor differences are obvious in a baby in a supine position on a firm support, with both hip and knee joints flexed in a right angle (Fig. 12–6).
- Asymmetric folds: The affected thigh shows more folds than the normal thigh. In dislocation the gluteal fold is higher than on the unaffected side. Vulva and gluteal bottom folds are dislocated toward the side of dislocation and the gluteal dimples disappear on the affected side.

  Asymmetric folds are often overemphasized. Approximately two-thirds of the children who are examined because of this symptom have normal hips. However, in unilateral dislocation of the hip a cranial motion of the femur against the pelvis can be expected as well as an increasing disproportion of the soft tissue—with increasing hip dislocation—and an asymmetry of the adductor, gluteal, and inguinal folds (Fig. 12–7).
- Changed shape of the bottom: The dislocation of the proximal femur against the pelvis causes a different shape of the bottom. In a position with flexed hip joints and caudal view an indentation between the ischial tuberosity and the greater trochanter can be observed, or at least palpated, in obese babies.

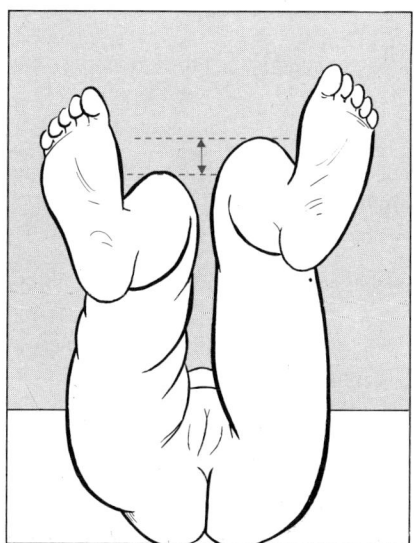

Fig. 12–6 Difference in leg length owing to dislocation of the right hip; note increased hip contour and gluteal indentation on the right side.

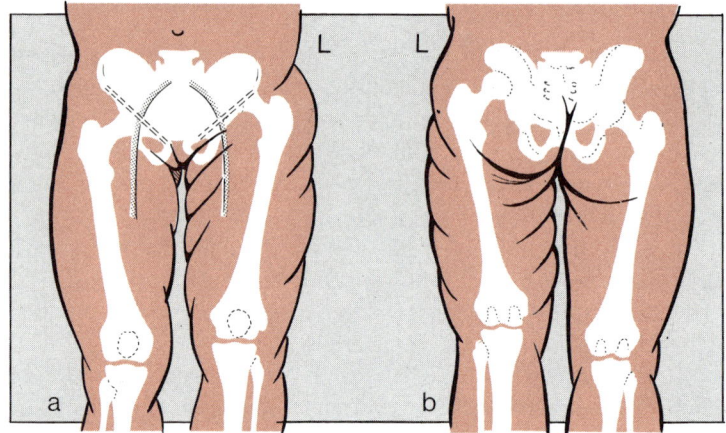

Fig. 12–7 Asymmetric folds in dislocation of the left hip. Vulva and rima ani are pulled toward the affected side. Femoral head is lateral to the intersection of the inguinal ligament and the femoral artery. Note the lateral deviation and elevation of the greater trochanter.

- Ortolani sign: Intraarticular snapping during the first week of life: in a dysplastic hip joint the femoral head jumps across a secondary rim during the examination.

Reliable Signs:

- Empty acetabulum: The dislocated head is palpated in the typical location; the acetabulum is palpated as empty.
- Elevated trochanter
- Abductor indentation: The child is in a prone position with extended thighs; a distinct depression can be felt in the inguinal area.
- Lateral deviation of the femoral head
- Hilgenreiner sign: The hip can be dislocated and put back in place with a loud snapping sound.
- Glissement: The femoral head, which is outside the acetabulum and opposite the pelvis, has shifted against the pelvis in a sliding motion.
- Radiograph: The pelvic survey allows a correct assessment of the situation and the course of the disorder.

Shape and position of the acetabulum, shape and development of the femoral epiphysis and neck, and position of the coxal part of the femur toward the acetabulum are evaluated. The evaluation is facilitated by use of accessory lines and angles (Figs. 12–8 and 12–9).

Hip Joint/Clinical Symptoms 241

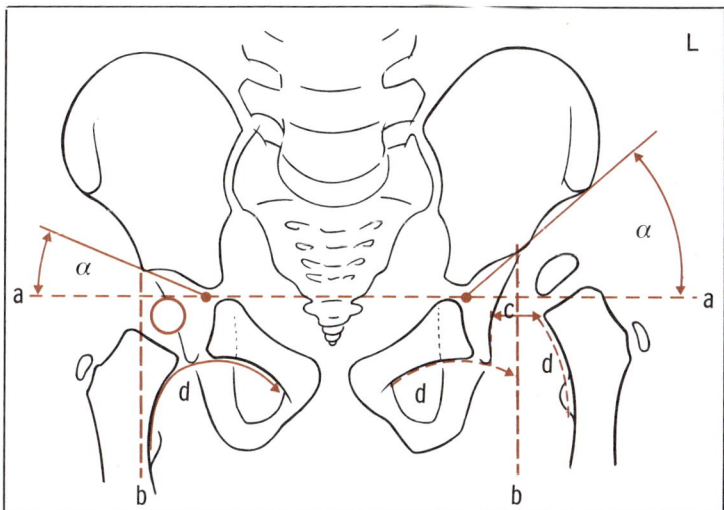

Fig. 12–8 Radiographic scheme of the pelvis in dislocation of the left hip. **a:** Hilgenreiner line; **b:** Ombredanne line; **c:** distance between the diaphyseal rim and the os ischii; **d:** Ménard-Shenton line; **d:** acetabular angle.

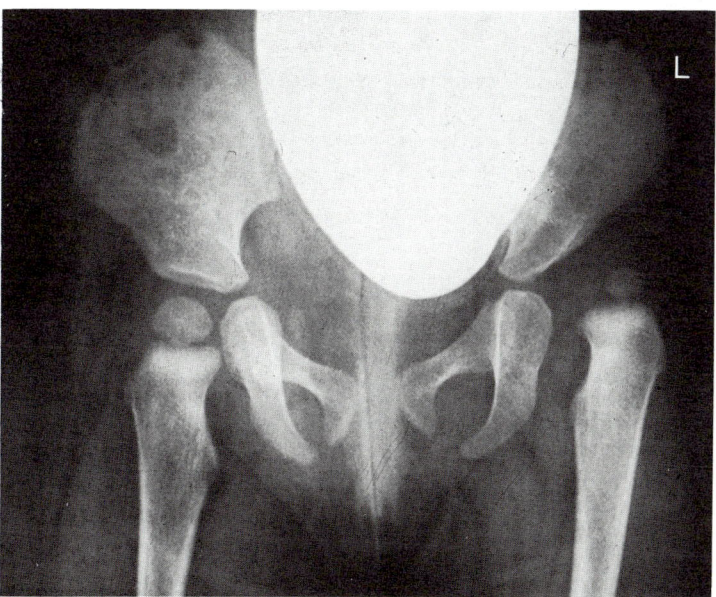

Fig. 12–9 Radiograph of the pelvis of a 15-month-old infant with dislocation of the left hip (from H. Cotta: Orthopädie, 4. Aufl., Thieme, Stuttgart, 1984).

A joint arthrography is recommended for an intraarticular examination, for instance, whether there is an obstacle interfering with a reposition or to determine the condition of the cartilage, which does not show up on the radiograph.

Conservative Nonsurgical Treatment. For physiologic reasons, the treatment of hip dysplasia, dislocation, and subluxation must be started early. The goal is a centered position of the femoral head within the acetabulum, to achieve better development of the acetabular cup by the formative stimulus.

Hip Dysplasia and Subluxation: Wrapping in abduction position is sufficient during the first 2 to 3 months if the signs are unreliable. A suspicion alone justifies the treatment, since there is no risk of damage such as disturbances of the remodeling of the femoral head.

After the diagnosis of a dysplasia or subluxation in a 3- to 4-month-old infant, a special abduction splint is put on (Fig. 12–10); it can be taken off for cleaning purposes but is worn day and night. This treatment is ended if the acetabulum has developed normally within the next 4 to 8 months (which would be confirmed by

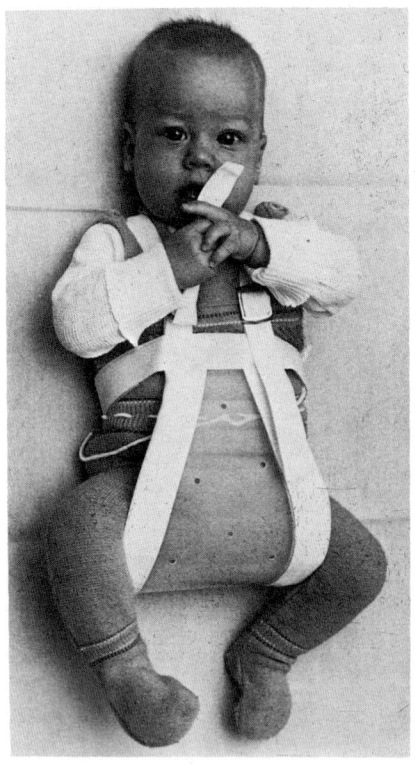

Fig. 12–10 Abduction splint.

radiographs). The abduction is continued with an adjustable splint if the healing process is still incomplete.

Dislocation of the Hip: Repositioning of the femoral head into the primary acetabulum is necessary in an infant or small child. After the successful reposition, the joint, which is still endangered, must be retained in the correct position.

Closed (Nonsurgical) Reduction. With conservative treatment, bandages that gradually bring the hip into a flexed position over 90° have proved successful. In this position the adductors push the dislocated femoral head gradually toward the acetabulum. As soon as this position has been reached, the hip joint is slowly moved into increasing abduction, which makes reduction of the femoral head possible in most cases (Pavlik splint, Fig. 12–11). An alternative to this approach is extension therapy, where the contracted soft tissue is prestretched first by extension. The femoral head is then reduced by changing the position of the extended leg. After the reduction a dislocation is possible within the next 3 months. Depending on the stability of the reduction, the corrected position is immobilized either by a cast (Fig. 12–12) or splints that eliminate movements that could trigger another dislocation.

Surgical Treatment. If the closed reposition attempt has failed, an arthrography must be performed to evaluate the type and extent of the impairment. The femoral head is centered in the acetabulum, and afterward (during the unstable reduction

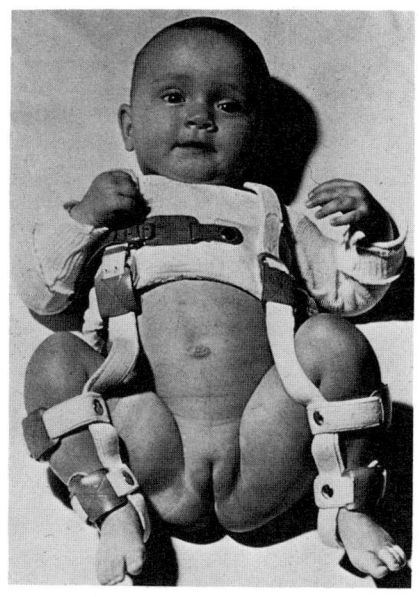

Fig. 12–11 Pavlik splint.

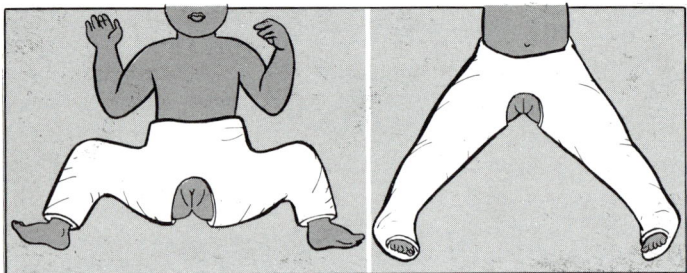

Fig. 12–12 Conventional casts to retain the hips after congenital dislocation. **a:** Lorenz position; **b:** Lange position (from P. Pitzen, H. Rössler: Kurzgefasstes Lehrbuch der Orthopädie, 14. Aufl., Urban und Schwarzenberg, München, 1980).

phase) the hip is immobilized in a cast for at least 6 weeks (stable retention phase). In a severe dysplasia, a plastic repair of the acetabular roof can be attempted to improve the shape of the acetabular cup.

An osteotomy for derotation and varus position is recommended as an additional measure for a severe coxa valga deformity.

After completion of the second year, surgical techniques are used to improve the acetabulum if the situation has been diagnosed too late and if earlier conventional therapy has failed to reverse the dysplasia, subluxation, or dislocation of the hip. These techniques (Fig. 12–13) include the following:

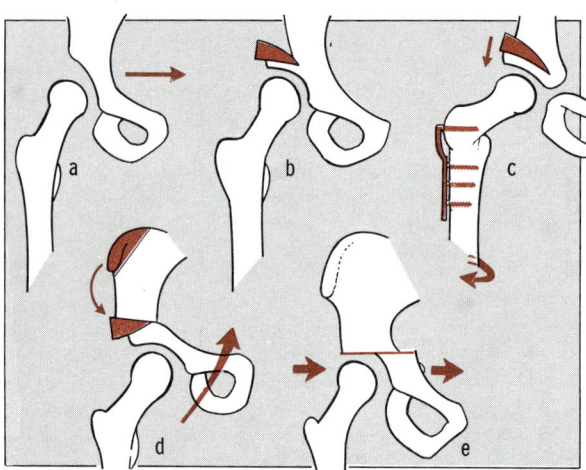

Fig. 12–13 Surgical procedures used to improve the acetabulum in dysplasia of the hip (see text after descriptions) (from P. Pitzen, H. Rössler: Kurzgefasstes Lehrbuch der Orthopädie, 14. Aufl., Urban and Schwarzenberg, München, 1980).

- Plastic repair of the acetabular roof in which the upper acetabular rim is carved out and bent down further with autologous bone chips (according to Lance) (Fig. 12–13b)
- Periacetabular osteotomy mobilizing the entire acetabulum down to the Y suture (according to Pemberton)
- Pelvic osteotomy in which the distal part of the transected pelvis, including the acetabulum, is bent downward across the femoral head (according to Salter) (Fig. 12–13d)
- Pelvic osteotomy in which the distal part of the pelvis is shifted medially; the sectional plane—separated from the femoral head by the joint capsule—functions as a deepened acetabular roof (according to Chiari) (Fig. 12–13e).

Frequently, an osteotomy of the coxal femoral part is necessary in addition to the plastic repair of the acetabulum to eliminate pathological antetorsion (derotation and varus osteotomy, Fig. 12–13c).

Arthritis of the Hip (Coxarthrosis, Arthrosis of the Hip)

Origin. Wear and tear of the joint, seldom idiopathic (owing to unknown reasons). In most cases it occurs as a sequel to an incongruity of the joint after a congenital hip dysplasia, Perthe's disease, epiphysiolysis of the hip, coxitis, necrosis of the femoral head, or fractures of the acetabular roof and the femoral head (see also basic discussion in Chapter 7).

Symptoms. Initial pain during walking, especially on uneven ground or climbing stairs. Range of motion in the hip joint is restricted in the sequence internal rotation, abduction, and extension. With hip contracture there is increased pelvic tilt and compensatory increased lumbar lordosis or unilaterally elevated pelvis.

Pain is felt mostly in the inguinal area, on the greater trochanter, along the front of the thigh, inside the knee joint, and in the lumbar area. The typical radiographic result is a narrow space of the hip joint and an uneven contour of the femoral head and the acetabular cup.

Conservative Nonsurgical Treatment

- Reduced weight bearing: Use of a cane, body weight loss, cushioning of the shoe heel, and possibly a change of profession
- Physical therapy
- Medication: antiinflammatory, analgesic, protection of the cartilage (also intraarticular injections). Steroid injections have a temporary effect but increase the risk of a necrosis of the femoral head.
- Radiation therapy
- Additional aids

Surgical Treatment

- Surgery to preserve the joint: The weight-bearing stress is altered by a corrective osteotomy; the parts of the joint that have barely been subjected to stress are moved into the area of highest stress.
- Surgery to destroy the joint: Arthrodesis of the hip (in high physical activity), maintained mobility of the opposite hip, the lumbar spine, and the knee joint)
- Resection of the femoral head and neck (possibly in combination with a derotation and angulation osteotomy) after removal of a total endoprosthesis: Unstable hip with severe shortening of the leg; walking ability supported by a cane
- Surgery to replace the joint: Total endoprosthesis, especially in patients over age 60.

Idiopathic Necrosis of the Femoral Head in Adults

Origin. Aseptic, possibly ischemic necrosis (see section on Epiphysiolysis of the Femoral Head in Chapter 6).

This condition may be caused by underlying metabolic diseases. The joint cartilage is not affected primarily, but can be destroyed secondarily by bony breakdown, resulting in an arthrosis of the hip.

Symptoms. Bilateral occurrence in more than 50 percent of patients, mainly in males (4:1). Onset of the disease occurs between ages 20 and 50. At first there is unspecific pain during weight bearing and after rest, as in arthritis.

Radiographs show a characteristic wedge-shaped dense area of bone with increasing demarcation and collapse of the articular surface.

Therapy. See Arthritis of the hip.

Acetabular Profusion

Origin. Severe excavation of the acetabulum, primarily caused by disturbed skeletal development and by disturbed bony consolidation (dysostosis, rickets). Secondarily, there is decreased mechanical stability of the acetabular floor. The pressure from the femoral head causes acetabular protrusion into the small pelvis.

Softening of the acetabular floor can result from to osteoporosis, inflammative diseases of the hip joint, neuropathic arthropathy, tumor, systemic skeletal diseases, or fractures.

Symptoms. Increased restriction of mobility in middle age, at first during abduction, then rotation, whereas flexion remains free even in the late stage. There is a tendency toward flexion contracture with a compensated increased lumbar lordosis. In early cases radiography reveals a deep acetabulum, which surrounds the femoral head more than usual. In addition, the typical clinical and radiological symptoms of an arthrosis start to develop.

Therapy. See arthritis of the hip. During the early stage a valgus osteotomy of the coxal femoral portion can reduce the stress on the acetabular floor.

Coxa Valga

Increased angle between the femoral neck and shaft (collum-diaphysis angle, CCD angle; see Fig. 12–14c). The CCD angle in a newborn is usually approximately 150°, decreasing to approximately 139° until age 9 and to approximately 128° with completion of the growth period. In older persons the angle can be reduced to 120°.

Coxa valga causes increased stress on the hip joint and must be considered a prearthrotic deformity—especially in combination with an insufficient acetabular roof—resulting in early arthritis.

Origin. Most often coxa valga is observed in combination with increased antetorsion in so-called congenital dislocation of the hip (see earlier). Coxa valga also results from to a disposition without an antetorsion. It can be acquired by a lesion of the growth plate of the femoral head (inflammation, tumor, trauma); by a change of forces, which influences the direction of the growth as in paralysis; by muscle diseases, owing to reduced weight bearing; and by a fracture of the femoral head, healed in a malposition.

Symptoms. No symptoms occur for a long time, except those caused by the underlying disorder. Accidental diagnosis is made from a radiograph. In late stages symptoms are similar to those of an arthrotic hip.

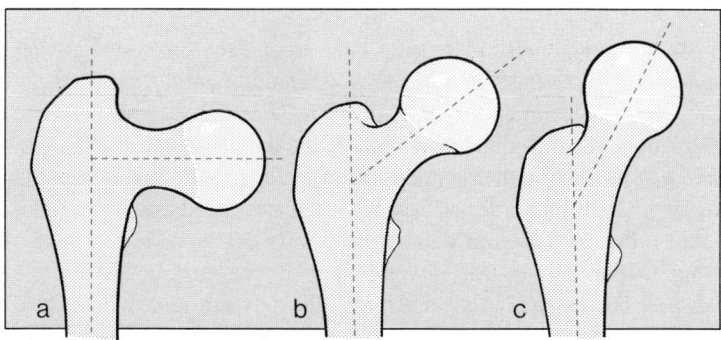

Fig. 12–14 a: Coxa vara; **b:** normal angle; **c:** coxa valga.

Treatment. During the growth period a spontaneous correction is possible. After childhood, varus osteotomy is done, possibly in combination with corrective surgery of the acetabulum (see Fig. 12–13c).

Coxa Vara

Decreased CCD angle below the normal age-related value toward 90° or less (for normal values see coxa valga; Fig. 12–14).

Origin. Congenital coxa valga (coxa vara congenita). Acquired as a stress-related deformity and from decreased stability of the bone, as in inflammation, tumor, rickets, dysostosis, aseptic necrosis; after lesions of the growth plate, as in aseptic necrosis, inflammation, tumor trauma; and from fractures, healed in a malposition.

Symptoms. Coxa vara congenita: The decreased CCD angle causes an elevation of the trochanter, leg length shortening, insufficient abductor muscles of the hip, and the resultant positive Trendelenburg sign. In infants the pathological changes are not obvious. When the child starts walking, a limping and waddling gait (with bilateral disease) indicates problems. Abduction and often rotation are restricted.

The symptoms in an acquired coxa vara are less pronounced than in the congenital form. Both types, however, lead to arthritis.

Treatment. Conservative treatment is important only with temporarily decreased stability of the bone (rickets); otherwise, surgical correction by intertrochanteric valgus osteotomy is needed.

Periarthrosis Coxae

Origin. As in periarthrosis humeroscapularis, degenerative changes of tendons, muscles, and ligaments create the preconditions for the deposit of calcium within the paraarticular and periarticular tissue.

Symptoms. Acute or gradually increasing pain around the hip joint (greater trochanter) radiating into the thigh and buttocks. Chronic, more diffuse pain can be sharply increased by mechanical stress. Pain during strong abduction, presence of the Trendelenburg sign, and pain during passive abduction indicate a disease of the abductor muscles of the hip, their tendons, or insertion points. Pain increasing during extension of the hip or internal rotation indicates the iliopsoas muscle. Overheated skin indicates calcium deposits (bursitis calcarea; Fig. 12–15). Inactivity owing to pain favors the development of contracture and muscle atrophy. The disease occurs unilaterally and bilaterally between ages 40 and 60. It is not unusual for a coxarthrosis to be predominant at the same time.

Therapy. See Periarthropathia humeroscapularis.

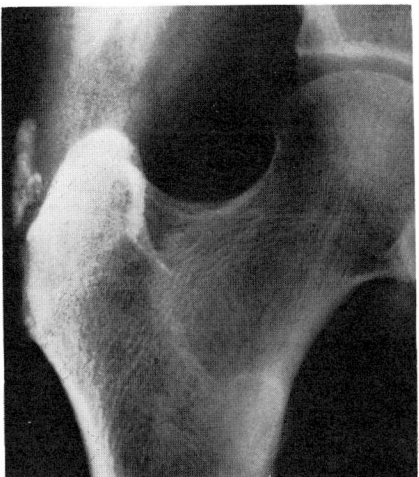

Fig. 12–15 Periarthrosis coxae. Calcified trochanteric bursa (from H. Cotta: Orthopädie, 4. Aufl., Thieme, Stuttgart, 1984).

Snapping Hip (Coxa Saltans, Jerking Hip)

Origin. Uneven tension of the fascia lata owing to a genetic disposition. Decreased elasticity and abnormal mobility of the iliotibial band (weak connective tissue). Traumatic or inflammative changes of the iliotibial band and the surrounding tissue and a congenital or acquired change of the shape of the greater trochanter (tumor, malposition after a fracture).

Symptoms. During walking the fascia lata and the iliotibial band do not glide continuously and smoothly across the greater trochanter; instead, there is a disturbing and uncomfortable jerking movement at a certain flexion position of the hip. This snapping or jerking during flexion and extension can occur unilaterally or bilaterally. Often it cannot be initiated passively, but it is noticed immediately when the patient is walking and the examiner puts a hand below the greater trochanter on the lateral thigh. Increased mechanical stress can cause painful inflammations, bursa formation, and pain during rest.

Treatment. As long as the patient is free of pain, strengthening of the hip abductors is done. In cases of pain, therapeutic attempt with a local anesthetic, possibly with additional steroids, is done. Surgically, in case of persistent discomfort, extirpation of the inflamed bursa between the fascia lata and greater trochanter, fixation of the split iliotibial band to the femur, and correction of the shape of the greater trochanter are options.

PHYSICAL THERAPY

Hip Dysplasia/Hip Dislocation

Conservative Treatment

Hip Dysplasia and Subluxation in Infants and Young Children. Abduction splints (Figs. 12–10 and 12–11) for the treatment of a permanent reduction of the hip can be used only if the hip joints are freely mobile and loose. Any restriction of abduction must be eliminated before the corrective immobilization of the hip joints to avoid disturbances of bone remodeling in the femoral head.

The abduction splint must fit exactly; it should be neither too tight nor too wide and should match the distance between the popliteal spaces with 90° of knee flexion, 90° of hip flexion, and 90° of external rotation of the hip joints. With abduction splints the legs have a defined range of motion, which stimulates the development of the hip joint. Flexion, abduction, and external rotation are allowed, but extension, adduction, and internal rotation are restricted.

Hip Dislocation in Infants and Young Children. The reduction is usually combined with a stay in the hospital. Pretreatment is necessary for shortened muscles, especially for the adductors. In a relatively short time the tensed and shortened muscles can be relaxed and stretched and all the muscles of the legs and hips can be stimulated and strengthened. After successful reduction, treatment is continued on an outpatient basis.

Cast, bandage, or splints, or a combination thereof, are commonly used; for instance, cast two times for 6 weeks, followed by a bandage. The bandage is wrapped crosswise ventrally, leading the legs from an abduction in a squatting position.

Advice for the parents is an essential part of this therapy: how to give the child enough care and attention, to prevent any psychomotor disturbance owing to the restriction of the child's natural need for activity. A baby should be given opportunities for activities and play according to its age and should be frequently moved around and stimulated.

After Completion of Conservative Treatment with Cast, Bandage, or Splint and with a Stable Retention. Joint contractures and/or soft tissue shortening are observed only temporarily in infants. However, the legs continue to assume the therapeutic position for some time after the treatment.

- Insufficient muscle strength
- Insufficient back musculature, depending on the pretreatment
- Occasionally a setback in the development of movement patterns according to age

Goals of Therapy

- Assist in "unlearning" the therapeutic position.
- Mobilize the joints and strengthen the leg muscles.
- Strengthen trunk musculature.
- Facilitate movement patterns through the developmental sequence.
- Initiate independent ambulation.

Therapy. Special physical therapy is often not necessary with sufficient advice and instructions for the parents on exercising with the child at home. However, therapy is needed if persistent contractures, delays in normal activity, or pain owing to an aseptic necrosis of the femoral head exists. If radiography is conclusive, the physician must order further therapy.

Accompanying diseases, such as infant cerebral palsy (ICP), are treated accordingly.

Sometimes a short stay in the hospital may be required after a long period in a cast, bandage, or abduction splint.

Although the child has learned to walk with the bandage or the splint, a normal gait is missing. (Up to the second year, walking with a bandage or splint is not possible.) Active exercises in warm water with a soft ball or on a pillow are started first. All the muscles of the feet and legs must be trained intensively; they are all equally important for stability.

Sometimes the muscles are so insufficient that the child cannot stand up without the splint. If the feet and leg muscles are not strong enough to support an upright position, additional aids and the therapist's hands can be used.

Walker, crutches, or canes are not suitable for a young child, who does not learn how to use them properly. The first attempts to walk should be scheduled in the therapeutic pool. In the water a walking aid might be useful. Without aids, standing and walking are developed from crawling and kneeling. These techniques are used in children who have never walked. The treatment can also be designed according to developmental aspects from neurology and kinesiology (Bobath and Vojta).

A satisfactory balance is provided for by strengthening the trunk muscles.

An even gait is improved by activities such as: walking along lines on the floor, stepping across obstacles, walking on stairs, changing the tempo or following a rhythm, clapping, and singing. The treatment should be playful. Usually sports activities are not restricted. Parents should observe often to develop their own ideas for handling the child at home. The stay in the hospital can be shortened considerably and further treatment might be unnecessary with the parents' cooperation.

The child will remain under orthopedic supervision for years. Continued physical therapy is required in cases of children with irregular moving patterns.

Surgical Treatment

Hip Dislocation and Remaining Dysplasia. Open surgical reduction to treat remaining dysplasia (intertrochanteric osteotomy for derotation and varus position, plastic repair of the acetabular roof, or pelvic osteotomy).

Before Surgery

Evaluation Results

- More or less severe restriction of abduction is obvious without prior treatment with an abduction bandage or splint, or in a dislocation diagnosed late.
- The legs are in a preconditioned position, depending on the type of immobilization.
- General muscle insufficiency is present if the child's motor development was restricted by the hip lesion.

Goals of Therapy

- Mobilize the hip joints to eliminate the restriction in abduction or an unphysiologic posture.
- Strengthen the muscles of the legs and trunk.

Therapy. Restricted abduction is the main problem. The adductors are carefully stretched several times daily, and passive manipulations cannot be avoided. Vibration and gentle massage prepare the stretching activity.

After Surgery

Evaluation Results—Depending on Child's Age

- Position of the hip joints is preconditioned, depending on the type and time period of the immobilization.
- All leg and trunk musculature is weak.

Therapy. The exercise treatment is strictly active. Mobilization of the joints strengthens the muscles at the same time and vice versa, aiming at complete adduction of the hips. The position of the pelvis must be observed and possibly fixated manually by the therapist. A therapeutic ball is a suitable support, if the legs are not yet weight bearing (Fig. 12–16a).

Exercises on a bolster are recommended to start weight bearing (Fig. 12–16b through d). The diameter is chosen according to the desired contact with the floor. A riding position on the bolster is also favorable for balance exercises (Fig. 12–16e and f). Balance in a sitting position must be improved, lateral deviation or kyphosis of the spine must be equalized, and symmetry must be pursued. The child should sit without help only if the trunk is sufficiently stabilized.

Exercise treatment in the therapeutic pool is started not sooner than 2 days after the removal of the stitches in children who did not receive a cast after the surgery. Young children are first placed in a bathtub and after a few days can go into the pool together with the therapist. Vigorous kicking and quick, strong motions in the water create resistance and stimulate mobilization and strengthening. Standing and walking can also be started in the pool.

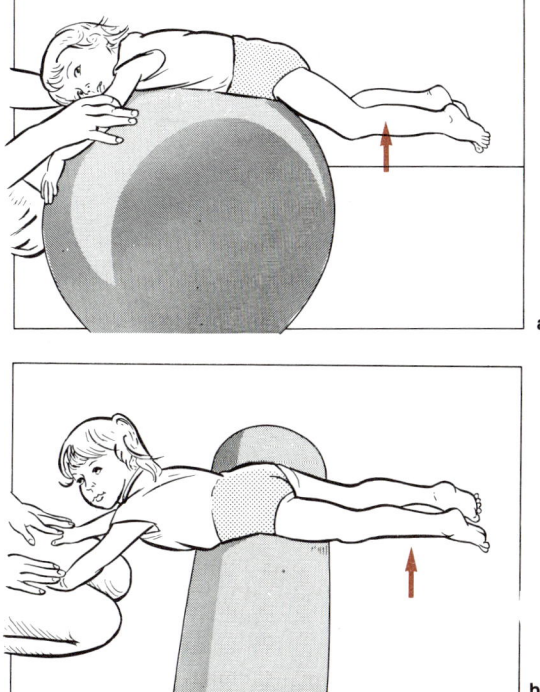

Fig. 12–16 Exercises on a therapeutic ball or bolster (**a-f**) *(continued)*

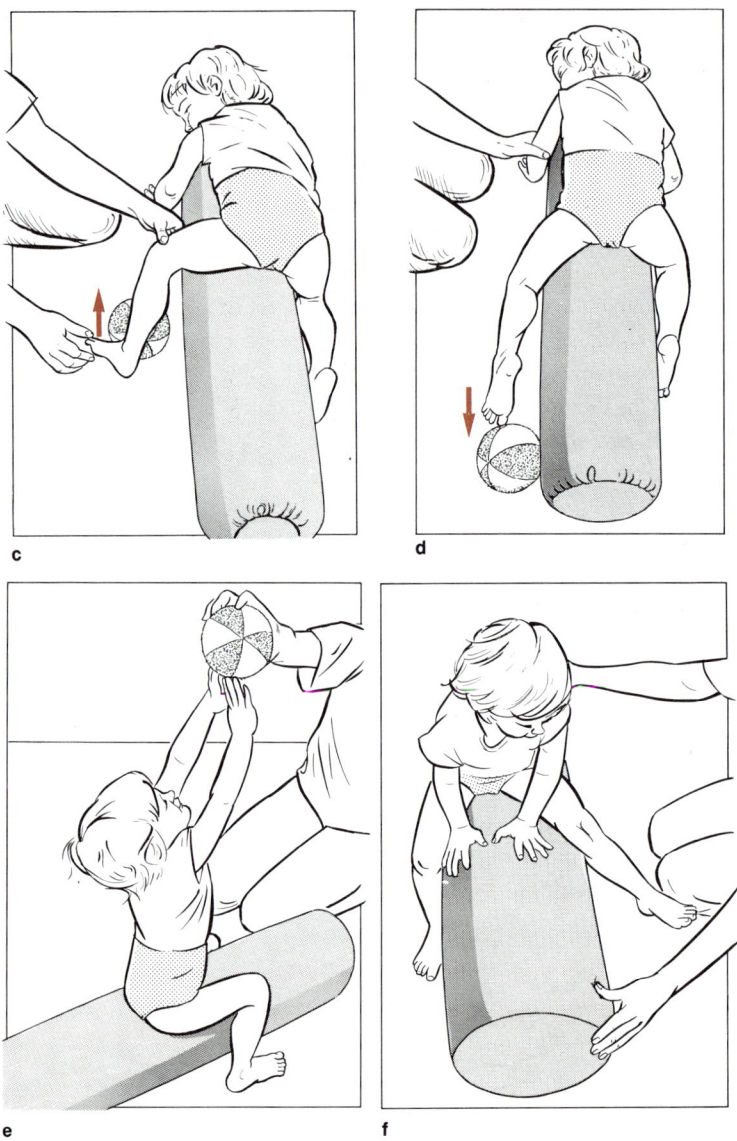

Fig. 12–16 continued

As soon as weight bearing is permitted for the hip, the child can exercise on a floor mat in quadriped or kneeling position. Crawling is started if the child had not been able to walk before surgery. The floor mat provides sufficient space for exercising playfully but at the same time aiming at various muscle groups. Two or more children together can stimulate one another. The younger the child, the more difficult it is to exercise sufficiently and to avoid continued pelvic deviations over the spine and the normal hip joint. The reason for this is insufficient strength of the muscles. The therapist tries to counteract this by facilitation and active (passively supported) resistance. For suggestions for gait training, see Conservative Treatment.

Limping. Depending on the degree of varus position, the origin and insertion of the muscles between the pelvis and the trochanter approach each other by elevation of the greater trochanter. These muscles become weak. During ambulation the Trendelenburg sign appears in the weight-bearing phase, often in combination with a Duchenne limp. In young children the limp is temporary and is eliminated by intensive exercises, which the parents should participate in after sufficient instructions.

Limping is also observed in older children and adolescents who had been walking normally before surgery. Parents and patients must be made aware of this fact before surgery to avoid disappointment. Intensive gait training must be pursued for months.

Trendelenburg Sign

Origin. Weakness or deficiency of the gluteus medius and minimus muscles.

Symptom. During weight bearing on the affected leg the pelvis drops to the opposite side.

During Walking

- Unilateral: Limping, lateral deviation of the hip (with adduction of the hip joint)
- Bilateral: Waddling

Duchenne Sign

Origin. As above.

Symptom. During weight bearing the trunk swings toward the affected side (supporting leg); the pelvis drops; the Trendelenburg sign is eliminated.

During Walking. The trunk swings toward the affected side (with abduction of the hip joint).

Physical Therapy. Therapy consists of intensive training of the gluteal muscles, matched to the ability of the muscles, to avoid compensating motion of the pelvis. All the muscles of the limb have to be included in the program. PNF exercises are recommended.

Electrotherapy should also be applied if a muscle test grade is below fair.

Exercises are done with weight bearing, if strength permits, in both kneeling and standing. The amount of weight bearing is dependent not only on muscle strength but also on the disease and the diagnosis of the hip joint.

Walking can be supported by swinging the arms vigorously; quick, rhythmic walking; walking barefoot (but not when a difference in leg length is present).

Use of exercise equipment: pushing a rod above the head with both hands, carrying a therapeutic ball on the affected side with a flat hand in a horizontal line or above the head. Simulating the use of a cane on the contralateral side, correcting the posture consciously; walking exercises in front of a mirror.

The use of a cane must also be matched to muscle strength. It should not take away more work than necessary from the gluteal muscles.

In children another incorrect habit during walking is a pronounced forward swinging of the leg; the hip and knee joints are not flexed sufficiently. This is improved by practice of stepping over obstacles and walking on stairs.

Open Reduction

Immobilization: Cast including the pelvis and leg in a squatting position
Hip joint: 90° to 100° flexion, 50° to 80° abduction, 10° to 15° internal rotation
Knee joint: 30° to 40° flexion

The foot remains free. The cast remains in place for 12 weeks, followed by a bandage or, less frequently, an abduction splint. The result of the clinical and radiographic examination determines the length of the treatment; 1 to 2 years is possible. The child can start walking with the bandage; the legs are brought gradually into the neutral position. The entire treatment period can be calculated based on the child's age at the beginning. It is approximately twice as long as the child's age.

Derotation and Varus Osteotomy (DVO)

Children Under Age 4:

Immobilization: Pelvis, leg, and foot cast; hip joint: flexion/extension 0° or slight flexion, rotation 0° or slight internal rotation, 20° adduction.

The knee and foot are in the neutral position.
After 4 weeks: The cast is bivalved, and exercises are started in the cast, which is put back after the treatment.
After 5 weeks: Addition of hydrotherapy and ambulation with partial weight bearing.

After 6 weeks: Increased weight bearing, depending on the radiographic result.
After 7 weeks: Discharge; radiographic followup.

Children Over Age 4:

Position: Traction, during the first week, day and night.
After 1 week: Exercises are started; traction only at night.
After 2 weeks: Addition of hydrotherapy and ambulation with partial weight bearing; controlling the leg length and adjusting shoes as necessary.

The exercises are gradually intensified. The intensity depends on the radiographic result.

Derotation and Varus Osteotomy and Plastic Repair of the Acetabular Roof (According to Pemberton) or Pelvic Osteotomy (According to Salter)

Immobilization: Pelvis, leg, and foot cast, as earlier.

After 2 weeks: After wound healing, discharge with the cast in place
After 5 weeks: Bivalve the cast; monitor with radiographs; begin exercises in the cast
After 6 weeks: Addition of hydrotherapy and ambulation with partial weight bearing, possibly adjustment of the shoes
After 7 weeks: Full weight bearing
After 8 weeks: Discharge; radiographic followup; continued control and physical therapy needed, depending on the situation

Pelvic Osteotomy (According to Chiari)

Immobilization: Pelvis, leg, and foot cast, as earlier
After 3 weeks: Bivalve the cast; radiographic control; start exercises in the cast for 3 days; after the fourth day, addition of hydrotherapy and partial weight bearing (5 kg).
After 4 weeks: Increased weight bearing and intensification of exercises
After 5 weeks: Controlling the leg length, possibly by adjusting the shoes; ambulation with 30-kg weight bearing; removal of the wire during the sixth week
After 6 weeks: Discharge; weight bearing of 30 kg for the next 4 months. Physical therapy is continued on an outpatient basis. In 4 months and after radiographic followup, full weight bearing is allowed.

Pelvic osteotomy according to Chiari is indicated for children over age 8, adolescents, and adults. The postoperative exercise program is the same for all age groups. Cautious movements are recommended as long as the wire is in place. A pillow should be used as a support as long as the osteotomy site is not quite consolidated and the hip flexion has not yet reached 90°.

Arthritis of the Hip

Conservative Treatment

Evaluation Results

- *Pain*
  - Depending on the severity: initial pain, pain during rest, activity, weight bearing, or constant pain
  - Different location: In the inguinal area or radiating from the greater trochanter over the knee along the lateral leg to the ankle (along the iliotibial band).
- Tension and increased tone in leg and back muscles, especially in the adductors, gluteal muscles, tensor fasciae latae, erector spinae, and quadratus lumborum. In a strong flexion contraction of the hip, pain is also felt in the triceps surae and the foot muscles.
- *Restricted Range of Motion:* Restriction of internal rotation occurs first and is most pronounced, followed by abduction and extension. Flexion and external rotation are not affected for a long time. Frequently, even considerably restricted ranges of motion are not realized in their full extent by the patient, who has become accustomed to the gradually increasing restriction, especially if he or she is not active. With the onset of limping the patient starts to notice the situation.
- Muscle shortening, especially of the adductors, external rotators, and flexors, including the rectus femoris muscle.
- Insufficient strength, especially of the gluteal muscles, but also the muscles of the thigh and the entire leg, depending on the severity of the disease. Decreased thigh circumference is visible and can be measured.
- *Gait Deviations:*
  - Uneven gait: Owing to the lack of extension of the hip, the step length on the unaffected or less affected side is shorter, the step length on the affected side longer.
  - Uneven weight bearing: Because of pain, the affected leg is taken off the ground quicker.
  - Insufficient stability of the affected leg: This is the result of restricted mobility and weakness, especially of the pelvic and trochanteric muscles. There is a positive Trendelenburg sign.

    The missing internal rotation and abduction of the pelvis is compensated by rotating the trunk during walking.
- Interference with daily routine, such as sitting down and getting up, sitting on hard or deep chairs, climbing stairs or walking on uneven ground, personal

care, using the toilet or bathtub, dressing and undressing, especially socks and shoes
- Dependency on additional aids and other persons
- Stressing other areas of the body, especially spine, shoulder girdle, and arms, by use of a cane.

Goals of Therapy

- Reduce muscle spasm and promote relaxation.
- Mobilize affected joints.
- Elongate shortened muscles.
- Promote ambulation training.
- Encourage activity of daily living training.

Treatment

- *Pain Relief:*
  —Reducing stress
  —Moist hot packs or whirlpool bath
  —Soft, gentle massage transverse to the direction of the muscle fibers in the area of the back, pelvis, and legs, especially over shortened and tensed muscles
  —Underwater massage
  —Electrotherapy
  —Hydrotherapy: while resting on floats, performance of slow motions within the pain-free range of the affected joint, the neighboring joints, and the spine
  —Permanent extension or traction in a relaxed position by pulleys, starting gently with a little weight, to avoid reflex tension of the muscles
  —Relaxation techniques, starting in a relaxed position
  —Vibration
  —Manual traction, matched to the radiographic result and after discussion with the physician.
- *Relaxation:* All pain-relieving techniques including use of PNF techniques to counteract the reflex tension of the muscles. Attempt ice applications. Usually patients with arthrosis do not tolerate cold well.
- *Stretching Shortened Muscles:* Brief application of ice along thigh muscles, such as the rectus femoris, is used before to careful stretching.

- *Mobilizing the Joints:* The mobilizations mentioned earlier are sufficient to eliminate the contracture of shortened soft tissue and mobilize the joint sufficiently without causing further damage by shearing forces.
- *Strengthening the Muscles:* Improve insufficient muscle strength to stabilize the achieved range of motion.

    —Static contractions for extension, abduction, and internal rotation, for instance, for the gluteus maximus: in prone position, support by a pillow to equalize the flexion contracture of the hip and hyperlordosis of the lumbar spine (Fig. 12–17); in supine position with active resistance (Fig. 12–18).
    —Dynamic exercises in a sling with traction (Fig. 12–19) to compensate for the lordosis and fixation of the pelvis over the opposite leg. Hip extension across a bench or box to compensate for the lordosis (Fig. 12–20). Exercises against resistance (Fig. 12–21).

    The gluteus maximus and minimus muscles are responsible for abduction and internal rotation of the hip, and stabilize the pelvis on the supporting leg.

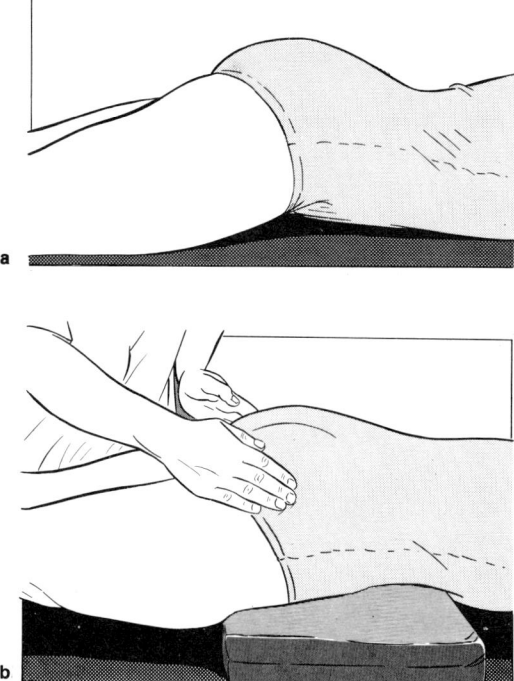

Fig. 12–17 Isometric contractions in prone position.

Hip Joint/Physical Therapy   261

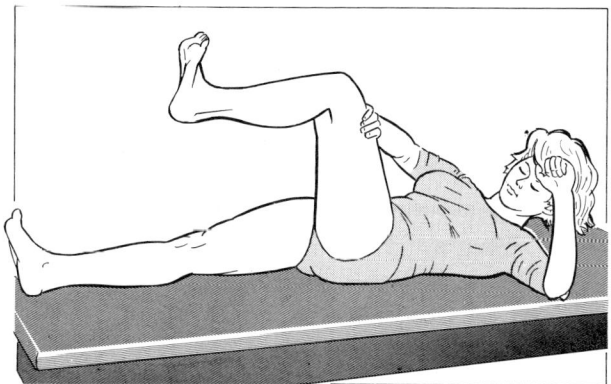

Fig. 12–18 Isometric contraction in supine position with active resistance.

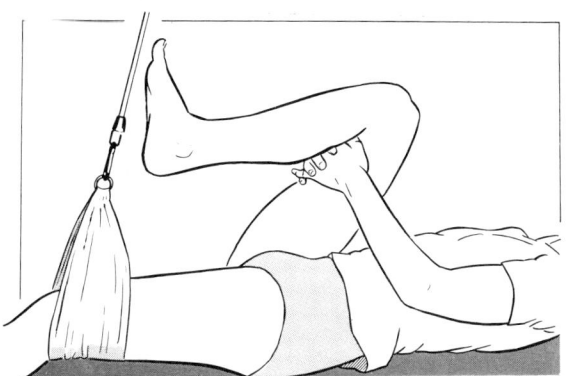

Fig. 12–19 Dynamic exercises in a sling with traction.

A maximum effect of the exercises can be attained by adapting to the forces, for instance:

—Isometric and active exercise in a sling (Fig. 12–22)
—With a controlled position of the pelvis and active resistance in side lying (Fig. 12–23)
—Against the resistance of a pulley (Fig. 12–24a and b); PNF techniques, hydrotherapy, and use of free exercises on a floor mat to increase muscle strength.

- *Gait Training:* To help develop a more economical way of walking, i.e., the patient should be able to walk without pain, using less energy, and with less

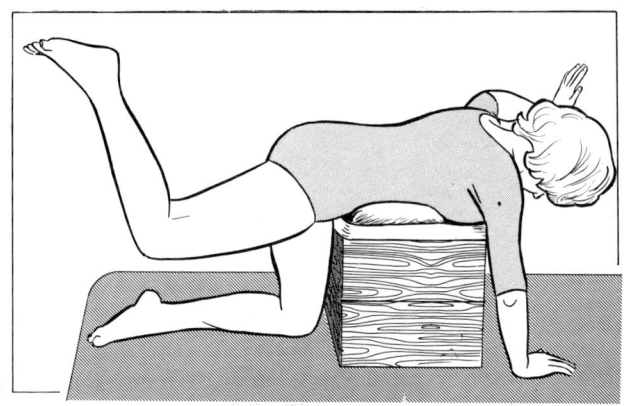
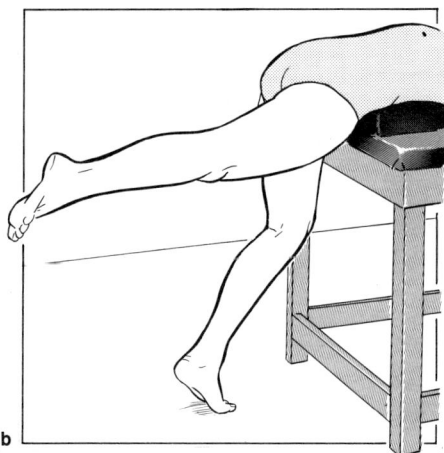

Fig. 12–20 Compensating lordosis across a box or bench.

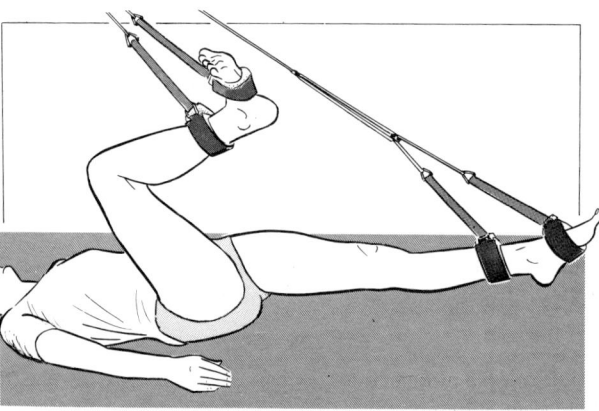

Fig. 12–21 Exercising against the resistance of a pulley in the supine position.

Hip Joint/Physical Therapy 263

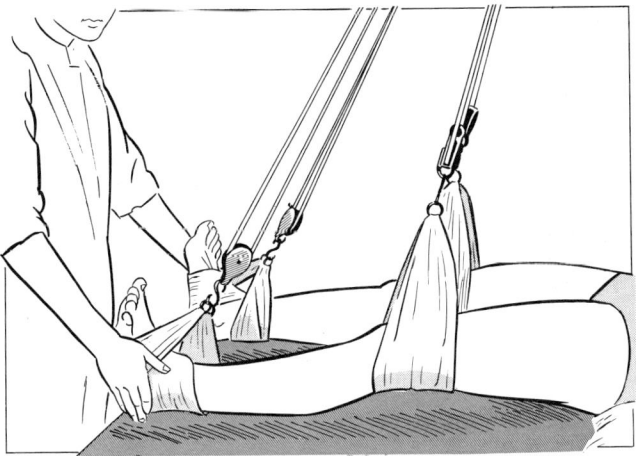

Fig. 12–22 Isometric and active exercises in a sling.

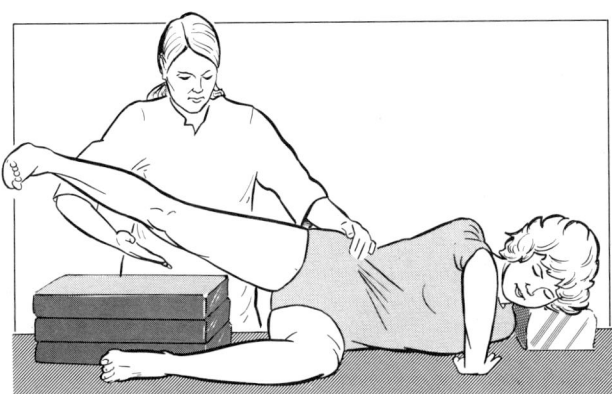

Fig. 12–23 Exercising in side lying position with active resistance.

stress on the joints. A certain degree of limping must be tolerated, depending on the diagnosis. The gait should be as normal as possible but not forced. Additional aids may be needed.

The degree and intensity of gait training are matched to the individual patient.

A gait analysis demonstrates the quality of the single phases and the deviations from the normal moving pattern.

The following parameters are evaluated:

264 Lower Limbs

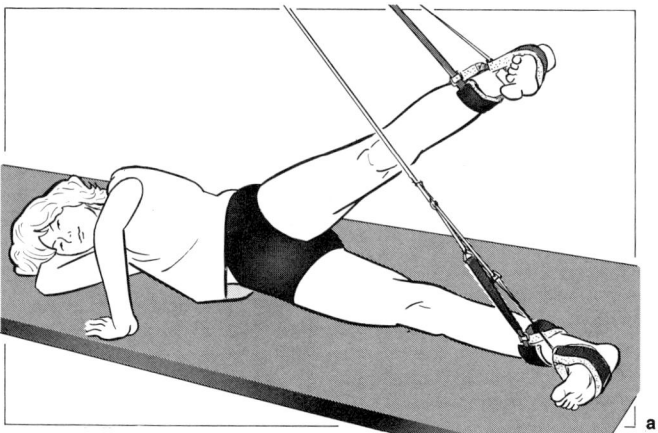

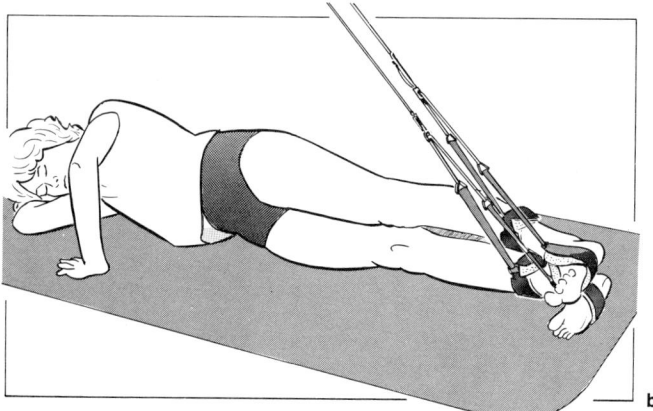

Fig. 12–24 Exercising against resistance, in side lying position.

—Use of supporting and saltatory leg; alternating between both legs; the rolling movement of the foot; the function of foot, knee, and hip joint, dynamically during the swing phase, statically during the weight-bearing phase
—Even lateral and forward motion of the center of gravity from the right leg to the left leg
—Perpendicular posture of the body above the supporting leg
—Even tempo during the phases
—Movement of all joints of the leg and the pelvis
—Muscle strength

—Rotation of the spine
—Simultaneous movement of the arms
—Overall impression of posture and movement.

The patient walks barefoot and wears clothes that allow observation of all movements. Visual control in front of the mirror helps the patient to recognize the presence of a limp and the possibilities for correcting it. Gait training can be done barefoot if there is no difference in leg length.

According to the examination result, single phases of the gait are corrected, with partial or full weight bearing.

Gait training at first is easier in the therapeutic pool.

Reciprocal walking can be practiced in slings (Fig. 12–25), shifting weight and stabilizing in quadriped and kneeling positions on a floor mat. Obstacles can be used to determine the stride, in an asymmetric pattern if needed. The use of equipment can improve the mobilization or stabilization of the trunk. The use of an ambulatory aid is learned. As soon as the walking aid is no longer necessary, the static and dynamic functions of the legs and pelvis are learned.

Gait deviations should be eliminated, whenever possible, since they cause stress on the joints.

An asymmetrical gait pattern, such as uneven stride length owing to lack of extension of the hip, cannot be corrected. A forced correction will fail and cause pain. The patient is advised to wear soft shoes. The heel can also be supported by a cushion. The rolling motion of the foot is facilitated and the stress on joints and spine, which cannot be relieved by the muscles, is eliminated.

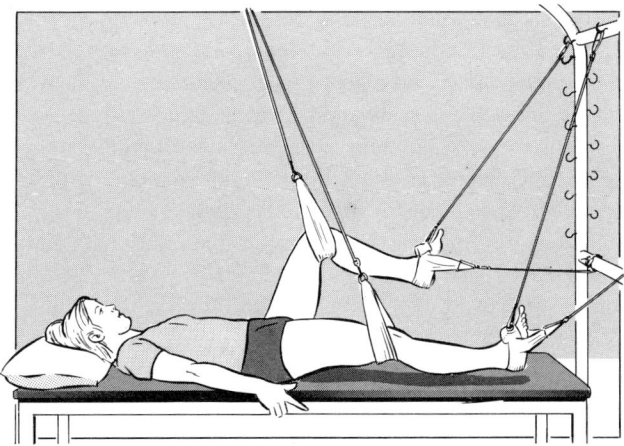

Fig. 12–25 Preliminary exercise for reciprocal walking.

- *Activities of Daily Living:* The patient learns the variety and complexity of body motions, exercises freely on the floor mat or a stool with or without equipment. Some movements forgotten by the patient are relearned. The patient gradually regains awareness of his or her body, coordination, and security.

    Gait training follows the same aspects. It should be scheduled outdoors, if at all possible. Uneven terrain is chosen; obstacles must be overcome or walked around, slopes must be walked on with changing use of the cane, sometimes even without it; the tempo is changed, and so forth. The therapist must observe the patient and adjust the activities to the patient's abilities. Ambition should not be overstressed.

- *Activities of Daily Living Training:* The program must be designed for the individual patient, if the patient is still restricted in some areas after treatment, or if there are permanent restrictions that would cause him or her to depend on someone else for assistance. An examination is a prerequisite. It must include a detailed discussion of the situation at home, the problems that might arise, and how to handle them. Equipment is tried out and chosen, and its use is taught, e.g., aids to put on socks and shoes (Figs. 12–26 and 12–27).

- *Compensating Exercises:* Shoulder girdle, arms, and especially the lumbar spine are affected by overstress. The use of walking aids results in tension of shoulders and arms, overload of the wrists, rigid posture of the trunk, and elimination of spinal rotation.

    The lack of extension at the hip joint is compensated by an increased lordosis of the lumbar spine. Each restriction of the hip results in additional stress on the spine. These problems can hamper the treatment of the original disease to a great extent and, when possible, must be prevented.

    Exercises performed on a daily basis also reduce the stress on exposed areas of the body. Intended for use as a home program, these exercises relax the muscles, mobilize the spine in non-weight bearing, and strengthen weak muscle groups, especially arm and abdominal muscles. Hydrotherapy and swimming are especially recommended. An individual program for the patient at home can be scheduled easily on the basis of the therapy program. Some exercises are good for all patients, others are used only with certain individuals. Sports can be continued or taken up gradually, without stress on the legs (swimming, water ball, or bicycling).

- *Therapeutic Schedule:* In the prestages of arthritis and in mildly affected patients the treatment can be scheduled on an outpatient basis. The therapy can be matched to the patient's daily life two or three times weekly. Therapeutic stimulus and rest should alternate and be equally emphasized. Frequently, the patient must be convinced that overactivity is not beneficial

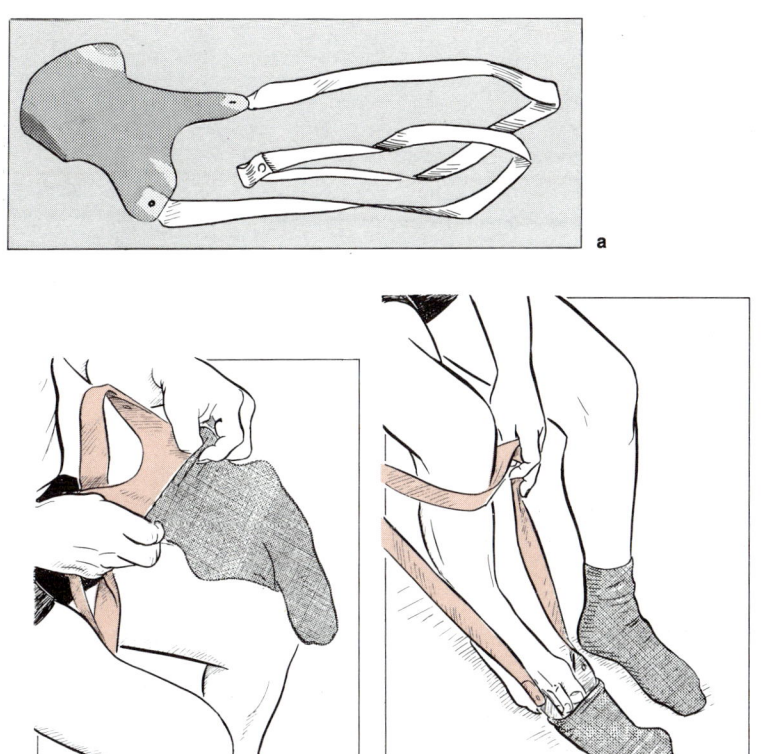

Fig. 12–26 Aid to put on socks.

and that the activity/exercise sessions should be distributed throughout the week.

Examples of various combinations of treatment are as follows:

—Heat, massage, traction, exercise
—Underwater massage, hydrotherapy, electrotherapy, exercise
—Swimming, traction, exercise.

A 4- to 6-week hospital treatment is indicated in severer disease with distinct radiological changes of the joint, restricted range of motion, and muscle atrophy. The patient must be able to be away from his or her daily activities and profession for the treatment period. Elimination of stress on the hip joint and general relaxation constitute the basis for the physical therapy.

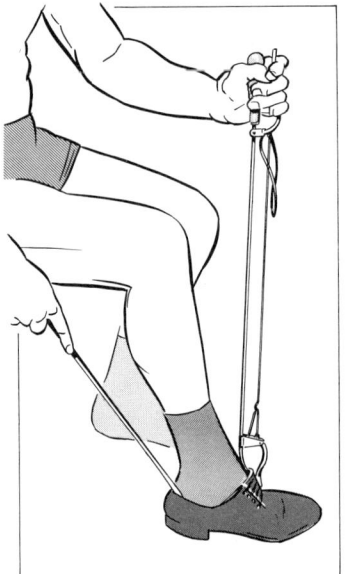 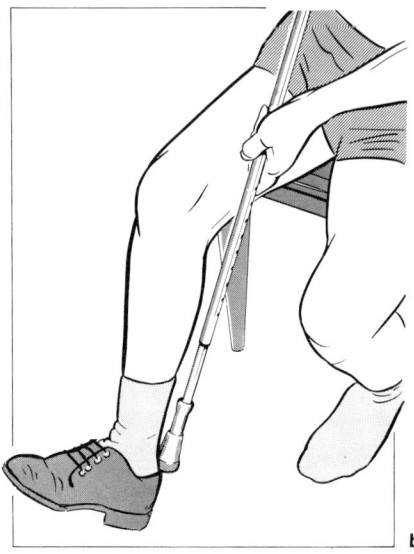

Fig. 12–27 Aids to handle shoes.

Position in Traction (Fig. 12–28)

- Pressure on the joint surfaces is temporarily relieved during the period of bed rest.
- The physician prescribes the weight and duration of the traction.
- The support for knee and heel may not interfere with the traction and must be controlled regularly. The rope carrying the weight must glide freely.

Permanent passive traction to eliminate a contracture is contraindicated in an arthrotic joint. Bone and cartilage can also be damaged by shearing forces. Controlled stretching is recommended for shortened muscles, but pain must be avoided by any means.

Position of the Leg during Bed Rest (Especially After Surgical Procedure on the Hip)

Supine position:

- Hip joint. Flexion/extension: Flexion should be minimal (Fig. 12–29). Usually, flexion during sitting is sufficient exercise. With free extension a neutral position should be taken. Abduction/adduction: Approximately 20° abduction; use of an abduction pillow to control the position of the pelvis.

Hip Joint/Physical Therapy

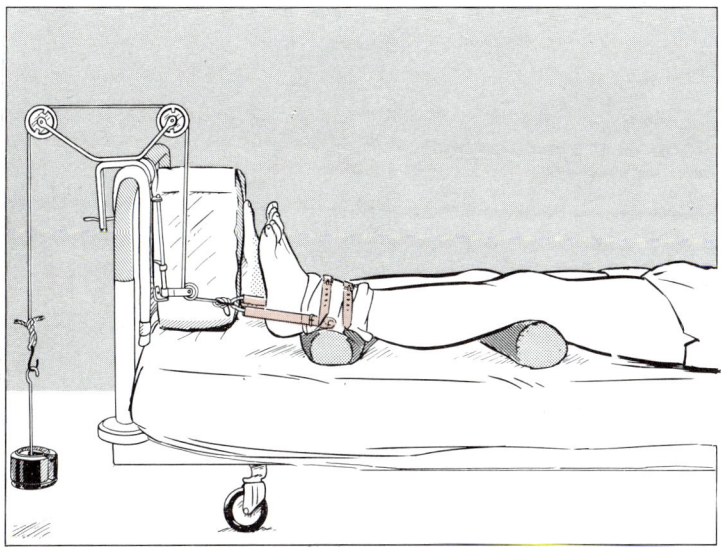

Fig. 12–28 Position in traction.

Internal/external rotation: Neutral position, if possible. Support for the trochanter and proximal thigh by a wedge, if the inward rotators are insufficient.

- Knee joint flexion/extension: Little support, depending on the size of the heel support. Temporarily the neutral position is maintained.
- Upper and lower tarsal joint: Neutral position; use of a heel support and foot rest. The blanket should not press down on the toes.

If contractures interfere with the positions, the positions must be modified, as closely as possible to the ideal position, in order to achieve muscle relaxation and comfort.

A permanent flexion position should also be avoided by using splints, especially if the patient is unable to change position alone. The pelvis should never sink into a soft mattress, resulting in flexion of the hip, and elevation of the head of the bed should not result in a permament sitting position (Fig. 12–30). Young patients should be in a flat supine position. Older patients need support under the head and chest. The position is changed several times during the day, and respiratory exercises are stressed. As soon as possible, the prone position should be tried for short periods.

A bivalved cast with a transverse rod can be applied to the lower leg in cases of rotary malposition of the hip joint or danger of postoperative dislocation of the

270 Lower Limbs

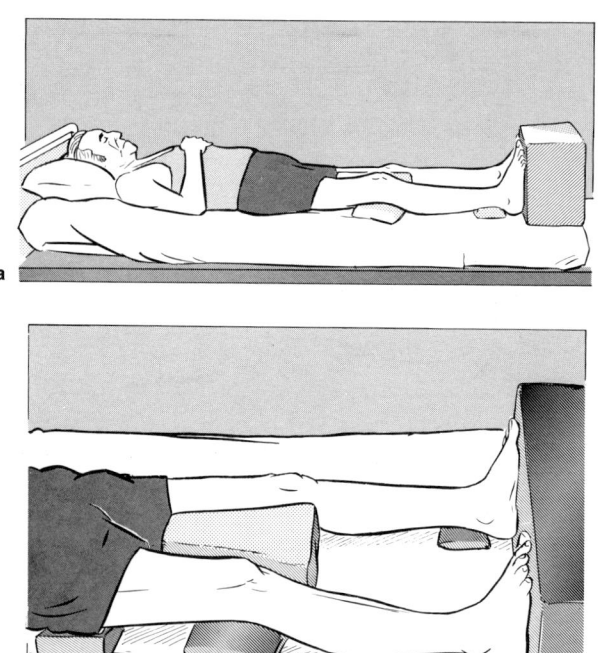

Fig. 12–29 Position of the leg after a surgical procedure on the hip.

Fig. 12–30 Incorrect bed position.

endoprosthesis. The bivalved cast is well cushioned, and the transverse rod maintains the corrected position. The knee joint must be supported above the cast to avoid problems (Fig. 12–31). The foot and lower leg are immobilized by the

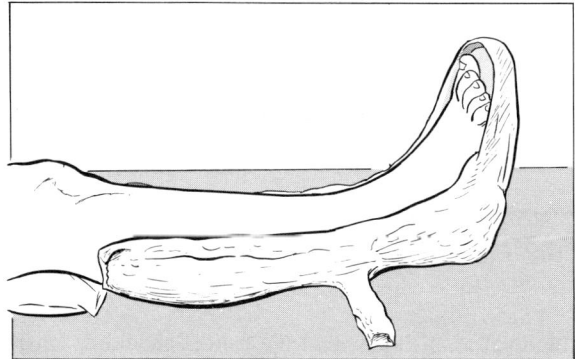

Fig. 12–31 Support of the knee joint in a lower-extremity bivalved cast.

cast, and the patient is informed that abrupt turning of the trunk can be detrimental to the hip joint.

Side Lying Position. The patient lies on the unaffected side. The affected leg on the upper side is not in adduction. Abduction must be maintained during position changes, especially after insertion of an endoprosthesis. The underlying unaffected leg is flexed to achieve a stable position. The upper affected leg should be in extension and placed on a support (foam block) behind the unaffected leg (Fig. 12–32). Material that can be compressed or displaced, such as a folded pillow, is not suitable. The foam block can replace the foot rest while in supine position and resists the plantar flexion movement of the ankle.

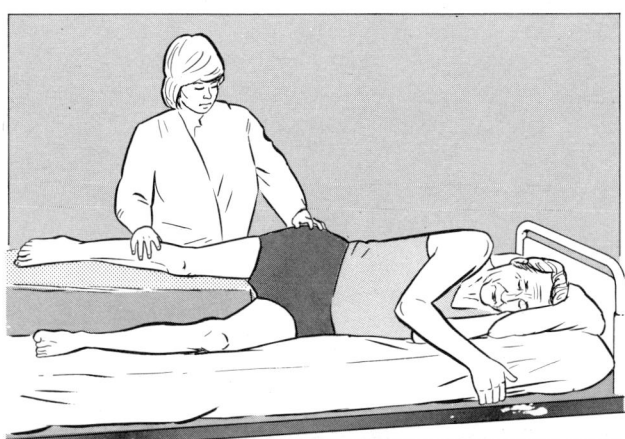

Fig. 12–32 Stable side lying position after hip surgery.

272 Lower Limbs

Prone Position

- Hip joint. Flexion/extension: Neutral position; sufficient support needed when flexion contracture exists (Fig. 12–33). Abduction/adduction: Approximately 20° abduction with a wedge pillow; inward/outward rotation in neutral position
- Knee joint. Flexion/extension: Flexion, depending on the size of the foot
- Foot joints. Neutral position; position change with support; no pressure on the toes

The iliac crests should be level at all times, and the patient should be made aware of the correct pelvic position which is adjusted repeatedly and controlled several times daily.

All position changes serve as decubitus prophylaxis and the initial position for exercises.

Surgical Treatment

Each day (after the patient's admission to the hospital and before the actual surgery) is used for preoperative physical therapy and preparation for the postoperative period. The patient learns what to expect the first postoperative day.

Preoperative Evaluation. A thorough examination and recording of the results helps in the assessment of the postoperative phase, outlines reasonable expectations, and determines the goals.

- *Respiration:* Respiratory rhythm, direction, restrictions, noises, costal mobility, use of accessory respiratory muscles.

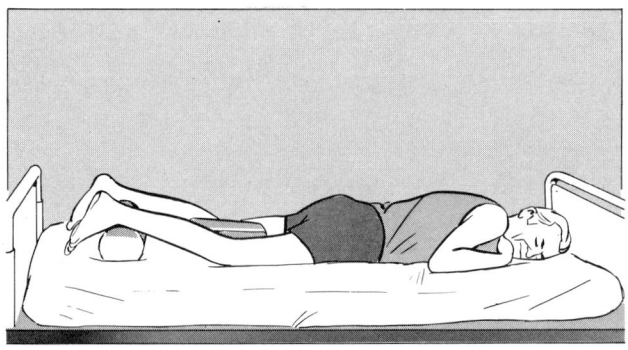

Fig. 12–33 Prone position after hip surgery.

- *Risk of Thrombosis:* Swelling of the legs, varicose veins, pains, fatigue of the legs.
- *Regulatory Disturbances of the Circulation:* Nausea during quick position changes.
- *General Strength and Mobility:*

    —Joint mobility of the lower extremity (recording range-of-motion measurements)
    —Muscle strength, muscle testing of all muscles of the hip and leg
    —Evaluation of gait deviations
    —Use of aids, extent of use, and type of aids
    —Problems in activities of daily living

Preoperative Therapeutic Aspects. These are basically the same as those for conservative or postoperative treatment.

- Reduce increased muscle tone.
- Mobilize all joints, including the joint to be operated on.
- Strengthen the muscles of the hip and legs.
- Influence the gait patterns. The patient increasingly uses the knee and tarsal joints and the spine because of the loss of hip function. Severe conditions like this, even bilaterally, can seldom be improved preoperatively.
- Modify daily routine moving patterns.
- Correct the use of equipment, avoid unnecessary aids.

Preparation for the Postoperative Phase:

- Learning active techniques for preventing pneumonia and thrombosis, for instance, breathing exercises and effective coughing and using the calf muscle pump
- Training relaxation; experiencing passive movement
- Learning to exercise single muscles or muscles in a group
- Learning active assisted movements
- Preparing for position changes, using the bedpan, changing bedsheets, sitting up, standing up; using special grips during position changes and turns; pulling oneself up with sufficient tone of abdominal and back muscles (Fig. 12–34); shifting the entire body (en bloc) toward the edge of the bed or across the bed, without moving the hip joints, to exercise knee flexion; sitting up and standing up with as little movement of the hip joint as possible

274 LOWER LIMBS

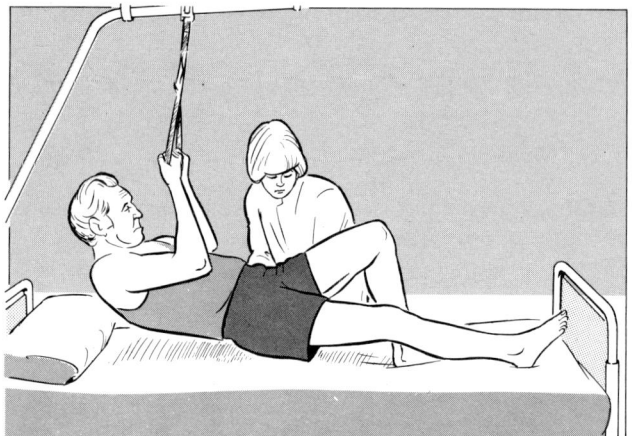

Fig. 12–34 Use of overhead trapeze for position changes.

- Exercising in preparation for walking with a walker or crutches with no or partial weight bearing; climbing stairs, always putting the affected leg down before the unaffected leg.

Aspects During the First Days of Bed Rest

The following conditions may exist, depending on the type of anesthesia, age and general condition of the patient, and extent of surgery:

- Pain at the operative site
- Risk of pneumonia
- Risk of thrombosis
- Disturbed circulatory regulation
- Risk of joint contracture owing to the immobilization of the affected extremity
- Risk of decubitus.

Aspects of Treatment During the First Few Days:

- Position control
- Pneumonia prophylaxis
- Thrombosis prophylaxis
- Decubitus prophylaxis

- Circulatory stimulation
- Mobilizing all nonaffected extremities and spine
- Strengthening nonaffected muscles
- Functional training depending on the type of surgery.

Management During the First Few Days:

- Pain reduction: Avoiding stress, comfortable position, changing positions
- Pneumonia prophylaxis: Techniques to deepen the respiration and relieve secretion. Passively: Cutaneous stimulation, vibrations, tapping, moderate stretching. Actively: Deep breathing, breathing through the nose, ventilating all segments of the thorax, simultaneous motion of the arms, coughing up mucus. External conditions: Clean air, relaxed position, avoiding chill.
- Thrombosis prophylaxis and circulatory stimulation: Use of elastic stockings; elevation of the foot end of the bed; isometric contractions of all leg muscles (not including muscles incised during surgery), quick strong motions of foot and toe muscles, calf muscle pump; active movements against resistance for the unaffected upper and lower extremities; getting up with additional wrapping around the elastic stockings. The legs are wrapped as soon as the patient gets up and as long as one leg is not subjected to full weight bearing; this is done until sufficient weight bearing activates the muscle pump again and there are no signs of swelling. The stockings are also used during exercise sessions; if there is an increased risk of thrombosis during the first days, the leg is kept wrapped.
- Decubitus prophylaxis: Changing between supine, prone, and side lying positions several times daily, if possible. The times in between are scheduled by the therapist and the nursing staff. Exercises can be performed in all positions.
- Improving mobility and muscle strength of the unaffected extremities and the spine: The patient can work isometrically and actively, in isolated motions or in more complex patterns. The affected hip joint should not be included.

    The unaffected leg and the foot and knee of the affected side are prepared intensively for standing and walking from the first day on. All foot muscles are moved against resistance, especially the gastrocnemius muscle group; isometric contractions for the quadriceps and gluteus muscles on the affected side; resistance on the unaffected side.

    The patient weight-trains upper extremity and trunk musculature with use of dumbbell weights. This will build up the endurance and strength of all the muscles used for supported standing.
- Functional training for the operation site: Each surgical technique has its own therapeutic rules; however, the motion allowed must be matched to the

individual patient. The surgeon must inform the therapist about the operation and postoperative treatment.

Varus Osteotomy (VO) in Adolescents and Adults

Position: Keeler splint with 20° abduction

Day 1 after surgery: Position control: maintaining abduction of the hip through correct pelvic position; pneumonia and thrombosis prophylaxis

After 2 days: Addition of isometric contractions for all leg muscles, resistive exercises for both feet and the unaffected leg

After 3 days: After the removal of the drain, addition of active assistive and active exercises for the affected leg

After 6 days: Walking with two crutches in a three-point gait, initially with 5-kg weight bearing; weight bearing increases as muscle strength improves. Evaluation of leg length is done, and if necessary, a lift is used.

After 2 weeks: Hydrotherapy initiated 2 days after suture removal

After 4 weeks: Ambulation with 20-kg weight bearing; discharge; continued therapy as an outpatient

After 6 weeks: Radiographic monitoring, 30-kg weight bearing; after 12 weeks full weight bearing may be allowed.

Exercises are continued until mobility, muscle strength, endurance, and the patient's gait pattern are satisfactory.

The metal is removed approximately 1 year after surgery.

From the second postoperative day, active exercises are possible without restrictions. Ambulation is started on the first postoperative day using crutches for at least 7 days. Therapy is continued for 1 to 2 weeks and is prolonged further, if necessary, on an outpatient basis.

Reinsertion of the Trochanter. Varus osteotomy and/or a Chiari pelvic osteotomy result in trochanteric elevation. Origin and insertion of the pelvitrochanteric muscles are approximated, which can cause muscle weakness. The weakness can be so persistent that even intensive exercises cannot improve the strength sufficiently and the patient continues to limp. This is an indication for reinsertion of the trochanter approximately 2 cm caudally.

Postoperative Treatment: Trochanter stable enough for exercises: Position in 30° to 40° abduction.

After 1 day: Position control; pneumonia and thrombosis prophylaxis

After 7 days: Active flexion and extension of the hip, maintaining abduction. The pelvitrochanteric muscles are not used. Flexion of the knees can be trained in a supine or prone position; standing and ambulation without weight bearing is allowed.

After 6 weeks: Radiographic control; ambulation with partial weight bearing (5 kg); active exercises—abduction, adduction

After 7 weeks: Intensification of exercises; discharge; treatment continued as an outpatient
After 8 weeks: Radiographic control; increased weight bearing (50 percent of the body weight) with gradual elimination of the use of the crutch or cane
After 12 weeks: Radiographic control; full weight bearing

Endoprosthetic Replacement. The primary purpose of the procedure is to eliminate pain; functional improvement is secondary.

Preoperative contractures (flexion, abduction, external rotation) are usually not completely eliminated by the prosthesis. Severer muscle contractures persist, unless they can be corrected during surgery. Severely weak muscles cannot be strengthened quickly and, in the older patient, not satisfactorily.

Because of the elimination of pain the patient is usually motivated to improve his or her ability to move and ambulate. However, overactivity should be curtailed. The patient should be comfortable for years to come, even if only limited function was obtained.

Preoperative Treatment: See section on Arthritis of Hip (earlier in this chapter).

Postoperative Treatment:

Position: During the first few days, abduction in a Keeler splint; after removal of the drain, position as described for arthritis.
After 1 day: Treatment includes circulatory stimulation, thrombosis and embolism prevention, standing with a walker; exercises for both feet and the unaffected leg; isometric exercise of all thigh and hip muscles of the affected leg and active assisted hip flexion and extension. Treatment is started carefully, considering the presence of sutures and the drain.
After 2 days: Exercises are intensified after the removal of the drain; position changes are used for exercises. Abduction of the hip is carefully maintained during all movement. The pain threshold sets the limit for all activities. Complex movements according to PNF are contraindicated. Knee flexion is exercised in side lying or prone position or on the edge of the bed. Restricted flexion owing to a tight iliotibial band may be present. Pain decreases with progressive healing of the wound.

Ambulation with toe-touch weight bearing depends on the patient's situation; a walker or two crutches may be used. Increased weight bearing depends on the type of prosthesis and the implantation technique and is prognosticated by the surgeon.

Controlled flexion of the hip in sitting position is done with use of a pillow. The feet are supported by a foot rest while sitting on the bed for just a short while (Fig. 12–35). Sitting on an arm chair with back support is preferable.
After 2 weeks: Hydrotherapy is started after suture removal, as is partial weight bearing (50 percent body weight). If there are no complications, the hospitaliza-

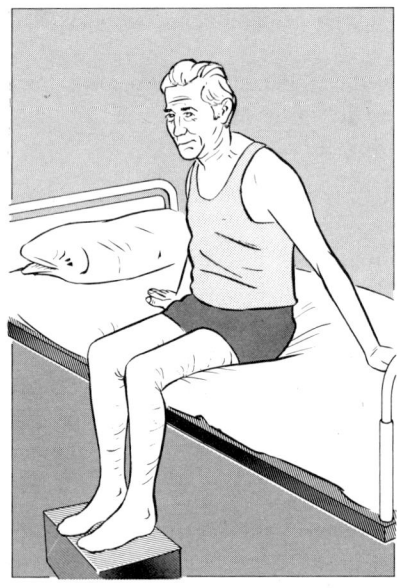

Fig. 12–35 Sitting on the edge of the bed with foot rest.

tion period ranges from 3 to 5 weeks. Continuing therapy after discharge is recommended. The transition to full weight bearing should be gradual as the strength of the hip and leg muscles increases. The program may be modified for the following reasons:

- Access to the joint by temporary dissection of the greater trochanter. During the first 5 weeks only active assisted movements in flexion and extension are done, maintaining abduction. All abduction and adduction movements and isometric contractions of the hip abductors and extensors are avoided. After 1 week the patient stands up and starts ambulation with toe-touch weight bearing. After 6 weeks, the normal program is resumed.
- Access to the joint by detaching the pelvitrochanteric muscles. During the first 3 weeks, exercises are the same as in dissection of the trochanter; then the normal program is resumed.
- Special care, for example, in severe acetabular protrusion and when there has been a change of endoprosthesis. The surgeon will then provide special instructions for position and physical therapy.

Resection of the Femoral Head and Neck (Girdlestone) or Removal of the Total Endoprosthesis (TEP)

Postoperative Treatment:

Position: Traction with 3.5 kg in neutral position of the hip joint during the first 3 weeks, day and night

After 1 day: Usual treatment initiated, including on the unaffected leg; isometric contractions of all leg muscles and equinus prophylaxis on the affected side

After 3 days: After removal of the drain, knee flexion on the edge of the bed once a day without movement of the hip. The traction position should reduce the elevation of the femur as much as possible. The bone defect must be bridged by a connective tissue scar, which should develop without disturbance. During this period the area of the hip is not mobilized.

After 3 weeks: Traction only at night; active assistive exercise, including flexion and extension of the hip, and non-weight-bearing ambulation

After 5 weeks: More intensive active flexion and extension.

After 8 weeks: Slowly increase partial weight bearing (5 kg). The difference in leg length is equalized. If the result is satisfactory, the patient is discharged. Exercises and gait training are continued after discharge.

After 12 weeks: Reevaluation is done; weight bearing to patient's tolerance. Use of a cane is necessary for most patients.

In TEP removal because of infection, the program is changed; there is a longer period of immobilization to improve infection control.

Arthrodesis of the Hip (Removal of the Joint Cartilage)

Preoperative Treatment: Examination results might lead to the following:

- Free mobility for feet and knee joints
- Best possible mobilization of the spine, especially the lumbar spine
- Strengthening all leg and trunk muscles

For further considerations, see section on preoperative arthritis earlier in this chapter.

Postoperative Treatment:

- Immobilization in a pelvis, leg, and foot cast
- Arthrosyndesis position of the hip joint: 10° adduction, 15° flexion, 0° to 5° external rotation

After day 1: General thrombosis and embolism prophylaxis; exercising of arm and trunk muscles

After 6 weeks: Cast is bivalved; mobilizing the knee joint (without any motion of the hip) for 2 days; walking with partial weight bearing. A shoe lift is used to compensate for missing knee flexion on the opposite side.

After 8 weeks: Discharge

After 12 weeks: Cast is bivalved; x-ray is taken. The knee is again mobilized for 2 days; application of full weight-bearing exercises are done. The patient is discharged.

After 16 weeks: Cast is bivalved; an x-ray is taken; exercises and gait training are permitted if the bony consolidation is sufficient. In case of insufficient consolidation, continue as above for 6 to 8 weeks.

Aspects of Treatment: Postoperative treatment goals are the same as those of preoperative treatment. The hip joint in a fresh arthrosyndesis is supported and immobilized after each position change. Mobilization can also be scheduled during hydrotherapy. The resistance of the water must be avoided during the first few days. Swimming is possible later.

Ambulation Training: The pelvis and femur of the affected side form a functional unit owing to the arthrosyndesis. Prerequisites for gait to be as normal as possible are good mobility of the foot and knee on the affected side, hyperextension of the normal hip joint, and free mobility of the lumbar spine. The affected leg, which should be 1 to 2 cm shorter in order to swing more easily, is moved forward by pelvic extension with hyperextension and rotation on the unaffected leg. Vigorous use of the foot and knee compensates for the lack of extension of the hip during the stance phase.

Other Diseases of the Hip Joint

Coxa valga, coxa vara, acetabular protrusion, and idiopathic necrosis of the femoral head are treated as prearthrotic conditions or, in advanced cases, as arthritis.

Ambulation Aids

Walker. The wide area of support of a walker offers the patient safety. However, the use of a rolling walker does not provide for safe partial weight bearing (Fig. 12–36). The walker needs to be resting on the ground before bearing on the affected leg. A walker can be used with elderly and weak patients who do not have enough balance to use another aid. A walker is also recommended for use on the first postoperative day if there was no time for preoperative gait training.

The additional use of platforms should be used only in special situations. Often the patient puts too much weight on the platforms and does not use the proper supporting muscles enough, thereby putting too much weight on the leg.

A standard or reciprocal walker is used if walking with crutches is not possible. The supporting area is less than that of a rolling walker, but there is no problem of uncontrolled rolling and safety is increased (Fig. 12–37). These walking aids are

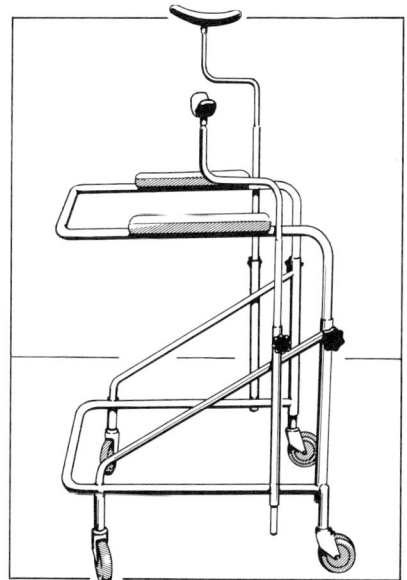

Fig. 12–36 Rolling walker.

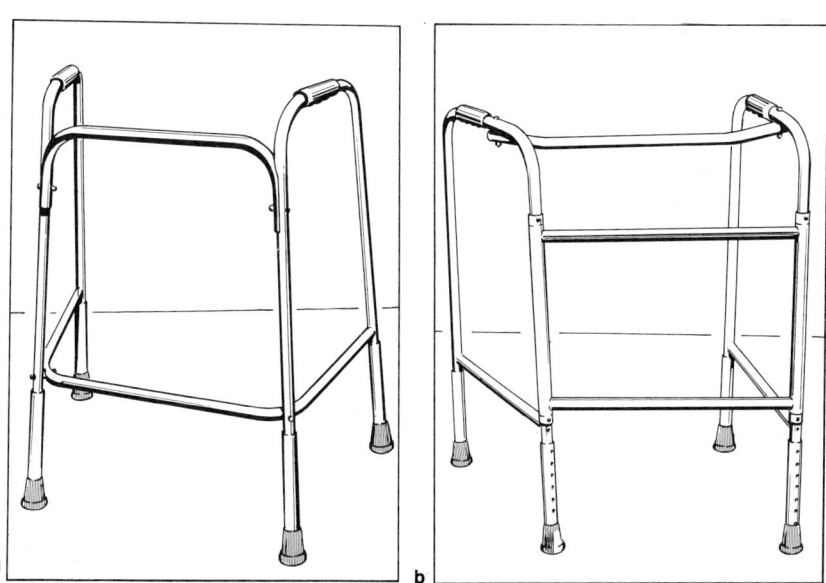

Fig. 12–37 a: Standard walker; **b:** reciprocal walker.

favored by elderly patients, especially elderly women. All walkers are useless on stairs.

Parallel Bars. An ideal aid for overcoming difficulties during the first attempts at walking, parallel bars offer the greatest safety and force the patient to use muscles of the arm and unaffected leg (Fig. 12–38). The patient can ambulate and stand independently and can rest in between. The patient can exercise with no, partial, or full weight bearing and use a three- or four-point gait pattern. The bars are useful for support, but not for moving forward.

The patient can usually advance from use of the parallel bars to crutches without much trouble, first changing from one bar to one crutch and then to two crutches.

Crutches. The area of support is relatively small, since the crutches are held close to the body. Ambulation with crutches (Fig. 12–39) requires good balance. With good training, crutches can be used for every form of weight bearing (Fig. 12–40). Correct adjustment of crutch height is crucial (see height adjustment discussion later in this section).

Wide- or Small-Based Quadcane (Four-Point Walking Aid). As with a cane, the forearm is not supported and the wrist is free. The cane is stabilized by the four points of support (Fig. 12–41). Elderly patients like this device, although it is rather bulky. They can be used on stairs if the stairs are not too narrow.

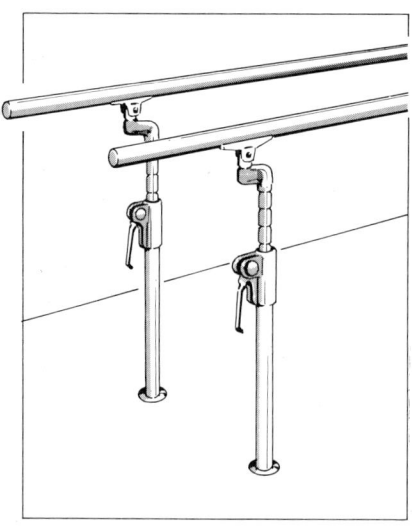

Fig. 12–38 Parallel bars.

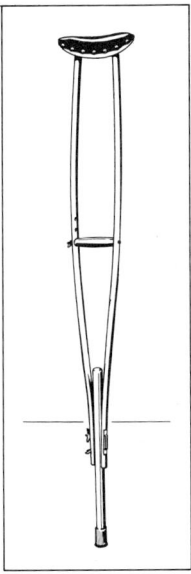

Fig. 12–39 Axillary crutch.

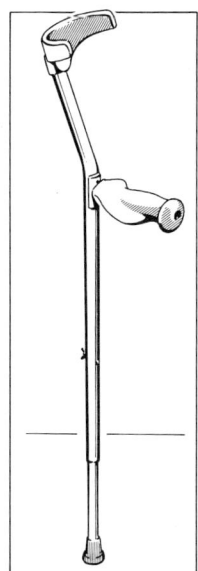

Fig. 12–40 Forearm crutch.

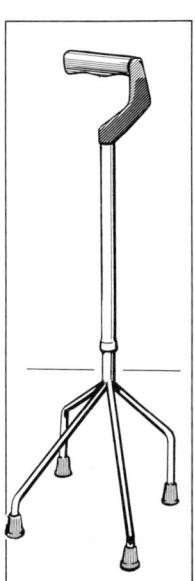

Fig. 12–41 Four-point walking aid: wide-base quad cane.

Platform Cane (Walking Aid for Rheumatic Patients). This is a special crutch with a support for the forearm and a handle (Fig. 12–42), designed for a patient who is unable to use his or her hand and whose elbow extension is restricted or eliminated. For certain patients, especially rheumatic patients, it is the only way they can support themselves during ambulation.

Cane. The wrist remains free; the patient has to use considerably more power for support. Partial weight bearing is still possible with two canes, however. One cane is commonly used with full weight bearing to support weak muscles (Fig. 12–43).

Height Adjustment of the Handles. With the scapula drawn down and the elbow in slight flexion, the hand is at the level of the greater trochanter. If the hand is too high, the supporting muscles are stressed too much and the shoulder girdle is pushed up, which causes painful tension and easy fatigue of the muscles. If the hand is too low, the trunk is flexed and the muscles cannot contract sufficiently.

Anatomical Handle. The hand is supported by an anatomically shaped surface, especially the thumb (Fig. 12–40). The handle is available for crutches and canes. A handle can also be manufactured according to an individual mold.

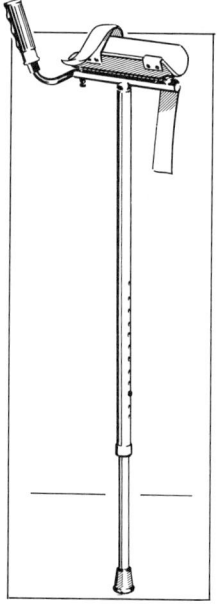

Fig. 12–42 Walking aid for rheumatic patients—platform cane.

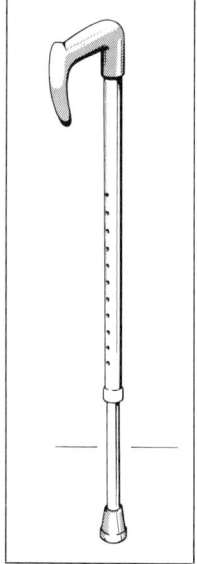

Fig. 12–43 Standard straight cane.

When Are Walking Aids Used?

- When bones and joints are not able to sustain full weight bearing
- When full weight bearing is possible but the muscles are too weak

Non-Weight Bearing vs Partial Weight Bearing. In non-weight bearing the affected leg does not touch the ground and the patient essentially "hops" on the unaffected leg. Partial weight-bearing begins with toe-touching and ends with full weight bearing. The weight bearing on the affected leg is determined by the physician. Weight bearing of 5 kg is analogous to a slight touch on the ground. Bilateral weight bearing is calculated and controlled by scales or more sophisticated equipment (Fig. 12–44). Partial weight bearing is performed by three- or four-point walking with two crutches or other aids.

Ambulation with a crutch on the opposite side takes about 30 percent of the body weight off the hip joint. The load on the hip joint is barely increased by replacing the crutch with a cane, but the posture is remarkably improved.

Walking on Stairs. Stairs do not complicate weight bearing, especially if they have hand rails. Most ambulation aids can be used. Climbing stairs should be included early in gait training and matched to the home situation.

KNEE

EVALUATION RESULTS IN PHYSICAL THERAPY

Typical and common results are joint effusion, contracture, muscle atrophy, and instability.

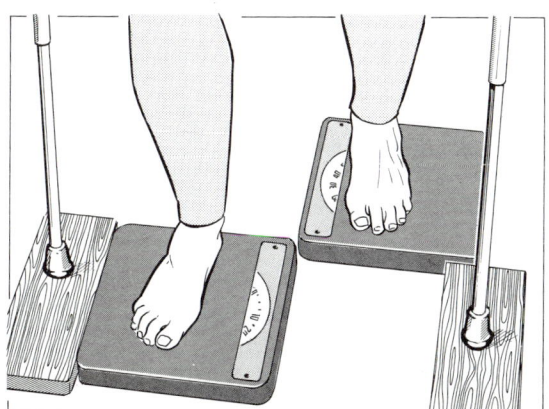

Fig. 12–44 Calculating bilateral weight bearing.

Joint Effusion

The interference with mobility depends on the amount of intraarticular fluid present. If there is irritation, it is accompanied by other symptoms of inflammation.

Checking the Effusion

The knee joint is placed in extension with a relaxed quadriceps muscle. The therapist puts a hand around the tibial head caudally and pushes cranially toward the joint space. The other hand holds the distal end of the thigh above the patella, compressing the upper recesses of the joint capsule. With the index finger the patella can be moved around on the increased joint fluid (''ballottable'' patella) (Fig. 12–45). In flexion of 25° to 30° the capsule is most relaxed. In severe effusion the joint will automatically assume this position. The patient in severe pain bends the knee joint automatically and flexes and externally rotates the hip joint.

A swelling of the joint capsule can mimic an effusion. The joint is thicker than normal and the circumference is increased. ''Ballotting'' of the patella cannot be induced, however. The swelling is not soft and elastic, but firm and doughy, especially in the lower area of the capsule. Swelling of the capsule cannot be treated by physical therapy; however, it is not a contraindication for exercising to the full extent.

Contracture of the Knee Joint

The examination results are typical for the origin of the contracture, i.e., the tissue structures that have changed the joint contours:

Fig. 12–45 Examination of knee joint effusion.

- Intraarticular and periarticular passive tissue (ligaments, capsule, menisci): If the capsule is affected, flexion is more restricted than extension (capsular pattern according to Cyriax); the mobility of the joint components against one another is restricted.
- Active tissue surrounding the joint (muscles with tendons): During passive movements, stretching is insufficient and the affected muscles are painful. The joint components may be freely mobile.

In a contracture of the knee joint the patella motion can be restricted, mainly in a distal direction owing to an extension contracture. Rotation is drastically reduced in severe flexion and extension contractures.

Measuring Knee Joint Range of Motion

The extension and flexion of the knee joint are measured in a supine position with flexed hip joint or by having the patient sit on the edge of the bed (Fig. 12–46). Pelvic deviation and a changed femoral position must be observed.

The rotation is examined in a supine position with knees and hips in flexion compared with the unaffected side. In knee flexion of 90° the rotation is best; it is also examined with the patient sitting on a stool with the feet on the floor.

Atrophy of the Knee Muscles

The quick atrophy of the quadriceps muscle is always surprising in painful knee problems and after immobilization, especially of the medial portion, the vastus medialis. The pain and stretch receptors in the joint capsule are responsible for this. Their impulses cause a decreased tone and activity of the knee extensors in

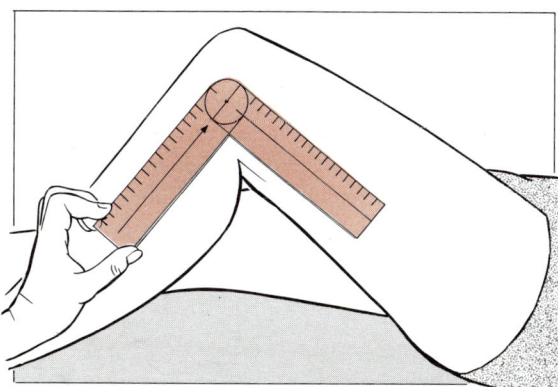

Fig. 12–46 Measuring knee joint range of motion.

combination with increased tone of the knee flexors. The distinct atrophy of the vastus medialis is also explained by another factor: A shortened rectus femoris muscle is in opposition to the vastus medialis together with the vastus lateralis, which it pulls the same direction. The patella is pulled laterally by each tension of the quadriceps. Physical therapy to strengthen the vastus medialis may be useless without stretching of the rectus femoris to its normal length. The exercises may even increase the traction of the lateral quadriceps portions, so that the atrophy of the vastus medialis worsens. The disproportion of strength within the quadriceps muscle also causes pressure on the gliding bed of the patella, which is especially important in patellar chondropathy.

Atrophic vastus medialis and sartorius muscles recover slowly. Despite free, passive joint mobility, a so-called extension deficit often remains for a long time.

Atrophy of the knee extensors favors contracture of the joint, which in turn further accelerates muscle atrophy.

Measuring the Circumference of the Leg

The measurement is taken in relation to muscle atrophy and joint effusion. The measurement sites are marked to compare both sides.

Thigh: The measuring tape is put around the thigh (relaxed quadriceps muscle) 10 and 20 cm above the medial joint space transverse to the joint axis.

Knee Joint: The measurement is taken at the level of the joint space.

Calf: The measurement is taken 15 cm below the joint space or around the thickest part of the calf.

Instability of the Joint

The instability becomes noticeable as a hypermobility into one or more directions. The joint does not move over the bony components, but over the menisci, capsule, ligaments, muscles, and tendons. If the passive and active tissue components are intact, the knee joint is stable, especially in extension, and the stability is maintained in other positions.

Considerable muscle strength is necessary to stabilize the knee joint. All muscles crossing the joint are involved in the stabilization, partly by a direct connection to the joint capsule. The tensor fasciae latae and the gluteus maximus muscles are involved essentially by their common tendon, the iliotibial band, as the strongest part of the fascia lata.

Muscles Stabilizing the Knee

Medially:

- Vastus medialis
- Muscles of the pes anserinus (gracilis, semitendinosus, and sartorius muscles)

- Semimembranosus
- Gastrocnemius, medial head

Laterally:

- Vastus lateralis
- Muscles of the iliotibial band
- Biceps femoris
- Popliteus
- Gastrocnemius, both heads

Posterior:

- Gastrocnemius, both heads
- Popliteus
- Biceps femoris, pes anserinus muscles

Anterior:

- Quadriceps with all portions

Vigorous use of the foot muscles should not be neglected. The strength of all foot muscles is examined.

CLINICAL SYMPTOMS

Discoid Meniscus

Origin. Disturbances mostly during the development of the lateral meniscus, which remains as a cartilage disk rather than taking a semilunar shape, also separating the intraarticular surfaces centrally.

Symptoms. There are often no symptoms until the discoid meniscus is affected by trauma or degeneration, causing the characteristic symptoms. Sometimes a snapping (audible and visible) occurs. The diagnosis can be confirmed by arthrography or arthroscopic procedure.

Treatment: Surgical removal.

Chondromalacia Patellae (Chondropathia Patellae, Retropatellar Chondropathy, Retropatellar Arthrosis)

Origin. Impact, fracture, subluxation, and dislocation. The varying shape of the patella and the surface of the corresponding femoral component are important, as it can cause cartilaginous damage by increased pressure on the lateral facet and decreased pressure on the medial facet.

Symptoms. Adolescents often complain about pain. The discomfort behind the patella or in the entire joint space becomes worse when climbing mountains or stairs. Descending results in the severest discomfort. The same problems arise when sitting with flexed knee joints, which the patient tries to avoid by stretching out his or her legs.

The patella shifting against the femoral condyles causes crepitation of the cartilage to various extents. Pain may be caused by pressure or percussion. The emerging joint facet can be palpated if the patella is passively shifted laterally. This is accompanied by pain. The joint can be irritated with capsular thickening and effusion. Disuse of the joint because of pain results in muscle wasting, especially of the medial head of the quadriceps.

Tangential radiographs of the patella reveal decreased joint space, subchondral sclerosis, and arthrotic marginal osteophytes (Fig. 12–47). The patellofemoral joint is dysplastic. The incongruity can be diagnosed. The angle formed by the facets of the patellar joints is normally 120° to 140° and is reduced in a patellofemoral dysplasia.

Conservative Nonsurgical Treatment. Possible body weight reduction; strengthening of the quadriceps muscle; hot packs; ultrasound and iontophoresis. Irritation and inflammation can be counteracted by application of ice or antiinflammatory medication. In cases of cartilaginous damage, drugs can be used that directly influence the metabolism of the cartilage.

Surgical Treatment. In a minor lesion of the patellofemoral joint the lateral retinaculum, i.e., the ligamentous connections between the lateral patella margin

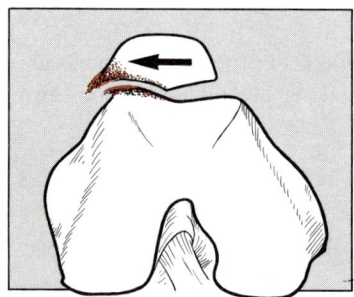

Fig. 12–47 Arthrosis of the patellofemoral joint (severer in the lateral portion) in recurrent or habitual dislocation.

and the vastus lateralis (lateral release) muscle, is split; in addition, there is removal of damaged cartilage layer. If the patellar joint surface is more severely damaged, the tibial tuberosity with the insertion of the patellar ligament is shifted ventrally, thus elevating the patella in its gliding bed and relieving pressure on the patellofemoral joint. In a severe lesion of the patellar joint surface the subchondral bone is drilled. The budding vascular connective tissue can undergo metaplasia into fibrous cartilage during postoperative exercises. The patellar joint surface is replaced or the patella is removed in cases of progressive arthrosis.

Dislocation of the Patella

We distinguish congenital dislocation, habitual or recurrent dislocation, acquired dislocation, and recurrent dislocation owing to recidivism.

Congenital Dislocation

Origin. Disturbed development and muscle balance, deformity of the patella and the femoral condyles.

Symptoms. Frequently the dislocation is bilateral, next to the lateral femoral condyle, and already in existence at birth.

Treatment. See habitual or recurrent dislocation.

Habitual or Recurrent Dislocation

Origin. Flattening of the lateral femoral condyle, elevated patella, deviation of the patellar shape, maltorsion of the thigh, genu valgum, constitutionally weak connective tissue, unphysiologic direction of traction by the quadriceps muscles, preexisting dysplasia, and instability in the patellofemoral joint.

Symptoms. Initial dislocation without external impact; the patella is partially or completely dislocated in movements during daily routine. There is often a spontaneous repositioning with extension of the knee joint. Girls in their late childhood are affected most often. In more progressive stages the patella constantly slips out of its bed across the flattened lateral femoral condyle during increasing flexion. In other patients, the patella is more movable owing to the weakness of the muscles, ligaments, and capsule.

The dislocation is usually accompanied by pain and effusion. Frequent dislocations cause painful irritation and, finally, an arthrosis of the patellofemoral joint.

Conservative Nonsurgical Treatment. Repositioning usually occurs spontaneously without any problems, by just extending the leg. After the initial dislocation, immobilization in a cast for 3 to 4 weeks is done to avoid another dislocation by shrinking of capsule and ligaments.

Operative Treatment. Repeated dislocations of the patella require surgery to avoid secondary joint lesions and restore the function of the leg.

- Passive fastening of the patella. A semilunar piece from the medial part of the fibrous joint capsule is moved laterally around the patella and sutured in place under corrective tension. Further passive correction is achieved by repairing the medial defect.
- Active fastening of the patella by a tendoplasty
- Transplantation of the gracilis tendon to the medial edge of the patella. The tension of the gracilis muscle then pulls the patella farther medially.
- Reinsertion of the tibial tuberosity in a medial and posterior direction, especially in a genu valgum
- Correction of an axial deviation of the knee
- Correction of a maltorsion of the thigh

Acquired Dislocation

Origin. Accident, paralysis.

Symptoms. Without a predisposing disease only considerable trauma can cause the capsule to tear with subsequent severe hematoma.

Treatment. Reposition, puncture of the effusion, immobilization in a cast for 3 to 4 weeks.

Dislocation Owing to Recidivism

Origin. Mainly theoretical classification as a separate type from a recurrent dislocation. It is based on an acquired dislocation, especially owing to insufficient treatment or extensive lesions of capsule and ligament during the initial dislocation. With an increasing incidence of dislocations the difference from the recurrent or habitual dislocation becomes inessential.

Congenital Dislocation of the Knee Joint

Origin. Developmental disturbance. The acquired dislocation of the knee joint, which is usually caused by an accident, is characterized by lesions of the ligaments and internal structures of the knee joint, unless it did not cause injuries to the vessels and nerves.

Symptoms. An entire complex of symptoms are found, from a congenital genu varum over the subluxation to the complete dislocation, especially anterior dislocation of the tibia.

Treatment. Closed, if necessary surgical, reduction during the first days of the infant's life.

Genu Recurvatum

Origin. Congenital or acquired.

Congenital:

- In a congenital dislocation of the knee joint
- Weak connective tissue (constitutional genu recurvatum)

Acquired:

- Overstretching the posterior knee joint capsule and ligaments by long-lasting effusions and extension of the lower leg, flaccid paralysis (knee can only be stabilized in a recurvatum); equinus (knee is in recurvatum) and shortening of the opposite leg
- Epiphyseal growth disturbances owing to unphysiologic weight bearing, inflammation, tumor, trauma
- Trauma without growth disturbances (ligament injuries, fractures close to the knee joint and healed in malposition).

If a recurvatum of the knee joint is manifest, the weakness of ligaments and capsule is worsened, increasing the recurvatum even more. Frequently hyperextension of the normal leg is chosen as a less strenuous position if severe leg length shortening cannot be compensated. This results in an overstretching of capsule and ligaments and formation of genu recurvatum. Overstretching of capsule and ligaments can be caused secondarily by overstress, if the genu recurvatum is not primarily caused by soft tissue changes, but by the changing shape of the femoral condyles or the platform of the tibial head.

Symptoms. Abnormal hyperextension of the knee joint, which can be the first stage of the development of an unstable knee joint by overstretching and loosening of the ligament apparatus. Patients complain about a feeling of insecurity in standing and walking, painful irritation, and later the typical symptoms of arthrosis of the knee joint.

Conservative Nonsurgical Treatment. Immediately after birth the congenital genu recurvatum is brought into flexion and immobilized in a thigh cast and later in a bivalved cast or splint. Less severe types of acquired genu recurvatum are treated by strengthening the flexor muscles of the knee joint. In severer cases, especially paresis, there is need for application of an orthosis that counteracts the hyperextension; also, the underlying disease and secondary symptoms, such as irritation of the periarticular tissue and inflammation need to be treated.

Surgical Treatment. In severe cases corrective osteotomy in the area of the tibial head. Surgical correction of the soft tissue, such as capsulorrhaphy, shortening of the tendons, muscle transposition, is not successful. An arthrosis of the knee joint that cannot be treated conservatively might be considered for an arthrosyndesis or an endoprosthetic replacement.

Genu Varum (Bow Legs)

Origin
Congenital: Physiologic (temporary) genu varum of the newborn, weak connective tissue, systemic diseases.

Acquired: Weight-bearing deformity in rickets (often in combination with coxa var, femur varum), in osteoporosis, and circumscribed loss of stability of the bone (Paget's disease). Faulty growth owing to asymmetric function of damaged growth plate (inflammation, trauma, or neoplasm). Lesions of the external ligament apparatus of the knee or fractures close to the joint and healed in a malposition.

Symptoms. Bowing of one or both legs, the apical point of the curve being in the knee joint. The extent of the deformity is determined by the angle between tibia and femur or measurements of the distance between the intraarticular components, the medial portions of the surfaces touching one another (standing or lying position).

Increased weight bearing can worsen the deformity if the axes do not normalize spontaneously during the first year of life. With increasing age the medial joint space develops a medial arthrosis of the knee joint owing to overstress.

Conservative Nonsurgical Treatment. Treat the underlying disease. Elevate the inner edge of the shoe to relieve the inner joint space. In a severe case of rickets the leg axis can be straightened in a cast after manual correction, if it is started before the antirachitic medication.

Surgical Treatment. Corrective osteotomy (Fig. 12–48).

Genu Valgum

Origin. Weak connective tissue, systemic diseases; acquired as a deformity owing to weight bearing or malfunction of the epiphyseal growth plate as in a genu varum.

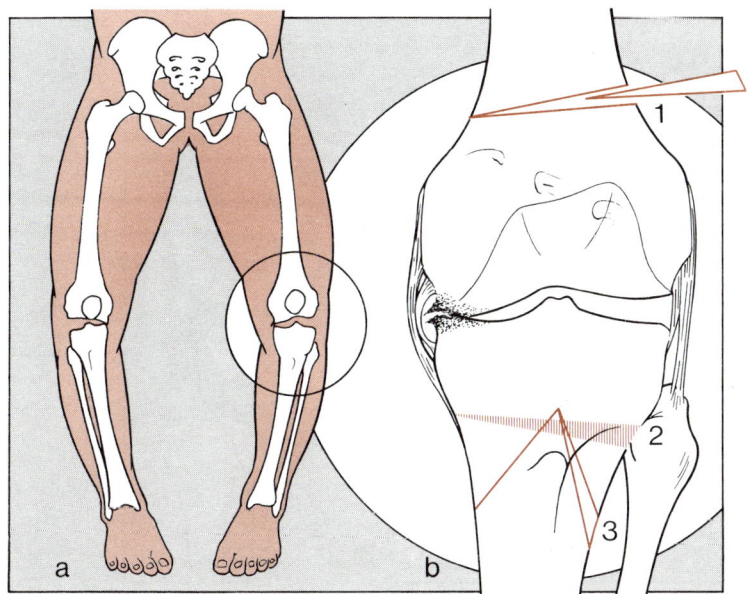

Fig. 12–48 Genu varum. Owing to overstress of the medial portion of the knee joint. Corrective osteotomy to adjust the unphysiologic load and the malposition, supracondylar in **1:** and in **2:** in the area of the tibial head, a wedge or swinging osteotomy is possible.

The genu valgum of early childhood develops physiologically from a genu varum in infancy, and later the leg axis becomes straight. The valgum position of elbow and knee joint—a secondary sex-linked characteristic—is more pronounced in females than in males.

Symptoms. Malposition of the knee joint. In an extended leg with the femoral condyles touching each other, the lower legs diverge. The extent of the deformity is determined by the angle between the femur and tibia or the distance between the intraarticular components in standing and lying positions. Genu valgum is frequently seen with talipes valgus and planus and genu recurvatum.

Classic type of prearthrotic deformity.

Treatment. See also genu varum. A conservative (nonsurgical) therapy cannot eliminate the cause, but can treat the symptoms by relieving the lateral joint space with an elevated inner edge of the shoe.

Surgical Treatment. Corrective osteotomy, especially in children; dome-type osteotomy (Fig. 12–49). In adults a stable osteotomy is indicated to avoid problems resulting from immobilization (plate osteosynthesis, external fixation). The correction of a severe genu valgum is often limited by the stretch on the fibular

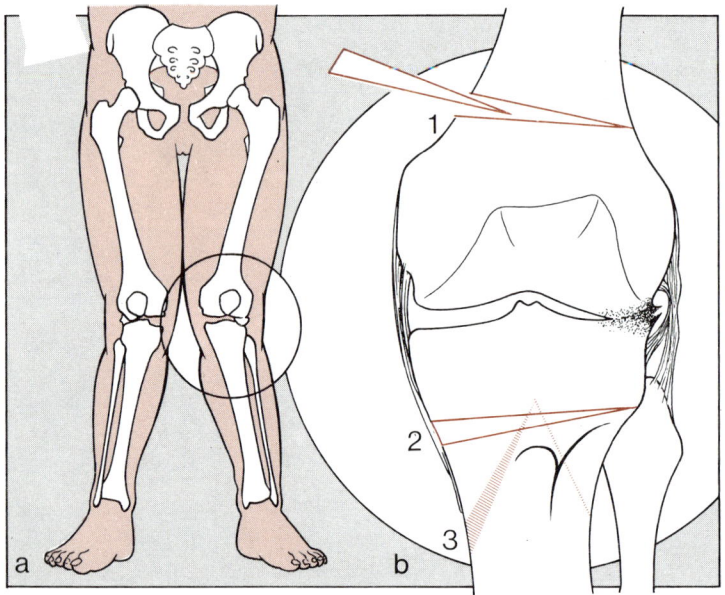

Fig. 12–49 Genu valgum. Typical valgus arthrosis of the lateral portion of the knee. Corrective osteotomy to equalize the malposition. **1:** in the area of the tibial head; **2:** as a wedge; or **3:** dome-type osteotomy.

---

nerve. In severe cases total replacement of the joint or an arthrosyndesis must be considered.

Crus Varum

Origin. Congenital in systemic diseases. Acquired as a deformity owing to overstress (rickets) and after fractures of the lower leg healed in a malalignment. (Crus varum congenitum must be regarded as a separate entity.)

Symptoms. Bowing of the lower leg; in contrast to genu varum, the apical point is not within the knee joint. Compensatory talipes varus/planus.

Conservative Nonsurgical Treatment. In mild cases corrective bivalved cast during the night and reinforcement by physical therapy. Rickets require correction in phases (see genu varum).

Surgical Treatment. Corrective osteotomy to avoid axial deviation of more than 15°.

Crus Varum Congenitum

Origin. Congenital disturbance of ossification in the lower third of the tibia. In infants an antecurvation and varus position are noted initially. Bone remodeling and spontaneous fractures result from weight bearing. The risk of pseudoarthrosis is great. A so-called pseudoarthrosis of the lower leg develops.

Symptoms. In most cases symptoms occur unilaterally. There is characteristic antecurvation of the lower leg; abnormal mobility is due to pseudoarthrosis.

Conservative Nonsurgical Treatment. Careful alignment; avoiding a fracture by splinting. Non-weight bearing in an apparatus.

Surgical Treatment. The chances of success by bridging the defect with autologous bone transplants improve with age until puberty.

Arthrosis of the Knee (Inflammation Gonarthrosis)

Origin. See Chapter 7, Aging of the Connective and Supporting Tissue; most frequent cause is axial deviation (see genu valgum).

Symptoms. Crepitation, pain, recurrent irritation, atrophy from disuse, progressive deformity of the knee.

Conservative Nonsurgical Treatment. Pain relief, reducing the tone of tensed muscles, improving mobility, preventing contractures, strengthening insufficient muscles, avoiding a disproportion between weight bearing and weight-bearing ability.

Surgical Treatment. Correcting axial deviation, partial or total endoprosthetic replacement.

PHYSICAL THERAPY

General Principles

Goals of Therapy

- Decrease joint effusion.
- Mobilize the knee joint.
- Strengthen leg muscles.
- Stabilize the joint.

Therapy

Joint Effusion

Immobilization: The technique and duration depend on the severity of the symptoms, for instance, the application of a splint or only the restriction of mobility and weight for a temporary period.

Controlled Position: Flexion owing to pain or effusion is not reduced passively by placing a sandbag on the knee; instead, it is reduced as much as possible with muscle relaxation. The leg is placed in the neutral position. Malpositions stressing the medial or lateral portion of the joint must be avoided. The foot is in a neutral position and the heel is supported in a ring or a narrow cushion under the Achilles tendon. Position should be changed regularly, perhaps at 4-hour intervals. The same is true when using a splint. The leg may be elevated by raising the foot of the bed. The support is reduced analogously to the reduction of flexion.

Treatment: Use of ice is beneficial. The ice pack must be changed as soon as it has reached the temperature of the joint; it can be changed by the patient.

Physical Therapy of the Effusion: The goal is to improve the tone, especially for the extensor muscles of the knee joint, if possible using an ice pack or ice massage. The toning exercises are slow and rhythmic, gradually increasing the muscle tension until the strongest contraction is attained, maintaining it for several seconds, gradually relaxing the contraction, break, and repeat. The patella should not be jerked or pulled strongly along its gliding bed, especially in already existent changes of the gliding bed or in a chondromalacia patellae.

Control Measurements: Before and after each treatment the circumference is measured at the level of the joint space and recorded in a graph depicting the course of the treatment.

The patient exercises independently 15 times daily.

The exercises are intensified by simultaneous active use of the foot and hip muscles by PNF techniques. Maintaining the best extension possible, all leg patterns can be taught concentrically and eccentrically with the hip joint as a pivot. The resistances must match the strength and should not be too great, in order to avoid any leverage on the knee joint. Flexion of the knee joint is omitted partially or completely as long as the effusion exists.

A compression bandage is also used to counteract the effusion. A ring or cross made of felt or foam surrounds the patella (Fig. 12–50) and is held in place with a firm but elastic bandage, avoiding strangulation. The bandage is taken off during physical therapy and put back on after it. During bed rest, moving about, and during the patient's independent exercises, it stays in place. It can be taken off as soon as the effusion has regressed.

Electrotherapy: Galvanic stimulation, diathermy, or ultrasound therapy may be used.

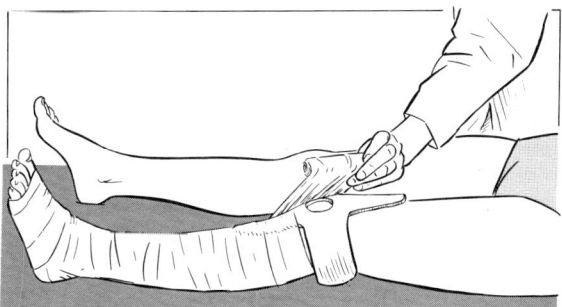

Fig. 12–50 Compression bandage for an effusion of the knee joint.

Puncture of the Knee Joint: This procedure is done aseptically to relieve pressure on the joint in case of an effusion resistant to therapy. It is followed by compression bandage treatment (see earlier).

Contracture. First, the restricted mobility of the patella must be loosened, facilitating further mobilization. The patella can be moved in cranial, caudal, lateral, and medial directions easily and without resistance if the joint is in a neutral position and the muscles are relaxed. If this is not the case, the patella is gently mobilized with the thumb and index finger by manual therapy techniques (Fig. 12–51) without pressure on the gliding bed and without breaking the resistance abruptly.

Manual therapy is also indicated if the mobility of the patella is restricted. The tibiofibular joint is also checked in this respect. Restricted rotation is carefully mobilized. Position is carefully changed every 30 minutes, using the knee flexion

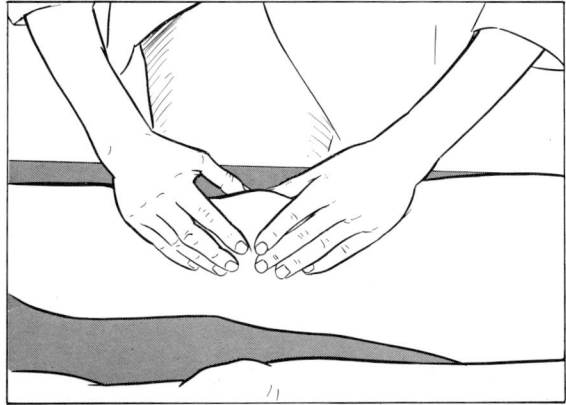

Fig. 12–51 Mobilizing the patella. *(continued)*

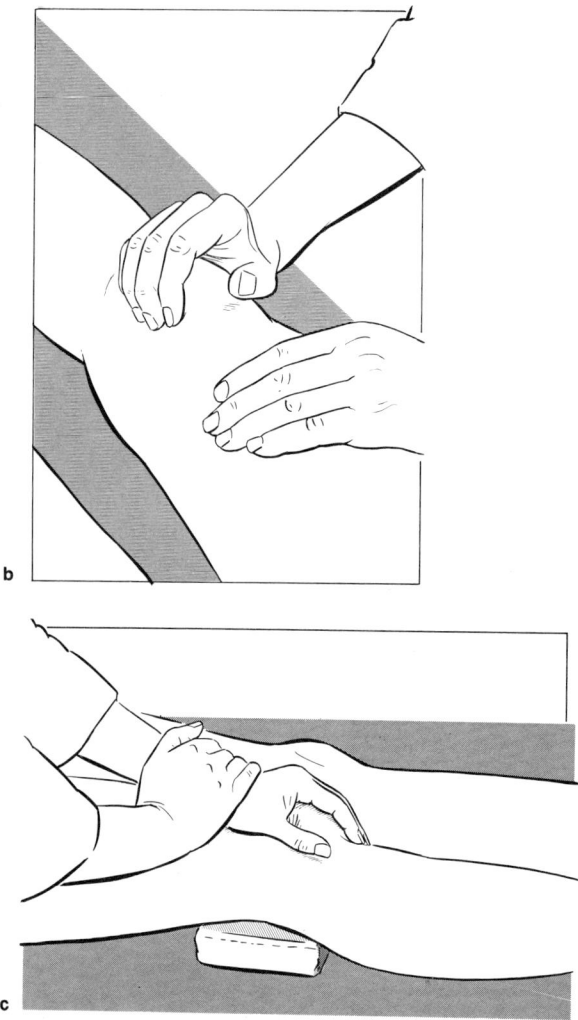

Fig. 12–51 continued

bench (full extension and gradually increasing flexion), which enhances mobilization (Fig. 12–52). The muscles are worked isometrically and actively to decrease the contracture. Shortened muscles are gently stretched.

The treatment is supported by ice application, which helps to relieve pain and stimulate the muscles.

Frequently the knee joint does not react favorably to the application of heat (including hydrotherapy) in preparation for mobilization, especially when there is a tendency to effusion. Active manipulation and manual therapy techniques are most important.

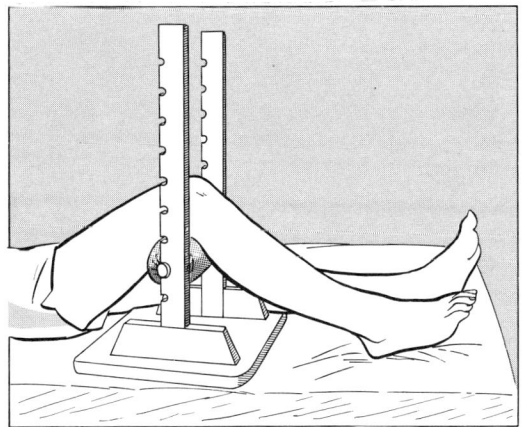

Fig. 12-52 Bench for knee flexion.

If there is no response, traction with a weight can be attempted. See Chapter 8, Contractures, for details of mobilization under anesthesia.

Atrophy. All muscles that cross the knee joint, including one or two joints, must be worked according to their function. The function may change with changing angle of the knee joint. Initial exercise positions must be chosen accordingly. Although the insufficient extensor muscles have priority, all other leg muscles, especially foot muscles, must be strengthened in order to achieve muscle balance.

Instability. Muscle training always has a stabilizing effect, especially strengthening the muscles that are connected to the passive structures of the joint or whose tendons serve as a reinforcement for certain capsular portions by their position and insertion.

Complete strengthening and stabilizing exercises for the knee joint are possible only in a standing position under weight bearing. However, weight bearing during standing and walking is problematic, and stability is impossible as long as the quadriceps muscle is so insufficient that a straight leg raise cannot be accomplished. (A knee extension deficit of 10° to 15° at the most is tolerated.)

During this period the patient walks with two crutches or a cane and partial weight bearing in a two-, three-, or four-point gait pattern, depending on the degree of instability. Exercises to develop stability can be performed with the patient supported by the parallel bars or on stall bars.

External stabilization with a splint or apparatus becomes necessary if the instability cannot be overcome by intensive practice or the muscle control of the joint cannot be regained. Operations to eliminate instability may involve the capsule, ligaments, or muscles, for instance, transposition of a muscular insertion to change the direction of the traction and tension. The muscle requires intensive postoperative strengthening, supported by electrotherapy.

Exercise Samples

Isometric Exercises for the Quadriceps Muscle. In supine position, the knee is supported by a small pillow. The therapist puts one hand above the patella on the quadriceps and the other hand on the dorsal aspect of foot.

- Toes and foot are elevated against resistance, keeping the heel on the floor. The patella is pulled up against the therapist's gentle resistance; the knees are pushed against the support; the heel is kept on the floor (Fig. 12–53a). If the heel rises slightly, a stronger support under the knee is indicated. Recurvatum of the knee joint must be avoided (Fig. 12–53b).

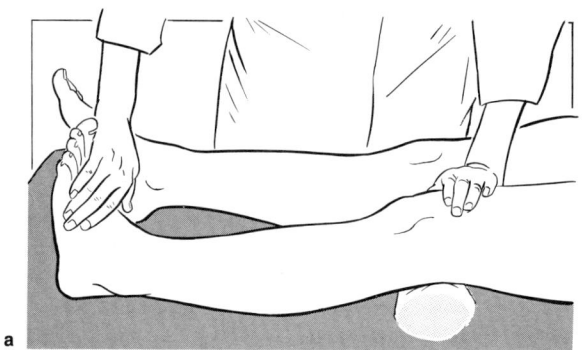

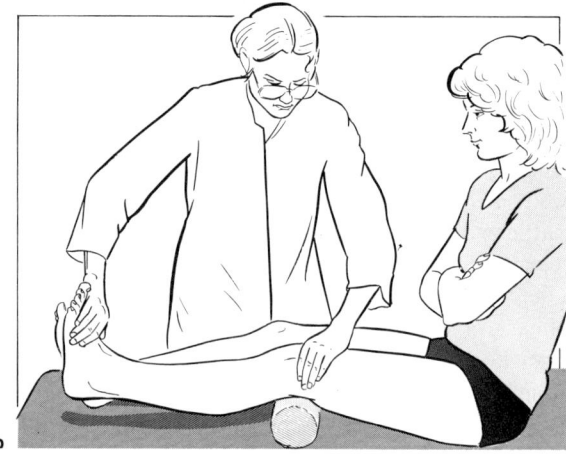

Fig. 12–53 Isometric exercises for the quadriceps muscle.

Tension of the quadriceps in combination with severe atrophy of the vastus medialis muscle causes a lateral shift of the patella. In this case the rectus femoris muscle must be checked for its ability to stretch, if the patient's condition allows it (see also Evaluation Results).

- Isometric training of the quadriceps without weight bearing and without knee flexion (Fig. 12–54)
- Training the vastus medialis muscle with various types of equipment (Fig. 12–55)
- Active exercise of the quadriceps at the edge of the bench (Fig. 12–56)
- Isometric and active exercise of the knee flexors (Fig. 12–57a)
- Isometric gastrocnemius muscle exercise (Fig. 12–57b).
- Stabilizing exercises with partial weight bearing on the therapeutic ball, combined with pushing (Fig. 12–58)

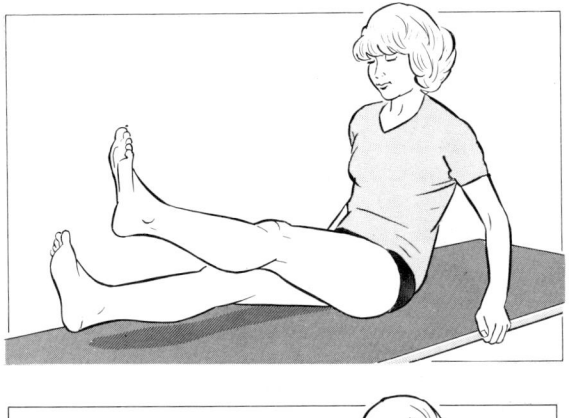

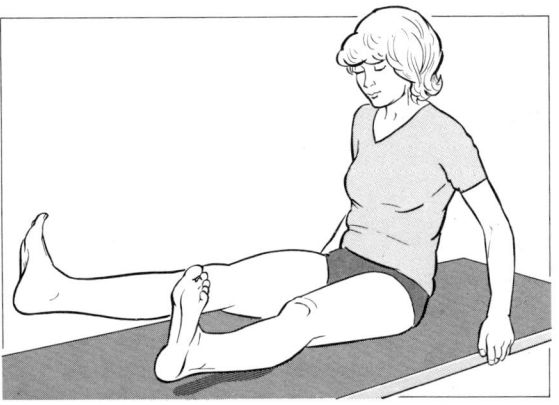

Fig. 12–54 Isometric training of the quadriceps without weight bearing (**a-d**). *(continued)*

304 Lower Limbs

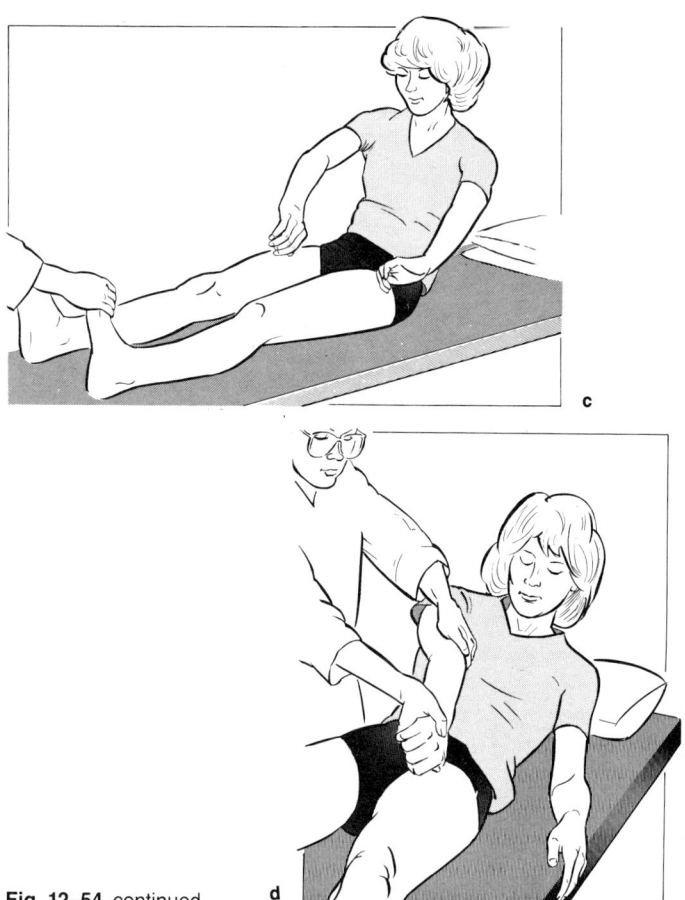

Fig. 12–54 continued

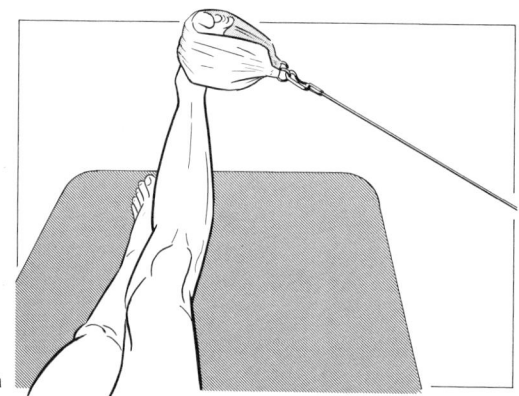

Fig. 12–55 Training the vastus medialis muscle with equipment. **a:** Pulley

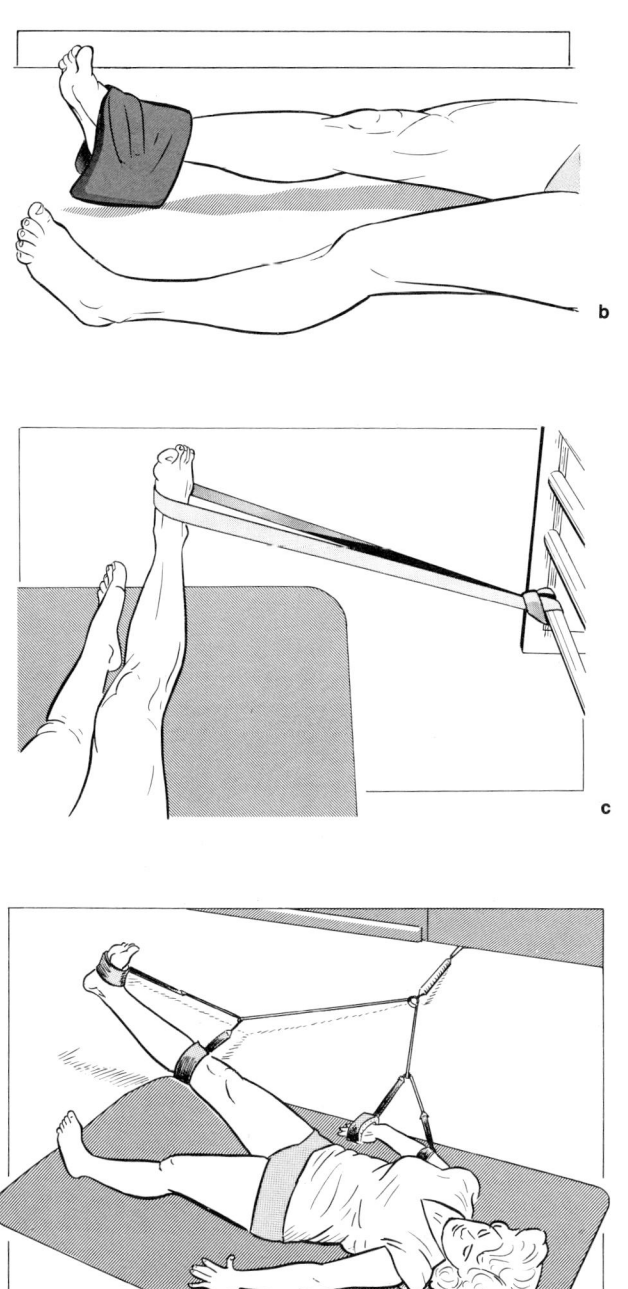

Fig. 12–55 continued; **b:** sandbag; **c:** theraband; **d:** resisted pulley.

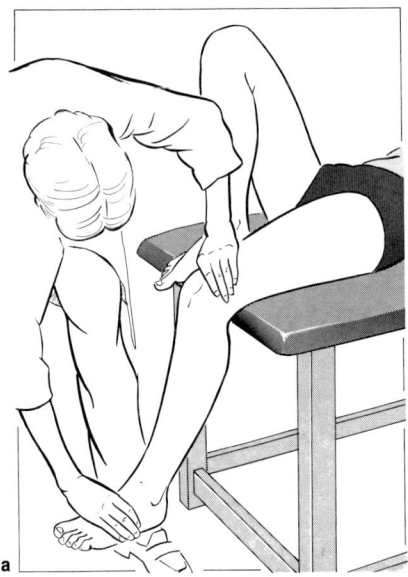

Fig. 12–56 Active exercises for the quadriceps on the edge of a bench.

- Stabilizing exercises with full weight bearing, with the therapist, with a tilt board and a block (Fig. 12–59)
- Isometric and active training for both legs with heavy weight bearing on flexed knees (only with normal joints) (Fig. 12–60)

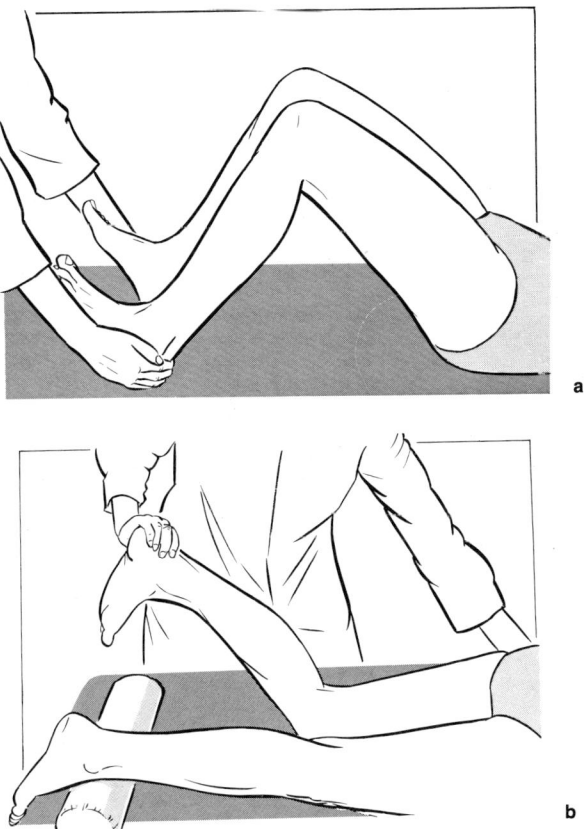

Fig. 12–57 Training the knee flexors against manual resistance.

Meniscectomy of a Discoid Meniscus

Postoperative Treatment

Treatment is basically the same as after posttraumatic meniscectomy.

For Patient up to Age 40. Immobilize the leg in a long cast.
After 3 days: The cast is windowed above the patella, especially in the cranial direction. Exercises for the quadriceps muscle are initiated. After the exercises the opening is wrapped again to avoid the development of edema in this area. The patient exercises independently by raising the trunk to a sitting position or lifting the cast.

308 Lower Limbs

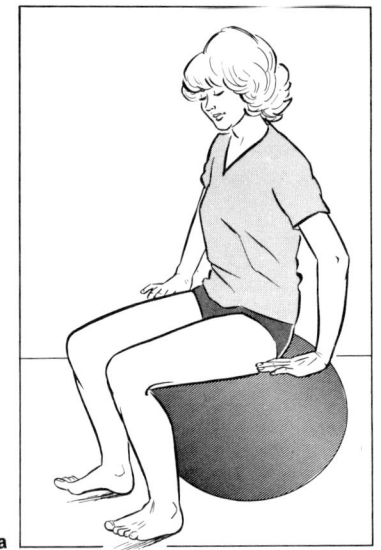
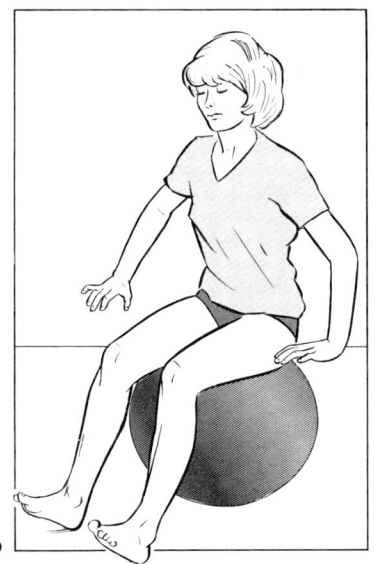
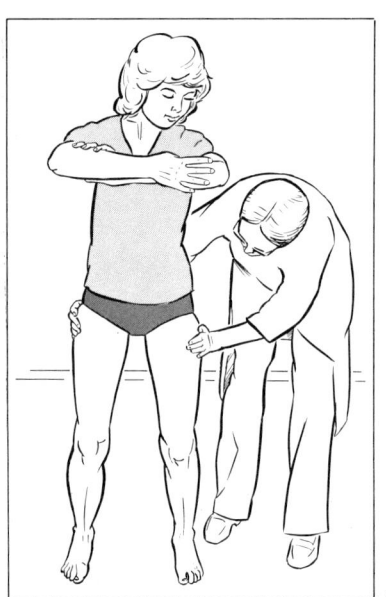
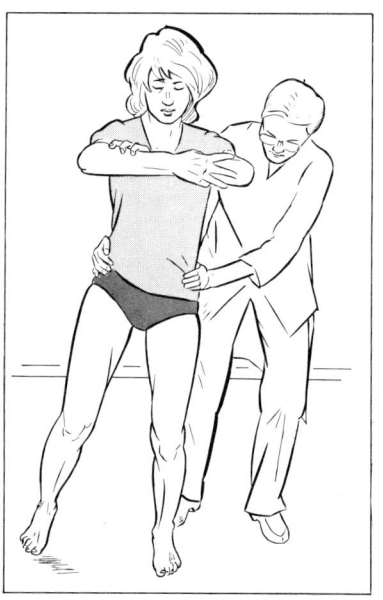

Fig. 12–59 Stabilizing exercises with full weight bearing (**a-e**).

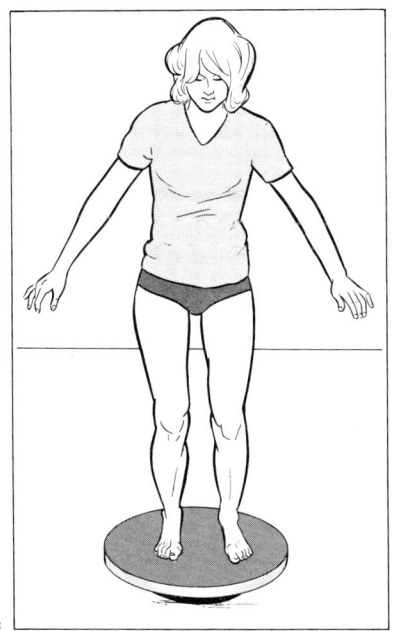
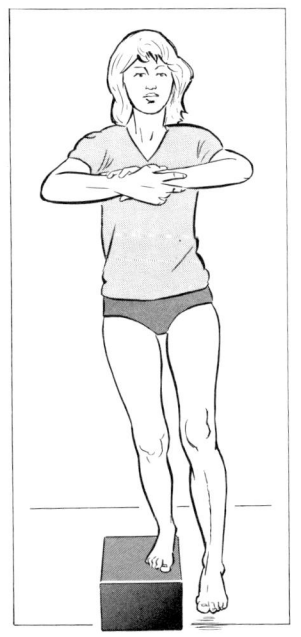
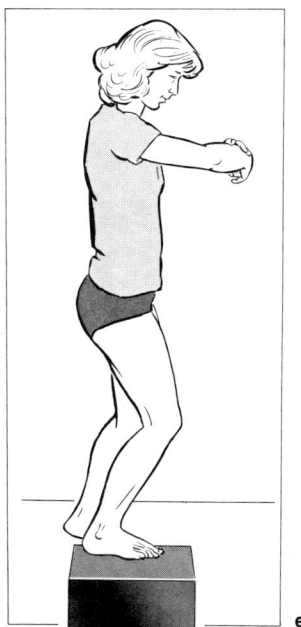

Fig. 12–59 continued

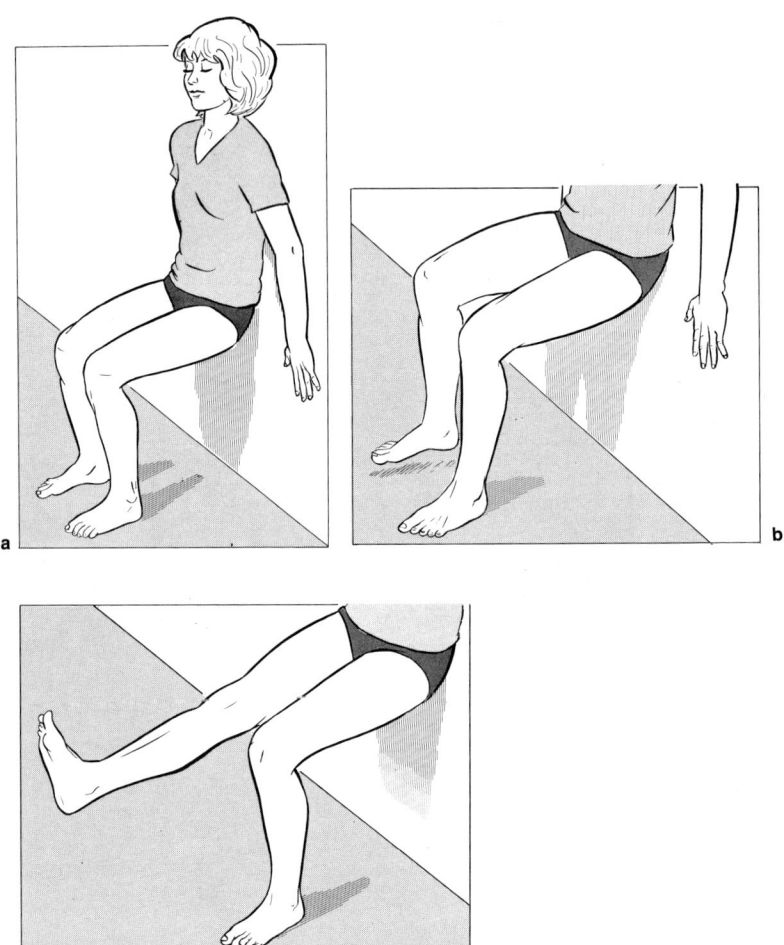

Fig. 12–60 Isometric and active training for both legs.

After 7 days: The cast is bivalved and mobilization of the knee joint is started. The quadriceps muscle is trained intensively. The knee is flexed actively. The goal is to increase knee flexion daily by 15°. At the end of each movement the muscles are contracted isometrically. In case of a joint effusion the treatment is applied as described earlier. The bivalved cast is still in place but is later taken off except for during the night. The extensor muscles are strong enough to elevate the extended leg from the bed against resistance. Usually knee flexion of 90° is achieved after the first week. The patient walks with two crutches with partial weight bearing with a three-point gait pattern. The ability to flex the knee to 90° is not essential for walking, but walking requires the vigorous use of all stabilizing muscles of the knee. The muscle training is intensified. An active knee flexion of 90° is usually sufficient for walking. When climbing stairs the patient should put the affected leg behind the normal one; otherwise, deviating movements are established over the lumbar spine and the pelvis. For normal stair climbing knee flexion of 120° is required.

After 2 to 3 weeks: The patient is discharged and continues to walk with two crutches until the fourth week; then a cane is used for another 2 weeks.

Any sports activity that would stress the knee is stopped for 3 months.

For Patients Older Than 40. No cast; splint is used. The physical therapy program is the same as outlined for those under age 40.

Dislocation of the Patella

Postoperative Treatment

The tibial tuberosity is transferred medially; the retinaculum is split laterally and partly transferred from medially to laterally.
Position: In a splint in 20° of flexion
After 3 weeks: Isometric contractions for the quadriceps muscle, active assisted exercises, ambulation starting with partial weight bearing that is slowly increased to 30 kg are initiated.
After 6 weeks: After radiographic check, active exercises are started and weight bearing is increased.

Chondromalacia Patellae

Conservative Nonsurgical Treatment

Evaluation Results

- Pain, especially during knee flexion, sitting down or squatting, climbing stairs, and riding a bicycle
- Atrophy of the thigh muscles, especially the quadriceps
- Legs tire easily during walking; endurance decreased
- Irritation of the joint in a more progressive stage

Goals of Therapy

- Decrease articular irritation.
- Strengthen the quadriceps muscle.

General Recommendations for Treatment. The patient is advised to keep the knee as unstressed as possible, avoiding such activities as sports that stress the knee: mountain climbing, extensive bicycling, swimming in frog style, carrying heavy loads, climbing stairs (preferably use elevators or escalators), taking long walks, taking long car rides, wearing high heels (frequently walk barefoot instead).

- *Pain relief:* Measures include application of ice pack or ice massage around the patella, application of moist heat, electrotherapy
- *Muscle strengthening:* If there is no irritation and the pain has decreased, training of the leg muscles is started, beginning with the foot. For stabilizing muscles of the knee joint, isometric contractions with the knee in extension or in slight flexion are begun.

The patient will need a home exercise program. Therapy is continued and intensified as long as there is no pain and the discomfort continues to subside.

Postoperative Treatment

Lateral Release
Position: Splint in extension
After day 1: Active assisted flexion and extension
After 3 days: Isometric contractions of the quadriceps muscle and unlimited active exercises; walking with partial weight bearing (5-kg weight bearing) with elastic bandage around the leg
After 2 weeks: Emphasis on exercises to the medial aspect of the knee; gradual approach to full weight bearing

Ventral Transfer of the Tibial Tuberosity (Stable Anchoring)
Position: Splint in 20° of flexion
After day 1: Isometric contractions of the quadriceps muscle
After 1 week: Active assisted exercises, including flexion; partial weight bearing ambulation
After 2 weeks: Exercises continue; ambulation with a removable splint around the leg; 20 to 30-kg weight bearing
After 6 weeks: After radiographic control, active exercise program started and weight bearing gradually increased

Genu Varum and Genu Valgum

Conservative Nonsurgical Treatment

Evaluation Results. Physiologic genu varum and genu valgum in infants requires treatment only if the deviation exceeds 30°. Under weight bearing a talipes valgus and talipes planus develop in the presence of a genu varum. A genu recurvatum and a talipes valgus and talipes planus are combined with a genu valgum. The leg muscles become insufficient and the knee joint loses stability. Children are unstable on their legs and tire easily. Poor posture may also be observed.

Goals of Therapy

- Prevent worsening of malposition. The malposition cannot be influenced by exercises. In a young child with only a mild deviation and ongoing growth, an increase of the deformity may be avoidable.
- Improve muscle insufficiency by general strengthening of the foot and leg muscles and by stabilization and gait training.
- Improve weak posture by general gymnastics and posture training.

Therapy

- Malposition: Passive manipulations as practiced in the past, such as the use of splints, are not successful in a genu valgum between the knees and in a genu varum between the ankles. The child should not sit on the floor playing in extreme malposition, nor should he or she crawl this way. Favorite positions like this are comfortable and occur automatically, but they must be avoided. Squatting and Indian sitting should be encouraged in genu valgum. A child with genu varum can sit on the heels with closed knees.
- Muscle insufficiency: Along with the general training of the foot and leg muscles, the muscles on the medial side of the knee must be built up, especially in a genu valgum; in a genu varum the muscles on the lateral side, and in a genu recurvatum mainly the stabilizing muscles in the back side of the knee (Figs. 12–61 and 12–62).

Postoperative Treatment

Corrective Osteotomy in Children. Dome-type osteotomies or supracondylar corrective osteotomy with fixation by Kirschner wires.
Position: Immobilization in long leg cast
After 10 days: Changing of the cast and radiographic check
After 2 weeks: Discharge with the cast
After 6 weeks: Radiographic check; bivalve cast if bony consolidation has started; initiation of exercises without the cast
After 7 weeks: Exercises and ambulation in the therapeutic pool; partial weight bearing; cast now worn only at night
After 10 weeks: Discharge; continuation of physical therapy
After 14 weeks: Radiographic check; physical therapy until stability of the knees is satisfactory

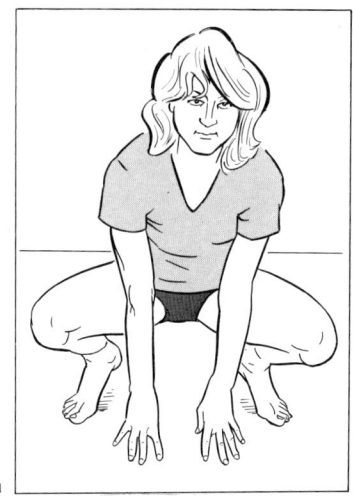 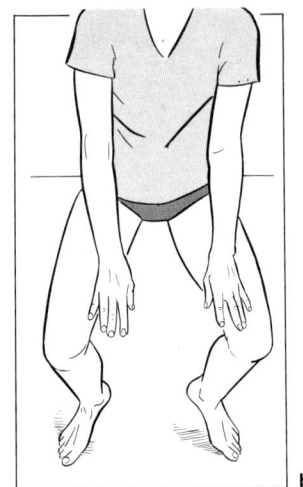

Fig. 12–61 Exercise for genu valgum—hopping like a frog.

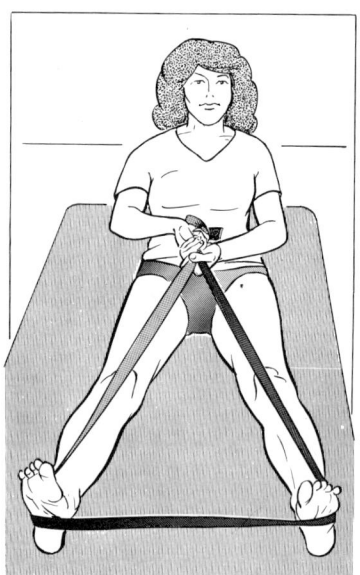

Fig. 12–62 Exercise for genu varum with use of theraband.

Corrective Osteotomy in Adults. Supracondylar correction osteotomy, fixation with an angled plate.
Position: Hip joint in a 90° flexion and knee joint in a functional (dynamic) splint

After day 1: Active extension of the knee as allowed by the splint; isometric exercises for the quadriceps muscle
After 2 weeks: Ambulation with a three-point gait pattern with partial weight bearing (approximately 5 kg)
After 6 weeks: After radiographic check, start active exercises against the weight of the lower leg; gradually increasing the weight to 50 percent of body weight.
After 8 weeks: Discharge; exercise in weight bearing
After 12 weeks: Radiographic check; depending on results, exercises continued, intensified, or ended

Infracondylar Corrective Osteotomy with External Fixation
Position: Immobilization in a splint
After day 1: Isometric exercises for the quadriceps muscle; active assisted flexion and extension of the knee and hip joint (if pain-free); general conditioning of arms and trunk
After 2 weeks: Active knee extension and knee flexion over the edge of the bed; non-weight-bearing ambulation
After 6 weeks: Radiographic check; possibly removal of the external fixation device; application of an external knee support; gradually increased weight bearing; discharge
After 8 weeks: Radiographic check; if bony consolidation insufficient, reapplication of cast for 4 more weeks; with sufficient bony consolidation, actual knee exercise and strengthening of the leg muscles, including hydrotherapy and gait training under weight bearing

Inflammation of the Knee Joint

Conservative Nonsurgical Treatment

In general, the therapy is similar to that for arthritis.

Evaluation Results

- Pain during moving and weight bearing until it is not possible to bear weight, especially climbing stairs or mountains
- Joint swelling and effusion
- Crepitation during motion
- Restricted range of motion in flexion and extension, later affecting the neighboring joints, the other leg, and the spine. A long-lasting flexion contracture of the knee causes impaired extension of the hip joint and compensatory increased lordosis of the lumbar spine. Functional shortening

of the leg leads to a pelvic tilt, negatively influencing the spine and the other leg.
- Muscle insufficiency, especially the quadriceps; lack of endurance
- Malposition of the joint, frequently in varus or valgus position
- Instability of the joint, less security during standing and ambulation
- Impaired ambulation, limping
- Interference with daily routine
- Overstressing other areas of the body

Goals of Therapy

- Mobilize the joint, bringing the restricted mobility back, if the changes have not progressed too far.
- Strengthen muscles to promote relaxation and stretch shortened muscles in the area of hips and knees.
- Promote correct positions during rest and use of splints during weight bearing to influence malpositions.
- Provide ambulation training.
- Promote joint protection.
- Provide aids for activities of daily living.
- Provide an exercise program for general conditioning.

Therapy

- All therapeutic techniques are aimed first at relieving pain by using moist heat, whirlpool baths, electrotherapy, or massage.
- Joint irritation is eliminated as described previously.
- Depending on the radiographic result, manual therapy is indicated.
- Active movement with no weight bearing, for instance, in a therapeutic pool is started. Swinging exercises can be done across the edge of the bed if there is sufficient ability for flexion; a weight cuff around the ankle can be added but only in a stable joint. Active treatment of the contracture may not exceed the pain threshold.
- The muscles are strengthened mainly with isometric contraction at the end of the flexion and extension range. They are trained intensively, considering the malposition. The knees are not actively moved against resistance.
- Gait training to modify deviations, such as consciously using the muscles of the toes, feet, and hips for compensation. The newly achieved or remaining

range of motion is used intensively. The exercises are controlled in front of the mirror, possibly barefoot.

- Protection for the joint: Avoid standing for long periods, crossing the legs in sitting position, and increased stress on the knee joint when climbing stairs or mountains and in sports. Body weight must be reduced. Heavy loads should not be carried (use a shopping cart). Shoes should be elastic with a soft sole, and a cane is recommended. Using a bicycle with a high seat in an early stage of inflammation is preferred to long walks. Later, riding a bicycle can cause discomfort.

Postoperative Treatment

Dome-Type Osteotomies. See section on corrective osteotomies earlier in this chapter.

Endoprosthetic Replacement. Surface replacement or hinge joint.
Position: In a functional splint in flexion of approximately 60°, no pressure (watch fibular head)
After day 1: Change position in full extension and increase flexion (twice daily for 2 hours). Possibly pain medication is needed. Start isometric contractions for the quadriceps muscle. Standing by the bed (no weight bearing). Possibly effusion prophylaxis by use of elastic bandage.
After 3 days: Continue flexion and extension exercises; active assisted and active exercises are intensified. Strengthening of the quadriceps is most important. Swinging exercises across the edge of the bed are started as soon as 90° is reached (the lower leg is wrapped). The splint is taken off; a splint may be applied at night. Partial weight bearing ambulation is started (5 kg) with use of a walker or two crutches.
After 2 weeks: Weight bearing is increased up to 50 percent of the body weight.
After 3 weeks: Full weight bearing is allowed, depending on the muscle strength; the type of walking aid is selected according to the patient's needs; a cane might suffice; discharge
After 6 weeks: Radiographic check and consultation.
A hinge endoprosthesis allows range of motion between 100° and 120° of flexion.

Arthrodesis of the Knee

Preoperative Treatment. The status of the neighboring joints, the other leg, and the spine is assessed. The physical therapy program should improve the preoperative situation. Mobilization and strengthening of the muscles, including the supporting muscles of the arm, are most important.

Postoperative Treatment. External fixation; position in a splint.
After day 1: General thrombosis and embolism prophylaxis; isometric and active

exercises for the trunk, shoulder girdle, arms, and unaffected leg. Affected side: Active foot and passive ankle exercise; isometric exercises for the hip muscles.
After 6 weeks: Radiographic check. The external fixation device is removed and a cast is applied. Comparison of leg lengths in a standing position is done, elevating the shoe if necessary. Ambulation with a three-point gait pattern is begun with increasing weight bearing.
After 7 weeks: Discharge
After 12 weeks: Radiographic check. An adhesive/elastic bandage is applied for 2 weeks if the arthrodesis is clinically and radiographically stable. If the stability is still questionable, a cast is reapplied until there is sufficient consolidation. A short stay in the hospital may be necessary after completion of the immobilization period, to initiate physical therapy and gait training.

Gait Technique with a Knee Arthrodesis. The stance phase does not cause problems. The foot and toes are vigorously flexed to push the leg off the ground. The foot is elevated quickly and the leg is swung with hip flexion and lateral flexion of the spine. The swing phase is facilitated by the moderate shortening of the leg. Limping becomes more pronounced if the difference in leg length increases. Depending on the patient's age and preoperative activities, skill training is included in the program, such as climbing ladders, hopping, jumping, walking, running, dancing.

The problem with the extended leg in a sitting position cannot be eliminated, which troubles the patient, especially in the beginning. The patient must get used to this and develop "tricks" to compensate for the problem.

Training to help oneself, including the use of additional aids, are required only if the function of adjacent joints is also affected. Full flexion of the hip joint and extension in the proximal tarsal joints are required.

Bilateral ankyloses of the knees is hard to overcome. The increased stress on the adjacent joints, the upper extremity, and the spine is an additional problem, especially in walking, sitting down, and standing up. This situation may be sufficient indication for endoprosthetic replacement.

FOOT

EVALUATION IN PHYSICAL THERAPY

The normally shaped foot has three main stress points: the calcaneus (os calcis) and the first and fifth metatarsal heads. These bones are the most plantar points on the foot, which consists of three elements. The posterior element contains the calcaneus and the talus (astragalus); the anterior medial segment contains the talus, the navicular (scaphoid), the three cuneiform bones, and the first three metatarsal bones; the anterior lateral segment consists of the calcaneus, talus, cuboid bone, and the fourth and fifth metatarsal bones.

The skeletal components form a medial and lateral longitudinal arch and an anterior transverse arch. This arrangement, adapted to the function of the foot, is reinforced by ligaments, tendons, and muscles. A delicate and highly differentiated compound is created, which can be disturbed by small changes in one component, resulting in changes of the position or shape of the foot. Changes in muscles or ligaments initially cause a malposition. This results in an overstress on the bones and joints and can even lead to disturbances in the growing skeleton. The onset of the disease and the earliest possible therapy are therefore crucial. Disturbances of the muscle balance are more serious for the growing foot skeleton in a child than for the mature skeleton in an adult.

The load transmission on the foot comes from the tibia and farther down over the talus to the calcaneus and, in an anterior direction, across the remaining tarsal bones to the metatarsal heads.

The flexor hallucis longus is the most important muscle; it prevents tilting of the calcaneus medially and flattening of the longitudinal arch. Its tendon runs directly under the sustentaculum tali of the calcaneus and is tensed in each step as the foot is loaded. The anterior foot joints have little mobility. However, there is a little motion of the rear foot and forefoot against each other. This can be done passively with the foot in a non-weight-bearing position; one hand fixates the calcaneus and the other hand moves the forefoot into pronation. This motion occurs during each step under weight bearing. The rolling motion of the foot is reversed again during the non-weight-bearing stance phase. It is intensified when standing on tiptoe.

The short and long flexors of the foot are more important for support than for motion. They are stronger than the extensors and work synergistically. In a standing position they keep the foot on the ground; during walking they lift the heel from the ground and push the foot up. During each step they lift the body weight against gravity. Their tone is initiated and modified as a reflex when touching the ground. They work constantly and with high endurance, especially in sprinters or ballet dancers.

The triceps surae muscle is important in this context. It is the strongest tendon in the body. Its performance in walking and jumping, together with the short and long flexors of the toes, is considerable. However, it is the antagonist in supporting the standing position. In a forward tilt of the trunk, especially with the knees in extension, it tends to flatten the longitudinal arch, the more so the farther the trunk is from the perpendicular line. The stress on the toe muscles increases, and the gastrocnemius muscle has to stretch considerably.

Unfortunately, the importance of training the foot muscles is as often underestimated in physical therapy as it is in sports and gymnastics. Frequently there is a disproportion between the body weight and the strength of the foot muscles.

The foot is evaluated in weight-bearing and non-weight-bearing conditions. Evaluation in a weight-bearing condition is concerned with the following:

- Standing on both legs, feet parallel and directed forward; the distance between the feet is the width of one foot: Position of the foot, supporting function of the muscles during the therapist's attempt to challenge the balance
- Standing on one leg with the position of the foot and using the muscles, especially the tibialis posterior and the flexors of the toes
- Moving forward: The type of foot motion in changing speed. Are the knees overextended and is the trunk tilted forward away from the perpendicular line?
- Influence on statics and dynamics of the entire body
- Performance of the foot in special movements, such as walking, running, hopping, jumping, balancing (e.g., on a horizontal bar), climbing (e.g., stall bars)
- Pain in the area of the foot or in adjacent joints under stress

Evaluation in a non-weight-bearing condition is concerned with the following:

- Active and passive joint mobility and the motion within the joint itself
- Strength of all toes and foot muscles, especially of the flexors, maintaining a position against resistance
- Mobility of the toes and feet, picking up items, using the short foot muscles in exercises with equipment (ball or rope)
- Pains in the area of the foot or adjacent joints

Each physical therapist can design an individual examination, based on his or her own experiences, that enables evaluation of the foot and its function within a few minutes.

More details must be assessed in cases of deformities of the foot and toes.

Measurements in degrees are restricted to the proximal tarsal joint. The goniometer is applied parallel to the lower leg and the sole (Fig. 12–63).

The range of motion in the distal tarsal joint is estimated in comparison with the normal side or the standard values.

CLINICAL SYMPTOMS

Congenital Clubfoot (Pes Equinovarus Excavatus et Adductus)

Origin

- Genetic lesion: This assumption is based on a constant sex-linked distribution (male to female, 2:1). The hereditary course is latently recessive with increased penetrance in males.

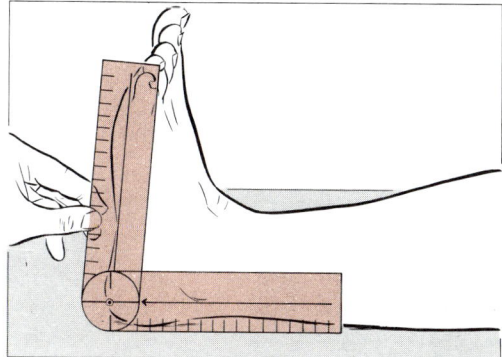

Fig. 12–63 Measuring the proximal tarsal joint.

- Space-taking processes in the uterus (deformities, twin pregnancies, tumor, lack of amniotic fluid, amniotic cords)
- Neuropathic theory: Owing to preexisting lesions of the nerves (myelodysplasia, spina bifida) the muscles in the area of their innervation undergo hypoplasia.
- The most widely accepted assumption is that the deformity is due to exogenously or endogenously caused arrest in an early embryonic phase. This is supported by the similarity of clubfoot to the fetal foot during weeks 5 to 12 of gestation. The initially inhibited muscle development in the uterus causes a characteristic deformity of the foot skeleton by interfering with the muscle balance. In a congenital clubfoot the single skeletal components have a normal shape at birth. However, their position is already pathological. The unphysiologic stress owing to the malposition causes pathological growth, and the malposition of the foot turns into a bony consolidated deformity.

Symptoms. Mostly bilateral complex deformity of the foot with the following single components:

- The entire foot is in plantar flexion (pes equinus).
- The back of the foot is in an increased varus position (pes varus).
- The forefoot is in more plantar flexion than the back foot, resulting in a high arched foot (pes excavatus).
- The soft tissue across the outside, convex part of the clubfoot is overstretched.

Within the medial, plantar, and concave parts of the foot the supinators, the plantar fascia, and the soleus muscle are shortened (Fig. 12–64).

322 Lower Limbs

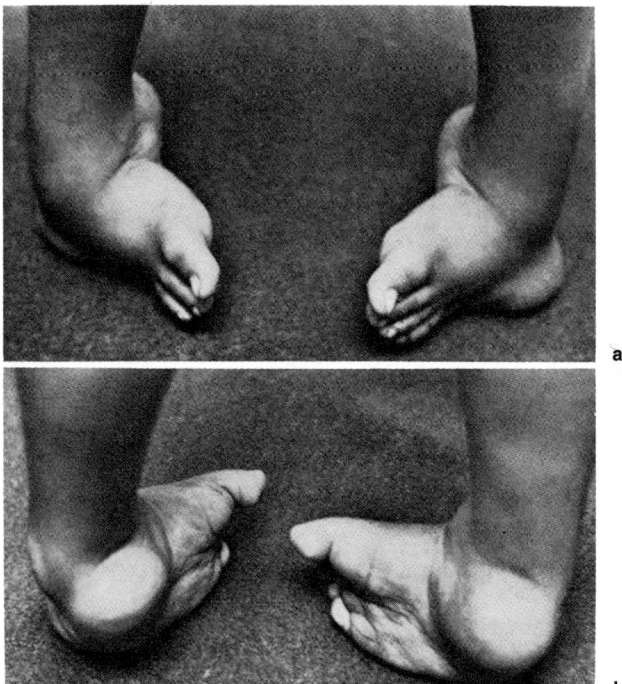

Fig. 12–64 Bilateral congenital clubfoot. **a:** Anterior view; **b:** posterior view (from H. Cotta: Orthopädie, 4. Aufl., Thieme, Stuttgart, 1984).

The calf muscles are already underdeveloped in the newborn; the muscle belly has shifted proximally (clubfoot calf, match calf). The toes might be in a flexion contracture. An outward rotation of the tibia can be combined with an inward rotation of the tarsal joint. The muscle balance influencing the foot is disturbed. The fibularis group and the extensors are weakened but not paralyzed. The tibial muscle group is rather hypertonic and shortened. The deformities present at birth will increase during the growth period if they are treated insufficiently or not at all. Muscles, tendons, and ligaments will contract more and more. In a severe deformity the foot is put on the floor with the lateral edge or in extreme conditions even with the dorsal part. Callosities and bursae develop in the area of increased stress. The subsequent overstress on the knee joint can cause further static problems. Late subsequent lesions are arthrotic changes not only of the entire foot, but also of the knee joint area.

In a normal skeleton the axis of the calcaneus and the talus form a dorsally open angle of 30° to 40° in a lateral view and a distally open angle of the same size in a dorsoplantar view (Fig. 12–65). In clubfoot, however, they are nearly parallel in

Foot/Clinical Symptoms 323

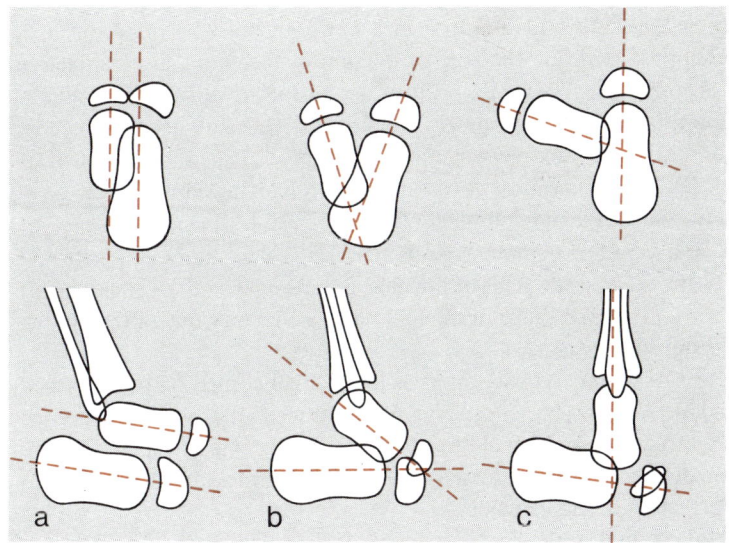

Fig. 12–65 Bilateral congenital clubfoot (from: H. Cotta: Orthopädie, 4. Aufl., Thieme, Stuttgart, 1984).

both views (Fig. 12–66). The navicular bone has shifted medially and plantar to various degrees and the cuboid bone is in supine position, such as the calcaneus and navicular bones. A subluxation is evident between talus, calcaneus, and navicular bones.

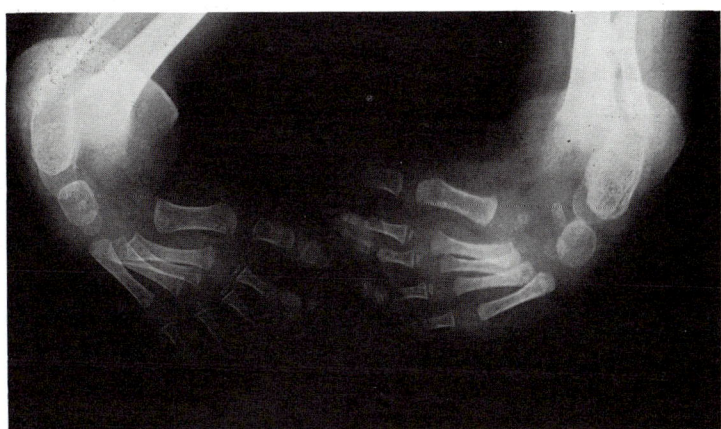

Fig. 12–66 X-ray of bilateral club feet.

A physiologic supination malposition in a newborn must be ruled out as a differential diagnosis (tickling the sole or dorsum of the foot causes an active correction). Another diagnostic possibility is clubfoot resulting from neural lesions (spina bifida, early brain damage, poliomyelitis, stroke), accompanied by typical neurologic symptoms and anamnesis. Clubfoot can also be found in systemic diseases, such as arthrogryposis multiple congenita, in which the clubfoot is severely contracted and combined with other deformities.

Treatment. Early initial treatment is crucial, since the clubfoot is soft and pliable only during the first few days of life. The initial conservative (nonsurgical) therapy is aimed at a normal shape of the foot with satisfactory functioning of the pronator and extensor muscles.

Conservative Treatment: As early as possible manual correction is performed on forefoot adduction, supination and varus position of the rear foot in knee flexion, before surgical correction of the elevation of the heel is considered. There is a risk of bending the forefoot dorsally, resulting in a rocking foot, owing to insufficient correction of the os calcis.

The corrected position of the foot is immobilized in mild cases during the first postnatal days with elastic bandages, but more often in a thigh cast with the knee in 90° of flexion. The cast is changed every 2 to 5 days with another manual correction. Permanent control of the blood circulation and mobility of the toes are important (Fig. 12–67).

If the treatment is started later, in an older infant or small child, two more therapeutic techniques may be indicated:

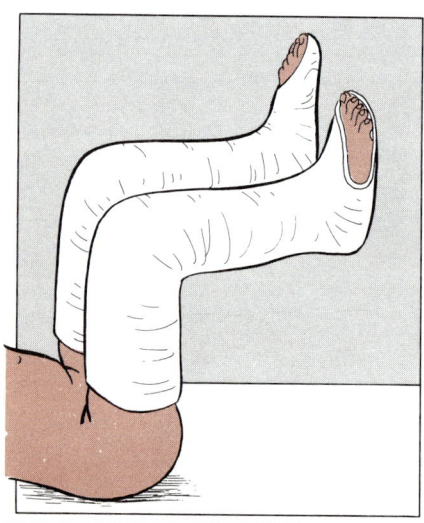

Fig. 12–67 Thigh cast with the knees in 90° of flexion allowing permanent control of circulation and mobility of toes.

- Cast correction: The cast consists of two parts, one containing some of the toes and the foot, the other containing the rear foot, lower leg, and thigh. Wedges are cut out dorsally and laterally according to the desired direction of the correction. The new position is reached gradually, by adapting and recasting the edges of the cut.
- Functional treatment in a splint according to Dennis-Browne: The clubfoot is fixed to a foot plate. A right and a left foot plate are connected by a bar and fixed on a ring in order to move hip and knee joints. The position of the foot plates on the bar is variable, to allow correction of the position.

To achieve satisfactory position of the foot over a period of 3 to 4 months, the foot must be immobilized by a bivalved cast or a splint in combination with vigorous physical therapy. Arch support (made from a mold) is prescribed as soon as the child begins to stand. The parents are informed accordingly, stressing the necessity for further exercises and checkups and the risk of recidivism. The treatment of a clubfoot is finished only if the foot has a normal shape and position and the strength of the pronator muscles matches the strength of the supinator muscles.

Surgical Treatment. Soft tissue surgery has two purposes:

1. Obstacles that interfere with the correction of the foot must be eliminated by tenotomy, capsulotomy, incisions of fasciae and ligaments.
   - Elevation of the heel: Open; sagittal Z-shaped tenotomy of the Achilles tendon, leaving the lateral portion distally attached to the calcaneus. Incision of the posterior contracted capsule of the talocalcaneal and talocrural joint. Correction of the calcaneus position and suture of the Achilles tendon in a corrected position of the foot. A wire extension can be applied to the calcaneus if it is difficult to achieve. Postoperative immobilization in a cast for 8 weeks. Application of special splints during the night and arch support.
   - Adduction position of the forefoot; complex medial tenotomy, the tendon of the tibialis posterior muscle is dissected at its insertion medially on the navicular and cuneiform bones. Tenotomy of the plantar fascia and medial capsulotomy of the joints between the talus, navicular, and cuneiform bones. Postoperative immobilization in a corrective cast after the treatment outlined.
2. Muscle balance of the foot is improved by the transposition of tendons. The supinators are stronger than the pronators. Transposition of the anterior tibialis muscle on the middle or lateral dorsum of the foot. Transposition of the muscle on the outside of the dorsum is also possible. Postoperative immobilization in a cast; electrotherapy for the transposed muscle and active exercises after 3 weeks.

Operations on the bones are done for two reasons:

1. Osteotomies eliminate bony fixated deformities. In a growing skeleton, care must be taken not to harm growth plates or joint cartilage in a clubfoot deformity owing to changes of the foot skeleton that cannot be corrected passively or by soft tissue surgery. In a growing skeleton a wedge osteotomy or an excochleation of the cuboid bone is performed (sparing the joints). If growth is almost complete (age 14), subtalar arthrodesis is necessary in addition to dorsolateral wedge osteotomy in the area of the ankle.
2. Subtalar arthrodesis provides for a stable and pain-free foot skeleton, able to bear weight. The muscles that stabilize the proximal tarsal joint must be trained postoperatively, after 12 weeks and under increasing weight bearing. Arch support and possibly orthopedic shoes with a double support for the ankle provide for stability during the postoperative phase or in frequent walks across uneven ground.

Acquired Clubfoot

Origin. Paralysis, fractures of the foot healed in a malposition, scar contraction, sequels of inflammative processes.

Symptoms. See Congenital Clubfoot; the extent of the deformity depends on the time of onset of the development.

Treatment. Early prophylaxis by active or passive exercises, possibly position in a bivalved cast or orthesis.

Sickle (or Crescent)-Shaped Foot (Pes Adductus, Metatarsus Varus)

Origin. Malposition in the uterus; mostly a remaining deformity after clubfoot treatment.

Symptoms. In mild cases only an adduction position of the big toe (metatarsus varus). The contracture progresses with growth and will eventually interfere with wearing normal shoes.

Conservative Nonsurgical Treatment. Manual correction as for a clubfoot, later on splints during the night, arch support, including the heels with a reinforced medial edge. Considerable risk of recidivism.

Surgical Treatment. Medial capsular incision into the joint between the first metatarsal bone and the first cuneiform bone. Tenotomy of the abductor hallucis muscle, followed by immobilization in a cast for 6 weeks and then splints during the night and arch support with a medially reinforced edge.

In a rigid deformity corrective osteotomy is performed near the base of metatarsal bones I through V.

Congenital Pes Calcaneus Congenitus (Contracted Foot)

Origin. Muscle imbalance. The frequent calcaneus position in newborns must be differentiated. The dorsum of the foot can also be brought in touch with the front of the calf; however, the plantar flexion is free and the arch of the foot is normal. The situation usually improves during the first weeks of life.

Symptoms. A unilateral or bilateral deformity, combined with other deformities, with increased dorsal extension in the proximal tarsal joint (until the dorsum of the foot touches the calf) and severely inhibited plantar flexion of the foot.

Conservative Nonsurgical Treatment. Early manual correction as for clubfoot and correcting casts in knee flexion, followed by splints during the night and physical therapy.

Acquired Pes Calcaneus and Pes Calcaneus Excavatus

Origin. Partial or total elimination of the calf muscles, scarry retraction on the dorsum of the foot, rigid malposition of the proximal tarsal joint.

Symptoms. Steep position of the calcaneus, increased dorsal extension with decreased plantar flexion, making standing on tiptoe impossible. The muscles of the soles are dominating and later are shortened. The longitudinal arch of the foot is more distinct. In an attempt to equalize the arch passively, the muscles of the sole and the plantar aponeurosis become tensed. A steppage gait, painful callosities on the heel by overstress, and arthrosis of the tarsal joints are noted.

Conservative Nonsurgical Treatment. Correcting casts during childhood.

Surgical Treatment. Subtalar arthrodesis with a correcting wedge osteotomy of the calcaneus. The tendon of the physiologically functioning muscles (peronei, tibialis posterior, flexor hallucis longus, flexor digitorum) can be transplanted on the Achilles tendon.

Excavated Foot

Origin. Muscle imbalance, especially in myelodysplasia, progressive muscle dystrophy, spastic paresis. A high instep, which is considered normal, must be differentiated.

Symptoms. Increased arch, which makes the foot appear plump and shortened; the ball of the big toe is protruding plantar. The plantar aponeurosis is tensed in the attempt to flatten the arch passively.

Excavated clawfoot: Special form with claw position of the toes and dislocation of the metacarsotarsal joints. Inelastic gait.

Conservative Treatment. Stretching exercises for mild cases, arch support and relief for painful pressure points, orthopedic shoes for severer cases.

Surgical Treatment. Tenotomy of the plantar aponeurosis to flatten the arch; wedge osteotomy in severer deformities combined with subtalar arthrodesis.

Equinus

Origin. Congenital: Abnormal position in the uterus (rare).
Acquired:

- Equinus contracture of the foot in long-lasting malposition, for instance, pressure from the blanket during long bed rest, in a cast, and as a compensation for a shortened leg.
- Paresis

  —Flaccid in poliomyelitis and peripheral nerve injuries
  —Spastic in infant cerebral palsy, apoplexia, brain trauma

- Posttraumatic

  —Scar contraction
  —Pathological growth after lesion of the growth plate
  —Fractures healed in malposition

Symptoms. The foot in plantar flexion cannot be brought into dorsiflexion beyond the neutral position either actively or passively. Because of an increased arch the foot is put down in the area of the toes, causing painful callosities and a widening of the forefoot. The risk of genu recurvatum is caused by touching the ground on tiptoes and overextension of the knee joint. The functional elongation of the affected leg can cause a pelvic tilt, predisposing a static scoliosis. The lower leg is lifted higher (steppage gait) to avoid stumbling over the forefoot.

Conservative Nonsurgical Treatment. Prophylaxis by correct position in a cast, physical therapy, avoiding pressure from the blanket, stretching shortened soft tissue by manual correction. In simultaneous shortening of the leg, the equinus can serve as a compensation for the length difference. Corrective treatment is not indicated, other than orthopedic shoes. Shoes or apparatus may be required, especially in flaccid or spastic paresis.

Surgical Treatment. Achillotenotomy with incision of the posterior capsule of the proximal and sometimes the distal tarsal joint. In spastic paresis the shortening and excessive tone of the plantar flexors are eliminated by myotomy and neurectomy of the motor nerves supplying those muscles. In flaccid paresis tenoplasty or tenodesis may be indicated.

A bony consolidated equinus can be corrected only by osteotomy. Arthrodeses are indicated to eliminate the pain of arthrotic joints that cannot be stabilized by other nonsurgical or surgical techniques.

Congenital Flatfoot (Vertical Talus, Talipes Planus)

Origin. Unknown.

Symptoms. Rocking foot, dorsiflexion of the forefoot with abduction and pronation. Characteristic radiographic result. Opposite deformity to congenital clubfoot.

Conservative Nonsurgical Treatment. Early manual correction and cast; later, splints and arch support.

Surgical Treatment. Elongation of the Achilles tendon, incision of the posterior capsule (talocrural and talocalcaneal joint); because of the risk of recidivism, permanent and carefully controlled splint use during the night with arch support, and physical therapy.

Splay Foot (Metatarsus Latus, Pes Transversoplanus)

Origin. Weak connective tissue, increased stress on the forefoot by badly fitting shoes, high heels, overweight, polyarthritis.

Symptoms. Flattening of the arch of the forefoot and lowering of metatarsal heads II through IV are accompanied by spreading of the metatarsal bones with subsequent widening of the forefoot. The direction of the traction by the tendons inserting on the toes is changed, resulting in a muscle imbalance and secondary toe deformities (hallux valgus, claw and mallet toe). It is the most common stress deformity of the foot.

Conservative Nonsurgical Treatment. Treatment of the underlying reasons, strengthening the muscles of the toes and sole. In a contracted splayfoot, an arch support is indicated.

Surgical Treatment. Treatment of the secondary deformities, such as hallux valgus, claw or mallet toe. In a polyarthritic splayfoot, a partial or complete resection of the metatarsophalangeal joints is possible.

Combined Talipes Valgus, Planus, Transversoplanus

Origin. Decreased stability (constitutional weakness of connective tissue and muscles, paralysis, overstress), compensatory development of a talipes valgus with genu varus, inflammative or traumatic deformity of the foot skeleton.

Symptoms. Depending on the stress, the development of the talipes valgus starts with an inward rotation of the articulating surface between the lateral and medial malleolus and subsequently the talus, which is not sufficiently stabilized by muscles and ligaments. With subluxation of the talocalcaneal joint the talus slides in a medial and plantar direction, pushing the calcaneus in a valgus position (talipes valgus). The forefoot touching the ground moves in an abduction position. In a permanent disproportion between weight bearing and weight-bearing ability the medial segment is spread, flattening the longitudinal arch (talipes valgus and planus). The malposition, initially compensated passively, turns into a bony consolidated malposition in a child and can no longer be equalized passively. During adolescence the joints are overstressed and react with irritation and inflammation. In adults the ligaments contract, resulting in an early arthrosis. Frequently the severely deformed, contracted flat foot of adults causes considerably less discomfort than the slightly deformed splayfoot with beginning muscle contracture. The end stage of a flat foot or splayfoot is less painful than its development.

Treatment. Avoid overstress. The hypoplasia of the toe and sole muscles is caused by life in civilization. A young child should not be pushed to stand and walk early. The inflamed and contracted talipes valgus and planus in adults requires temporary immobilization, antiinflammatory medication, arch support, and increasing training under weight bearing.

Adults with severe, unresponsive discomfort require arch support, orthopedic shoes, and possibly subtalar arthrodesis.

Hallux Valgus

Origin. Sequel to a pes transversoplanus, injuries, paralysis.

Symptoms. Mostly bilateral toe deformity in combination with pes transversoplanus. Women are affected more than men. The big toe is subluxated laterally (abduction and pronation in the metatarsophalangeal joint). Because of the adduction of the first metatarsal bone and the abduction of the big toe, caused by shoe pressure and traction of the flexor tendons, the head of the first metatarsal bone is projecting medially. The shoe causes chronic irritation, capsular inflammation, and, finally, formation of osteophytes. The valgus position of the big toe can be so strong that it is pushed above or below the second or third toe inside the shoe (Fig. 12–68).

Conservative Nonsurgical Treatment. Foot exercises, comfortable shoes with flat heels, correcting splint during the night, special arch support to restore the anterior transverse arch, possibly orthopedic shoes to correct severe deformations.

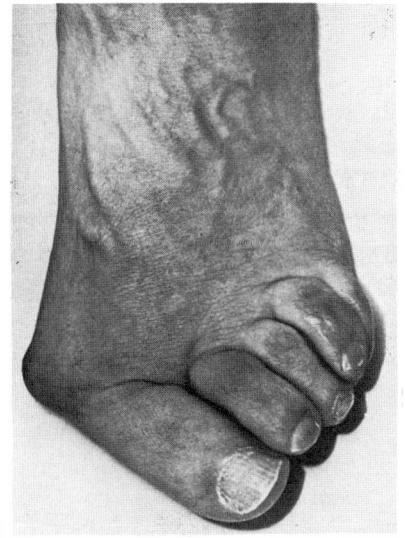
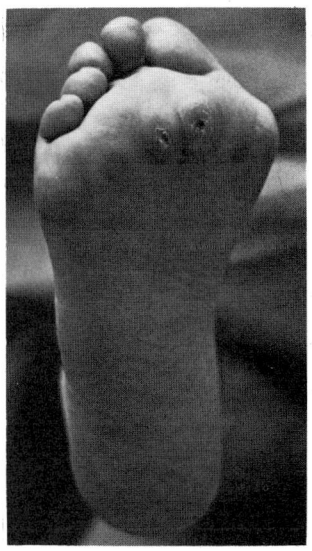
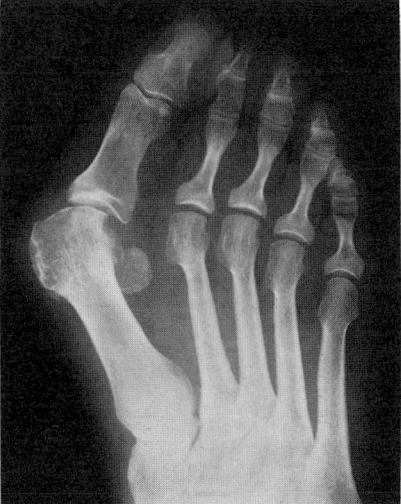

Fig. 12–68 Splayfoot. a: With hallux valgus and claw toe formation; b: typical callosity on the sole; c: onset of arthrosis in the proximal joint of the big toe (from H. Cotta: Orthopädie, 4. Aufl., Thieme, Stuttgart, 1984).

Surgical Treatment. In younger patients subcapital corrective osteotomy of the first metatarsal bone, transposition of the abductor hallucis muscle, and medial capsulorrhaphy (Fig. 12–69b). In a severe deformity with progressive arthrotic changes in the proximal joint of the big toe:

- Modified operation according to Brandes: Resection of the proximal phalanx of the big toe; distally, a pedicle capsuloperiosteal flap is turned as an interposition into the resection gap; the exostosis on the metatarsal head is dissected (Fig. 12–69c).
- Resection of first metatarsal head interposition according to Brandes
- Dissection of the medially protruding "exostosis" as a palliative procedure (Fig. 12–69a).

After the first two operations, immobilization in a cast, traction through the nail of the big toe for 12 days, followed by arch support and splints during the night.

Hallux Rigidus

Origin. Arthrosis, growth disturbances, or inflammation of the proximal joint of the big toe.

Symptoms. Restricted elevation in the proximal toe joint with increasing stiffness in flexion position. Considerable restriction in rolling the foot through the weight-bearing phase.

Treatment. As in hallux valgus.

Claw Toe, Mallet Toe

Origin. Malposition of the toes due to tight socks and shoes, complicated by splayfoot; inflammation of the toe joints with polyarthritis; disturbed muscle balance.

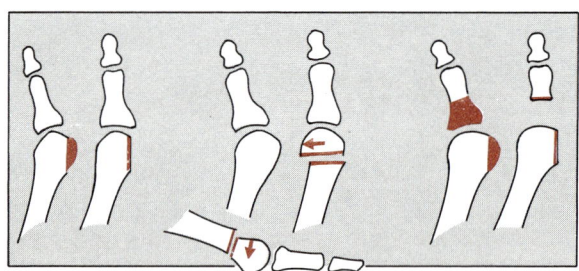

Fig. 12–69 Graphic illustration of different surgical techniques that have proved successful in hallux valgus. **a:** Simple dissection of the "exostosis," protruding medially from the first metatarsal bone, correction of the position of the big toe by a distally connected capsuloperiosteal pedicle flap (only a palliative surgery in mild cases); **b:** subcapital osteotomy of the first metacarpal bone; hallux valgus, splayfoot can be corrected at the same time by shifting the dissected metacarpal head in lateral and plantar direction; **c:** as in **a** and partial resection of the proximal phalanx of the big toe according to Brandes-Keller, which is a commonly used technique (from P. Pitzen, H. Rössler: Kurzgefasstes Lehrbuch der Orthopädie, 14. Aufl., Urban und Schwarzenberg, München, 1980).

Symptoms. A malposition of the toe is called claw or mallet toe (Fig. 12–70) if the proximal joints are in overextension in combination with a flexion of the middle and distal joints. The situation can be associated with subluxation or luxation. In a standing position or during walking the toes might not be in touch with the floor. Painful callosities owing to the pressure of the shoe start to develop along the dorsal surface of the toe joints.

A mallet toe is extended in the proximal joint (Fig. 12–70b) in combination with flexion (often 90°) of the middle and distal joints. Callosities cannot only form along the extension side of the toe joints, but also on the tip of the toe. If the big toe is affected, the condition is called hallux malleus.

Conservative Nonsurgical Treatment. Correction of the splayfoot by arch support and training the toe muscles. Stress relief of the callosities by felt or rubber rings.

Surgical Treatment. Resection arthroplasty by resecting the head (proximal joint) and tendopathy of the extensor tendon.

Digitus Quintus Varus Superductus

Origin. Mostly congenital, occasionally a splayfoot deformity as in hallux valgus.

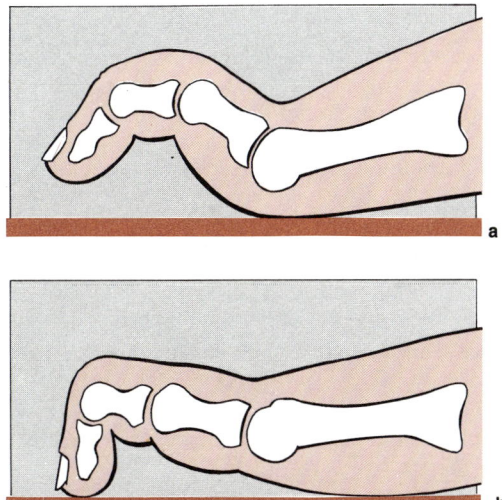

Fig. 12–70 a: Claw toe; **b:** mallet toe.

Symptoms. The head of the fifth metatarsal bone projects with a strong adduction of the fifth toe owing to the pressure of the shoe and sock. The fifth toe can be pressed under or above the other toes.

Conservative Nonsurgical Treatment. Correction in infants by bandages, splints at night, and arch support.

Surgical Treatment. Subcapital correcting osteotomy of the fifth metacarpal bone and shifting the metatarsal head medially.

Morton's Neuroma (Metatarsalgia)

Origin. Compression and neuroma formation of the plantar nerves.

Symptoms. Piercing pains of the soles by nerve compression between the second, third, and fourth metatarsal heads.

Conservative Nonsurgical Treatment. Arch support.

Surgical Treatment. Extirpation of the neuroma.

Dorsal Hump

Origin. Formation of a marginal bulge along the dorsal joint facets between the navicular and medial cuneiform bones (especially in a hollow or flat foot).

Symptoms. Hump on the dorsal foot interfering with the shoe; early arthrosis.

Conservative Nonsurgical Treatment. Pressure relief inside the shoe.

Surgical Treatment. Dissection of the bulging margins, possibly extirpation of the bursae.

Haglund Exostosis

Origin. Different shape of the calcaneum with a stronger development of the upper posterior edge of the calcaneus.

Symptoms. The area of the Achilles tendon insertion is irritated, possibly causing inflammation and callosities.

Conservative Nonsurgical Treatment. Avoiding pressure from the shoe (by use of a lateral cushion or removal of the stiff cap for the heel).

Surgical Treatment. Dissection of the so-called exostosis.

Spur (Calcaneal Exostosis)

Origin. Bony overgrowth owing to a tendopathy of the insertion at the origin of the short foot muscles (lower exostosis or spur).

Symptoms. The bony overgrowth is directed along a tendon and does not push against the sole. It seldom causes trouble, although it can be diagnosed in 20 percent of adults.

Treatment. Supporting the longitudinal arch, possibly creating additional relief by a special support, sparing the painful area.

March Fracture (Metatarsal Fatigue)

Origin. Fatigue fracture of one or more metatarsal bones.

Symptoms. Increasing pain in the forefoot. The radiograph is often inconclusive during the early stage; later, a fissure or fracture line appears surrounded by spindle-shaped callus.

Treatment. Non-weight bearing for 3 to 4 weeks and then gradually increasing weight bearing.

Achillodynia (Paratenonitis Achillae)

Origin. Degenerative changes of the tendinous sheaths and fibers.

Symptoms. Discomfort in the area of the tendon insertion, swelling and heat along the tendon. A spindle-shaped thickening can be palpated, and the insertion at the bone is painful to pressure.

Treatment. Temporary non-weight bearing (bilateral elevation of the heel). Stimulation of the blood circulation (for example, histamine iontophoresis), possibly temporary immobilization. In case of persistent discomfort surgical revision of the tendon sheath.

Rupture of the Achilles Tendon

Origin. Closed rupture of the tendon within the endangered middle portion. The cross section of the tendon is smallest and there is a marginal area of blood supply, coming from the origin and insertion of the tendon.

Symptoms. Frequently the tendon ruptures with a loud popping sound during increased stress. Minor stress can also cause a rupture, based on previous lesions. Even in a complete rupture of the tendon, plantar flexion is possible with no weight bearing by means of the tendon of the plantaris muscle.

Conservative Nonsurgical Treatment. Immobilization for several weeks (as well as after surgery) runs the risk of a relative elongation of the tendon.

Surgical Treatment. Surgical treatment during the early stage allows an end-to-end adaptation. Afterward, immobilization in a thigh cast in 30° of knee flexion and equinus at the ankle for 3 weeks; another leg cast for 3 weeks, followed by bilateral elevation of the heel (2 cm) for 3 months with gradually increased weight bearing.

PHYSICAL THERAPY

Congenital Foot Deformities in Infants

Congenital deformities include clubfoot, equinus, contracted foot, pes planus, and sickle foot.

Goals of Therapy

- Stretch shortened, contracted muscles.
- Mobilize joints.
- Restore muscle balance.
- Instruct parents on how to exercise with the child.

Conservative Treatment

Treatment of an elastic, minimally affected foot that has not been immobilized in a cast consists of the following:

- Manual correction (see earlier)
- Active exercises
- Use of elastic bandages, if necessary
- Possible use of night splint.

The treatment is repeated several times daily in this sequence. The parents are instructed in detail and take over most of the treatment, if they are able to, as soon as the bandages can be taken off.

Manual correction is done carefully and intensively.

Clubfoot. At first the posterior part of the foot is corrected from a varus into a valgus position; then the forefoot is adjusted with the other hand from adduction/supination to abduction/pronation; finally, an attempt is made to reduce the elevation of the heel (the most difficult part of the procedure).

Equinus (Rare). The calcaneus is pulled down to stretch the Achilles tendon. The stretching fingers touch the back of the heel with the hand fixating the entire sole. Common mistake: Only the forefoot is straightened.

Contracted Foot. The entire foot is pulled down by holding the foot dorsally right below the ankle; the valgus position of the posterior foot and the pronation of the forefoot are adjusted at the same time.

Pes Planus (Flat Foot). Cast correction is usually required. Several times daily manual correction is used in preparation for the cast, at first correcting the plantar flexion of the calcaneus and then decreasing the pronounced dorsiflexion, pronation, and abduction of the forefoot.

Sickle Foot and High Arch. Response to physical therapy is poor; correction is not successful. Passive motion of single segments of the foot by manual therapy can prevent contractures and activate all foot muscles.

Active Exercises with Infants

Single insufficient muscles or muscle groups are stimulated to contract, using the reflex reactions to exteroreceptive and proprioreceptive stimulation. The skin can be stimulated by gentle strokes with the fingertips, dull or pointed wooden sticks, soft or medium-hard brushes, etc. The choice is based on the result, and a change is recommended.

In treating the various deformities there are typical and favorable areas in which to achieve the desired muscle contraction.

Clubfoot. Lateral edge of the foot or lateral part of the sole, from the heel to the small toe; between the third, fourth, and fifth toes; along the outside of the lower leg.

Equinus. Sole, plantar side of the distal phalanges, or also dorsal foot and tibial edge.

Contracted Foot. Sole (especially under the heel), starting under the small toe across the sole to the heel.

Talipes Valgus, Transversoplanus. Inner edge of the foot, middle of the medial sole, between the first and second toes, under the heel.

This information does not necessarily applying to every patient; the stimulation points must be found individually.

Active Exercises with Young Children

As soon as the child shows conscious reactions and performs its own activities, stimulation of reflex contractions is no longer necessary. Now the therapist can work actively with the child, making him or her move the foot and toes in a playful but correcting way. Attractive, colorful toys of suitable size and shape, made of appropriate material, are used to roll, push, grab, lift, and coordinate foot and hand as well as both feet.

The infant is placed on a table for the exercises; the young child is placed on a floor mat. The moving space is enlarged gradually and the feet are prepared for weight bearing. Partial weight bearing is started, sitting on the therapist's knee, on a cylindrical pillow, on a stool or a ball, and moving around on a tricycle without pedals. The therapist supports and corrects the child by manual stimulation.

The child learns to understand better and follow instructions independently to exercise single muscles. In certain movements manual resistance against some directions can also be applied. It is difficult to keep the child's attention.

As soon as the child is walking, exercises against the body weight are more useful. The floor consistency is now important, and opportunities for balancing are stimulating, especially for the short foot muscles. Correction must also be kept in mind during weight bearing.

Clubfoot. Rolling motion across the medial segment of the foot, balancing on the horizontal bar, walking in a squatting position, crossing the feet, etc.

Equinus. Rolling the foot along the floor from the heel to the forefoot, swinging the knees forward; squatting with the heels touching the floor, walking up a slope, tilt board.

Contracted Foot. Rolling the foot from the toes to the heel, standing and walking on tiptoes, walking down a slope.

Talipes Valgus and Transversoplanus. Rolling along the lateral edge of the sole, pressing the toes against the floor, exercising the short foot muscles and the flexor hallucis longus muscle. The muscles are stimulated by shifting the center of gravity into various directions, from one leg to the other, etc.

Treatment After Cast Correction

Evaluation Results

- The foot is in a neutral or overcorrected position.
- Usually there is no contracture in this position.

- Some muscle positions might be tensed and shortened.
- All muscles of feet and legs are weak.
- There is a general lack of activity.

Goals of Therapy

- Mobilize the foot.
- Maintain the result of the correction and avoid recidivism.
- Strengthen the correcting muscles.
- Strengthen the entire leg muscles.
- Promote general gymnastics for infants.

Therapy

As described previously.

Clubfoot

Postoperative Treatment

Soft Tissue Manipulation; Elongation of the Achilles Tendon

Position: Long leg cast in a corrected position with the knee joint in 70° to 80° of flexion.
After 2, 8, and 14 days: Change the cast.
After 3 weeks: Change the cast again and prepare a mold for a splint to wear at night; possibly arch support; discharge patient.
After 6 weeks: Change the cast and fit the splint on an outpatient basis.
After 8 weeks: Cast removal; apply the splint for use at night. Instruct the parents in exercises to mobilize the knee joint, generally strengthen the leg muscles. Parents are advised regularly and the exercise procedure is corrected during the recheck every 3 months.

Transposition of the Tendon of the Tibialis Anterior Muscle

Position: Cast and splint as in achillotenotomy
After 3 weeks: Electrotherapy for the transplanted muscle and active exercises as described previously
After 6 weeks: Weight bearing.

Bone Surgery. Wedge osteotomy and subtalar arthrodesis after completed bone growth.
Position: Long leg cast

After 2 days: Radiographic check and cast change
After 2 weeks: Radiographic check, cut down cast; discharge
After 6 weeks: Radiographic check; remove cast, mold for orthopedic shoes (or arch support including the heels), reapply cast; readmission to the hospital for removal of fixation wires
After 12 weeks: Radiographic check; remove cast; fit shoes; mobilization of all toe joints and proximal tarsal joint; general strengthening of the leg muscles; walking exercises

Normal Development of the Infant Foot

During the second year of life the apparent talipes valgus develops from an apparent pes planus of a newborn. This is necessary for balance as the child starts to walk. At the same time and for the same reason a genu valgus starts to develop and the feet are rotated inward. During the fifth to sixth year the temporary physiologic malpositions start to disappear. They do not require therapy at any time.

Acquired Pes Valgus and Pes Planus and a Combination of Both

Conservative Treatment

The therapist observes these deformities mostly as a sequel to decreased weight-bearing ability and overstress of the foot during childhood, adolescence, and adult life. The normal foot adapts to an uneven surface; however, it must be used constantly in order to maintain this ability. The foot that is compressed in a shoe all the time is unable to function properly. Permanent exercises are required to maintain or restore sufficient muscle strength:

- Unconsciously, allowing the foot enough space for natural movement
- Consciously, by regular muscle training

The parents are made aware of the necessity to provide natural movement for the foot as part of daily care. Shoes and socks are taken off during playing, walking, running, and climbing on natural ground and across obstacles. A few selected exercises are demonstrated for daily use at home. Only severely affected children need regular physical therapy.

Adults can easily learn how to strengthen the muscles of foot and leg. However, the foot gymnastics are successful only with constant exercises and correction of the foot.

Evaluation Results in Considerable Deformities in a Later Stage

- Easy fatigability of feet and legs
- Pain
- Overstretching and weakness of muscles
- Tension and shortening of muscles
- Restricted range of motion
- Gait deviations
- Affection of adjacent joints and the spine

The flexors of the toes and foot, the anterior tibialis and posterior tibialis muscles are weak and overstretched at the same time. Frequently, the extensors of the toes are tensed and shortened.

The reason for the pain must be evaluated before physical therapy, since exercise is contraindicated in cases of inflammation and arthrosis of the tarsal bones. First the pain is eliminated by immobilization; then the muscles are strengthened gradually by isometric contractions, which are later turned into an exercise program.

Goals of Therapy

- Mobilize restricted joint function and stretch shortened muscles.
- Strengthen muscles, train posture and endurance.
- Promote normal movements of the foot.
- Correct gait deviations.
- Initiate general gymnastics and sports activities, training all muscles of the legs, abdomen, and back.

Therapy

Non-Weight Bearing. The painfully tensed muscles are relaxed by use of contrast foot baths. Two tubs are required, since the water level should reach below the knee. Toes and foot joints are moved actively in warm water.

Foot massage (Fig. 12–71), which includes the short foot muscles, can be learned and applied independently by adult patients. This is only partly true for techniques of manual therapy to stretch the shrunken part of the capsules and ligaments. The shortened muscles can also be stretched under ice application to relieve any pain.

342 Lower Limbs

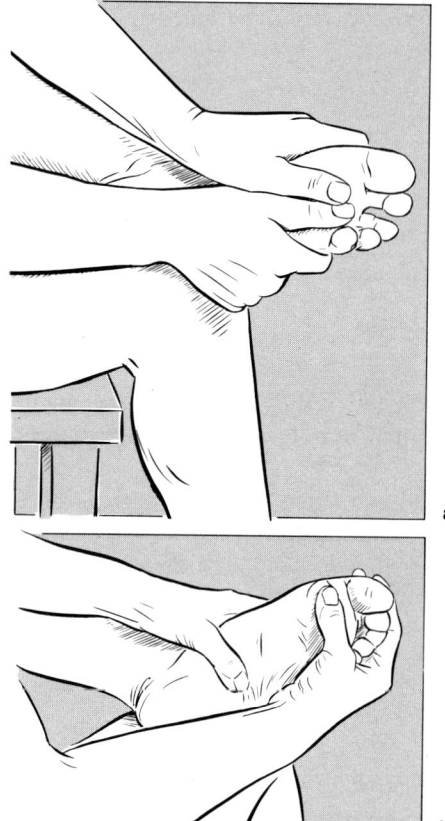

Fig. 12–71 Foot massage.

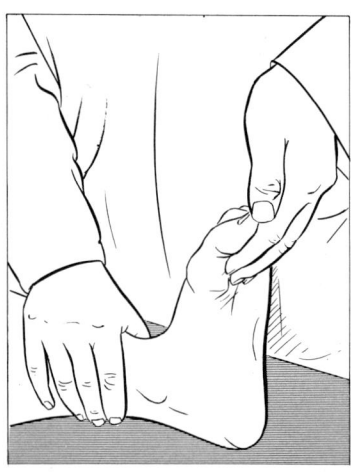

Fig. 12–72 Special training for the flexor hallucis longus muscle.

Foot/Physical Therapy   343

PNF exercises can be used to train insufficient muscles (Fig. 12–72) or muscle groups against controlled manual resistance. In particular, the extension pattern of the legs is indicated, emphasizing the use of toes and foot in the plantar direction.

Non-weight-bearing exercises for the foot can be done using marbles or pebbles, wooden sticks, cubes, paper, towels, elastic rubber bands, rope, ball, and hoop (Fig. 12–73)—the imagination is unlimited. Long-forgotten mobility is restored to the joints of foot and toes; in particular, the short foot muscles are stimulated. At the same time the blood circulation is actively improved. The exercises also relieve pain caused by muscle weakness and tension. They are necessary to prepare for exercises under weight bearing, which allow effective work on the stability of the foot.

Partial Weight Bearing. Knee and hips are flexed at a right angle, the weight bearing is evenly distributed on both feet; for example, strong tension of the transverse and longitudinal arch. The foot becomes "shorter"; with flexion of the

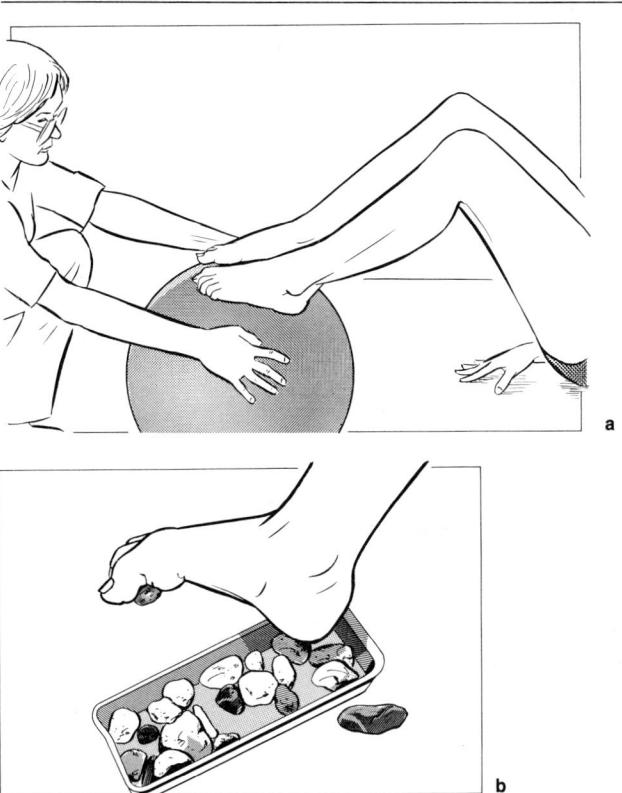

Fig. 12–73 Foot gymnastics without weight bearing, using various equipment. *(continued)*

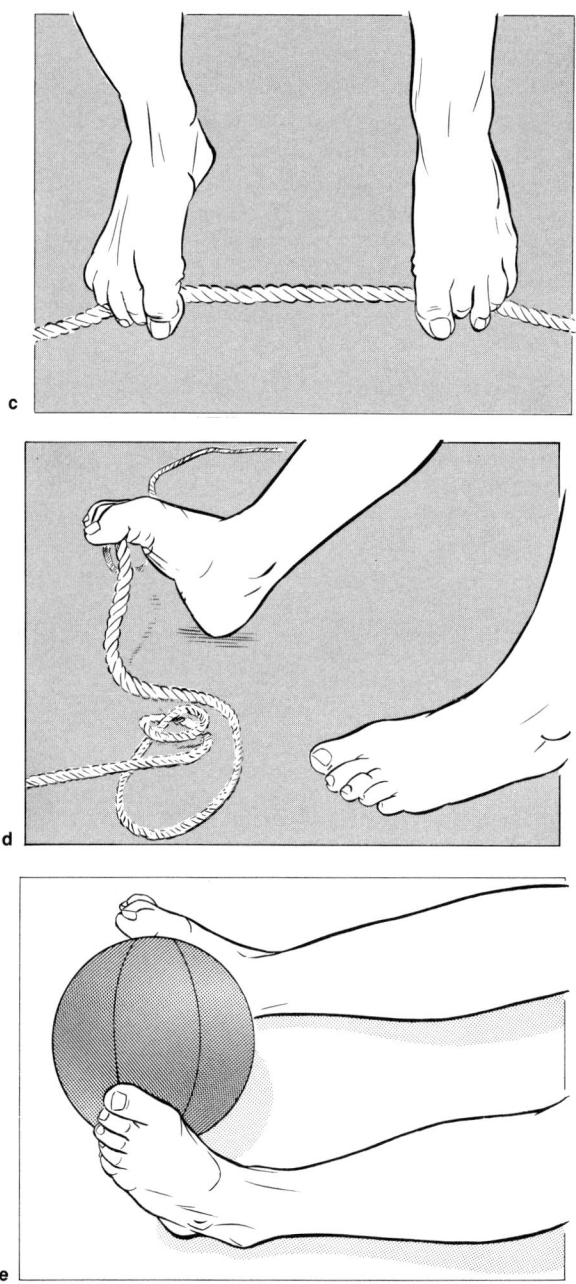

Fig. 12–73 continued

proximal toe joints and extension of the middle and distal toe joints the toe tips approach the fixed heel.

From the same initial position the foot is moved into tiptoe position. The exercise is intensified by the resistance of a sandbag on the distal thigh or by pushing strongly with the hands (Fig. 12–74a). At the same time the buttock muscles are tensed and the trunk is maintained in an upright position.

In a kneeling position on one knee, the foot remains tightly on the floor with tension of the arches, and the therapist challenges the balance by manual resistance (Fig. 12–74b).

Full Weight Bearing. The same principle is also valid: Maintaining the tension of the arches with the shift of body weight. The therapist or partner stabilizes the different strides, balancing on a tilt board or spinning top.

The tiptoe position is exercised only if there is sufficient muscle strength (Fig. 12–75), first supported, for example, on stall bars, with a walking aid, or placing one leg on a stool or chair. In an extreme tiptoe position the heel is in strong supination. The body weight is above the perpendicularly directed first metacarpal bone, if the position is correct (Fig. 12–76). The following muscles are used: flexor hallucis longus, all short foot muscles, tibialis posterior, and triceps surae. The extreme tiptoe position should be especially exercised in children, but adolescents should also maintain this ability.

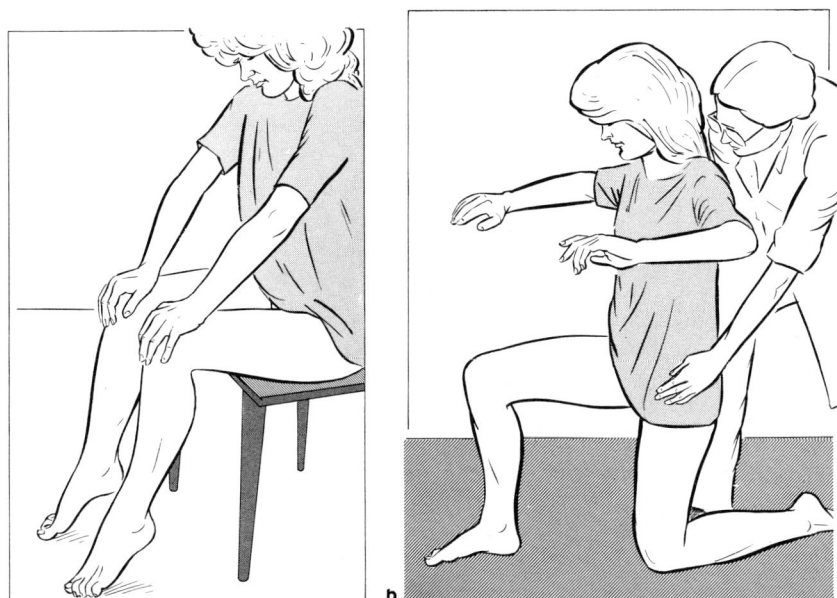

Fig. 12–74 Foot gymnastics with partial weight bearing.

346 Lower Limbs

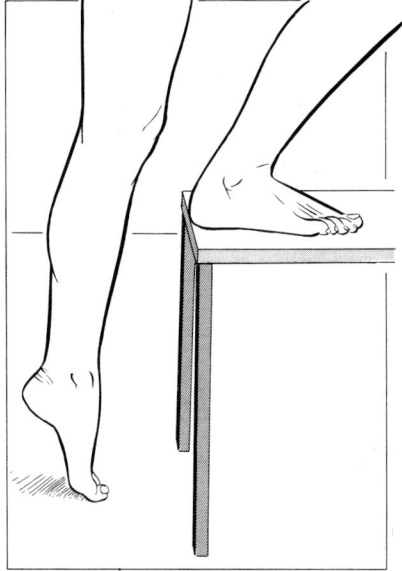

Fig. 12–75 Extreme tiptoe position, supported by one leg.

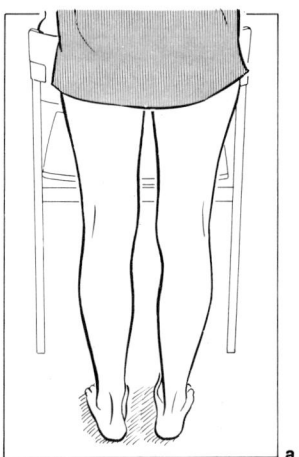
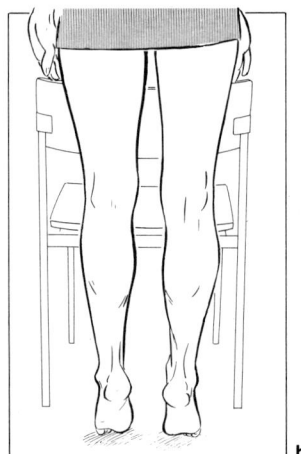

Fig. 12–76 Extreme tiptoe position.

Examples for Exercises

- Walking with special tension of the longitudinal arch and weight bearing on the lateral edge of the foot, avoiding walking on the lateral edge of the tilted foot

- Practicing various gaits in slow motion, for example, crawling, walking like a stork, wide stride, walking in squatting position
- Balancing on horizontal bars (Fig. 12–77), forward and to the sides
- Jumping on a mat, outside on the lawn, pushing with the toes elastically, not stamping
- Climbing stairs, swinging on outer tiptoes
- Walking barefoot up a slope on uneven ground, the steeper the better
- Exercising the spontaneous use of the foot in various gait combinations, changing directions, tempo, posture, rhythmic background (tambourine, music, dancing barefoot on natural ground).

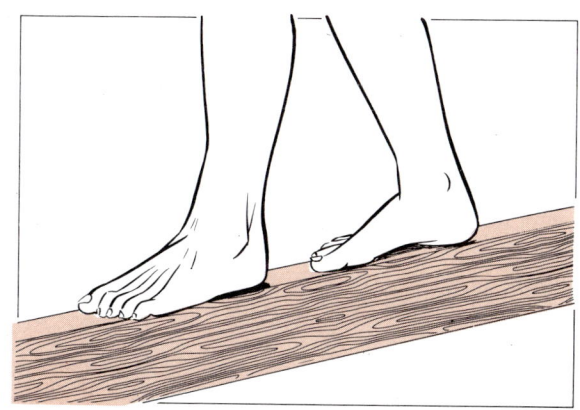

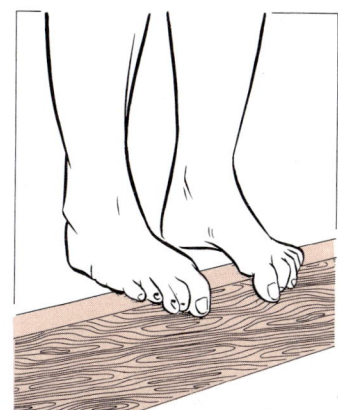

Fig. 12–77 Walking on a balance beam.

In addition to the exercises, advice for patients or parents is important. Shoes with an elastic, soft sole are recommended, and they should be changed several times daily—even the height of the heel. The foot should never be compressed in shoes that are too small or too narrow. The same is true for the size of the socks or stockings.

A few effective and easily understandable exercises should be chosen to instruct the parents. The physician and the therapist should review the success of the treatment at regular intervals.

Contracted Malpositions

Talipes Valgus. The posterior foot is fixed in pronation; the remaining parts of the foot are pliable.

Talipes Planus. The longitudinal arch cannot be restored, either actively (tiptoes) or passively.

Talipes Planus and Valgus. The fixed flat foot cannot be brought in supination either. An attempt with careful physical therapy and exercises can be made if the contractures are responsive to manual therapy without pain.

In a complete malposition of the foot, which causes no problems, local mobilization is avoided. Static effects such as discomfort in the neighboring joints and up the spine are included in the physical therapy and treated according to the symptoms.

Postoperative Treatment

Physical therapy in the postoperative period is the same as in a conservative treatment. Its timing and intensity are based on the type of surgery, the postoperative course, and the individual symptoms. The treatment is aimed at preservation of the surgical result. In addition, splints during the night, arch support, or orthopedic shoes can be used.

Operation in Infant Pes Valgus and Pes Valgoplanus. Procedure according to Schede-Neiderecker.

Position: Long leg cast

After 2 to 4 days: Change the cast.

After 2 weeks: Change the cast and discharge.

After 6 weeks: Change the cast again and cast a mold for an inside shoe; bandage the lower leg.

After 12 weeks: Remove the cast, fit the shoes, and supply them. Exercises are started with mobilization of the foot and intensive strengthening of the transplanted muscle.

Operation of the Pes Valgoplanus in Adults. Arthrodesis of the distal tarsal joint according to Grice.
Position: Long leg cast
After 2 weeks: Change the cast and discharge.
After 6 weeks: Change the cast again, radiographic check. If the result is satisfactory, the shoes are fitted and supplied. Usually physical therapy is not required, except for obviously weak leg muscles. Gait training.

Splayfoot (Talipes Transversoplanus)

Evaluation Results

- Burning pain in the anterior sole of a fatigued foot. Pressure pain below the second through fourth metatarsal heads
- Restricted flexion of the proximal toe joints
- Weak and possibly overstretched flexors of the big toe and especially of the lumbrical muscles. A severe insufficiency is characterized by muscle cramps during unusual stress, which subside as soon as the muscle is actively used again.

Goals of Therapy

- Mobilize the proximal toe joint and the transverse arch.
- Increase muscle strength.

Therapy

- Heat or heat alternating with foot baths in which the toes are moved intensively eliminates the burning of the sole, improves the blood circulation, and relaxes the muscles
- Massage of the short foot muscles, shifting the metatarsals against each other (Fig. 12–78a), passively shaping the arch (Fig. 12–78b)
- Special exercises for the lumbricales and the flexor hallucis brevis muscles; flexing the proximal toe joints with extended middle and distal toe joints. The transverse arch is elevated, whereas the toes remain tightly on the floor. Resistance should also be applied, for example, pulling a weighted towel with the toes (Fig. 12–79).
- General gymnastics for the foot.

Patients exercise with partial or no weight bearing. The exercises have only prophylactic value. A complete splayfoot requires additional arch support.

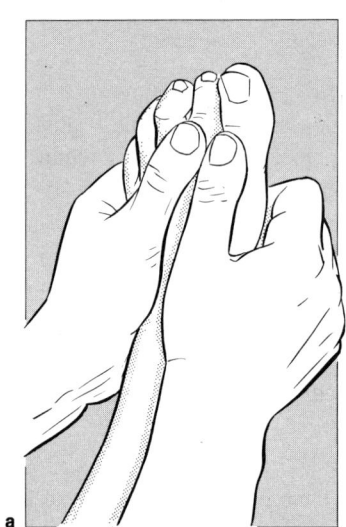 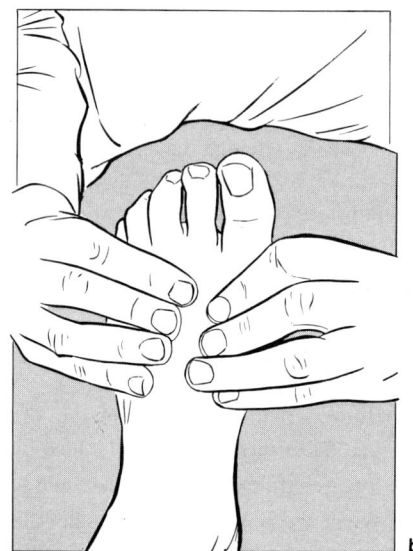

Fig. 12–78 Passive treatment of splayfoot.

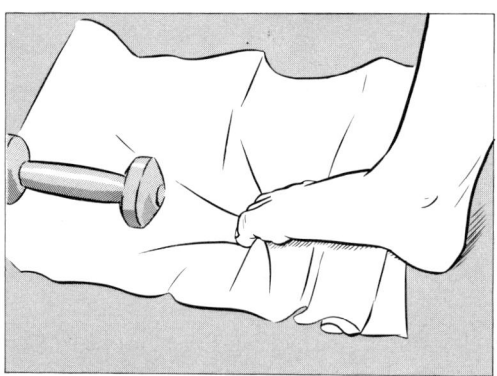

Fig. 12–79 Active exercises for splayfoot.

Hallux Valgus

Evaluation Results

- Pressure pain on the medial side of metatarsal head I increased by irritation. The pain is piercing, frequently occurring in episodes unbearable for the patient.

Foot/Physical Therapy 351

- Pain during motion, non-weight bearing or weight bearing, in already existing arthrotic changes of the proximal joint of the big toe
- Restricted abduction but also flexion and extension
- Weak abductor hallucis and shortened adductor hallucis muscle
- Malposition of the big toe. Unfavorable and increased traction of the extensor hallucis longus by its changed position from the joint with increasing malposition. The rolling motion over the big toe is restricted.

Goals of Therapy

- Stretch the shortened adductor hallucis muscle and possibly the extensor hallucis longus muscle.
- Strengthen the abductor hallucis muscle.
- Provide passive correction of the big toe.

Conservative Nonsurgical Treatment

Vigorous daily treatment is indicated only in the initial stage of the deformity to avoid the development of a severe deformity.

Besides the thorough treatment of the splayfoot, which includes use of an arch support, manual therapy is also used:

- Pain relief through application of ice
- Muscle strengthening: Under traction with the toe in outward rotation perform passive stretching of the adductor hallucis muscle. If there is still no subluxation, perform gliding motions to the side to avoid lateral shrinking of the capsule and ligament.
- Muscle strengthening: Active medial shifting of the big toe by isolated contraction of the abductor hallucis (Fig. 12–80)

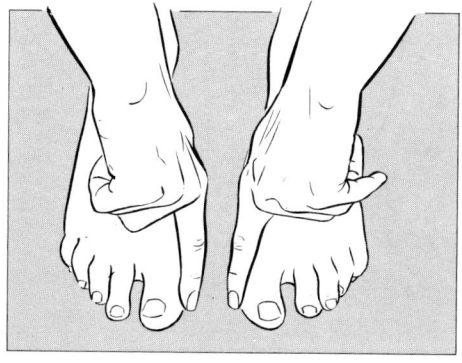

Fig. 12–80 Strengthening the muscles in hallux valgus.

- Passive correction of the position: Wearing a hallux splint at night (Fig. 12–81) and a special sandal (Fig. 12–82) for several hours a day; possibly application of a wedge (Fig. 12–83); avoiding tight shoes and stockings

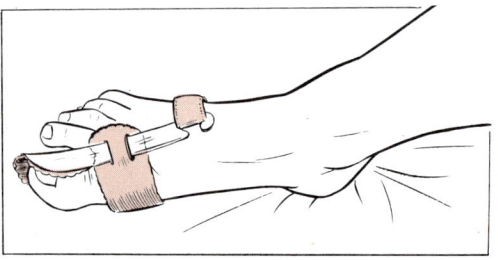

Fig. 12–81 Hallux splint at night.

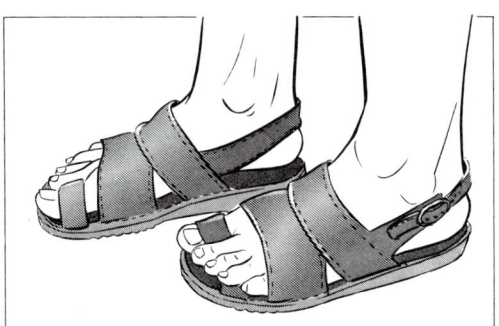

Fig. 12–82 Special sandals for hallux valgus.

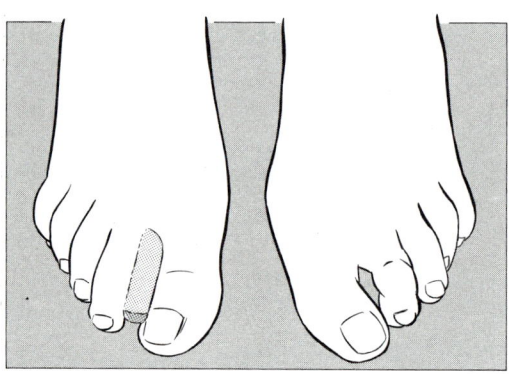

Fig. 12–83 Wedge placed between the toes.

Postoperative Treatment

Surgery According to Brandes

Position: Fixation of the corrected big toe by a wire extension in a cast shoe
After 2 days: Move the legs and change position; sitting up over the edge of the bed
After 12 days: Remove the cast shoe. The hallux splint is applied at night and must be worn at least 3 months, until the correction that has been achieved is secured by scar tissue. At first the foot is mobilized in general. The big toe is moved only actively, in flexion and extension exclusively. Extension of 20° and flexion of 10° are sufficient. No abduction or adduction exercises or any type of mobilization along this plane is avoided. The exercises are brief and performed in preparation for the rolling motion necessary for walking.
After 2 weeks: Walking—during the first few weeks with crutches and gradually increasing weight bearing. Wide sandals are worn, since the foot may still be swollen.
After 3 weeks: Molding of an arch support after the swelling has gone down; discharge; intensive foot exercises at home

Corrective Osteotomy of the First Metatarsal
Position: Short leg cast
After day 1: Standing up, walking without weight bearing
After 2 weeks: Change cast and radiographic check; discharge
After 6 weeks: Change cast and mold arch support
After 12 weeks: Remove the cast, fit the arch support, and supply it to the patient. Start exercises to mobilize all joints of the foot and toes and instruct the patient how to exercise independently. Strengthening of the abductor hallucis muscle and conservative treatment is most important.

Hallux Rigidus

Evaluation Results

- Contracted flexion position of the proximal joint of the big toe
- Restricted rolling motion, possibly painful
- Weakness of the toe elevators

Goals of Therapy

- Mobilize the proximal joint of the big toe.
- Increase muscle strength.

Therapy

- Relieve pain by mobilizing the joint; ice application, traction, and gliding manual therapy techniques; stretching of flexor hallucis longus brevis muscles
- General exercises for the foot.

Postoperative Treatment

Surgical procedure according to Brandes. Postoperative course as in hallux valgus. Intensive strengthening of the levators of the big toe is needed.

Claw and Mallet Toes

Evaluation Results

- Flexion in the middle and distal joints of the toes, more or less contracted; frequently associated with hallux valgus and splayfoot
- Shortened muscles
- Weak muscles
- Pressure pain, increased with the formation of callosities.

Goals of Therapy

- Decrease the contracture and maintain joint mobility.
- Increase the strength of the extensor digitorum longus and lumbrical muscles.

Therapy

- Traction and gliding manual therapy techniques; stretching the flexors of the toes.
- Active exercises against resistance, for the long extensors of the toes
- Treating the splayfoot and general exercises for the foot
- Temporary application of a Hohmann bandage with adhesive tape; excision of calluses and possible application of felt rings until the malposition and the risk of pressure are eliminated
- Arch support
- Avoiding tight shoes.

Postoperatve Treatment

Surgical Procedure According to Hohmann

Position: Correctly applied Hohmann bandage, which must be examined daily and possibly corrected and changed; elevation of the leg

After day 2: Standing up, short walks, circulatory training, moving and elevating the legs

After 3 weeks: Removal of the bandage and molding of an arch support if the foot is no longer swollen; discharge; no local exercises; continue foot exercises for the splayfoot and general muscle weakness

After 6 weeks: Recheck by the physician; fitting and supplying of the arch support.

Fatigue (March) Fracture

After the cast immobilization, manual mobilization of all extensors of the foot and toe joints and foot exercises as in the treatment of pes planus, transversoplanus, and valgus. Strengthening of all muscles of the leg is necessary.

Chapter 13
Typical Orthopedic Surgical Procedures

H. Cotta, G. Rompe, and G. Koester

SURGICAL PROCEDURES OF TENDONS

A tendon repair requires immobilization for 3 weeks and non-weight bearing for another 3 weeks (exception: repair of the flexor tendon with dynamic splinting).

Tenotomy

- Closed tenotomy: A sickle-shaped knife (tenotome, from the Greek *tenon*, tenton; *tome*, cut) is pushed through the skin, led around the tendon, and then pulled back through the tendon (Fig. 13–1).

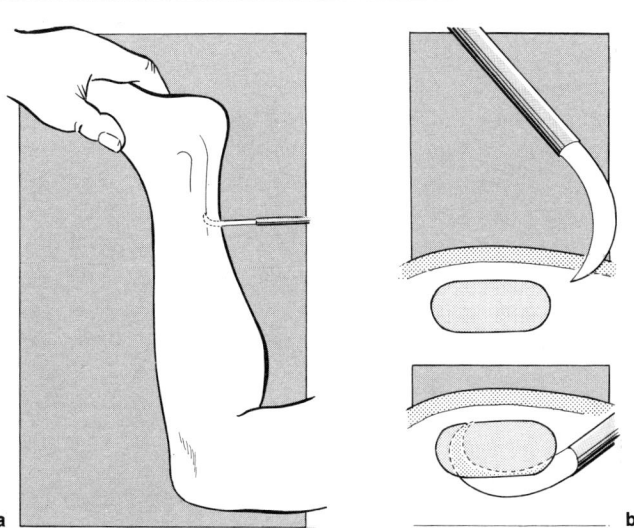

Fig. 13–1 Subcutaneous tenotomy of the Achilles tendon (after Lange).

- Open tenotomy: Operative dissection of the tendon, for instance, to incise the tendon partly or Z-shaped for elongation (Fig. 13–2).

Tendon Suture

- End-to-end suture (Fig. 13–3)
- Pull-out suture: End-to-end suture, using two wires, which permit the sutures to be pulled out after the tendon has healed completely (pull-out wire) (Fig. 13–4)
- Free tendon transplantation: To bridge a tendon defect by an end-to-end suture with the two sections. If at all possible, autologous tendon tissue is used (tendon of the palmaris longus or plantaris muscle).
- Flap tendon transplant: Transposition of a tendon insertion after dissection from the original insertion point on the tendon of a (paralyzed) muscle, or to replace a ligament (e.g., radialis replacement); transposition of flexors from the wrist in a radial paralysis to the extensors of the hand and finger joints (Fig. 13–5)
- ''Pencil box'' plasty (split tendon plasty): Elongation of the tendon by splitting off part of a strong tendon (Fig. 13–6)
- Suture of the flexor tendon with dynamic splinting: End-to-end suture with an additional circular adaptation suture without complete immobilization. A dynamic splint provides for flexion of the wrist and the proximal finger joints, avoiding suture dehiscence. The injured finger is kept in flexion passively with a rubber band fixed to the fingernail. The finger can and should be

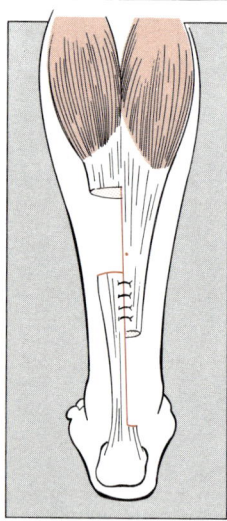

Fig. 13–2 Z-shaped elongation of the Achilles tendon in the sagittal plane.

Surgical Procedures of Tendons 359

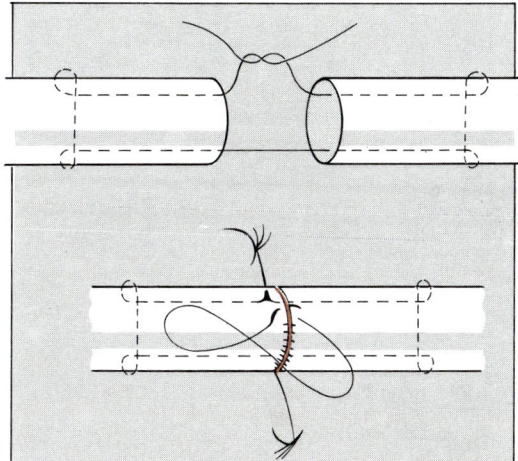

Fig. 13–3 Graphic scheme of the end-to-end suture.

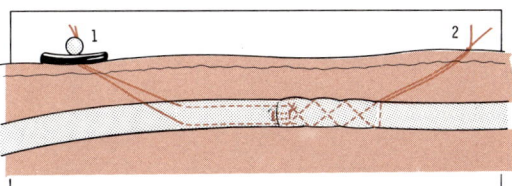

Fig. 13–4 Pull-out suture according to Bunnell. Two wires are used; the first one is used for the tendon repair itself. After being anchored in one tendon section, the wire is pulled transversely through the other tendon section and then pierced through the skin and secured with a knot through a button. The second wire is connected by a loop to the base of the anchored first wire and pierced through the skin at the shortest distance possible. After complete healing of the tendon the first wire is cut at the button and pulled out with the second wire (after Buck-Gramcko).

actively extended toward the splint (immediately postoperatively). Complete extension of the middle joint is especially important to avoid flexion contractures. Flexion is achieved passively with the rubber band. (See Fig. 13–7.)

OPERATIONS OF THE BONES

Osteotomy

Surgical osteotomy (from the Greek *osteon,* bone; *tome,* cut, sawing) is used for the correction (alternating varus-valgus position) of congenital or acquired bony

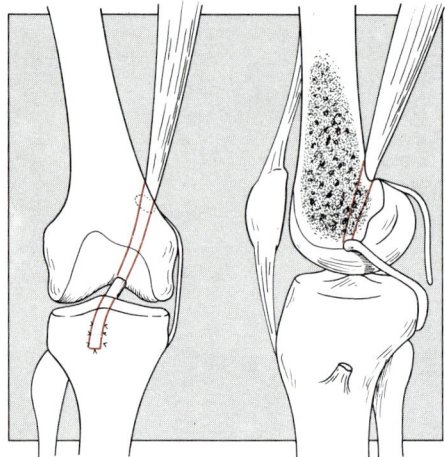

Fig. 13-5 Posterior cruciate ligament plasty according to Lindemann. The tendon of the gracilis muscle is separated from its insertion and as a replacement for the posterior cruciate ligament it is pulled through a drilled canal in the femoral condyle and attached to the posterior tibial surface (after Lang).

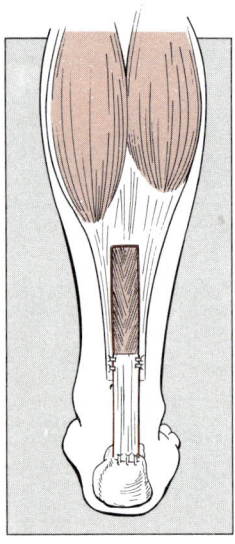

Fig. 13-6 Split tendon plasty ("pencil box"). The central third of the tendon aponeurosis is shifted caudally like a lid of a pencil box (after Lang).

malpositions. Chisels, drills, saws, or laser beams are used and the cuts are straight, wedge-shaped, V- or Z-shaped, or curved (Fig. 13-8).

Healing of an osteotomy can be compared with healing of a fracture and is dependent on age, site, and primary or secondary disease.

Operations of the Bones   361

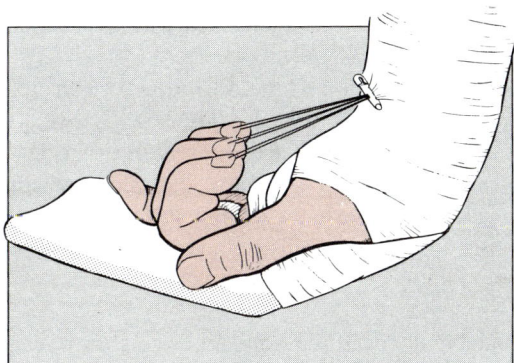

Fig. 13–7 Dynamic splint used after flexor tendon repair. The wrist is placed in 50° of flexion and the proximal finger joint in 30° of flexion (after Buck-Gramcko).

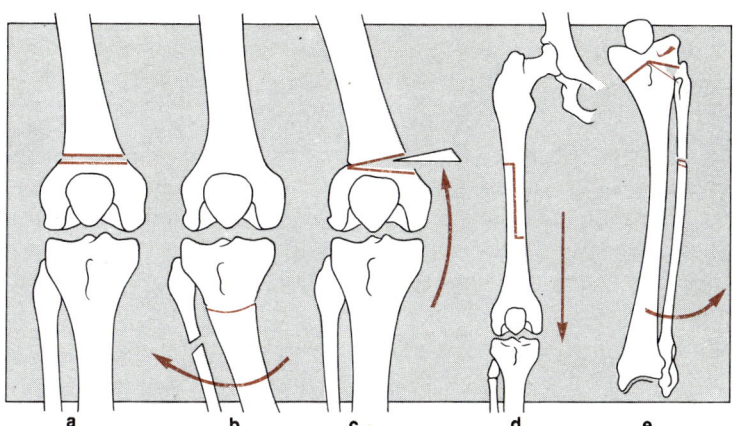

Fig. 13–8 Osteotomy. **a:** Straight; **b:** wedge; **c:** curved; **d:** Z-shaped; **e:** V-shaped.

In the majority of cases the osteotomy is stabilized by an osteosynthesis, preferably by compression plates, intramedullary nailing, or external fixation. Casts affecting the adjacent joints can be avoided in this way, and active assisted exercises can be started postoperatively. Increases in weight bearing are based on the radiographic result. Partial weight bearing is usually not allowed before the twelfth postoperative week. Early partial weight bearing is possible, however, for an osteotomy that is only subjected to compression.

Occasionally an osteotomy cannot be stabilized. An adapting osteosynthesis with nonstable internal wire fixation (Kirschner), plates, nails, or screws can prevent the dislocation of the fragments only if supplemented with an external fixation device or a cast.

Internal fixation is not necessary if the surface of the osteotomy is wide and consists of spongy bone (for instance, through the tibial head or right above the femoral condyles (see Fig. 13–8b, c, and e). The osteotomy will be bridged rapidly by spongy bone, and a second operation to remove the osteosynthetic material is not necessary. Younger patients especially are immobilized in a cast. As soon as bony consolidation is verified radiologically, partial weight bearing is permitted; according to the further radiologic results there is a gradual increase of weight bearing.

Osteosynthetic material implanted in the bone is usually removed after 1 year, since the implant alters the transmission of force and the elasticity of the bone. Especially after the removal of plates and screws, the stability of the implant bed is significantly decreased (screw holes) and weight bearing is affected, owing to the risk of a refracture.

External fixation is removed as soon as possible, i.e., when bony consolidation can be verified.

Elongation Osteotomy

Unilateral elongation osteotomy is mostly done in a Z-shape (see Fig. 13–8d) and is stabilized by osteosynthesis; the more the bone is elongated, the more difficult this is. The abrupt stretching is not well tolerated by the soft tissue (which is actually shorter) and especially nerves and vessels.

More phasic elongation osteotomy using an external device according to Wagner permits a daily increase of the distance by 0.5 to 2 mm with external fixation at the same time (Fig. 13–9a and b). The stretching of the soft tissue is distributed over a longer period and, with appropriate external fixation, permits a

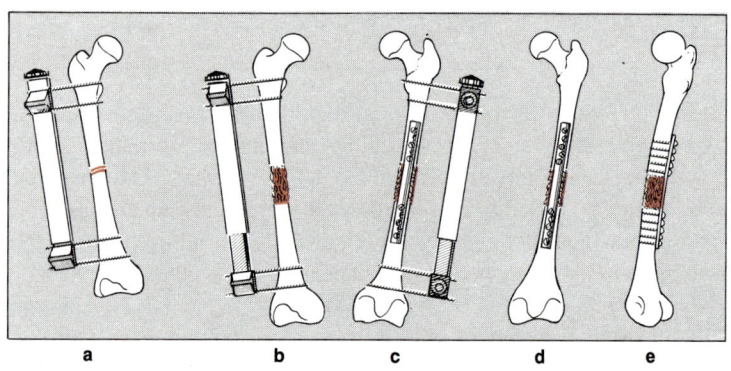

Fig. 13–9 Elongation of the femur with a Wagner apparatus.

lengthening of 5 to 10 cm. After the desired or possible length is reached, external or internal stabilization (Fig. 13–9c through e) is required until the elongated bone shows structural consolidation.

A shortening osteotomy on the contralateral side can be performed instead of an elongation. The shortening is usually achieved at one time (e.g., varus osteotomy or Z-osteotomy) with a stable compression osteosynthesis. Shortening osteotomy on the legs causes a decrease in height. A decrease of more than 2 cm weakens the muscles, since their insertions and origins are closer together. Intensive muscle strengthening is required.

SURGICAL PROCEDURES OF THE JOINTS

Arthrotomy

A joint is opened surgically (arthrotomy, from the Greek *arthron,* joint) to expose pathologic changes, to drain effusions and remove free bodies (osteochondrosis dissecans), or to take biopsies and samples for microscopic and bacteriologic evaluation.

The mobility of contracted joints is improved by incising the joint capsule (capsulotomy). In unstable joints and ligament lesions, capsule and ligaments are tightened and torn ligaments are repaired with autologous material (tendon, fascia skin) or heterologous material (lyophilized dura).

A simple arthrotomy is immobilized for 8 to 10 days until the wound has healed. After surgery to relieve contractures, the joint is placed in the position achieved and actively assisted exercises are started on the next day. After surgery (capsulorrhaphy, ligament plasty), strict joint immobilization is required for several weeks, according to the type of surgery.

Arthrolysis

Stiff joints are released (arthrolysis, from the Greek *lysis,* loosening) by elongation of contracted tendons, sufficient resections of the capsule, sparing the ligaments in order to change the contracted position of the joint into a more favorable, functional position and at the same time to improve mobility.

Postoperatively, the joint is placed in a position opposite to the contraction. Four to six times daily the newly created range of motion is performed, to avoid adhesions. On the fifth day active assisted exercises are started with free motion and passive techniques, as in the treatment of contractures in the third week.

Arthroscopy

This technique (from the Greek *skopein,* to look inside) enables the joint to be viewed through a small skin incision. Different optical devices provide for examination of joint components, which are not visible during a common arthrotomy. For example, a medial arthrotomy of the knee joint allows a good view of the anterior two-thirds of the medial meniscus and the articular cartilage in this area. However, the articular surfaces of the patella and the cruciate ligaments are only partially visible. Almost nothing can be found out about the lateral part of the knee joint and the situation of the posterior part of the medial meniscus.

In atypical clinical symptoms of the knee joint it has proved useful to start the operation with an arthroscopy and choose the surgical approach according to the result.

A simple arthroscopy does not require immobilization or followup treatment. The skin incision is sutured and covered with a sterile dressing.

Arthrodesis

The surgical immobilization of a joint (from the Greek *desis*, connection, rigidity) is achieved by resecting the joint cartilage and compressing the components by internal (Figs. 13–10 and 13–15) or external (Fig. 13–11) fixation.

The joint must be immobilized in a cast if an accurate compression of the polyaxial articular surfaces is impossible (arthrodesis of the distal tarsal joint—subtalar arthrodesis). Bony consolidation is enhanced by roughening the articular surface after removal of the cartilage and implanting spongy bone in the resection gap.

The healing period is usually 16 weeks, during which (as in the healing of osteotomies and fractures) shearing and bending forces must be avoided but axial compression is encouraged.

Stiffening of the spine is called spondylodesis, and it can be performed between the vertebral bodies (ventral spondylodesis) or between the small vertebral joints (dorsal spondylodesis).

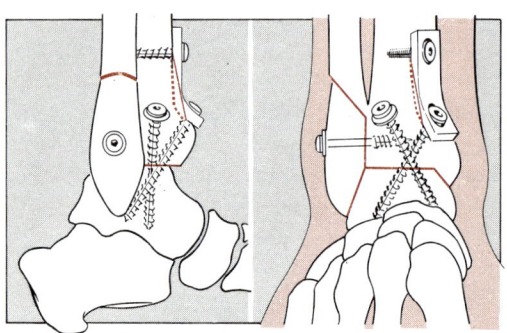

Fig. 13–10 Arthrodesis of the proximal tarsal joint with internal fixation (after Baumgartner).

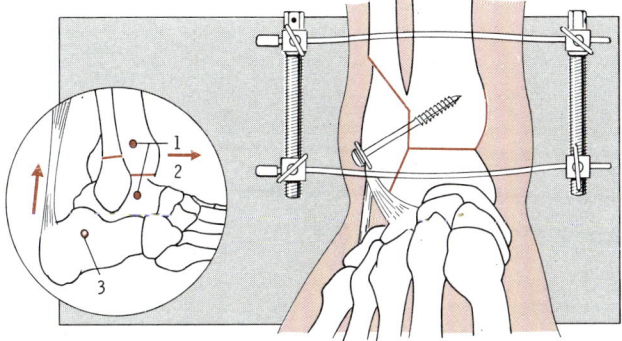

Fig. 13–11 Arthrodesis of the proximal tarsal joint with external fixation. **1:** Position of the Steinmann pins ventrally in tibia and talus. Tension band effect on the Achilles tendon. **2:** Ventral shifting of the tibia. **3:** Location of the third Steinmann pin in case of instability.

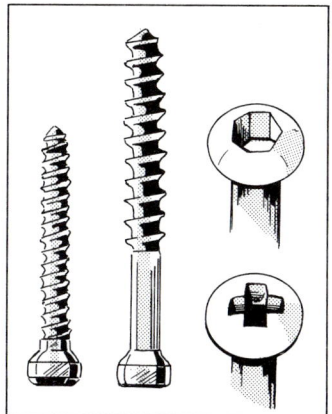

Fig. 13–12 Screws. **a:** Cortical screw; **b:** lag screw; **c:** inner hexagon and Philips cross slit.

Arthroplasty

Joint-forming procedures (from the Greek *plastos*, shaped) in earlier times restored the shape of the stiff joint surgically, after the articular cartilage had been lost. The chances of success are considerably worse (stiffness, instability) than with modern endoprosthetic replacement.

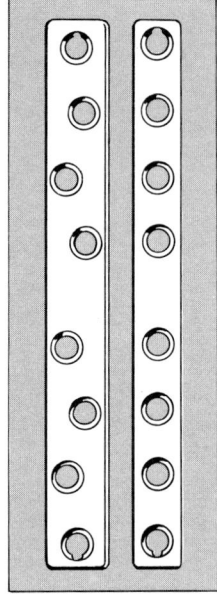

Fig. 13–13 Straight plates. **a:** Wide plate; **b:** narrow plate.

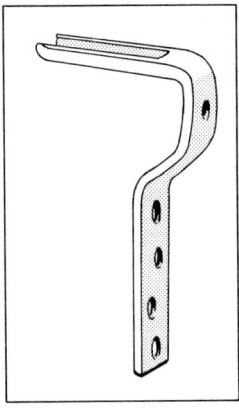

Fig. 13–14 Angled plate. Standard 90° hip plate for adults.

ALLOPLASTIC IMPLANTS

Biomaterials are used for the production of implants (from the Latin *implantare*, to plant). The materials are called alloplastic, since they are made from foreign (artificial) material (from the Greek *allos*, foreign; *plasto*, shaped). They are classified as follows:

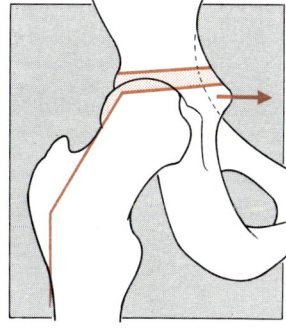 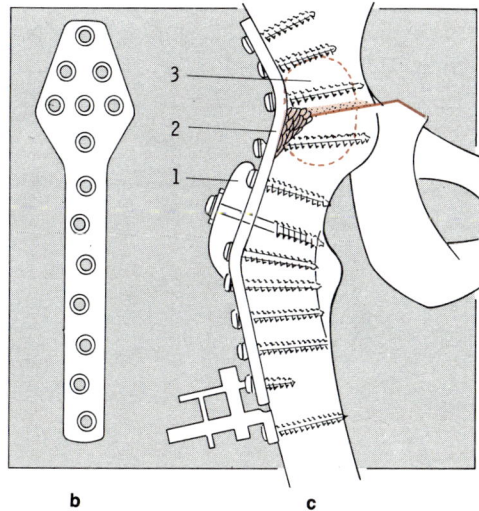

Fig. 13–15 Arthrodesis of the hip. **a:** Planning the osteotomy (modification with pelvic osteotomy); **b:** dorsal view on the buttress plate; **c:** greater trochanter; **1:** fixated by plate and malleolar screws; **2:** addition of spongy bone; **3:** alternatives to stabilize the trochanter (after Baumgartner).

- Short-term implants, which are in place not longer than 1 to 2 years (e.g., implants to stabilize bone fragments during the healing of fractures, osteotomies, arthrodeses)
- Long-term implants, which are supposed to function for a lifetime (replacing joints, ligaments, vessels)

Alloplastic materials cause a foreign-body reaction around the implant. As a protective reaction, the body surrounds it with a connective tissue capsule. Foreign material is not accepted by the body; at best it is tolerated. Testing of biomaterials for compatibility is therefore mandatory before their use. Compatibility and stability of metal implants are based on their corrosive properties. Corrosion is the electrochemical degradation of a material by ion exchange (for instance, between the body and the implant material).

Short-term implants are wires, nails, screws, or plates used to adapt, stabilize, and fixate bone fragments in fractures, osteotomies, and arthrodeses (Figs. 13–12 through 13–15). The compound of fixation material and bone is called osteosynthesis. Because a resorption develops between the bone fragments, the osteosynthesis must align them not only in touch, but also under compression, which secures the alignment after the resorption and prevents the osteosynthetic material from keeping the fracture ends apart.

Endoprostheses (from the Greek *endon*, inside; *prosthesis*, addition) are long-term implants and have become important procedures in orthopedics (Figs. 13–16 through 13–18).

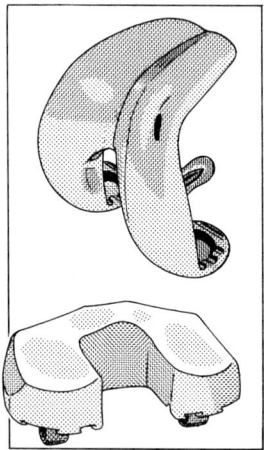

Fig. 13–16 Surface replacement for the knee joint (sledge endoprosthesis).

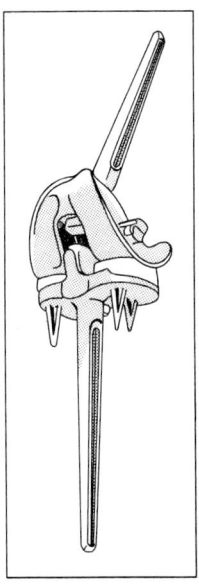

Fig. 13–17 Axial (hinge) endoprosthesis for total replacement of the knee joint.

Alloplastic Implants 369

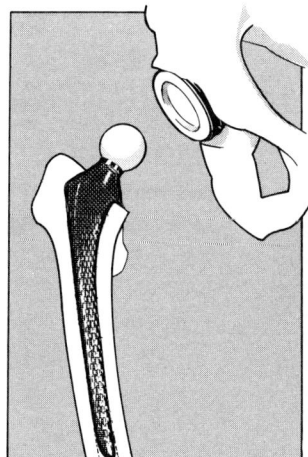

Fig. 13–18 Total endoprosthesis for the hip, implanted without cement.

Endoprostheses for all joints of the body are available for partial and total replacement. They are made of metal, plastics, ceramics, or carbon. Long-term problems are wear of the gliding surfaces and corrosion and fatigue of the materials, causing deformation and breakage of the implants in the body and increased foreign-body reaction of the implant bed. The implant will eventually become loose. Pain-free functioning of a joint is possible only with an absolutely tight fit of the prosthesis inside the bone.

Many endoprostheses are anchored with bone cement. Recent advances have been made to avoid the cement and achieve direct fixation of the endoprosthesis in the bone by using coarsely structured surfaces, fine pores, etc. The bone is expected to grow under compression on and into the structured implant surfaces, resulting in permanent fixation. If weight bearing is delayed, a better body implant bed can be developed.

Chapter 14

Amputations, Prostheses, and Orthoses

E. Marquardt, L.W. Friedmann, and G. Koester

REHABILITATION

Rehabilitation is never based on the efforts of a single person or specialty, but depends on the teamwork of several professional groups and the patient, with the intention of reintegrating the patient with the family, society, and work as much as possible. In this respect even an amputation, if indicated, is not a failure, but the beginning of a rehabilitation process, in which the physical therapist must fulfill an important task. In coordination with the surgeon, the following professionals are involved in the patient's care: the physiatrist, physical therapists, occupational therapists, prosthetists, orthopedic technicians, social workers, psychologists, employers, recreation workers, and teachers.

In amputations, the therapist is challenged, especially during the early phase, with using a prosthesis as early as possible. The reason for this is that the longer one delays the process, the poorer the end results for the patient. Because the therapist must be aware of the entire process of which he or she is a part, a special chapter will deal entirely with this subject.

The defect in amputations should not be emphasized exclusively. One needs to stress also the function of the remaining part of the extremity and the normal extremity. More than that, the stump is part of a whole human being. That truism means that there are other biomechanical considerations. The posture and function of the spine must also be assessed, since each amputation requires a compensatory use of trunk muscles. Furthermore, rehabilitation implies the optimal use of the patient's brain, hands, and social and vocational skills. Each therapist must view the patient as a person with a defect and problem, not as a stump to be fitted and treated.

Patients using orthoses must be evaluated with respect to their unassisted ability to function (in the legs to bear weight) without the orthosis before treatment. The function of the remaining part of the extremity and the normal extremities is crucial to decision making and must be emphasized.

For all patients, the patient and the health care professional must make many cost-benefit judgments. Is the proposed device/treatment worth it to me (the patient)? The cost is not only monetary but also in appearance, comfort, convenience, time lost from work for repairs, and so on. The benefit is improved function. Do I want/need that improved function? Do I want it enough to pay the prices? Am I getting it to please someone else (doctor, spouse, child), or is it really for me?

Amputations

The term amputation refers to the removal of parts of the body. If an extremity or part of an extremity is removed at a joint, this is called a disarticulation.

The indication for an amputation is usually to preserve life, for instance, after an accident or illness (arterial occlusion, malignant tumor, unresponsive infection, etc.). A functional indication might also be to correct an acquired or congenital deformity.

In approximately 10 percent of patients the upper extremity and in 90 percent the lower extremity is amputated. According to Baumgartner (1973), the number of leg amputations owing to problems of the arterial blood circulation in Switzerland has increased within the past 40 to 50 years from 31 percent to 90 percent. In Western nations the cases of arterial occlusion leading to amputation constitute about 80 percent to 90 percent of the total number of amputations. Some of the major causes are eating habits in combination with lack of exercise, diabetes mellitus, smoking, and longer life expectancy. In the Orient, vascular disease is far less common.

Patients requiring amputations because of malignant tumors are mostly children and adolescents. Amputations after accidents mostly involve adolescents and middle-aged patients. Amputations resulting from problems of the arterial blood circulation are mainly indicated for patients who are prematurely aged or over 60 years old and who suffer from arterial circulation disturbances of the remaining leg, coronary disease, diabetes mellitus, urologic and cerebral problems, and general geriatric symptoms, which must be considered during the treatment, since they complicate the care that is rendered and worsen the prognosis.

During recent years amputation techniques have improved considerably. Most important are subtle plastic-surgical techniques such as myoplasty (Dederich, Burgess), osteomyodesis (Weiss), or osteomyoplasty (Ertl). In a myoplasty, antagonistic muscle groups are united across the bony end; in an osteomyodesis (Fig. 14–1), the muscle ends are fixed to the bone by wires pulled through drill holes. The muscles work physiologically after the operation, since the length-tension relationship has been almost restored, and sensory feedback to the brain is

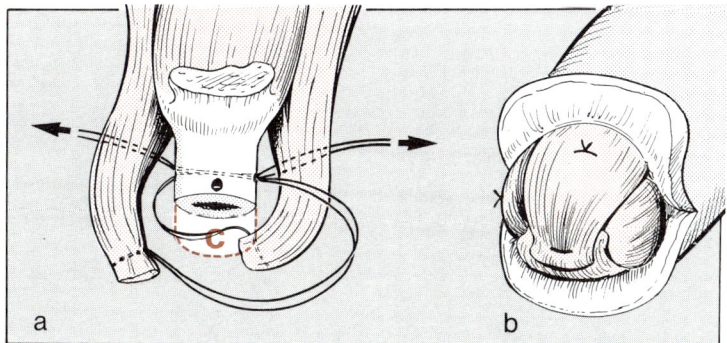

Fig. 14–1 Myodesis and myoplastic coverage of the amputated limb.

more normal, creating favorable conditions for wearing the prosthesis, weight bearing, and the blood circulation in the amputated limb. The lower extremity can be expected to gain full weight-bearing ability only if amputation is at the level of the posterior foot (e.g., modified Pirogoff stumps according to LeFort or Spitzy), Syme stumps, or disarticulation at the knee joint.

The level of amputation of an upper or lower extremity is not based on a general scheme of "sites of election," but is oriented toward the accident or the underlying disease. Amputations at levels owing to prosthetic deficiencies are uncommon today, except that enough room should be left for an internal knee unit in the above-knee ablation if a true knee disarticulation is not possible.

In the upper limb, all length that can be preserved should be, with few exceptions. The exceptions apply mainly to secondary revisions for deeply considered functional and cosmetic reasons, in consultation with the patient. Because the upper limb is not weight bearing, scars can be almost anywhere, and grafts, even split thickness grafts, which are often disastrous on the leg, are useful.

Special Surgical Techniques for Upper Extremity Amputations

Krukenberg Plasty. This operation transforms the amputated forearm into a plastic, sensate, prehensile organ (Fig. 14–2a and b; Krukenberg, 1917). It markedly improves the function of patients with a bilateral loss of the hands and is especially advantageous for blind patients.

Angular Osteotomy of the Humerus. This procedure facilitates a stable fit of the prosthesis. It leaves the shoulder free. The complete active motion of the shoulder joint and shoulder girdle can be harnessed to activate the prosthesis (Fig. 14–3a and b; Marquardt, 1972). This has sensory as well as motor and functional implications. The above-elbow patient can use the limb behind the back and above the head and always knows where the terminal device is in space. The sensory

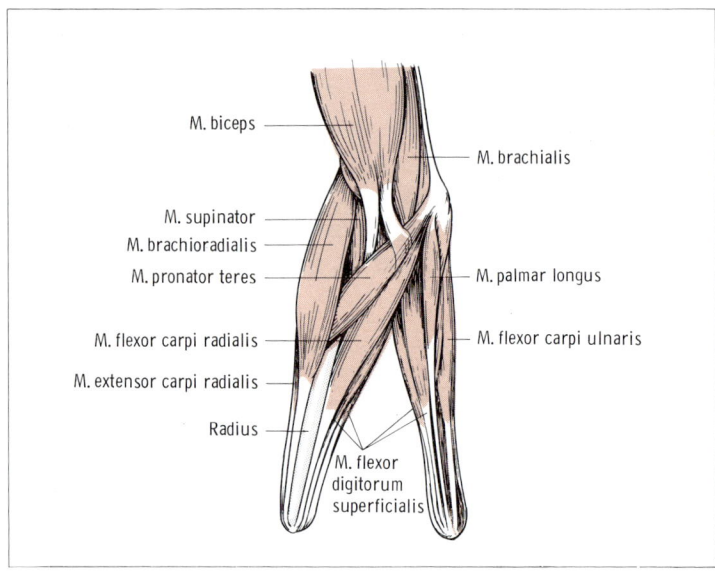

Fig. 14–2 a: Krukenberg plasty (according to Krukenberg, 1917). **b:** Combination of a body-powered cable controlled below elbow prosthesis with a standard hook as a terminal device (top) and a Krukenberg prehensile forearm (bottom).

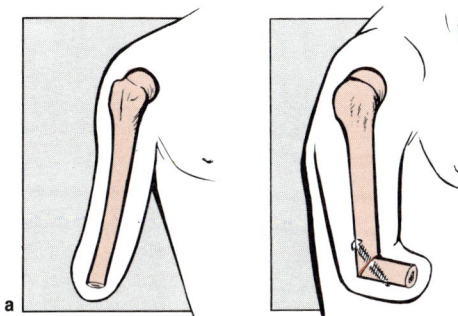

Fig. 14–3 a: Long above-elbow stump before; **b:** after an angulation osteotomy according to Marquardt.

importance of what we do prosthetically often eludes us, more often in the legless than in the armless.

Plastic Coverage of the Bony Amputation End with a Cap. This is the method of choice in pending bone penetration through the distal end of the upper arm or the lower leg during childhood and adolescence. The cap on the bone end facilitates partial weight bearing and helps to avoid further reamputations during prosthetic use (Figs. 14–4a and b and 14–5a and b; Marquardt, 1975, 1981). This is used after failure of skin traction used all day and night (Friedmann and Friedmann, 1985).

Postamputation Care Methods

There are many purposes for postoperative care. The most important is to ensure rapid wound healing with minimal scarring or adhesion to the underlying bone. Another is to diminish the size and volume of the stump so that better prosthesis control can be attained. The size of the stump depends on such factors as the muscle mass, its fluid content, and the subcutaneous fat. There is muscle atrophy with disuse, which occurs more quickly if the muscles are not reattached. There is shrinkage in stump size because of muscle atrophy and edema reduction at the same time the subcutaneous fat accumulates, since the patient is generally inactive. The fat disappears most rapidly with pressure. Which process is predominant in the individual depends on body structure, activity level, treatment method, and so on. Early after amputation, healing is the primary concern. Prompt healing by "first intention" is the quickest, safest, and cheapest item on the therapeutic agenda.

Postoperatively, the application of a prosthesis as early as possible is desired. The prognosis of the amputee is based not only on his or her age and the reason for

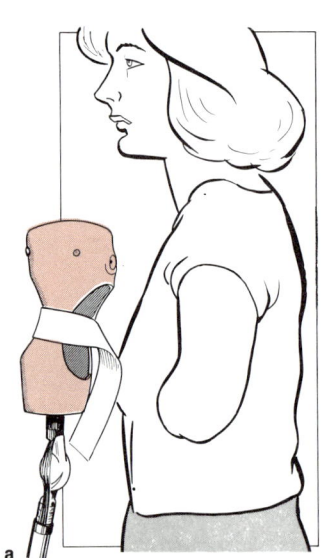 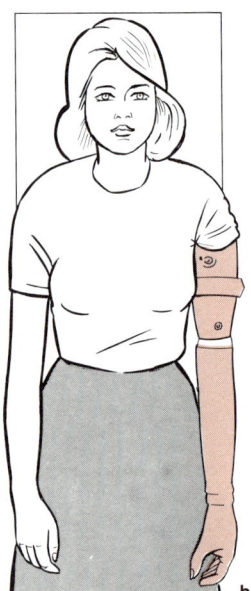

Fig. 14–4 After an angulation osteotomy a myoelectric above-elbow prosthesis is fitted to the stump, leaving the shoulder free. **a:** The prosthesis is still uncovered; **b:** the same person wearing the finished prosthesis.

the amputation, the level of the surgical intervention and number of necessary procedures, the technique, the wound healing, and the prosthesis, but also on the amputee's mental attitude toward the changed body image, self-image, and the further course of rehabilitation.

Many methods are in use to achieve prompt healing with subsequent stump shrinkage, avoidance of postsurgical complications, and gait training.

A method that is now diminishing in popularity is the rigid total contact dressing with or without a prosthesis immediately attached. The socket prevents edema and helps the stump to heal. It is especially useful for an immediate prosthesis for children, for upper limb amputees, or traumatic amputees. For vascular cases, immediate ambulation can cause serious damage in the elderly except under the most meticulous circumstances. An amputee team must be available 24 hours a day, 7 days a week. The principle of the rigid dressing used without a prosthesis immediately is excellent. Fitting the prosthesis with a delay of 2 weeks is safe and does not significantly delay discharge. After 3 months of artificial limb use, the gait pattern is no better for the person who has had immediate prosthetic fitting than it is for the individual who has been fitted after a 2-week delay. A variant is casting the stump with a hard polyurethane foam in the operating room. It is placed inside a zippered casting stocking.

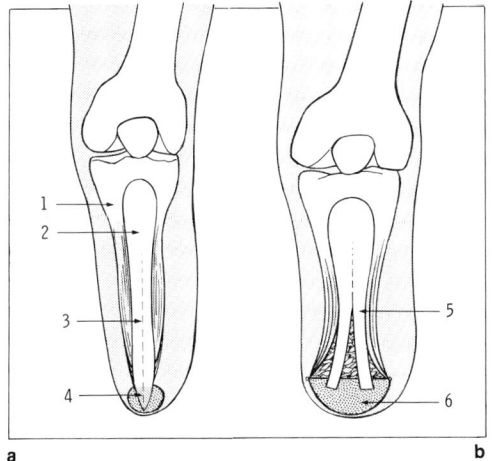

Fig. 14-5 Stump capping surgical procedure. **a: 1:** Tibia; **2:** anterior edge of the tibia; **3:** longitudinal osteotomy; **4:** spike of bone, protruding into the bursa shortly before perforation. **b:** Two bony pillars are built by a longitudinal osteotomy and are spread carefully **5**. They are fit **6** into an autogenous bone-cartilage transplant (fibular head, iliac crest, or if possible from the amputated material). The transplant will be temporarily fixed with two crossed Kirschner wires and be anchored with periosteal-muscle sutures. (Atlas of Limb Prosthetics, Mosby 1981).

A less dangerous and more easily applied technique is that of using the Unna semirigid dressing. It is more easily changed and has fewer instances of wound breakdown. It is vital that the "nip-and-tuck" technique used for plaster of Paris not be used. When the direction of the bandage must change, the material should be cut. The dressing should usually go over the proximal joint, but in some instances this is not practical. The Unna dressing may be used in place of a cast of the stump. If desired, it may also be used with a provisional leg.

The technique of controlled environment treatment developed by Redhead (1973) uses a machine that supplies air at a controlled humidity, pressure, and temperature that is cleansed of bacteria. The limb is covered with a clear sterile plastic bag of special design. The pressure control is important for edema prevention. This provides a perfect environment for primary wound healing. It does not cause the stump to shrink. The amputee can be placed in a walker with ischial tuberosity weight bearing above (or through) the proximally tightly fitted plastic bag and early walking can be started. Favorable results have been reported using this technique. The advantage of Redhead's technique is continuous wound control during standing and ambulation activities. The technique is experimental. At some future time, with further improvements, this may become the treatment of choice.

Hyperbaric oxygen treatment is excellent for increasing wound healing but is costly. The Topox unit only gives 1.06 atm of pressure, which is not enough to adequately stimulate growth of cells. Equally as good is using a plastic bag into which oxygen flows from a tank or wall distributor. Healing is considerably speeded, especially in vascular cases.

Another technique is airbag compression. A variation is to use a temporary prosthesis with an airbag inside it. The best of these is the Roehampton design, which has an additional inner airbag to support the distal tissues, to avoid reopening the wound. Healing and shaping can go on concurrently. The stump must be observed to assure that excess walking is not causing damage. These limbs should be differentiated from pneumatic walking aids, which do not have a circumferential airbag, but are merely above-knee temporary limbs that adjust in size by means of one or more air-filled bags. The former encloses the stump.

Simple dressings on stumps are used for draining wounds. For open amputations, skin traction must be used immediately and continuously and not be interrupted. The only exception to using traction is when the stump is much too long and will need to be shortened, so the inevitable bone death is not important, and the decision to surgically revise the stump later has been made.

Stumps may be shrunken slightly with elastic dressings. Elastic bandages are theoretically the best means of shrinking the stump by means of elastic compression. They must be put on correctly all the time. They can act as a tourniquet if not properly applied. They predispose to "window edema" if the turns slip when the patient turns in bed, or if even one aide or the patient applies it incorrectly. For this reason we prefer elastic stump-shrinking socks so that proximal compression is always less than distal compression. When pulled up high so that they are in contact with the entire surface of the stump, they are useful. They are prevented from rolling down by a garter belt or a built-in belt. When more pressure is tolerated, they should be overlaid with an elastic bandage. If the wound is still partly open or fragile, a ventilated sheath next to the skin and adherent paper tape over the wound margin prevents the wound from opening when the socks are pulled on.

The best method of shrinking and shaping a stump is the artificial limb itself. The early use of the permanent leg is not advisable, since rapid shrinkage is common, requiring multiple modifications and replacement of the limb in a short period of time. It is better, both medically and economically, to use a temporary provisional prosthesis. It has a custom-made socket in its best formulation. This is attached to leased components that the patient eventually returns to the prosthetist. Modification or replacement of the socket is inexpensive.

Temporary prostheses can be of many types. There are prefabricated limbs available of many materials, shapes, and sizes. Because the thigh is muscular and easily deformed, it is easier to get a good fit for the above-knee stump than for the below-knee stump. Adjustability of the socket is the rule for the above-knee prosthesis. Prefabricated below knee limbs have not been used, as the bony stumps are hard to fit properly. Stock sizes as with above-knee limbs are not possible.

For better-fitting above-knee sockets and all below-knee sockets, custom molding is needed. Different methods are in use. One is to make a conventional female cast of plaster and attach a limb to it. That cast may also be used as a mold to make a male and then a female plastic socket, either thermoplastic or thermosetting. A thermoplastic socket can be made directly on the stump with certain materials

A newer method is to use glass or plastic beads in a bag around the stump. When the surrounding air is evacuated, the beads form a rigid cast around the tissues. The cast may be used either to make a socket directly or as the female mold mentioned earlier.

Shape-sensing methods using contour mapping and laser sensing have been used experimentally, sometimes with computerized shape modification in tandem with automated milling machines to make thermoplastic sockets.

The best design for the socket has yet to be worked out, either for the below-knee or for the above-knee limb. Research is still being done because of inadequate satisfaction with present designs for some individuals. The above-knee socket should be more or less quadrilateral but have more rounded contours than usual. There should be no undercutting of the brims. The brims should have larger radii of curvature than normal. The ischial seat should not be parallel to the floor, but be angulated upward 20 degrees. The distal circumference of the socket should be smaller than for the final limb to "plug in" the tissues as they shrink. In this manner the body weight, during walking, is used to apply pressure to atrophy the fat. As the atrophy proceeds, the socket is redesigned by pads inserted into it to continue the process. Overall shrinkage is compensated for by adding stump socks. The stump is thus shaped as well as shrunken.

The below-knee temporary socket is the same in design as the permanent socket but has the following modifications. The anterior lower socket below the tibial tubercle is rounded to fit the contour of the stump. The end of the stump may be left free in an air chamber to avoid contact with the end of the stump, although it is best to have soft and then firm total contact. As the stump shrinks, pads will need to be inserted to take up the space of the atrophying tissues, especially along the sides of the tibial crest and in the popliteal space. The tissues around the patellar tendon and the medial tibial flare also shrink slightly. As shrinkage proceeds, pads on either side of the tibial crest will be needed to prevent pressure over the sensitive crest. Support for the medial tibial flare is needed.

The below-knee limb usually has a solid ankle cushion heel (SACH) foot, while the above-knee limb usually has either a lightweight SACH foot for the elderly or a single-axis foot for middle-aged persons who need stability, especially during standing. The above-knee limb for the elderly has a knee unit that can be locked for stability while learning to walk. Where it might be possible for the patient to later learn to walk with the knee unit open, a knee unit that has a constant friction unit should be chosen. In most cases we use the same knee unit for the temporary limb as we expect to use in the permanent, if payment for it can be arranged. We sometimes have to change units if the patient experiences difficulty with a complex or heavy unit.

The patient starts to learn to walk with the temporary prosthesis. It is a treatment method as well as an ambulation aid. As the stump shrinks because of the pressure of the body weight in the limb, adjustments must be made to the socket and the alignment. It helps to maintain the patient's vascular and nervous reflexes. Because the individual can stand and walk, it helps to prevent both emotional and physical deconditioning and the adverse consequences of bed rest. It teaches the person how the limb looks and works. Thus it shows both what it can and cannot do. It allows the patient and the team to set appropriate achievable goals. It also should be used to evaluate the need for special components as the patient learns effective limb use. In some instances the provisional limb serves as a permanent limb for a debilitated individual.

The patient is discharged from the hospital ambulating with the temporary limb. He or she uses it at home and on the job for between 3 and 6 months, until the stump is more or less its final size. The amount of time required depends on the patient's weight and activity level. When the patient is ready for the permanent prosthesis, he will be able to wear it at least 1½ years before it needs to be replaced. Our preference with all new amputees is to use a provisional artificial limb just as soon as the wound is healed. If wound healing is delayed, we use the bypass prosthesis described below. Some research reports use the time between surgery and provision of the "permanent" artificial limb as the measure of success. In our review this is erroneous, since the limb then needs to be replaced soon because the stump size changes rapidly. It is the efficacy of the ambulation, the safety, and the comfort that determine how successful the patient is.

The effective use of an artificial limb depends on the patient's neuromuscular coordination and cardiovascular state. This can be estimated by asking the patient about his or her previous agility. As a rule of thumb, if a patient cannot learn to walk well with a walker without an artificial leg, she often has great difficulty using an artificial leg. It is better to over-prescribe temporary artificial limbs and to use those limbs for their predictive value. This is medically best and most cost-effective. Early ambulation maintains coordination.

Endurance is best enhanced by use of the temporary artificial leg. The use of the provisional limb prevents contracture formation.

Where there is a delay in wound healing from any cause and the healing time is estimated to be more than 1 month, a bypass prosthesis may be constructed so that the patient may ambulate and continue training. This method, originated by Allen Russek, helps to reduce deconditioning while not keeping the wound from healing. The bypass limb has no socket for the stump, but leaves it open and free to heal. Weight bearing is proximal to the stump end. The below-knee bypass may bear weight on the patellar tendon if the open wound is distal, or on the ischial tuberosity if it is proximal. Above-knee bypass limbs bear weight on the ischium. After the wound is healed, conventional temporary prostheses are used, followed by permanent ones, following the usual criteria. The indications for the bypass limb include not only the as-yet unhealed stump, but also whenever weight should not be borne by the stump. Examples include ununited fractures or fusion, malunions, severe arthritis of the proximal joint, neuropathic arthropathy, chronic skin lesions over the weight-bearing surfaces, severe osteomyelitis, or a chronic painful stump.

Immediate Postoperative Prosthetic Fitting in Lower Limb Amputees

If the institution has the proper staffing, and the team to do immediate prosthetic fitting is available, especially in young amputees and arm amputees, after tumor or trauma, with a primary wound closure, a cast is applied, enclosing the stump and the adjacent joint. The procedure is done on the operating room table, relieving the cast over projecting bony portions such as the patella or the fibular head. The cast for an above-knee amputation must fit properly to the ischial tuberosity and for a below-knee amputation, to the patellar tendon, to avoid disturbed wound healing caused by weight bearing on the end of the amputation site. Then a trial prosthesis is attached to the cast. The patient gets out of bed on the first postoperative day, assisted by two persons, according to his or her strength, and uses parallel bars, a walker, or crutches for support. On the second day, if possible, the first steps are tried, putting no more than 10 percent of the body weight on the prosthesis; from the fourth postoperative day on, the prosthesis is loaded increasingly in standing, balancing, and ambulation activities.

It is detrimental for the stump to slip within the cast. Therefore, the therapist must watch continuously to be sure that the cast remains in the correct position during ambulation activities. The postoperative wound pain is usually less than in the traditional treatment, if the cast fits properly. Contractures can be avoided with the immediate application of a prosthesis for early standing and ambulation. The muscle coordination important for balance and walking with the final prosthesis starts to develop immediately after the amputation. Patients with strong muscles and no circulation problems will soon be able to change from the walker to crutches and canes. In our experience they become independent rather quickly, using their trial prosthesis. However, the immediate application of a prosthesis requires careful observation of the patient. The physician in charge must be informed about any rise of temperature, increased pulse rate, or pain, for the cast must then be bivalved and the wound inspected.

The first postoperative cast will be changed 2 days after surgery. The drains will be removed, and new sterile dressings will be applied. A new cast and prosthesis are manufactured after the removal of the stitches (approximately 3 weeks after surgery), which at that time are no longer needed to immobilize the adjacent joint. This joint is then actively exercised every day under the therapist's supervision. The trial prosthesis can be taken off for therapy and during sleep (Fig. 14–6a and b).

Ambulation training is started with standing and balancing in order for the patient to get used to the prosthesis and to relearn balance. Walking is a process during which one loses one's balance on one foot and catches it on the other foot. For this reason the achievement of balance is crucial to ambulation training. Special training and techniques are used according to the level of amputation and the type of prosthesis used. With each, the preliminary training in parallel bars is most important and often short-changed.

The trial prosthesis should usually have the same prosthetic knee joint as the permanent prosthesis. In debilitated individuals sometimes a locked knee is used early, which can later be replaced by a friction knee. We use it for 3 to 6 months, until stump shrinkage, conditioning, and training are completed. The patient goes home to work with the temporary limb. The permanent leg is then fabricated after

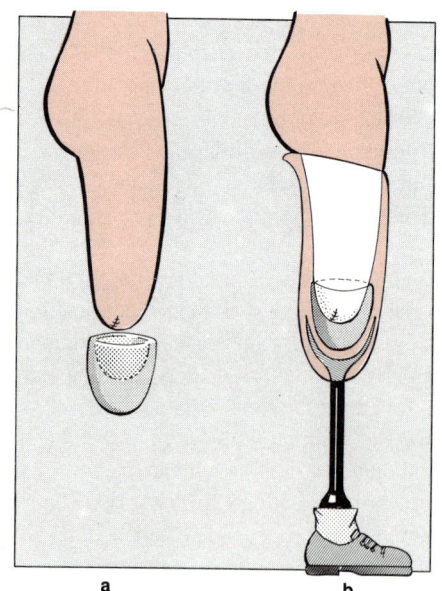

Fig. 14–6 Early application of a postoperative prosthesis (here still without a knee joint) after an above-knee amputation.

the patient has really become used to the prosthesis. It can then be used for years with minimal adjustments. In amputations resulting from trauma, while a permanent prosthesis can be supplied to patients 6 to 8 weeks after surgery, we prefer to have the patient use the provisional limb for about 3 months so that stump shrinkage and conditioning are well advanced. In tumor patients it is advisable to use an adjustable prosthesis until the completion of the chemotherapy, since the treatments usually cause fluctuations in the size of the amputated limb.

Amputees undergoing chemotherapy treatment may exhibit high pulse frequencies during the exercises; frequencies up to 160/min have been recorded telemetrically. The internist or pediatrician in charge should tell the physician or physical therapist what frequency should not be exceeded, to avoid cardiac problems. The same supervision is necessary for patients with arterial occlusion.

In our clinical routine, immediate application of a prosthesis has been abandoned for amputees with arterial occlusion, especially when there is subsequent tissue necrosis. A trial prosthesis is applied only when the wound shows primary healing.

For knee disarticulations or below-knee amputations resulting from arterial occlusion, immediate application of a bypass prosthesis is recommended. This was developed during the 1950s by Allen S. Russek at New York University. The amputation stump is wrapped with a thin bandage and hangs free without any weight bearing below the ischial tuberosity. The prosthesis essentially consists of two metal uprights, a thigh cuff, hinged knee joint, and prosthetic foot (Fig. 14–7a through c). This orthoprosthesis usually matches the principle of a Thomas splint with a locking knee joint and a prosthetic foot. The cast for the thigh cuff with ischial weight bearing should be taken before surgery from a patient with arterial occlusion in whom one suspects that closure will not be possible, so that the prosthesis can be provided immediately after the operation. We also use it whenever we estimate that wound healing will take more than 1 month. It is followed by a provisional limb, as described earlier, and then the permanent. Although this process sounds expensive, it is actually far cheaper than extended hospitalization while waiting for the wound to close.

Subsequent replacement by another temporary socket is necessary whenever there is a decrease in edema that cannot be compensated for by stump socks or socket relining.

The patient must get out of bed the day after surgery (unless there is a medical contraindication), regardless of which method of postoperative care is used. If the amputated limb has not been placed in a cast or semirigid dressing to control edema, it has to be wrapped accurately with an elastic bandage.

The periods of temporary prosthetic use are based on the patient's general condition and the healing of the limb. During the rest of the time the limb is wrapped in an elastic bandage or stump shrinker, or a removable cast is placed over the amputated limb.

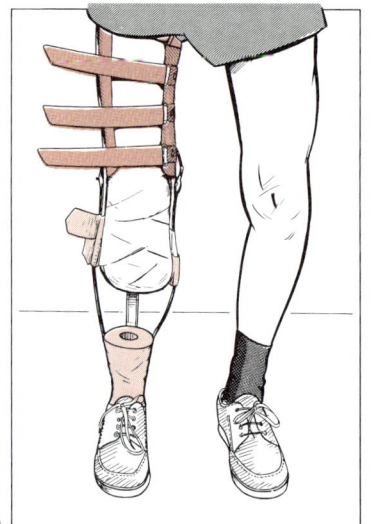
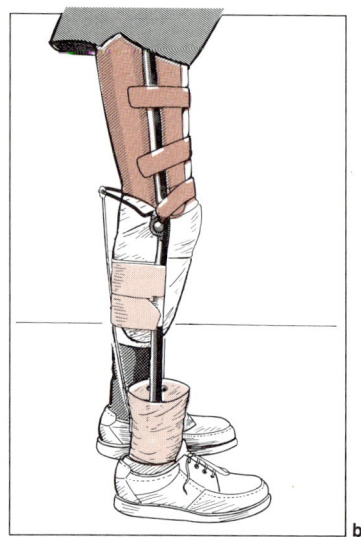
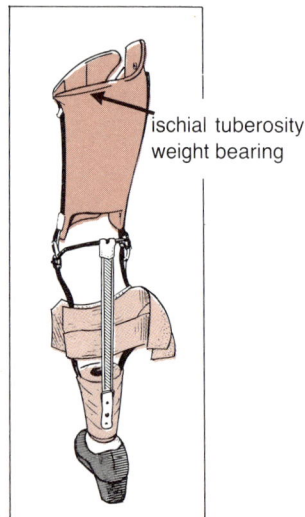

Fig. 14–7 Bypass prosthesis according to the principle of the Thomas splint.

Temporary prostheses are mandatory for inactive or geriatric patients to determine whether the use of a permanent prosthesis is feasible or whether a wheelchair is needed in addition to the prosthesis. The trial prosthesis must fit and be aligned properly if the trial results are to be at all useful.

Permanent Lower Extremity Prostheses

After amputations of single toes, only an arch support (foot orthosis) is needed. After the loss of all toes, a complete toe filler is needed. The toe filler may be attached to a foot orthosis. From the transmetatarsal level to the tenoplastic and myoplastic Chopart levels (Marquardt, 1973), a prosthesis placed inside an orthopedic shoe is used. Lisfranc and Chopart levels, which cannot be treated by tenomyoplasty, cause severe problems because of the development of equinus and supination contractures. For this reason most sources say they should not be performed at all. Those levels are indicated under special circumstances. If the scar is on the weight-bearing area, it must be protected by supporting part of the body weight on the patellar tendon. The Pirogoff and the Syme levels are able to function under weight bearing but require a prosthesis. The Boyd or the modified Pirogoff level is more favorable for full, prolonged weight bearing than the Syme because the heel fat pad mechanism that acts as a shock absorber is intact. With the Syme procedure the skin flap of the heel is attached to the surface of the tibia and fibula right above the proximal tarsal joint. The heel pad is never normal, so although the patient can do full weight bearing for limited distances, patellar support is required in the limb. The Syme amputation level remains an excellent choice for appropriate cases, when performed as originally described.

The amputated below-knee limb is placed (depending on the situation) in a rigid, total contact socket. The socket is made of plastic in most instances. Bony prominences such as the anterior tibial crest and the fibular head are carefully protected. Weight bearing is primarily transmitted to the area of the patellar tendon and the medial tibial flare, but where the patient is obese or carries heavy loads, is athletic, or has knee problems, weight is often partially carried by the thigh through a thigh corset. We fit each patient with a patellar tendon-bearing (PTB) prosthesis or a variant, such as the PTS or supracondylar-suprapatellar (SC-SP) first. If experience shows that the patient is not satisfied, or can do better with a trial thigh corset, we then provide it.

For padding and shock absorption, stump socks or an inner liner may be used. Various plastic formulations are in use. Each has special characteristics that may be of use in a particular individual. In addition to the common polyethylenes, rubbers, and so on, for patients with adherent, insensate, or friable skin who may not be able to tolerate shear stress, a gel liner made with silicone or other gel between two thin flexible layers of leather will absorb the shear. A slip socket, which has a spring to keep apart the outer structural layer of the double wall socket and the inner socket (Fig. 14–8a and b), is also used.

During the swing (non-weight-bearing) phase the below-knee PTB prosthesis is kept from falling off by a suprapatellar cuff or by a supracondylar or suprapatellar socket design (Fig. 14–9a through c). These suspend the limb by a clamping and

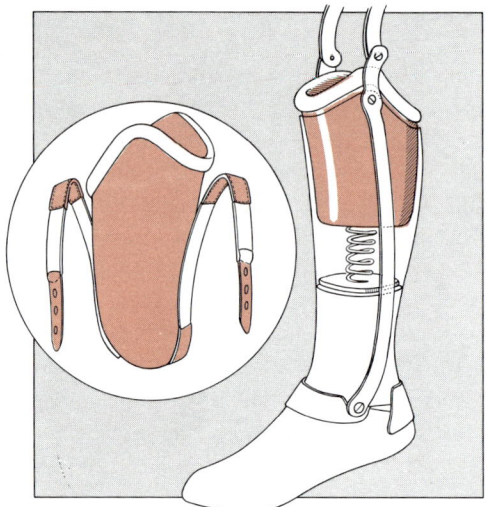

Fig. 14–8 a: Leather total-contact insert suspended by rubber elastic. **b:** Insert pressed against stump by metal spring.

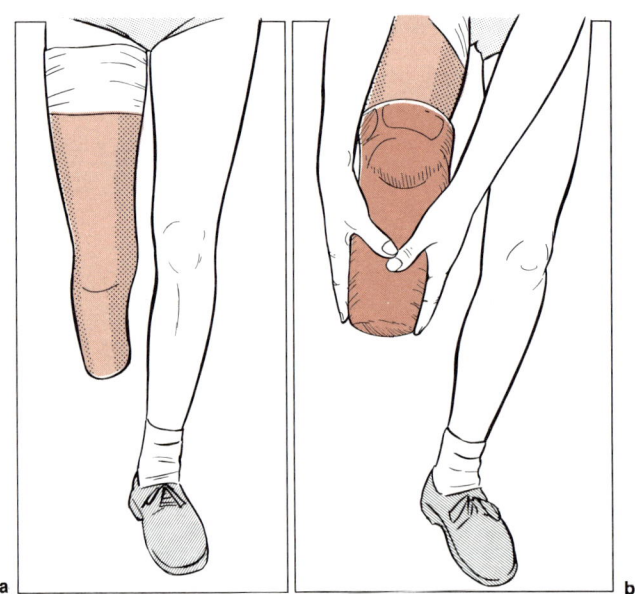

Fig. 14–9 The PTS prosthesis of Botta. **a:** Prosthetic sock; **b:** soft insert.

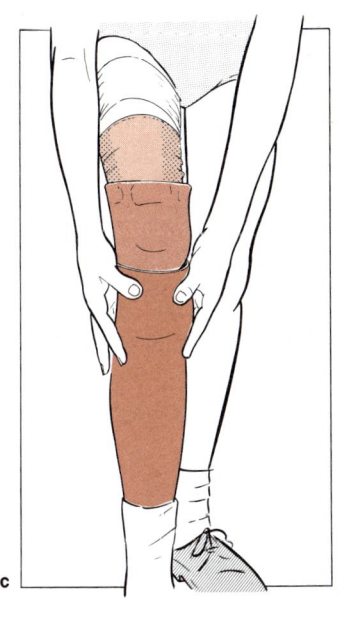
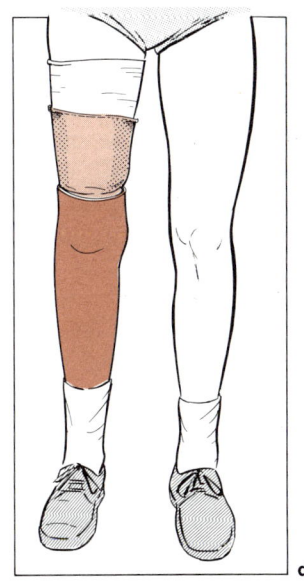
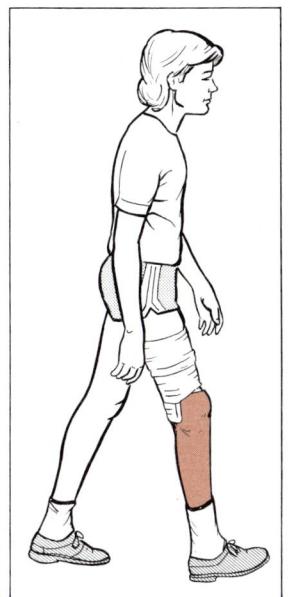

Fig. 14–9 c and **d:** hard socket prosthesis; **e:** patient wearing the prosthesis.

hooking action over bony prominences. The thigh corset (Fig. 14–10) is indicated only in special cases, such as sensitive stumps or if there is damage of the knee ligaments. Today nonathletes and geriatric patients can be treated more successfully with a PTB or SC-SP or PTS prosthesis than with a conventional prosthesis.

In addition to the supracondylar socket design, the strong muscles of the limb will contract inside the socket and hold the prosthesis on the limb during the swing phase of gait, especially if the socket is undercut for the muscle bulges. This is called muscular grasp suspension, which, in some young persons, can be the sole suspension.

Prosthetic feet will be selected based on functional or cosmetic requirements, such as the relatively light and agreeable-looking SACH foot or uniaxis or multi-axis feet. The latter are more functional but heavier. Newer sport feet, which store energy for pushoff, are now being marketed. Examples are the Seattle, S.A.F.E., STEN, and Flex feet.

If the leg cannot be salvaged below the knee, in recent years knee disarticulations have gained favor in comparison to above-knee amputations because of progress in surgical and prosthetic fitting techniques (Fig. 14–11a and b). A knee disarticulation is a less dangerous operation than an above-knee amputation (no myotomies with large muscle cross sections, no cutting through bone thereby opening the medullary canal, minimal bleeding). The result is a limb suitable for full weight bearing that provides a rotatory stable and self-bearing fit of the

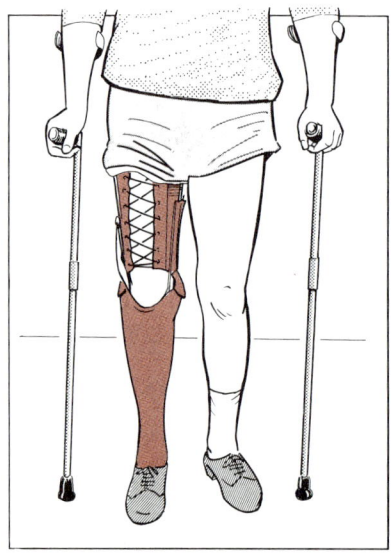

Fig. 14–10 Conventional thigh corset prosthesis.

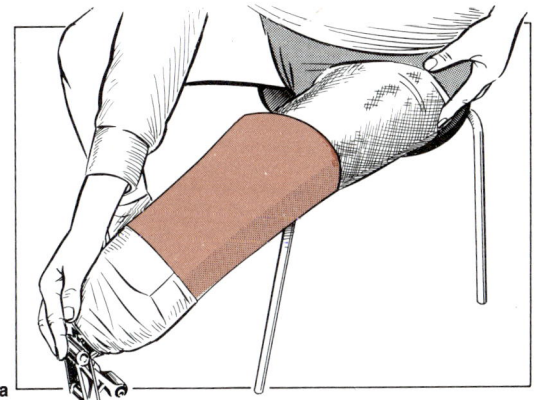

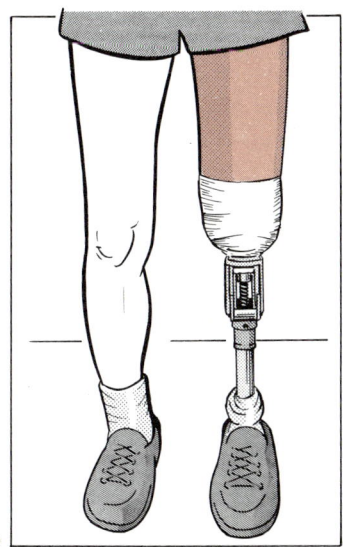

Fig. 14–11 Knee disarticulation prosthesis without cosmetic cover.

prosthesis to the remaining condyles. The weight-bearing ability of the limb can be fully used in the soft insert. The outer socket is hard distally and softer toward the proximal part, without ischial tuberosity support. This is far more comfortable than with an above-knee amputation in both standing and sitting and during ambulation. The new prostheses with polycentric knee units shift the knee axis back of the condyles, which largely solves the cosmetic problem during sitting that was the major defect of the conventional knee joints.

The above-knee prosthesis is provided with a total contact socket made of plastic (or rarely wood). Figure 14–12 shows an above-knee prosthesis with a wooden socket; the posterior wall is not visible. The shape of the socket is important for the fit of the prosthesis to the limb. The socket of a well-fitting prosthesis should not slip off the limb during the swing phase of gait, even if the suction valve is left off (Hepp, 1957). The rotary stability of an above-knee prosthesis is ensured by its shape (Fig. 14–13c). The body weight is more or less transmitted to the ischial tuberosity, depending on the limb, the shape of the socket (which until recently has usually been of a modified quadrilateral shape), and the alignment of the prosthesis. If the limb is physiologically adducted, the lateral wall of the socket also takes some weight. This is emphasized in the Iceland-Sweden-New York (ISNY), the normal shape-normal alignment (NSNA), and the controlled adducted trochanteric-controlled alignment method (CAT-CAM) designs even more than in the quadrilateral design.

The total contact socket supports some of the weight, depending on the surgical quality, the condition of the stump, and the fabrication and alignment of the socket, but in some persons it can take a fairly large proportion (Fig. 14–13a and b). In contrast to the total contact socket, the distal end of the limb in an "air chamber" socket hangs free inside the socket, which is held on by a Silesian or

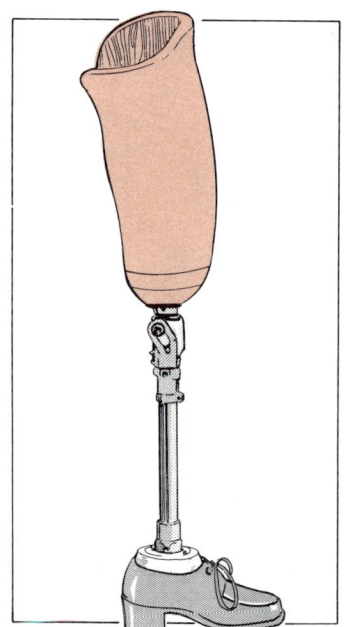

Fig. 14–12 Above-knee prosthesis with wood socket.

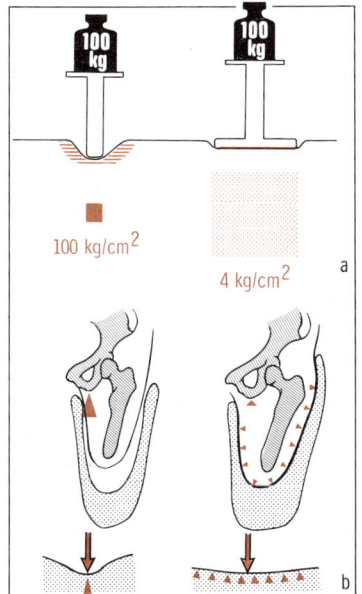
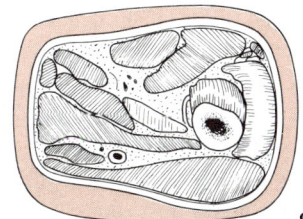

Fig. 14–13 Force and pressure. **a:** A strong force concentrated in a small area results in strong pressure, which is not tolerated well by tissue. The same strong force distributed over a larger surface results in less pressure, which is tolerated better by the tissues. **b:** Classic total contact socket. The socket (left) does not surround the stump completely; the stump is floating, lacking stability. The entire body weight is exclusively on the ischial tuberosity. The total contact socket (right) distributes the forces over a larger area, the pressure to the ischial tuberosity is minimized and will be tolerated well. **c:** Quadrilateral socket. The contracting muscles form not a cylindrical but an irregular changing shape; therefore, this socket type is not oval, but modified and changeable.

---

pelvic band. A "suction socket" has an airtight valve that permits air to exit from the socket but not return. The limb is held on by atmospheric pressure. It may be of the air chamber or total contact design. Circulatory problems are likely if the proximal fit is too tight.

Stumps with scars in the femoral triangle that contraindicate suction suspension or with a short bone must have additional suspension by means of a pelvic or Silesian band. It is always necessary to avoid heavy pressure on the femoral triangle in patients with arterial occlusion. If surgery has been done in the femoral triangle, the quadrilateral socket shape is contraindicated. Pressure in this region may be avoided by using either the old plug fit design socket or one of the newer above-knee shapes that have a narrow mediolateral and wide anteroposterior dimension. Such socket shapes include the NSNA and the CAT-CAM. The flexible-insert ISNY socket can also be used.

Optimal design of the socket and choice of the prosthetic components with proper construction are crucial for maximum function. The choice of knee unit design depends mostly on the patient's age and activity level. Flexion and abduction contractures of the hip joint require modification of the alignment of the prosthesis and sometimes a change in socket design as well. Alignment is facilitated by use of adjustable joints, an endoskeletal construction using tubing, and suitable adaptive connections. Use of a cosmetic cover improves the look of the prosthesis and is softer to the touch.

The Canadian hip disarticulation prosthesis (Fig. 14–14a and b) is now the standard design used to fit the unilateral hip disarticulation amputee. The prosthetic socket surrounds the iliac crest on the affected side and is held in place by straps or parts of the socket that lie between the iliac crest and the greater trochanter on the contralateral side. In a unilateral hemipelvectomy the socket encloses the opposite iliac crest and the lower ribs on both sides. A secure standing position without an additional locking device is made possible by the extreme anterior position of the axis of the artificial hip and slight posterior location of the knee joint. Pelvic tilt motions originating from the lumbar spine are transferred to the prosthesis and initiate the swing phase of gait. Walking with the Canadian hip disarticulation limb is learned surprisingly quickly by most patients.

Patients with bilateral disarticulation of the hip, or children with amelia or phocomelia of the lower limbs are provided with special prostheses for rotary or

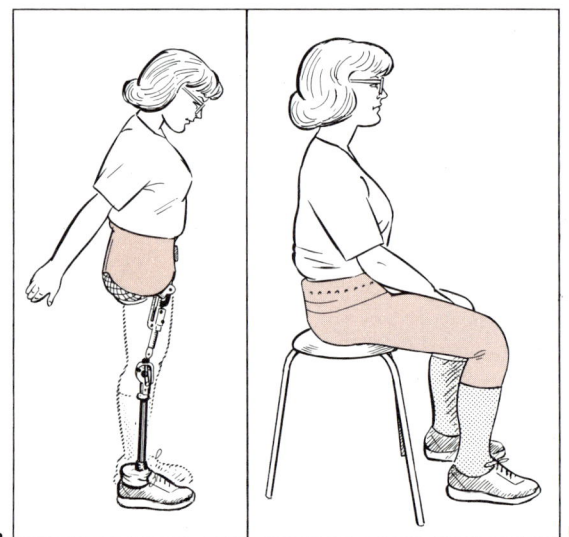

Fig. 14–14 Canadian hip disarticulation prosthesis (McLaurin) made with modular technique.

reciprocating walking, or a swing-through gait, depending on the function of the upper extremities. For instance, a child born without lower limbs, in his 12th month, will receive a "stubby" prosthesis consisting of a bucketlike socket and pylons for standing (Fig. 14–15). The child can stand at a table, play, or move around. If the child has normal arms and no legs, he can learn to ambulate with special prostheses—at first without hip and knee joints and then, from 4 to 6 years of age, with unlocked hip and knee joint units (Fig. 14–16a and b).

It is important for cerebral development that children with congenital deformities of the lower limbs start to move around on their legs according to their developmental age, approximately in the 12th month. Brain development depends on appropriate sensory input. This in turn depends on stimuli received in the upright posture. Preparatory surgery is always necessary for tibial defects and often for fibular defects (Fig. 14–17a and b). This should be done before the onset of walking. Prostheses for these children should be neither bulky nor heavy, nor should they be just a smaller version of an adult prosthesis. They must be matched to the special static and dynamic development of the individual child (Marquardt and Martini, 1979).

For all limb-deficient patients, congenital or acquired, the ability to walk must be evaluated initially as well as during treatment. This is most important for patients with complicating problems, such as geriatric patients, amputees under chemotherapy, and patients with several amputations or other handicaps. Additional aids such as wheelchairs may need to be used. The patient's car may also have to be modified.

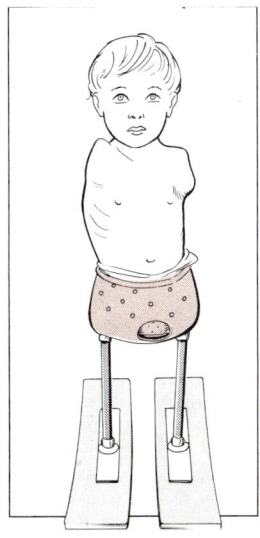

Fig. 14–15 A stubby prosthesis for the complete amelic.

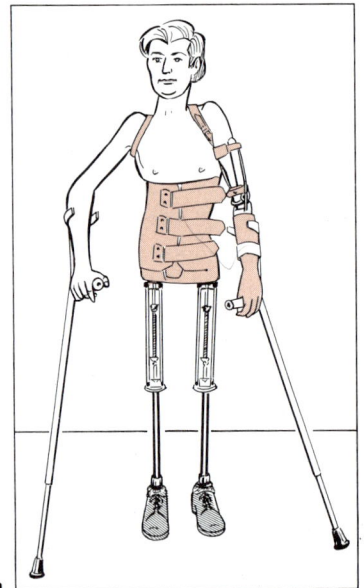
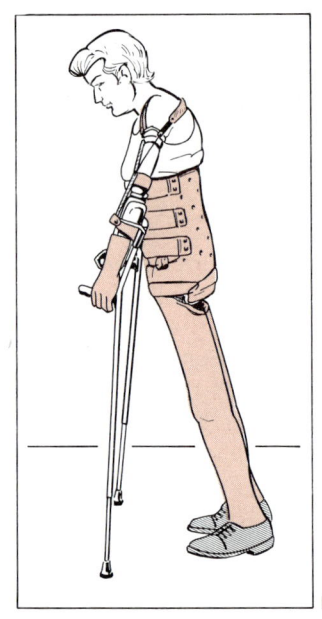

Fig. 14–16 Bilateral amelia of the lower extremities and transverse deficiency of the left forearm fitted with functional prostheses.

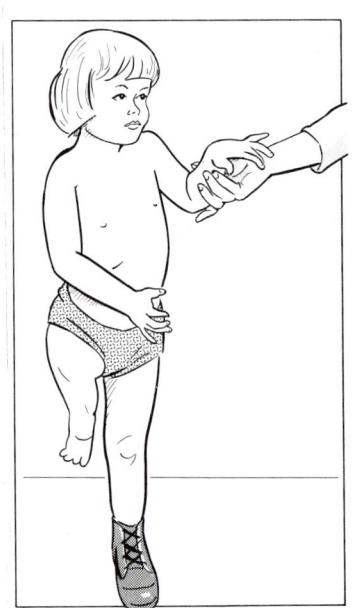
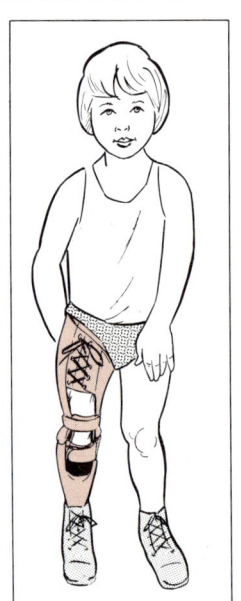

Fig. 14–17 Child wearing an orthoprosthesis for a subtotal femoral and total fibular deficiency (right).

The rehabilitation process for retraining amputees in their professional life should be started early, in order to save time between therapy and return to work.

Immediate and Early Postoperative Prosthetic Fitting in Upper Limb Amputees

If the upper limb amputation can be completed by primary wound closure, a padded cast is fitted on the operating table that immobilizes the joint proximal to the amputation site. On the day after the operation the temporary prosthesis is attached to the cast, and prosthetic training is started in the department of occupational therapy (Fig. 14–18). The physical therapist works on the mobility of the joints, sitting balance, and posture. Approximately 3 weeks after the amputation the cast for the final prosthesis can be applied, since shrinkage in the upper limb is minimal. The myoplasty requires 3 weeks to heal. Afterwards, pronation and supination are also exercised. Discharge with the final prosthesis and complete training to handle the prosthesis and independent daily living skills should be possible in 6 to 8 weeks.

Prostheses for Upper Limb Amputees

The hospital in which the amputation was performed may not be able to supply the patient with a prosthesis immediately; however, application of a trial pros-

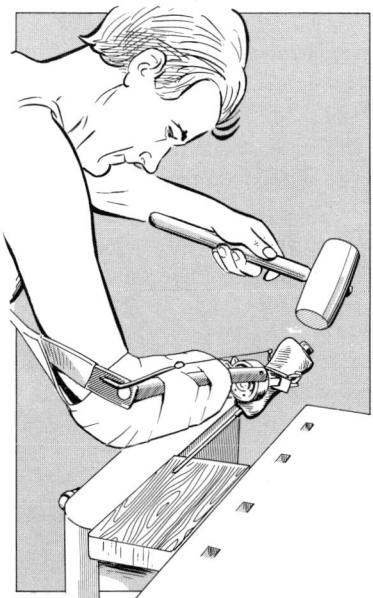

Fig. 14–18 Postoperative arm training in occupational therapy with a temporary prosthesis fixed to a plaster of Paris cast.

thesis as early as possible is an important goal (Fig. 14–18). The socket should be fitted as soon as the healing is complete after a skin graft or when the wound had to be left open because of the risk of infection. The course of therapy is delayed, on average, in comparison to the immediate application of a prosthesis, by about 2 to 3 weeks in a child and 4 weeks in an adult patient. Immediate or early prosthesis application is not possible after Krukenberg plasty, angular osteotomy, or plastic coverage of the bony amputation end by a cap. However, because most of these patients are amputated bilaterally, the opposite side should be fitted with a prosthesis before the plastic surgery and the patient should be trained to be independent.

The first prosthesis prescribed is a body-powered prehensile arm. Myoelectric prostheses are prescribed later, if at all. Myoelectric prostheses can be applied primarily for particular purposes when strong prehension and a good cosmetic effect is required. It is costly but sometimes advisable.

Approximately 5 to 6 weeks after the amputation, a cast of the stump for the final prosthesis is taken for a patient who has had an early trial prosthesis. After the prosthesis is finished, the prosthetic training has to be continued to accustom the patient to the final components and design (Fig. 14–4). Training with the prosthesis, in combination with self-help training and the use of technical aids, is an important aspect of occupational therapy practice that cannot be covered in this chapter.

Prostheses for replacement of the upper limb are classified in two groups: passive and active. They may be used in combination.

Passive Prostheses

Cosmetic Arms and Hands. Cosmetic arms and hands (Fig. 14–19a and b) are light prostheses that are used mainly for appearance. It should be realized that cosmesis is a function, albeit often a passive one. If someone is a salesclerk, appearance is all important. Many customers will be dissuaded from coming back to a store where the clerks are obviously disabled. We spend billions of dollars on enhancing our appearance because we know it is important for those who are normal. Those who are disabled already have one strike against them in being hired. If we can help to minimize the prejudice against them by diminishing the noticeability of their defect, we do them a favor.

Passive Work Arms. Passive work arms are stable functional prostheses, mainly used by patients with an amputated forearm but sometimes with higher ablation. Terminal devices may passively hold tools, or the tool itself may attach to the wrist unit. Examples of passive tool holders are a ring used to hold a rake handle, a hook to grab hay bales, a screw-down clamp to hold an object to be drilled in a drill press, or a spade holder (Fig. 14–20). A cosmetic hand is easily interchanged at the wrist. A specific tool may be used, such as a knife blade, a fork,

Rehabilitation 397

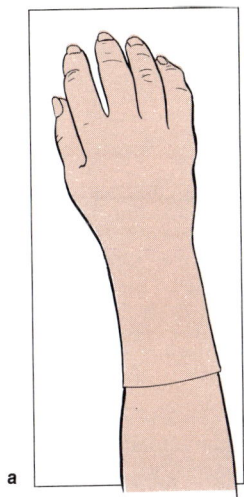 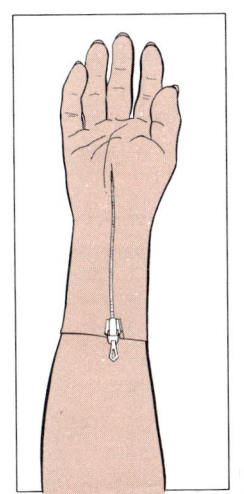

Fig. 14–19 Cosmetic hand. **a:** Dorsal view; **b:** volar view.

Fig. 14–20 Passive work arm with ring terminal device.

a soldering iron (adapted), or a crutch (for the multiple amputee). These passive arms have proved successful for farmers, gardeners, and metalworkers.

Active Arm Prostheses

Body Powered. The main characteristic of an active prehensile body-powered prosthesis is use of the body movements, for example, of the shoulder girdle, to transmit the body work to the movable joints of the prosthetic terminal device (Fig. 14–21) and to the prosthetic elbow joint in the above-elbow limb. The work of the body (muscular force × bony distance [range of motion]) is translated into prosthetic work. Although the motor power is sufficient below the elbow, it is barely adequate above the elbow. The big advantages of body-powered devices are that they are cheaper and easier to maintain and provide sensory feedback that is far superior to that which the patient gets from any externally powered limb. Active prehensile arms are mainly supplied to patients with unilateral or bilateral below-elbow amputations and those with one above-elbow amputation. All amputation lengths can be treated with active prehensile arms; however, the effectiveness of the prosthesis decreases with higher amputation levels.

The passive wrist joints are of a number of varieties. Some can be locked in different positions, while others can be adjusted gradually with rotation.

Various terminal devices can be connected to the wrists. One can use one or more of the following: the passive devices mentioned above, a prosthetic hand, hook, cosmetic hand, and so on.

Rotation of the prosthetic arm is possible by means of a passive turntable device located just superior to the prosthetic elbow. Abduction and forward motion in the artificial shoulder joint of the prosthesis for the shoulder disarticulation and the forequarter amputee are achieved passively (Fig. 14–22a and b).

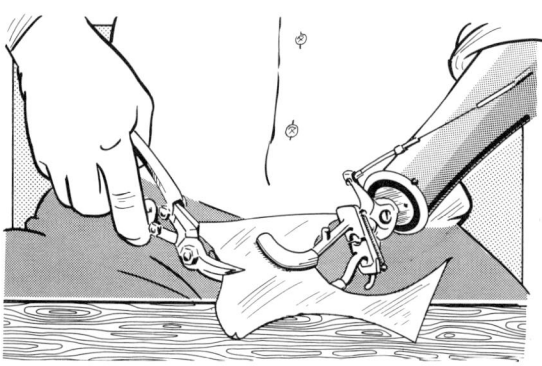

Fig. 14–21 Training in the use of a body-powered cable-controlled below-elbow prosthesis (the standard hook can be replaced at the wrist unit with an active prosthetic hand).

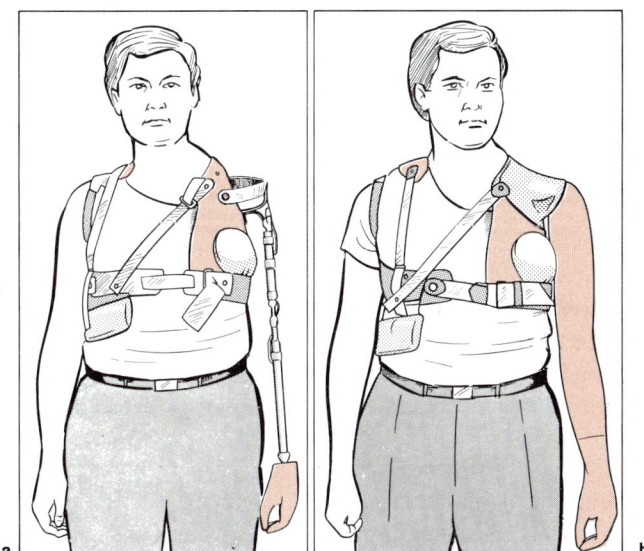

Fig. 14–22 Cosmetically acceptable prosthesis with electric hand worn by a patient with a unilateral forequarter amputation. **a:** Three weeks after surgery the patient is fit with an endoskeletal prosthesis with freely swinging and passively locking shoulder and elbow joints, passive rotation of the upper arm, passive rotation of the hand, and an electric hand operated over a twofold pull switch. **b:** Patient with the complete prosthesis after training.

In patients with an elbow disarticulation with normal condyles or a distal humeral angular osteotomy in a long above-elbow stump, full voluntary motion of the shoulder joint through the shoulder girdle musculature is transferred to the prosthesis, provided there is a correct fit. Any additional prosthetic aid for rotation is usually not necessary. The prosthesis can then be used behind the back, above the head, and in the groin with ease.

Externally Powered. Pneumatic and electric-powered components may be inserted in a prosthesis to help add power where the body cannot adequately supply enough power to do the tasks the patient wants done. The power must be controlled by the patient. Unfortunately, the higher the level of amputation, and thus the more the amputee can benefit from this type of limb, the more inefficient are the control sites.

The energy source for a pneumatic arm prosthesis (Heidelberg design by Haefner) is liquid carbon dioxide stored in a pressure-safe container made of aluminum or steel. For an electromechanical prosthesis it is electricity, supplied by a nickel-cadmium storage battery. Even patients with bilateral shoulder disarticulation can operate the prosthesis with remaining shoulder motions. Electromechanical prostheses are indicated especially for patients with bilateral acquired or congenital loss of the arms and for bilateral phocomelia (Fig. 14-23a and b).

In phocomelias, touch valves and switches are used for control. For higher impaired patients, switches, valves, or electromyographic potentials may be used for control. The control may be on-off or proportional. Depending on personal choice or professional needs, an active prehensile arm can be supplied with a prosthetic hand or standard hook, an electromechanical prosthesis operated by a touch switch or myoelectric control, or just a light cosmetic hand. The patient may need more than one device to satisfy different needs.

The myoelectric control functions by use of action potentials originated by muscle contraction. These are received by a contact electrode as differences in voltage. This information is then transformed electronically into a signal for the motors to act in one direction or the other, thus activating the electric hand or grasper (Fig. 14-24).

Agonist and antagonist muscles must learn how to contract and relax independently because signals of the flexor muscles will interfere with the extensor muscle function and vice versa, since the body is an excellent volume conductor of electricity. Electronic blocking of the channels is designed to make only one signal

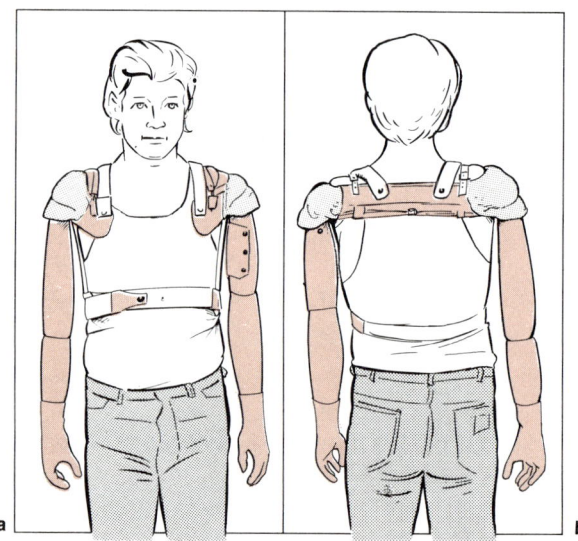

Fig. 14–23 Electromechanical Heidelberg prosthesis (right) and cosmetic arm (left) attached to a Simpson frame for a patient with bilateral disarticulation of the shoulders after an accident. The active functions (hand opening and closing, hand rotation, elbow and shoulder locking, and release) are operated from both shoulders by microswitches (pulling and pressure). Nickel-cadmium storage battery is located in the left arm section. The patient wears the prosthesis all day at a fulltime job.

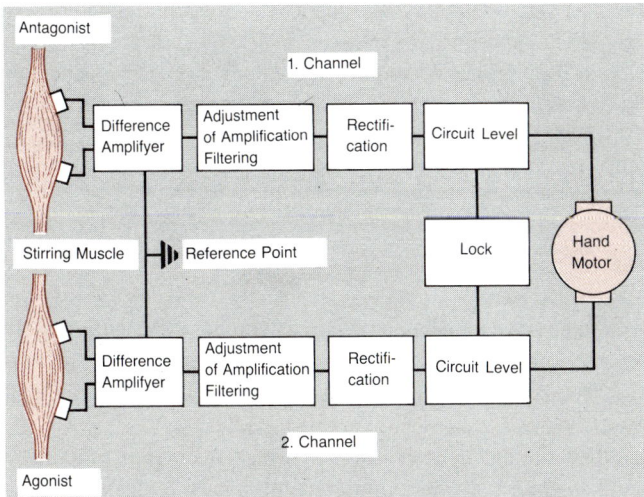

Fig. 14–24 Function of a myoelectric prosthesis (H. Roesler).

accessible at a time. Fine tuning is needed, adjusted to the individual's muscle potentials. This prosthetic system, in combination with appropriate training results, is an optimum human-machine combination.

A myoelectric prosthesis is indicated if the amputee needs an agreeable-looking hand with good prehension and does no heavy labor, e.g., for white-collar work. The cosmetic glove, which is vital for the appearance for which the hand is obtained, is fragile. Heavy or dirty work will ruin it almost immediately. For times when such work is needed, an exchangeable electrical prehensile hook or grasper is available, e.g., for hobbies, handicrafts, cooking, and other housework.

The application of prostheses and training in their use for children with amputations of the upper limb or congenital anomalies are matched to the child's development with special prosthetic designs and technical aids. The training is always use training for daily activities and play according to the child's age.

For patients with bilateral loss of the hand, the use of two powered limbs is less effective than the plastic surgical transformation of the forearm into "pliers" according to the surgical method of Krukenberg.

PHYSICAL THERAPY

Preliminary Remarks

The immediate and early application of prostheses after amputations is most important in modern clinical management. The prerequisites are to help lower limb amputees move around as soon as possible and to train the remaining muscles of all amputees to control the appropriate prosthesis.

The treatment of lower limb amputees should be concluded with intensive gait training.

The prosthetic treatment of the upper limb should include intensive training in how to use the prosthesis, usually in occupational therapy, within a functional exercise program led by a physical therapist.

Lower Limb Amputees

The treatment and immediate care of an amputee (owing to accident or tumor) has already been described. The treatment of geriatric patients with leg amputations owing to arterial occlusion requires a great deal of physical therapy and gait training and will be emphasized in the following discussion.

The treatment should be initiated before the amputation. The therapist should be informed about general weakness, cardiovascular disturbances, lung emphysema or bronchitis, contractures, muscle atrophy, disturbed coordination, pain, and psychological problems. The preoperative treatment is aimed at the patient's general conditioning. The patient should be ambulated before the operation, if at all possible.

A limb with necrosis or gangrene of the foot cannot be subjected to weight bearing because of pain. Vitali introduced a preamputation prosthesis to facilitate ambulation. The prosthesis is adjustable and can be used again for other amputees. The patient learns beforehand how to walk using this simulated prosthesis (Fig. 14–25).

The treatment of the unaffected limb is of equal importance. It will be subjected to increased weight bearing, especially during the initial training with the prosthesis, since the patient will need time to get used to pressure on the amputated limb.

The therapist needs to know the circulation and weight-bearing ability of both the affected and the unaffected limbs and choose techniques accordingly, such as supporting the circulation by connective tissue massage, elastic stockings, and so on. In vascular cases hot packs are contraindicated, although they may be of value in traumatic cases. Exercises that overstress the muscle and cause an additional oxygen deficit are contraindicated.

The following gait training protocol follows the interval principle. Distances are set and sufficient rest is given between treatment sessions. Numerous places to rest need to be made available. Exercises for the arms, shoulder girdle, and trunk are used to prepare them for sufficient support functions with crutches and canes, to maintain a good upright posture and good coordination, and to improve the blood supply to the unaffected limb.

The patient can be familiarized with the therapist and the treatment program if there is enough time for preoperative treatment.

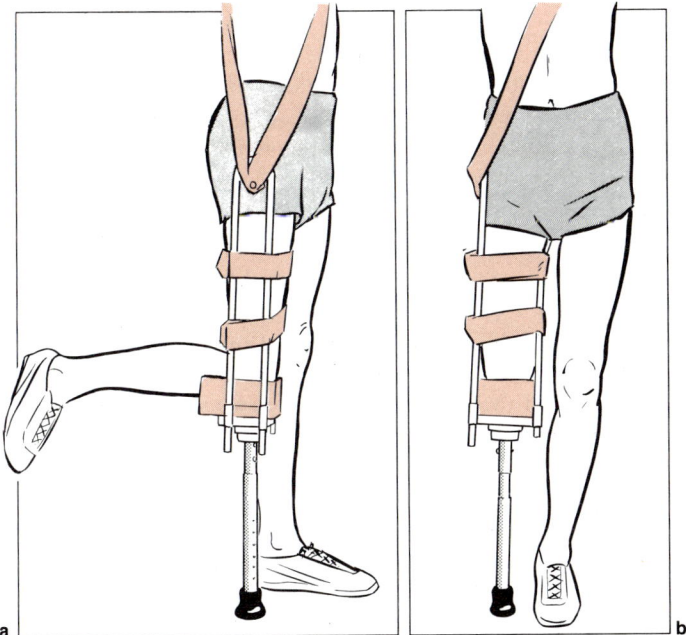

Fig. 14–25 Preamputation prosthesis (Vitali) for preoperative gait training. **a:** lateral view; **b:** frontal view.

Aspects of postoperative treatment, besides those mentioned above, are the prevention of malposition of the amputated limb and the consequent development of contractures, which are mostly caused during the first postoperative weeks by careless positioning.

After an amputation of the lower limb, knee flexion contracture is triggered by an immediate postoperative position, supported by a pillow, which is comfortable and less painful for the patient. Permanent flexion contracture of the knee also causes a flexion contracture of the hip joint. Restricted extension of both joints is a subsequent severe potential problem that might restrict or inhibit walking.

After an above-knee amputation, the sectioning of the adductor muscles while the abductors stay intact, and some of the extensors while the flexors are mostly intact, causes malposition in flexion, abduction, and external rotation of the hip joint, worsened by a soft mattress and support of the amputated limb by a soft pillow. Malpositions are also increased by long periods of sitting in a wheelchair and ambulation without a prosthesis. Rarely a surgeon may create a hip flexion contracture by doing a myoplasty while the hip joint is flexed. It should be done in hip extension and slight adduction. It is difficult to correct such a contracture by physical therapy. A pillow under the pelvis, not the stump, or a cast right after surgery will prevent this problem.

Development of contractures is increasingly a problem with shorter stumps. Preventive measures include correct and regularly controlled position changes, mobilization of the joints that move the amputated limb, strengthening of muscles by active movement and by controlled resistance (i.e., after a below-knee amputation, stress exercises for the extensors of the knee and hip joint; after an above-knee amputation, stress exercises for extension and adduction). Abduction exercises will be needed for prosthesis activation.

Special treatment is required for existing contractures, possibly in combination with passive techniques (e.g., sandbags or pulleys). While the wound is still healing, the sutures must be watched. Any tension during exercises that could result in loosening or dehiscence must be avoided. Contractures can best be prevented by using the myoplastic amputation technique and applying the prosthesis as early as possible. If the contracture is not responsive to conservative treatment, surgical intervention should possibly be considered. Minor to moderate contractures can be accommodated in the alignment of the prosthesis, but cosmesis is compromised. Figures 14–26 and 14–27 demonstrate unacceptable contractures, which should be avoided by early constant care.

An untreated contracture of the hip forces the above-knee amputee into an extreme lumbar lordosis. A static scoliosis is pending if the prosthesis is also

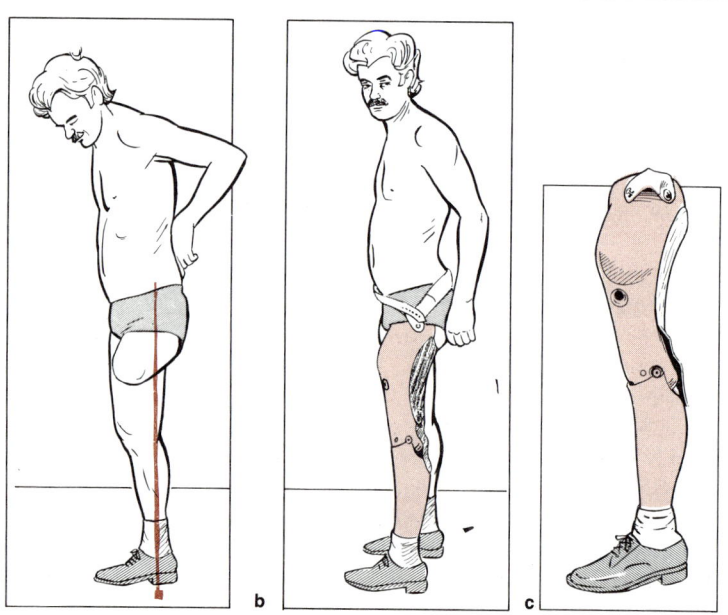

Fig. 14–26 Above-knee amputee with a fixed flexion contracture of the hip joint. His prosthesis accommodates the contracture, but his endurance to ambulation is greatly compromised.

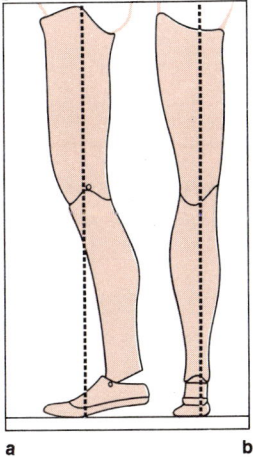
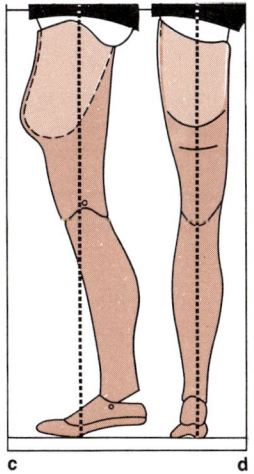
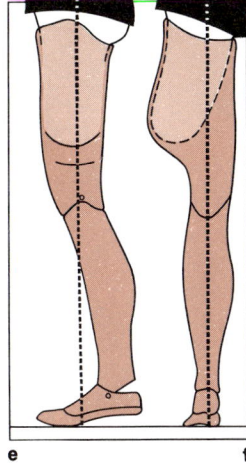

Fig. 14–27 The alignment of an above-knee prosthesis. **a:** Lateral view; **b:** frontal view; **c** and **d:** flexion contracture, lateral and frontal view; **e** and **f:** abduction contracture, lateral and frontal view. Frequently flexion and abduction contracture are seen together.

---

considerably shorter, possibly in combination with an uncorrected abduction contracture. Older patients may suffer from serious back problems as a result.

The position of the pelvis of an above-knee amputee using an unlocked prosthetic knee joint must be level. However, a prosthesis with a locked knee joint should be 1 to 1.5 cm shorter than the normal level, to facilitate swinging through.

Bandaging the Amputated Limb

Postoperative edema can be controlled by elastic bandaging during the time of healing and as long as the patient does not yet wear a prosthesis. The bandage is wrapped from distal to proximal with decreasing tightness in figure eight-shaped loops (Figs. 14–28 and 29). If the bandage slips, it is removed immediately by the patient and rewrapped. The patient should learn to wrap the limb independently.

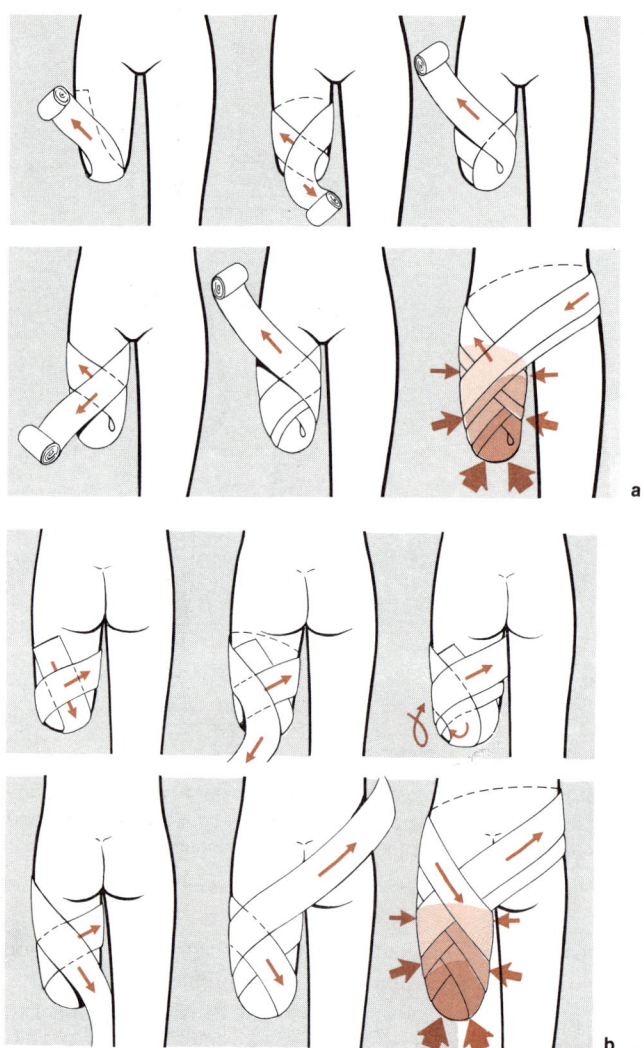

Fig. 14–28 Elastic bandage technique for the above-knee amputee. **a:** frontal view; **b:** posterior view (R. Baumgartner).

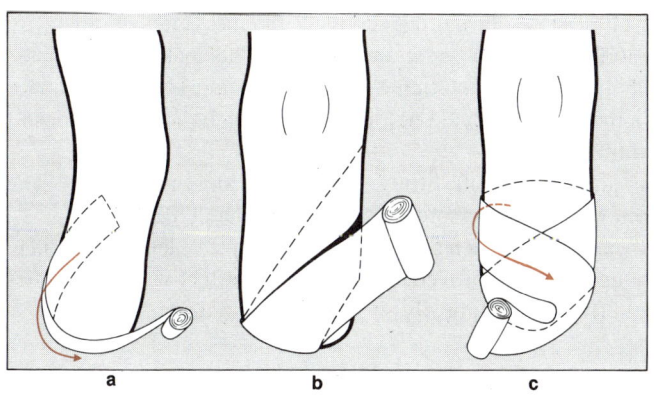
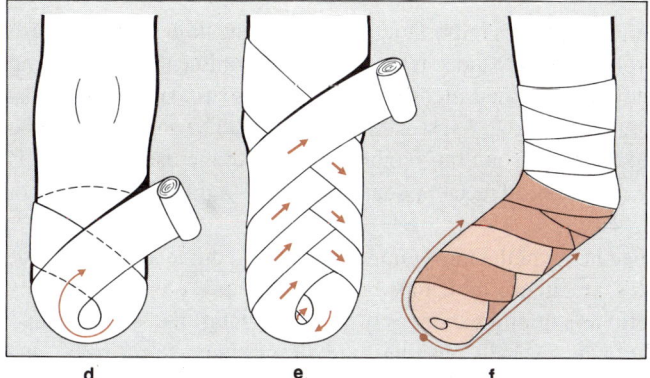

Fig. 14–29 Elastic bandage technique for the below-knee amputee. Note that compression is decreased proximally. (R. Baumgartner)

Wearing a compressive sock is less problematic than wrapping the limb. For a severely edematous stump a semirigid Unna bandage that must be changed every other day has proved successful. Isometric muscle contractions also help to reduce the edema.

Massage of the Stump

To encourage edema reduction, centripetal massage is useful to reduce the stump volume. This can be done manually or mechanically. While the wound is still unhealed, only manual massage should be used, with the wound edges held closed with one hand.

Massage is important psychologically. Amputees routinely do not like to look at the stump or touch it. They think it is ugly. Early massage by nurses, therapists, and the patient himself after doctor's orders conveys the message that others are not repulsed by the look, since they see it and touch it. This makes the amputee more willing to touch it and handle it. Often we look at the almost healed stump for no other reason than the psychological one, in cases in which the patient doesn't accept the residual limb.

Occasionally scars are treated with lifting massage, to loosen adhesions. The massage is performed only after the suture line has completely healed.

Connective tissue massage has been recommended to improve leg circulation in vascular cases. Although it has not proved to be adequately effective, some studies do show a beneficial effect and, clinically, it helps in some instances.

Hygiene and Skin Lesion Prevention

Maintenance of skin integrity is important. Washing of the limb with lukewarm water and soap, thorough rinsing, and soft toweling are recommended. The stump socks and socket should be washed nightly with a bland soap. The stump socks should be dried flat and allowed to "rest" for 3 or 4 days. The socket should be washed with a damp washcloth and thoroughly rinsed with the damp cloth. It is then allowed to dry overnight. Traces of soap should not remain on the limb or inside the prosthetic socket.

Exercises are aimed at strengthening, improvement of endurance, and balance activities. Examples are many and may be found in any physical therapy textbook. Some useful less traditional ones are pushing against the sheets or mat, rolling away a light or heavy ball, pushing the ball and bouncing it back, and balance exercises in the sitting, kneeling, and standing positions. These procedures are contraindicated for patients with vascular occlusion, unless special precautions are instituted, since they must be treated carefully to protect the skin.

The therapist must always examine the limb for possible pressure areas or breakdown during the exercises. The below-knee amputated limb is especially at risk. During the surgery the end of the anterior tibial edge, which is prone to pressure problems, is sawed off. This bony prominence is later placed in an area of reduced stress in the prosthesis. Before fitting, the area may be damaged by traction of the weight of the posterior soft tissues in the supine position in the obese patient, rolling in the bed or therapy, trauma on the ward, and so on.

Gait Training

Gait training for a patient with a lower limb amputation starts with partial weight bearing using both a three-point and a four-point gait pattern. These are taught in the parallel bars. The single most common error in training is to take the patients out of the bars to use a walker or crutches too early, to "encourage" them. This predisposes to gait deviations later. Details of the training are in standard textbooks. Later a two-point pattern is also taught. Full weight bearing is approached only if the skin exhibits tolerance to prosthetic wear.

Gait deviations must be checked out immediately. They may arise from incorrect prosthetic fabrication, inadequate training, patient problems, or habit. Diagnosis of the etiology of the problem(s) may require evaluation by the whole team.

Example of a Gait Deviation

The above-knee patient has a normal stance phase but circumducts and toe vaults during swing: the prosthesis is too long.

Prosthetic causes:

- The suspension is too loose.
- The patient is getting groin pain because he is in too far (large socket, too few stump socks).
- The knee friction is too great.
- The extension aid is too tight.

Amputee causes:

- Weight loss
- Edema reduction
- Fat and muscle atrophy
- Hydradenitis suppurativa in groin
- Painful adductor roll
- Habit

Other gait deviations and their causes and corrections may be studied in standard textbooks on amputee training.

A neuroma is a normal response to cutting of a nerve. It is not a serious pathological condition in itself. It causes discomfort only if it is incorporated in the scar or if it is subjected to pressure or tension, usually by the prosthetic socket. First an attempt should be made to reduce pressure on this area within the prosthetic socket. Neuromas that cannot be relieved of high-pressure socket areas or are incorporated in scar tissue should be resected, and the nerve ends should be placed high in muscle not subject to significant socket pressure. Neuromas covered by muscles are usually not painful.

Upper Limb Amputees

The remaining joints and muscles of the arm must be strengthened and mobilized. Because the unamputated side will now be the dominant limb, it also should be exercised. If the dominant limb was excised, then a switch of dominance is needed, and must be learned. An immediate prosthesis is the best therapy.

In addition, the influence of the weight of the arm on the posture should be considered, especially in unilateral amputations of the upper limb and disarticulation of the shoulder. Development of a scoliosis may be triggered by trunk tilting. The tilt is usually toward the amputated side because of the weight of the normal arm. To compensate for the unbalanced weight of the remaining arm, the person consciously leans toward the amputated side. The tilt is due to a static-dynamic compensation of the body for the missing limb. Preventive and conditioning exercises are required to strengthen the trunk muscles and train posture and balance. The patient is advised to participate in sports activities and swimming lessons. This effect is minimized by the wearing and use of a prosthesis, but a weight equal to that of the normal arm would be uncomfortable and poorly tolerated.

Training to Control Body-Powered and Myoelectric Prostheses

The use of a prosthesis requires muscular action. The work input must overcome frictional losses and then supply adequate work output. The work is the muscular force times the distance the force is applied. The patient must have sufficient force and be able to apply it for enough time and endure for long enough to get the job done. For this training, both physical and occupational therapy are needed. Even where an additional source of energy is being supplied, the control of the work requires special training.

The myoplasty requires a healing period of 3 weeks before the training. Start with isometric contractions of the muscles, originating from imaginary movements simultaneously with the normal arm. The therapist presses his finger with controlled resistance against the muscle to be trained; the patient must overcome the resistance without tension of the antagonistic muscles. After 2 to 3 weeks the necessary muscle potentials to control the myoelectric arm can usually be reached by this method. The most favorable contact points are marked, and a cuff is made, which will contain the contact electrodes. The patient can observe the success of the muscle contraction on the prosthetic hand itself or a toy for a child (Fig. 14–30). When the forearm amputee is able to control the closure and opening of the hand, he must learn to vigorously pronate and supinate the elbow and move the shoulder without involuntary triggering of the prosthetic hand. The above-elbow amputee has to learn isolated tension and complete relaxation of the

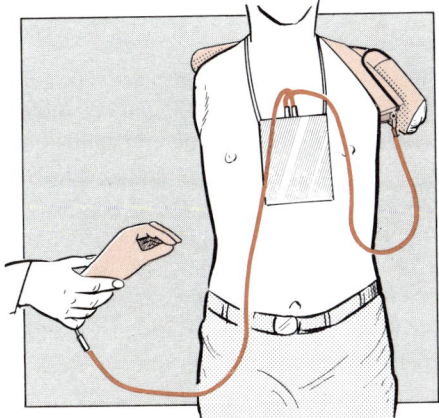

Fig. 14-30 Exercise cuff for contact electrodes with connected myoelectric prosthetic system of the first generation.

biceps and triceps brachii muscles during strong movements of the shoulder joint or the shoulder girdle.

Krukenberg Plasty

The Krukenberg operation making a pincer from the radius to oppose to the ulna has as its usual indication the bilateral loss of the hand and is mainly used for the blind. This gives sensate prehension in a situation in which conventional prostheses cannot be used, since they need visual feedback. For patients who need sensate prehension, it is an excellent procedure even for the sighted. While the appearance is not good, the function is superior. For social occasions it can be covered with a cosmetic glove, or the individual can use an electromechanical switch-controlled limb with a glove.

Postoperative Treatment

Wound bandage and wrapping are conventional, except that the opening between the two branches of 20 to 25 degrees is maintained by padding between the radius and the ulna. The elbow is kept in flexion at 90 degrees.

After day 1, one should maintain elevation of the arm during rest. The patient may get up, except where skin was removed from the inguinal area to cover the defect. The shoulder joint must be moved in all directions at least four times daily, raising the arm above the head frequently.

After 3 weeks active elbow flexion and extension and the transfer of pronation and supination to opening and closing of the branches with the elbow flexed to

90 degrees should be performed with assistance, then actively, and finally against resistance.

The following muscles open the branches: brachioradialis, biceps brachii, and both radial extensors of the hand. With increasing strength, the patient should attempt elevation of the radius away from the ulna, with fixation of the ulna on a support manually, first with active assisted and then with active motion. Electrotherapy may be needed to stimulate weak or alienated muscles.

The opening angle of the branches should be 20 to 30 degrees (Fig. 14–31). Careful passive stretching can improve an insufficient opening. The stretching should not be forceful because of the risk of injury to the supinator muscle. The use of the inhibition of antagonist technique of proprioceptive neuromuscular facilitation is most helpful. Temporary maintenance of stretching with fitted wedges of felt or cork is useful, especially at night and on weekends.

The branches are initially closed passively and then actively. The most important muscle is the ulnar portion of the supinator. A fitted cuff may be necessary to keep the tips together temporarily if they do not close sufficiently.

During opening or closing of the branches (pincers), shearing motions in pronation or supination should be avoided. This is initially achieved by manually supported and controlled movements. During the initial phase the muscles can be additionally trained by "phantom" exercises:

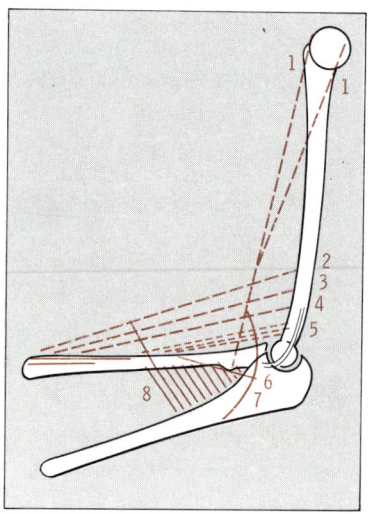

Fig. 14–31 Scheme of a Krukenberg prehensile forearm. **1:** biceps brachii; **2:** brachioradialis; **3 and 4:** extensor carpi radialis longus and brevis; **5:** pronator teres caput humeri; **6:** pronator teres caput ulnae; **7:** biceps brachii aponeurosis; **8:** supinator (according to Volkmann).

- Opening the branches: Abduction of the thumb and radial deviation of the hand
- Closing the branches: Adduction of the thumb and ulnar deviation of the hand

As soon as the movements are controlled, and the muscles are contracting appropriately, and the suture has healed properly, occupational therapy can be started, using small daily utensils and equipment.

ORTHOSES

An orthosis is a medically prescribed device applied to or around a body segment or manipulated by the body to aid function. The purposes of orthoses are as follows:

- Relieve pain
- Support the body weight or the weight of a body part
- Increase function or capacity
- Limit activity
- Prevent or correct deformity
- Reeducate muscles
- Stabilize joints

An articulation is a joint between rigid parts.

Immobilization restricts motion in a joint. It is seldom complete. Immobilization is used:

- to allow healing;
- to provide stability at proximal joints to allow effective muscular action at more distal joints;
- as a preoperative testing measure before arthrodesis;
- for pain relief.

Restriction in a brace ordinarily limits the available range of motion by means of stops. Stabilization maintains the alignment of two parts of the body by preventing unwanted motion.

A static splint is an unhinged brace that is used for positioning. Night splints and resting splints are examples. A dynamic splint is an articulated device that has a provision to replace the motive action of a muscle. A supportive orthosis has force characteristics to assist weak muscles with structural support. The inductive orthosis induces a reflex response to have the patient voluntarily or involuntarily move the body into a corrective position. It produces a physiologic change or response to counteract deformity. The mechanical forces exerted by the brace are insufficient by themselves to result in the desired response.

Serial casting, or bracing, which stretches slowly is much more effective than intermittent rapid stretch. Rapid stretch causes a reflex contraction of the muscles of the antagonist muscles, thus inhibiting stretching. Slow stretch fatigues the muscles on the contracted side, thereby allowing motion to the maximum that the joint is capable of at that time.

In the body the force exerted on a moving member (bone) depends on the force exerted by the muscle (which is determined by the cross-sectional area of that muscle) and the angle that that muscular force subtends to the bone. Muscular contraction is strongest when the muscle is stretched somewhat beyond its resting length. The resultant force will be the result of all of the forces acting on the part of the body under discussion. These forces are gravity, muscular contraction, and inertia.

Kinesthetics is the study of sensations by which muscle tensions, positions, and movements are perceived. Cybernetics is the science of communication and control in animals and machines. This is important, since all voluntary and involuntary motion in the human body is by muscular force. Muscular force is determined by the contractile effort willed and the sensations that are perceived from the muscles, joints, tendons, proprioceptors, and so forth. This information is conveyed to the central nervous system and "biases" the muscle spindles that modify muscular force. The process is then one of a constant interaction between sensation, central nervous system integration, and muscle action.

Brace prescription should be as detailed and specific as prescription of a medication. Each component of an orthosis or prosthesis should serve a specific patient need, depending on the patient's physical disability, his vocational, avocational, and social needs, and his intellectual capacity. It will be modified by economic constraints. The brace prescription should be specific as to type of brace or prosthesis in terms of function desired, the length, its components, the fasteners, the specific type or name, and the length of time that it is to be used. A brace or prosthesis is only one of a number of methods of treatment. It is to be used in conjunction with total patient care. It should be useful enough so that the patient will feel that it is worth the effort to purchase and use it. The patient should understand why the device is ordered, what it is like, and what is to be expected from its use. He should also understand that it has deficiencies, such as cost, weight, skin irritation.

Deformity is the result of persistent position. Soft tissues contract whenever they are not moved. The contraction is rapid. Contractures seldom develop when a joint is moved through its full range of motion more than twice daily. In order to assure that the joint is moved at least this amount, usually the prescription should be for moving the joint at least four times daily. Positioning encourages contracture unless it is combined with repeated motion. It does not prevent deformity, but it may be useful to encourage deformity in a more functional position. Positioning to restrict contracture in one direction should be alternated with motion to prevent contractures in the opposite direction. A flexed joint that is not moved allows the connective tissues to contract on the concave side of the curve and stretch on the convex side.

Night splints are of much greater importance than day splints, since prolonged immobility encourages contractures to develop. During the day, patients are moved, both for activities of daily living and during treatment. After therapy sessions stop until the next day when they restart, patients tend to be immobile. On weekends and holidays the time of immobility may be great. This is the most important time for orthoses to be used.

Soft tissues stretch best under gentle, slow, constant tension. This is best accomplished by a dynamic splint, or traction, used either all day or certainly after the last therapy session of the day until therapy resumes.

The force applied by an orthosis to the body is equal and opposite to the force the body applies to the brace by muscle action, gravity, and inertia.

As a rod is bent by the forces applied to it, one must take up the slack in a dynamic orthosis to continue to exert the same force. This is usually done by the three-point pressure principle with two points of pressure in one direction, one on either side of a force in the opposite direction. Dynamic splinting should always be done with a minimal force possible. The forces should generally be measured in grams rather than kilograms, even for the large joints. Splints need to be worn for many hours daily and, for this reason, must be comfortable to wear. Any orthosis that is uncomfortable will be discarded and useless. One must use the minimal force possible. A brace worn full time is better than one taken off for discomfort.

Balanced traction and skeletal fixation are occasionally useful methods for splint attachment that permits motion of the joints and prevents contractures without pressure on open areas, skin grafts, and so on.

One may control position of a body part in a number of ways. Immobilization is one type of position control. It is used (a) to allow healing, (b) to provide stability, (c) to transfer muscle function, and (d) for preoperative testing.

The position of rest for any joint is that position by which there is an absence of muscle activity as recorded electromyographically. Static alignment is for pain relief, promotion of desirable contractures, and preoperative testing. Active alignment is tracking stability to prevent motion in undesired directions while allowing motion in the desired plane. It is also used for prevention of deformity.

Motion control may be (a) total (immobilization); (b) endpoint control, which allows motion in one or more planes but stops the motion at a certain point for prevention of deformity or damage or for function; (c) guidance or tracking control, or control with assistance to motion in one or more planes. Assistive control acts by storing body power or by using external power forces.

The principles of bracing are as follows:

- Apply forces over an adequate surface area.
- Put the joint in the proper position.
- Use lever arms of proper length for the purpose to be achieved.
- There should be no pain or constriction of the body part.
- The body part should be in the desired position for function.
- Weight-bearing should be relieved if this is a function desired.
- The patient should preferably be able to apply the device himself, or any individual aiding him should be able to apply it consistently in a proper manner.
- The patient needs to be trained in donning and doffing the orthosis, in how it is to be used and maintenance.
- The appearance should be the optimal capable of being obtained, considering the function to be achieved.
- It should have minimal weight, complexity, and cost.

There are a number of avenues of orthotic approach. One is to modify the end-support conditions by supporting the end of a body part. An example of this is the Milwaukee brace. A second avenue is to unload the body part by supporting. An example of this is the back braces that "unload" the spine by restoring the intra-abdominal pressure. Another approach is to unload the supporting musculature by preventing deviations from a balanced posture (i.e., one in which electromyographic potentials are absent). Another avenue is to reduce motion, permit healing, reduce pain, and reduce muscle spasm. Another avenue of approach is to induce posture and deformity, correcting reflex responses and inductive brace.

Basically, orthotic joints can be classified into box joints that have one rod within, articulating with a more or less U-shaped insert on the outside rod, and lap joints in which two rods overlap each other.

Care of orthoses should be at least weekly. They should be washed with an appropriate cleansing soap. Leather should be washed with saddle soap. The dirt should be removed from joints and the joints should be oiled if they are metal. Any orthosis should be inspected for wear and missing parts or parts starting to wear or break. The alignment should be checked and the shoes and attachments should be proper. The patient should be told not to bang them. Plastic braces should be kept away from sources of heat such as the trunk or the back window of an automobile. Growing children should see the physician at least every 3 months to assure that the size remains proper.

There are dangers to use of orthoses as well as prostheses. Some of these dangers are (a) skin irritation or ulceration, (b) pressure atrophy of fat and muscle,

(c) restriction of function, (d) psychological problems, (e) possible distal deformities, (f) an orthosis may create its contractures if a child is allowed to grow out of the brace.

UPPER EXTREMITY ORTHOSES

The normal individual has a number of patterns of grasp that can be classified in a number of ways: palmar grasp (like pliers), lateral grasp, fingertip pinch, three-jaw chuck, hook grasp, cylindrical grasp, and spherical grasp.

Purposes of Hand Splints

Hand splints may be used to support and align the wrist and fingers in functional positions to provide rest and prevent deformity.

One of the purposes of hand splints is to adapt the hand to hold appliances (i.e., to supply programmed motions by adding dynamic movements to the hand). This may be for the purposes of correction of deformities or to add motive power.

There are a number of hand splint modifications to assist function and prevent deformity. Among those are (a) forearm extension, (b) lumbricales bar, (c) finger extension assist, (d) elastic opposition assist, (e) first dorsal interosseous assist, (f) finger flexion assist. These may be metal or rubber. A hand splint may hold appliances for the hand rather than have the hand hold the appliance.

There are three types of basic designs of hand splints: Georgia Warm Springs, Rancho Los Amigos, molded.

If one wishes to have various devices attached to the splint, one may attach, for example, a swivel "spork," a pencil holder, an electric shaver holder, or a typing device.

Another purpose of a hand splint may be to induce activity in an alienated muscle. This should not be done in muscles that are markedly weak. Hand splints may also be used for preoperative diagnosis.

Typical Conditions for Hand Splint Use

Flacidity
- peripheral nerve injury, congenital or acquired
- quadriplegia

Spasticity
- cerebral palsy
- acquired upper motion neuron disease

Inflammatory joint disease

Contractures

- burns
- fractures
- tendon damage

When there is no intact skin for finger traction, hooks may be glued to the fingernails for controlling finger position, or the skeletal fixation-balanced traction system may be used.

Tenodesis splints may be finger-driven, wrist-driven, or cable-driven. They may also be externally powered. Many designs are available. They may have locks or length-tension modifiers.

For hand splints, rubberband traction is generally better than spring-wire traction because it is more easily adjustable and replaceable.

Assistive control acts by storing body power or using external power sources, either pneumatic or electrical. The pneumatic orthosis uses carbon dioxide gas in the "McKibben muscle."

There are various "feeder" devices that allow a patient in a wheelchair, and sometimes ambulatory, to feed himself when he does not have adequate muscle power to bring objects to the mouth (Fig. 14-32). Among the types are (a) elastic suspension, (b) balanced forearm orthoses, (c) pneumatic or electrical. There are also programmed arm-carrying devices such as those devised at the Case Institute by Reswick and that devised at Rancho Los Amigos by Nickel.

Orthoses are indicated in the following types of cases:

Prevention of contractures, malpositions, and deformities:

—Bivalved splints in rheumatic diseases, pareses, or myopathies
—Correction of malpositions, contractures, or deformities. Early, uninterrupted treatment is desired.

- The three-point dynamic splint with traction may be used to treat ischemic contractures of the wrist and fingers.
- The static splint for the club hand is used to maintain the result achieved by serial correction or by surgery.

Temporary and permanent stabilization of one or more joints to provide for the function of a paralyzed extremity

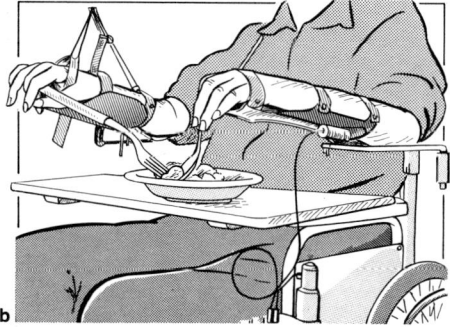

Fig. 14–32 Quadriplegic poliomyelitis patient with absent motor power on the left and weakness on the right. The arms are supported and moved by balanced forearm orthoses activated by trunk motion. Left lateral pinch is obtained by a pneumatic hand orthosis operated by left thigh abduction.

- Temporary stabilization of the shoulder and elbow joint in an adjustable work position by external locks (Fig. 14–33).
- Three-ring writing aid for paralyzed fingers (Fig. 14–34).

Replacement of Lost Active Mobility

Lost active mobility can be replaced by compensatory body motions, stored energy, or external power.

The principle can be explained in more detail by considering the example of paralyzed upper limbs. Shifting the weight of the trunk, which is still largely possible in a sitting position even for a severely paralyzed patient, is utilized by

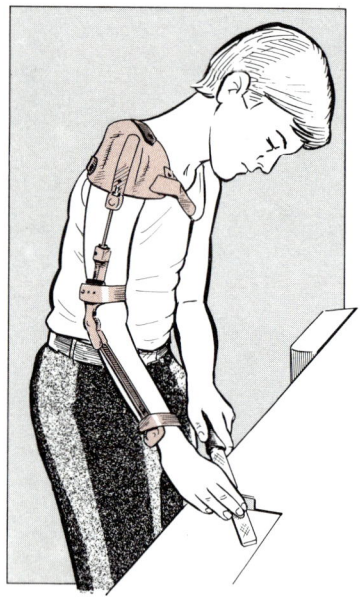

Fig. 14–33 Paralysis orthosis for the upper extremity with a Hosmer outside locking elbow joint. The shoulder cap is needed because of a paralyzed deltoid muscle. The lateral rod is used for passive rotation of the upper arm. This patient still has remaining function of the hand.

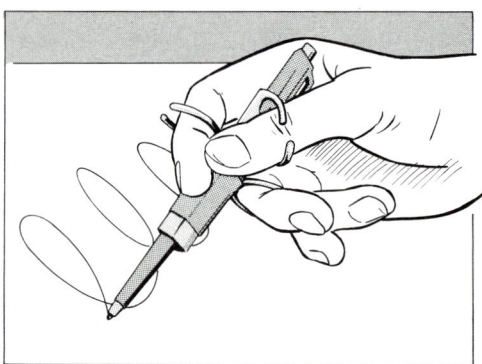

Fig. 14–34 Three-ring writing aid.

means of ball-bearing arm supports (balanced forearm orthoses), which facilitate finely controlled motions of shoulder and elbow joints within a certain radius, while supporting the weight of the arm. Excellent control of function and even a rapid change of direction are possible, for instance, in a poliomyelitic patient whose sensation is intact. For such patients only the lack of grasp and holding functions must be replaced.

A light orthosis can be worn on the body if the patient is able to walk. Orthoses with an external source of energy are useful for patients with complete loss of muscles of both shoulders and arms (Fig. 14–35). However, the orthosis may be a burden and could interfere with respiratory function. Training of the foot as a prehensile, sensate grasping organ and as an important replacement for the hand should not be overlooked for a young patient with bilateral paralysis of the arms.

LOWER LIMB ORTHOTICS

Orthoses may be simple; for example, temporary use of an elastic bandage to correct for a drop foot (Fig. 14–36) and peroneal spring (Fig. 14–37) exemplify energy storage in springs.

The materials of which an orthosis is made may vary from plaster of Paris, leather, wood, metals, to simple thermoplastic or esoteric thermosetting composite plastics (e.g., clubfoot splints for night use during the postoperative period to avoid recurrence, which need to be taken off during treatment).

Malpositions of the foot may be treated by an arch support (foot orthosis). The type must vary, depending on the patient's condition and age and other variables.

Fig. 14–35 Pneumatic orthosis for paralyzed muscles of the shoulder girdle and upper arm and minor pareses in the area of the forearm and hand muscles.

In the flexible pes valgus of an infant, we aim at a true correction. This can be secured only by an orthosis and additional physical therapy. In the adult with a fixed deformity, accommodation is required.

The application of orthoses is indicated as early as possible for instability and paralysis.

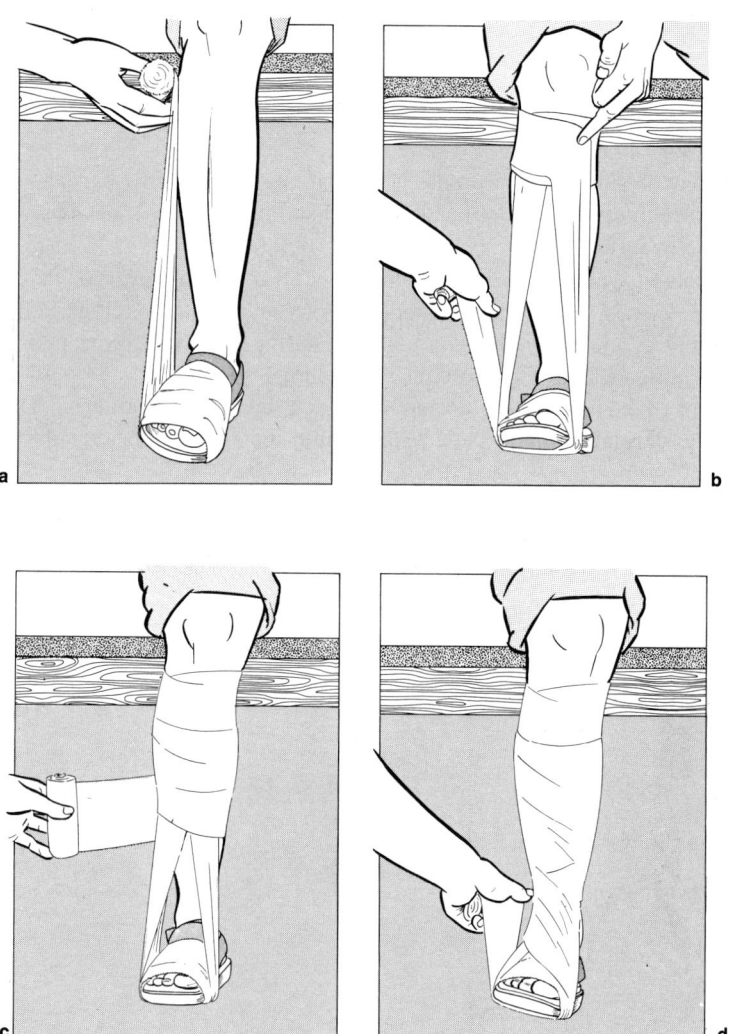

Fig. 14–36 Temporary corrective bandage for an equinus. *(continued)*

Lower Limb Orthotics 423

Fig. 14–36 continued

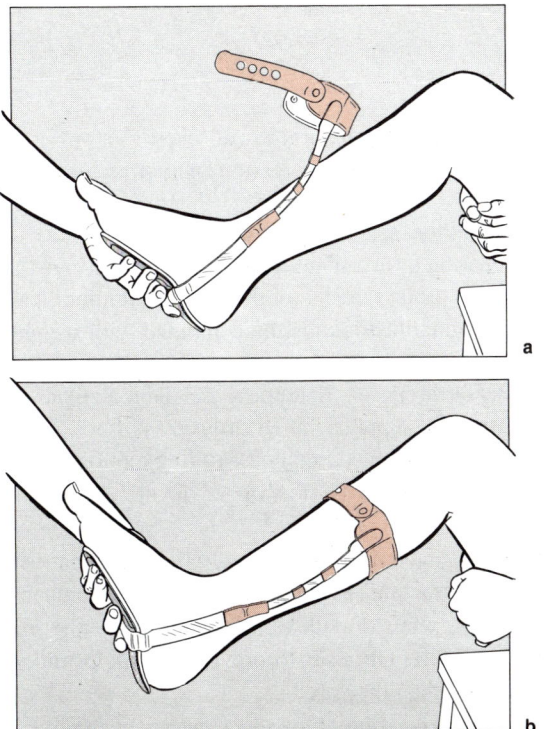

Fig. 14–37 Finlandic peroneal spring orthosis. (continued)

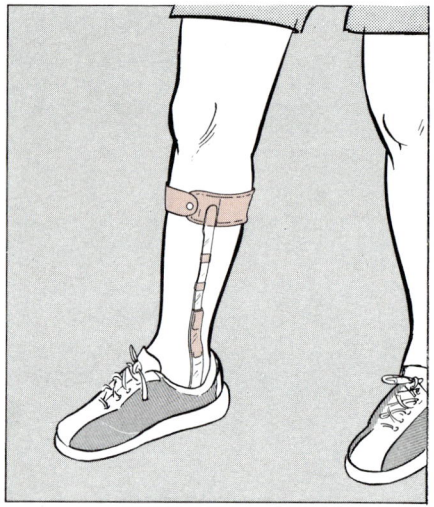

Fig. 14-37 *continued*

Weight Relief

Relief of a calcaneal exostosis (spur) or other painful exostoses by foot orthoses helps to maintain the shape of the foot while keeping pressure away from sensitive areas.

The Thomas splint or its modification according to Volkert (Fig. 14-38) is another example. During weight bearing or in a standing position, body weight is transmitted to the ischial tuberosity to protect the femoral head. The immobilization required by inflammation or pseudarthrosis must be combined with weight relief.

Immobilization is required after arthrodesis. Examples are internal fixation during surgery, an external arthrodesis support, or an arthrodesis boot. In a modified way, the principle of immobilization is used in the rolling motion of the foot inside the shoe with painfully restricted flexion of the great toe (hallux valgus).

Ankle dorsiflexion contractures are much more damaging to gait than contractures in mild plantar flexion, since contractures in plantar flexion can be compensated for by high heels and a shoe lift, while dorsiflexion contractures cannot be adequately compensated for by a toe lift. Orthoses to prevent foot deformities should be used much more commonly than they are.

Compensation for shortening of a leg is required to reduce energy expenditure and poor appearance in gait, and to prevent back and leg pain. Ways of doing this

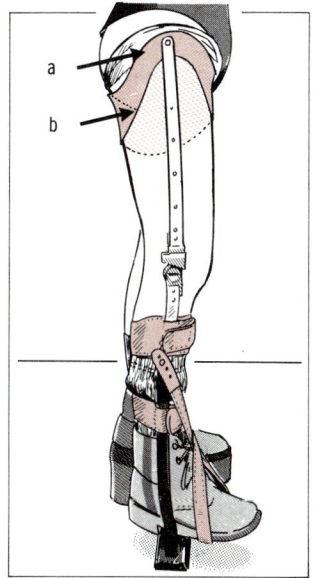

Fig. 14–38 Individual distribution and weight relief in the hip joint can be indicated and achieved with the splint system of the Mainz hip joint orthosis according to Volkert. Adjustments (a and b) facilitate surface coverage of the area of the femoral head.

may vary, depending on the amount of shortening and the individual's wishes, from orthopedic shoes with shoe lifts (external or internal), orthoses with shortening compensation, to an orthoprosthesis. If the deformed extremities are shortened severely, the structural and functional corrections (growth, mobility, stability, weight relief) of the deformed extremity are achieved with an orthosis, below which a prosthesis is attached to compensate for the shortening. Such a combination of orthoses and prosthesis is called orthoprosthesis (see Fig. 14–17).

In leg shortening and in orthoses for weight relief and immobilization, the compensation must be achieved with maximal spinal stability.

Patient function is improved by stabilizing joints that cannot be voluntarily controlled. Examples are, for instance, temporary fixation of the knee joint in extension with the Swiss lock; elimination of motion in the distal tarsal joint and an equinus strap on the mobile proximal tarsal joint in paralysis of the lower limb.

Orthoses of the lower limb require gait training; orthoses for the upper extremity need a functional occupational therapy program.

An orthoses is contraindicated if it interferes with the patient's remaining ability to stabilize his joints or to move in a controlled manner. The paralyzed or musculodystrophic patient can still shift his center of gravity. This may enable the patient to function adequately. A musculodystrophic patient may not need an orthosis, for example, if he can shift the axis of his knee joint back behind the weight-bearing line by assuming a slight talipes equinus position during weight bearing, or if he can contract his gluteus maximus muscle. The same patient will become dependent on an orthosis postoperatively if the equinus is eliminated completely and the weak quadriceps muscles can no longer stabilize the knee joint.

SPINAL ORTHOSES

Deformities

The Milwaukee, Boston, and similar braces are highly valuable in treating scolioses. They are initial remedies. Scoliosis braces are described in detail elsewhere in this book.

Bibliography

Atlas of Limb Prosthetics, Surgical and Prosthetic Principles, ed. by American Academy of Orthopaedic Surgeons. Mosby, St. Louis, 1981.

Baumgartner, R.: Beinamputation und Prothesenversorgungen bei arteriellen Durchblutungsstörungen. Enke, Stuttgart, 1973.

Baumgartner, R.: Amputation und Prothesenversorgung beim Kind. Enke, Stuttgart, 1977.

Baumgartner, R.: Beratung von Beinamputierten. Rehabilitation 21 (1982) 10–16.

Baumgartner, R., P.E. Ochsner, A. Schreiber: Checkliste Orthopädie. Thieme, Stuttgart, 1983.

Becker, E.: Skoliosen- und Diskopathienbehandlung, 6th Edition. Fischer, Stuttgart, 1973.

Benninghoff, A., K. Goerttler: Lehrbuch der Anatomie des Menschen, Bd. 1, 13th Edition. Urban & Schwarzenberg, München, 1980.

Bernbeck, R., J. Pramschiefer, H.D. Stolle: Technische Kinderorthopädie. Thieme, Stuttgart, 1982.

Bold, R., A. Großmann: Stemmführung nach R. Brunkow, 2nd Edition. Enke, Stuttgart, 1983.

Cotta, H.: Orthopädie, 4th Edition. Thieme, Stuttgart, 1984.

Daniels, L.: Muskelfunktionsprüfung. Fischer, Stuttgart, 1974.

Debrunner, H.U.: Orthopädisches Diagnostikum, 4th Edition. Thieme, Stuttgart, 1982.

Dederich, R.: Amputation der unteren Extremität. Thieme, Stuttgart, 1970.

Evjenth, O., J. Hamberg: Muskeldehnung warum und wie. Remed, Zug/Schweiz, 1981.

Frick, H., H. Leonhardt, D. Starck: Allgemeine Anatomie s. spezielle Anatomie I. Thieme, Stuttgart, 1980.

Frisch, H.: Programmierte Untersuchung des Bewegungsapparates. Springer, Heidelberg, 1983.

Gillert, O.: Elektrotherapie, 2nd Edition. Pflaum, München, 1983.

Groves, R., D.N. Camaione: Bewegungslehre in Krankengymnastik und Sport. Fischer, Stuttgart, 1977.

Harff, J., A. Großmann, U. Haeusermann: Übungsbehandlung für Säuglinge und Kleinkinder, 2nd Edition. Enke, Stuttgart, 1977.

Heipertz, W.: Sportmedizin, 6th Edition. Thieme, Stuttgart, 1980.

Heipertz, W., E. Schmitt: Wirbelsäulenerkrankungen. Springer, Berlin, 1978.

Hoepke, H., A. Landsberger: Das Muskelspiel des Menschen. Fischer, Stuttgart, 1979.

Hohmann, D., R. Uhlig: Orthopädische Technik, 7th Edition. Enke, Stuttgart, 1982.

Janda, V: Muskelfunktionsdiagnostik. Fischer, Heidelberg, 1979.

Jentschura, G.: Haltungsschäden bei Kindern und Jugendlichen. Enke, Stuttgart, 1977.

Jentschura, G., H.-W. Janz: Beschäftigungstherapie, 3rd Edition. Bd. I/II. Thieme, Stuttgart, 1979.

Kaeppel, R.G.: Das Schlingengerät in der Praxis der Krankengymnastik. Kohlhammer, Stuttgart, 1971.

Kaltenborn, F.: Manuelle Therapie der Extremitätengelenke. Norlis, Oslo, 1977.

Keller, M.: Die krankengymnastische Betreuung von Skoliose-Patienten im Milwaukee-Korsett. Krankengymnastik 27 (1975) 3/4.

Kersten, H.: Gehschule für Beinamputierte, 2nd Edition. Thieme, Stuttgart, 1975.

Klapp, B.: Das Klappsche Kriechverfahren, 11th Edition. Thieme, Stuttgart, 1982.

Klein-Vogelbach, S.: Funktionelle Bewegungslehre. Springer, Berlin, 1978.

Klein-Vogelbach, S.: Therapeutische Übungen zur funktionellen Bewegungslehre. Springer, Berlin, 1978.

Klein-Vogelbach, S.: Ballgymnastik zur funktionellen Bewegungslehre. Springer, Berlin, 1980.

Knott, M.: Komplexbewegungen. Fischer, Stuttgart, 1970.

Krämer, J.: Bandscheibenbedingte Erkrankungen. Thieme, Stuttgart, 1978.

Kuhn, G.G.: Kunstarmbau in Gießharztechnik. Thieme, Stuttgart, 1968.

Kucera, M.: Krankengymnastische Übungen. Fischer, Stuttgart, 1978.

Lehnert-Schroth, Chr.: Dreidimensionale Skoliosebehandlung. Kaschuge, Duisburg, 1973.
Lewit, K.: Manuelle Medizin im Rahmen der medizinischen Rehabilitation. Urban & Schwarzenberg, München, 1984.
List, M.: Eisbehandlung in der Krankengymnastik, München, 1978.
List, M.: Die Krankengymnastische Behandlung in der Traumatologie. Springer, Berlin, 1978.
Malick, M.H.: Dynamic splints for the hand. Harmarville, Rehabilitation Center, Pittsburgh, 1978.
Marquardt, E.: Steigerung der Effektivitat von Oberarmprothesen durch Winkelosteotomie. Rehabilitation 11 (1972) 244.
Marquardt, E.: Die Chopart-Exartikulation mit Tenomyoplastik. Z. Orthop. 111 (1973) 584.
Marquardt, E.: Plastische Operationen bei drohender Knochendurchspießung am kindlichen Oberarmstumpf. Z. Orthop. 114 (1976) 711.
Marquardt, E., A.K. Martini: Orthesen und funktionsverbessernde Operationen für Kinder mit Gliedmaßenfehlbildungen der unteren Extremität. Therapiewoche 29 (1979) 3132–3146.
Marquardt, E., H. Roesler: Prothesen und Prothesenversorgungen der oberen Extremität. In Witt, A.N., H. Rettig, K.F. Schlegel, M. Hackenbroch, W. Hupfauer: Orthopädie in Praxis und Klinik Bd. II. Allgemeine Orthopädie. Thieme, Stuttgart, 1981 (16.1–16.39).
Marquardt, E., S. Heyne: Beratung von Amputierten der oberen Gliedmaßen. In Sonderband 1: Rehabilitation Behinderter-Hinweise für Beratungsdienste. Rehabilitation 22 (1983) 56.
Matev, I.B., St. D. Bankov: Rehabilitation der Hand. Thieme, Stuttgart, 1982.
Matzen, P.F.: Orthopädie für Studierende. Barth, Leipzig, 1977.
Moberg, E.: Orthesen in der Handtherapie. Thieme, Stuttgart, 1982.
Neumann-Neurode, D.: Säuglingsgymnastik, 30th Edition. Quelle & Meyer, Heidelberg, 1979.
Peters, A.: Bewegungsanalyse und Bewegungstherapie im Säuglings- und Kleinkindalter. Fischer, Stuttgart, 1977.
Rabl, C.R.H., W. Nyga: Orthopädie des Fußes. Enke, Stuttgart, 1982.
Scharll, M.: Orthopädische Krankengymnastik, 7th Edition. Thieme, Stuttgart, 1984.
Schede, F.: Grundlagen der körperlichen Erziehung, 5th Edition. Enke, Stuttgart, 1969.
Tittel, K.: Beschreibende und funktionelle Anatomie des Menschen. Fischer, Stuttgart, 1974.

Trebes, G., U. Rolf, H. Röttgen, J. Groth: Die Armschulung. Thieme, Stuttgart, 1970.

tum Suden, A.: Unterwassergymnastik. Krankengymnastik 24 (1972) 257.

tum Suden, A.: Kryotherapie in der Orthopädie. Krankengymnastik 32 (1980) 70.

tum Suden, A.: Bücktraining in der Gruppe? Krankengymnastik 34 (1982) 527.

Vleeming, A., D. Winkel, O.G. Meijer: Schematisch handboek voor onderzoek en behandeling van weke delen aandoeningen van het bewegingsapparaat. Deel 1: Anatomie in Vivo. Nederlandse Akademie voor Orthopedische Geneeskunde, Delft, 1982.

Wagner, M., R. Schabus: Funktionelle Anatomie des Kniegelenkes. Springer, Heidelberg, 1982.

Winkel, D., S. Fischer: Schematisch handboek voor onderzoek en behandeling van weke delen aandoeningen van het bewegingsapparaat. Deel 2: diagnostiek. Nederlandse Akademie voor Orthopedische Geneeskunde, Delft, 1982.

Zielke, A.M., u.a.: Mobilisationsgymnastik mit Skoliosepatienten in der Halo-Extensionsgruppe. Krankengymnastik 26 (1974) 246.

Fachzeitschriften

Der Orthopäde. Springer, Berlin.

Medizinisch-orthopädische Technik. Gentner, Stuttgart.

Orthopädietechnik. Hrsg. vom Bundesinnungsverband für Orthopädietechnik, Dortmund.

Prosthetics and Orthotics International. Publ. by International Society for Prosthetics and Orthotics (ISPO), Kopenhagen; produced by the National Center for Training and Education in Prosthetics and Orthotics, University of Strathclyde, Glasgow.

Zeitschrift für Orthopädie und ihre Grenzgebiete. Enke, Stuttgart.

Orthopädische Praxis. Medizinisch Literarischer Verlag, Uelzen.

Index

A

Abdominal muscles, exercises, 100
Acetabulum, profusion
  origin, 246
  symptoms, 246-247
  therapy, 247
Achilles tendon, rupture, 335-336
  nonsurgical treatment, 336
  origin, 335
  surgical treatment, 336
  symptoms, 336
Achillodynia, 335
  origin, 335
  symptoms, 335
  treatment, 335
Achondroplasia, 12, 120
  manifestations, 12
  origin, 12
  symptons, 12
  treatment, 12
Acquired systemic disease
  clinical manifestations, 19-21
  evaluation, 19
  physical therapy, 22
Acromegaly
  partial, 25-26
  true, 25-26

Aging
  connective tissue, 49-51
  musculoskeletal system, 49-55
  supportive tissue, 49-51
Alloplastic implant, 366-369
Ambulation aid, 280-285
Amelia, 24
  prosthesis, 392-393
Amputation, 372-414
  bandaging, 405-407
  gait training, 409-410
  hygiene, 408
  indications, 372
  lower limb
    contractures, 403-405
    immediate prosthesis fitting, 381-384
    physical therapy, 402-405
  physical therapy, 401-414
  plastic cap, 375
  postoperative care, 375-381
    airbag compression, 378
    bypass prosthesis, 380-381
    controlled environment treatment, 377
    custom molding, 379
    early prosthesis application, 375-376

elastic dressing, 378
goals, 375
hospital discharge, 380
hyperbaric oxygen, 378
immediate prosthesis fitting, 381-384
limb shaping, 378
rigid contact dressing, 376
simple dressing, 378
skin traction, 378
socket design, 379
temporary prosthesis, 378-379
Unna semirigid dressing, 377
walking, 380
wound healing delay, 380-381
rehabilitation, 371
skin lesion prevention, 408
stump massage, 408
techniques, 372
toe, 385
upper extremity, 373-375
upper limb
early prosthesis, 395
immediate prosthesis fitting, 395
Ankylosing spondylitis, 79
Arachnodactyly, 14, 121
origin, 14
symptoms, 14
treatment, 14
Arm, prosthesis
body powered, 398-399
cosmetic, 396
externally powered, 399-401
passive work, 396-398
Arthritis, 211
hip, physical therapy, 258-280
luetic (syphilitic), 74-75
metabolic disturbance, 79-80
physical therapy, 85
origin, 211
symptoms, 211
treatment, 211
unspecific, 71
Arthrodesis, 364

hip, 279-280
Arthrogryposis, 14
origins, 14
physical therapy, 18
symptoms, 14
treatment, 14
Arthrogryposis multiplex congenita, 14
Arthrolysis, 363
operative, 64
Arthropathia hemophilica, 15-16
origin, 15-16
symptoms, 16
treatment, 16
Arthropathy, luetic (syphilitic), 74
Arthroplasty, 365
Arthroscopy, 363-364
Arthrosis, 51-55
hand, physical therapy, 231
knee, 297
nonsurgical treatment, 297
origin, 297
surgical treatment, 297
symptoms, 297
medication, 55
origin, 52-53
physical therapy, 55
symptoms, 53-54
treatment, 54-55
conservative, 54
surgical, 55
Arthrosyndesis, shoulder, physical therapy, 207-209
Arthrotomy, 363

B

Back muscles, exercises, 99-100
origin, 178
physical therapy, 179-183
evaluation, 180-181
exercises, 182-183
goals, 181

therapy, 181–182
symptoms, 179
treatment, 179
Bell-shaped chest, 111
Biofeedback, 2
Blood type incompatibility, 24
Bone
  inflammative diseases, 65–85
  operations on, 359–363
Bone cyst
  aneurismatic, 31
    origin, 31
    symptoms, 31
    treatment, 31
  solitary, 30–31
    origin, 30
    symptoms, 30
    treatment, 31
Bone density change, 12–14
Bone necrosis
  clinical manifestations, 35–45
  evaluation, 35
  localization, 36–37
  physical therapy, 45–47
  spine, 122–127
Bone remodeling disturbance, 12–14
Bone tumor, secondary malignant, 33–34
  origin, 33–34
  symptoms, 34
  treatment, 34
Bow legs, 294
Brace. See Orthosis
Brittle bone disease, 12–14, 121
  origin, 12
  symptoms, 13
  treatment, 14
Bypass prosthesis, 380–381, 383

C

Calcaneal exostosis, 335
Calcaneus, 318
Canadian hip disarticulation prosthesis, 392

Cane, 284
  handle, 284
  height adjustment, 284
  platform, 284
Cartilaginous exostosis, 28
  multiple, 28, 29
  origin, 28
  symptoms, 28
  treatment, 28
Cervical syndrome, 154–158
  origin, 154
  physical therapy, 155–158
    evaluation, 155–156
    goals, 156
    therapy, 156–158
  symptoms, 154–155
  treatment, 155
Chondrocalcinosis, 79–80
Chondrodystrophia calcarea, 12
  origin, 12
  symptoms, 12
  treatment, 12
Chondrodystrophia calcificans, 12
  origin, 12
  symptoms, 12
  treatment, 12
Chondrodystrophia fetalis, 12
  manifestations, 12
  origin, 12
  symptoms, 12
  treatment, 12
Chondromalacia patella, 290–291
  nonsurgical treatment, 311–312
  origin, 290
  postoperative treatment, 312
  symptoms, 290
  treatment
    nonsurgical, 290
    surgical, 290–291
  origin, 28
  symptoms, 30
  treatment, 30
Chondrosarcoma, 32–33
  origin, 32
  symptoms, 32
  treatment, 33

Chondrosis, 152–154
  origin, 152
  physical therapy, 153–154
    examination, 153
    goals, 153
    therapy, 154
  symptoms, 152
  treatment, 152–153
Chromosome aberration, 24
Claw toe, 332–333
  nonsurgical treatment, 333
  origin, 332
  physical therapy, 354–355
  surgical treatment, 333
  symptoms, 333
Cleidocranial dysostosis, 121
Clubfoot
  acquired, 326
    origins, 326
    symptoms, 326
    treatment, 326
  congenital, 320–326
    conservative treatment, 324–325
    origin, 320–321
    physical therapy, 336–338, 339–340
    surgical treatment, 325–326
    symptoms, 321–324
    treatment, 324
Congenital systemic disease
  evaluation, 11–17
  physical therapy, 16–17
Connective tissue, aging, 49–51
Contractile structure, 2
Contracture
  acquired, 57–59
    intraarticular dysfunctions, 58
    periarticular dysfunctions, 58–59
  clinical manifestations, 57–59
  congenital, 57
  evaluation, 57
  exercise
    active, 60
    active/passive, 61–63
    passive, 61
  physical therapy, 59–64

  conservative, 59–63
  joint manipulation under
    anesthesia, 63–64
  operative arthrolysis, 64
Coordination exercises, 100–102
Correction, evaluation, 2
Coxa saltans, 249
Coxa valga, 247–248
  origin, 247
  symptoms, 247–248
  treatment, 248
Coxa vara, 248
  origin, 248
  symptoms, 248
  treatment, 248
Coxa vara adolescentium, 39–41
Coxa vara epiphysarea, 39–41
Craniotabes, 19
Crus varum, 296
  nonsurgical treatment, 296
  origin, 296
  surgical treatment, 296
  symptoms, 296
Crus varum congenitum, 297
  nonsurgical treatment, 297
  origin, 297
  surgical treatment, 297
  symptoms, 297
Crutches, 282

D

Daily activity level, 10
Deformity
  deficient development, 24–25
  endogenous factors, 24
  evaluation, 23–26
  excessive development, 25–26
  exogenous factors, 24
  physical therapy, 26
  spine, 105–120
Degenerative diseases, spinal, 150–154
Derotation, 256–257

Digitus quintus varus superductus,
  333–334
  nonsurgical treatment, 334
  origin, 333
  surgical treatment, 334
  symptoms, 334
Disarticulation, 372
Discoid meniscus, 289
  exercises, 307–311
  origin, 289
  postoperative treatment, 307–311
  symptoms, 289
  treatment, 289
Dorsal hump, 334
Drug, deformity etiology, 24
Duchenne sign, 255–256
Dupuytren's contracture, 221
  origin, 221
  physical therapy, 231–232
    goals, 231
    postoperative treatment, 232
    therapy, 231–232
  symptoms, 221
  treatment, 221
Dysplasia, skeletal, 12

E

Ectromelia, 24
Elbow
  clinical symptoms, 210–211
  evaluation, 209–210
  physical therapy, 211–213
Enchondromatosis, 28–30
Endoprosthesis, 368–369
  replacement, 277–278
  total, removal, 278–279
Epicondylitis, 211
  origin, 211
  physical therapy, 211–213
    conservative, 212
    evaluation, 211–212
    goals, 212

  postoperative, 213
  symptoms, 211
  treatment, 211
Epicondylopathia humeri, 211
Epiphysiolysis
  femoral head, 39–41
    origin, 39–40
    physical therapy, 46–47
    symptoms, 40–41
    treatment, 41
Epiphysiolysis capitis femoris, 39–41
Epiphysis, 12
Equinus, 328–329
  nonsurgical treatment, 328
  origin, 328
  physical therapy, 336–338
  surgical treatment, 328–329
  symptoms, 328
Evaluation
  acquired systemic disease, 19
  bone necrosis, 35
  congenital systemic disease, 11–17
  contracture, 57
  correction, 2
  deformity, 23–26
  documentation, 2
  elbow, 209–210
  finger, 213–220
  foot, 318–320
  hand, 213–220
  hip joint, 233–237
  individual, 1
  joint, 2
  joint effusion, 286
  knee, 285–289
  knee joint contracture, 286–287
  movement, 2
  musculoskeletal system aging process,
    49
  pelvis, 233, 234
  posture, 2
  shoulder, 189–192
  spine, 89–94
  thumb, 213
  tumor, 27–34

Evaluation sheet, 2
Exercise program, 97

F

Fatigue man's disease, 127
Femoral head
  epiphysiolysis, 39–41
  idiopathic necrosis, 246
    origin, 246
    symptoms, 246
  resection, 278–279
Finger
  evaluation, 213–220
  sensory function, 215–218
  trigger
    origin, 221
    physical therapy, 232
    symptoms, 221
    treatment, 221
Fissure, vertebral, 118–120
Flat back, 96
  exercises, 102–104
Flatfoot, congenital, 329
  nonsurgical treatment, 239
  physical therapy, 336–338, 340–348
  surgical treatment, 239
  symptoms, 329
Foot
  clinical symptoms, 320–336
  evaluation, 318–320
  excavated, 327–328
    excavated clawfoot, 328
    nonsurgical treatment, 328
    origin, 327
    surgical treatment, 328
    symptoms, 327
  infant
    normal development, 340
    physical therapy, 336–338
  physical therapy, 336–355
  prosthesis, 385, 388
  sickle (or crescent)-shaped, 326
    nonsurgical treatment, 326
    origin, 326
    physical therapy, 336–338
    surgical treatment, 326
    symptoms, 326
  split, 24
Funnel chest, 111–112
  physical therapy, 113
    exercises, 114
    goals, 113
    techniques, 114

G

Gait training, amputation, 409–410
Ganglion, 30
  origin, 30
  symptoms, 30
  treatment, 30
Genetic mutation, 24
Genu recurvatum, 293–294
  acquired, 293
  congenital, 293
  nonsurgical treatment, 293
  surgical treatment, 294
  symptoms, 293
Genu valgum, 294–296
  nonsurgical treatment, 312–313
  origin, 294–295
  postoperative treatment, 313–315
  surgical treatment, 295–296
  symptoms, 295
  treatment, 295
Genu varum, 294
  acquired, 294
  congenital, 294
  nonsurgical treatment, 294, 312–313
  postoperative treatment, 313–315
  surgical treatment, 294
  symptoms, 294
Gonarthrosis, inflammation, 297
Gout, 79
Grip, 216–217

H

Haglund exostosis, 334–335
Hallux rigidus
  origin, 332
  physical therapy, 353–354
  symptoms, 332
  treatment, 332
Hallux valgus, 330–332
  nonsurgical treatment, 330
  origin, 330
  physical therapy, 350–353
  surgical treatment, 331–332
  symptoms, 330
Hand
  clinical symptoms, 220–221
  club. See Club hand
  evaluation, 213–220
  physical therapy, 221–232
    arm position, 230
    evaluation, 221–222
    exercises, 223–228
    goals, 222–223
    intensity, 226–230
    technique, 226–230
    therapy, 223
  prosthesis, cosmetic, 396
  sensory function, 215–218
  split, 24
Hand splint, 418–421
  activity mobility, 419–421
  conditions, 418–419
  purposes, 418
Harrison's groove, 20
Hemophiliac joint, 15–16
  origin, 15–16
  symptoms, 16
  treatment, 16
Hip
  arthritis, 245–246
    conservative treatment, 258–272
    nonsurgical treatment, 245
    origin, 245
    physical therapy, 258–280
    surgical treatment, 246, 272–280
    symptoms, 245
  arthrodesis, 279–280
  jerking, 249
  snapping, 249
    origin, 249
    symptoms, 249
    treatment, 249
Hip dysplasia/dislocation, 237–245
  closed (nonsurgical) reduction, 243
  incidence, 237–238
  nonsurgical treatment, 242
  origin, 238
  physical therapy, 250–257
  surgical treatment, 243–245
  symptoms, 238–242
    reliable, 240–242
    unreliable, 238–240
Hip joint
  abduction, 234–235
  adduction, 234–235
  clinical manifestations, 237–249
  congenital dislocation, 237–245
  evaluation, 233–237
  extension, 234
  flexion, 234
  rotation, 235–236
Hump, dorsal, 334
Humpback, 20
Hydrotherapy, shoulder, 204

I

Implant
  alloplastic, 366–369
  long-term, 367, 368
  short-term, 367
Infection, 24
Insertion, 2

J

Joint
  evaluation, 2

hemophiliac, 15–16
  hemorrhage, 17
  origin, 15–16
  physical therapy, 17
  symptoms, 16
  synovitis, 17
  treatment, 16
inflammative diseases, 65–85
manipulation under anesthesia, 63–64
surgical procedures, 363–365
Joint capsule, 2
Joint cartilage removal, 279–280
joint effusion
  abacterial, 71–72
    origin, 71–72
    physical therapy, 80–82
    symptoms, 72
    treatment, 72
  bacterial, 73
    origin, 73
    symptoms, 73
    treatment, 73
  evaluation, 286
  physical therapy, 298–306
    contracture, 299–302
    control measurements, 298
    exercises, 302–306
    immobilization, 298
    position, 298
    puncture, 299
    treatment, 298
Joint mobility, progression, 2, 10
Joint rheumatism, acute, 75
  origin, 75
  symptoms, 75
  treatment, 75
Joint tuberculosis, 73–74
  origin, 73–74
  symptoms, 74
  treatment, 74

K

Keeled chest, 111, 112–113
Knee
  arthrodesis, 317–318
  clinical symptoms, 289–297
  contracture, evaluation, 286–287
  evaluation, 285–289
  physical therapy, 297–313
  prosthesis, 388–389
Knee disarticulation, 388–389
Knee joint
  congenital dislocation, 292–293
    origin, 292
    symptoms, 292
    treatment, 293
  inflammation, 315–317
    evaluation, 315–316
    goals, 316
    nonsurgical treatment, 315–317
    postoperative treatment, 317
    therapy, 316–317
  instability, 288–289
Knee muscle, atrophy, 287–288
Köhler-Freiberg's disease, 43–45
Köhler II disease, 43–45
Krukenberg plasty, 373
  physical therapy, 412
Kyphosis, 20, 96
  juvenile, 122–126
    origin, 122–123
    physical therapy
      exercises, 125–126
      goals, 124–125
      techniques, 125
    symptoms, 123–124
    treatment, 124
Kyphosis/lordosis, 96
  exercises, 104–105

L

Leg, length differences, 236–237
Leg deformity, 20
Lesion, tumorlike, 28, 31
Ligament, 2, 87
Lumbar syndrome, 159–171
  origin, 159

Index 439

physical therapy, 163-171
  evaluation, 163, 164
  exercises, 165-171
  goals, 163-164
  therapy, 163-164, 164-165
symptoms, 159-160
treatment, 161-162
Luxatio coxa congenita, 237-245

M

Mallet toe, 332-333
  nonsurgical treatment, 333
  origin, 332
  physical therapy, 354-355
  surgical treatment, 333
  symptoms, 333
Marble bone disease, 122
March fracture, 335
  physical therapy, 355
Marfan's syndrome, 14, 121
  origin, 14
  symptoms, 14
  treatment, 14
Meniscectomy, discoid meniscus, 307-311
Meniscus, discoid, 289
  exercises, 307-311
  origin, 289
  postoperative treatment, 307-311
  symptoms, 289
  treatment, 289
Metaphysis, 12
Metatarsal fatigue, 335
Metatarsal head, 318
Metatarsalgia, 334
Metatarsus latus, 329
Mobility
  active, 2
  passive, 2
Mobilization, shoulder, 199-202
Morquio-Brailsford disease, 14-15
  origin, 14
  symptoms, 15
  treatment, 15

Morton's neuroma, 334
Movement
  against resistance, 2
  evaluation, 2
Mucopolysaccharidosis, 121
Mucopolysacchariddosis IV, 14-15
  origin, 14
  symptoms, 15
  treatment, 15
Muscle, 2. *See also Specific type*
Muscle strength, documentation, 3-9
Muscle strengthening, shoulder, 202-204
Musculoskeletal system aging process
  clinical manifestations, 49-55
  evaluation, 49
  physical therapy, 55
Myoelectric prosthesis, training, 410-412

N

Neuroma, Morton's 334
Noncontractile structure, 2

O

Orthopedic technician, 10
Orthosis, 414-425
  care, 417
  lower limb, 421-425
    weight relief, 424-425
  principles, 416-417
  purposes, 414
  spinal, 425
  upper extremity, 417-421
Osgood-Schlatter's disease, 43
Osteitis, 65
Osteitis deformans, 21, 70-71
  origin, 21
  symptoms, 21
  treatment, 21
Osteoarthritis, shoulder joint, 193
  symptoms, 193
  treatment, 193

Osteochondroma, 28, 29
    origin, 28
    symptoms, 28
    treatment, 28
Osteochondrosarcoma, 32
    origin, 32
    symptoms, 32
    treatment, 32
Osteochondritis dissecans, 42, 43
    origin, 42
    symptoms, 42
    treatment, 42
Osteochondritis of calcaneal apophysis, 43
    symptoms, 43
    treatment, 43
Osteochondritis of metatarsal head, 43–45
    origin, 45
    symptoms, 45
    treatment, 45
Osteochondritis of tibial head apophysis, 43
Osteoclastoma, 31
    characteristics, 31
    origins, 31
    symptoms, 31
    treatment, 31
Osteochondrodystrophy, 14–15
    origin, 14
    symptoms, 15
    treatment, 15
Osteodystrophia deformans, 21, 70–71
    origin, 21
    symptoms, 21
    treatment, 21
Osteofibrosarcoma, 32
    origin, 32
    symptoms, 32
    treatment, 32
Osteogenesis imperfecta, 12–14, 121
    origin, 12
    physical therapy, 16
    symptoms, 13
    treatment, 14

Osteogenesis imperfecta congenita Vrolik, 13
Osteogenesis imperfecta tarda, 13
Osteogenesis imperfecta type Lobstein, 13
Osteoma, osteoid, 31
    origin, 31
    symptoms, 31
    treatment, 31
Osteomalacia, 21, 173–174
    origin, 21
    physical therapy, 174
        evaluation, 174
        goals, 174
        therapy, 174
    symptoms, 21
    treatment, 21
Osteomyelitis, 65
    acute exogenous, 67
        origin, 67
        treatment, 67
    acute hematogenous, 66–67
        origin, 66
        symptoms, 66
        treatment, 67
    classification, 65
    infant, 66–67
    physical therapy, 80
    posttraumatic, 67
    primary chronic, 68–70
        origin, 68
        symptoms, 68–70
        treatment, 70
    secondary chronic, 67–68
        origin, 67
        symptoms, 67
        treatment, 67–68
    specific, 70
        origin, 70
        symptoms, 70
        treatment, 70
Osteoporosis, 21, 172–173
    origin, 21, 172
    symptoms, 21, 172
    treatment, 21, 172–173

Osteopsathyrosis, 12–14
    origin, 12
    symptoms, 13
    treatment, 14
Osteopsathyrosis Lobstein, 13
Osteosarcoma, 32
    origin, 32
    symptoms, 32
    treatment, 32
Osteotomy, 313–315, 359–363
    angular of humerus, 373–375
    elongation, 362–363
    pelvic, 257
Oxygen deficiency, 24

P

Paget's disease, 21, 70–71
    origin, 21, 70
    symptoms, 21, 70–71
    treatment, 21, 71
Parallel bar, 282
Paratenonitis Achillae, 335
Patella, dislocation, acquired, 292
    congenital, 291
    habitual, 291–292
    postoperative treatment, 311
Patient history, 2–10
Pelvis
    evaluation, 233–234
    osteotomy, 257
Periarthropathia humeroscapularis, 193–195
    acute shoulder stiffness, 193
    ankylosing shoulder stiffness, 194
    origin, 193
    pseudoparalytic shoulder stiffness, 194
    radiographic findings, 194
    ruptured rotator cuff, 194
    simple periarthritis, 193
    treatment, 194
Periarthrosis coxae, 248, 249

    origin, 249
    symptoms, 248
Peromelia, 24
Perthe's disease, 38–39
    physical therapy, 46
    symptoms, 38
    treatment, 38–39
Pes calcaneus, 327
    nonsurgical treatment, 327
    origin, 327
    surgical treatment, 327
    symptoms, 327
Pes calcaneus congenitus, 327
    nonsurgical treatment, 327
    origin, 327
    symptoms, 327
Pes calcaneus excavatus, 327
    nonsurgical treatment, 327
    origin, 327
    surgical treatment, 327
    symptoms, 327
Pes equinovarus et adductus, 320–326
Pes planus, physical therapy, 336–338, 340–348
Pes transversoplanus, 329
Pes valgus, physical therapy, 340–348
Phocomelia, 24
    prosthesis, 392–393
Photography, 2
Physical therapy
    acquired systemic disease, 22
    amputation, 401–414
        upper limb, 410–413
    bone inflammation diseases, 80–85
    bone necrosis, 45–47
    cervical syndrome, 155–158
    chondrosis, 153–154
    congenital systemic disease, 16–17
    contracture, 59–64
        conservative, 59–63
        joint manipulation under anesthesia, 63–64
        operative arthrolysis, 64
    elbow, 211–213
    foot, 336–355

foot deformity, infant, 336–338
hand, 221-232
hip arthritis, 258–280
hip dysplasia/dislocation, 250–257
infant scoliosis, 144–150
joint inflammation diseases, 80–85
juvenile kyphosis, 124–126
knee, 297–313
lumbar syndrome, 163–171
postural weakness, 96–105
recurrent shoulder dislocation, 205–207
scoliosis, 131–144
shoulder, 196–205
shoulder arthrosyndesis, 207–209
spine malposition, 96–105
torticollis, 107–111
tumor, 34
Platform cane, 284
Polyarthritis, chronic, 75–76
  juvenile, 77–78
  origin, 75–76
  physical therapy, 82–85
  symptoms, 76
  synovectomy, 84–85
  treatment, 76
Polyarthritis rheumatica acuta, 75
Polydactylia, 25
Posture
  evaluation, 2
  habitual, 94
Prosthesis
  above-knee, 379–380, 390–392
  amelia, 392–393
  arm
    body powered, 398–399
    cosmetic, 396
    externally powered, 399–401
    passive work, 396–398
  below-knee, 379–380, 385-386
  body-powered, training, 410–412
  foot, 388
  hand, cosmetic, 396
  immediate fitting, 381–384
  knee, 388–389
  lower extremity, permanent, 385–395
  phocomelia, 392–393
  socket design, 379
  upper limb, 395–401
    active, 398–401
    passive, 396–398
Pseudoacromegaly, 26
Pseudogout, 79
Psoriatic arthritis
  origin, 79
  symptoms, 79
  treatment, 79

Q

Quadcane, 282
Quervain's disease, 220–221
  origin, 220
  symptoms, 221
  treatment, 221

R

Rachitis, 19–20
  origin, 19
  symptoms, 19–20
  treatment, 20
Range of motion
  elbow, 210
  finger, 218
  forearm, 210
  knee joint, 287
  wrist, 218
Reaction exercises, 100–102
Rehabilitation, 371
Reiter's disease, 78–79
  origin, 78
  symptoms, 78–79
  treatment, 79
Resting position, 94–95
Reticulosarcoma, undifferentiated, 33
  etiology, 33

origin, 33
symptoms, 33
treatment, 33
Rheumatic arthritis, 75–79
Rheumatoid fever, 75
Rhizarthrosis, 231
Rickets, 19–20
  adult, 21
  origin, 19
  renal, 20
  symptoms, 19–20
  treatment, 20

S

Sarcoma
  Ewing's, 33
    etiology, 33
    origin, 33
    symptoms, 33
    treatment, 33
  osteogenic, 32
    origin, 32
    symptoms, 32
    treatment, 32
Scalenus syndrome, 192
  origin, 192
  symptoms, 192
  treatment, 192
Schlatter's disease, 43, 44
  origin, 43
  symptoms, 43
  treatment, 43
Scoliosis, 127–150
  classification, 128
  conservative treatment, 131–136
    evaluation, 131–132
    exercises, 135–136
    goals, 132
    therapy, 133–135
  infant, 144–150
    physical therapy, 144–150
  neuropathic, 130
  origin, 127–128

physical therapy, 131–144
preoperative treatment, 140–142
  exercises, 141–142
  goals, 140–141
  therapy, 141
treatment after spondylosyndesis, 142–144
treatment in braces, 137–140
  exercises, 139–140
  goals, 137
  therapy, 138–139
Scoliotic position, 95
Sensory function, hand, 215–218
Shoulder
  clinical manifestations, 192–209
  evaluation, 189–192
  mobilization, 199–202
  muscle strengthening, 202–204
  pain relief therapy, 198–199
  recurrent dislocation, 195–196
    origin, 195
    physical therapy, 205–207
    radiographic findings, 195
    symptoms, 195
    treatment, 195–196
  stiffness, physical therapy, 196–197
Spider fingers, 14
  origin, 14
  symptoms, 14
  treatment, 14
Spinal syndrome, 154–171
Spine, 87–187
  bone necrosis, 122–127
  deformity, 105–120
  degenerative diseases, 150–154
  evaluation, 89–94
  function, 87–88
  hypermobility, 89
  malposition, 94–96
    physical therapy, 96–105
  orthosis, 425
  postural weakness, 94–96
    physical therapy, 96–105
  structure, 87–88
  tumor, 184–187

Splay foot, 329
  nonsurgical treatment, 329
  origin, 329
  physical therapy, 349
  surgical treatment, 329
  symptoms, 329
Spondylarthrosis
  origin, 151
  symptoms, 151-152
  treatment 152
Spondylodesis, scoliosis, 142-143
  goals, 142, 143
  therapy, 143
Spondylitis, 175-177
  specific, 175-176
    origin, 175
    symptoms, 175
    treatment, 175-176
  unspecific, 177
    course, 177
    symptoms, 177
    treatment, 177
Spondylolisthesis, 115-118
  origin, 115
  physical therapy, 116-118
    evaluation, 116
    exercises, 117-118
    goals, 116
    techniques, 116-117
  symptoms, 115-116
  treatment, 116
Spondylolysis, 115-118
  origin, 115
  physical therapy, 116-118
    evaluation, 116
    exercises, 117-118
    goals, 116
    techniques, 116-117
  symptoms, 115-116
  treatment, 116
Spondylosis, 151-152
  origin, 151
  symptoms, 151-152
  treatment, 152
Spur, 335

Still's disease, 77-78
  origin, 77-78
  symptoms, 78
  treatment, 78
Strümpell-Marie-Bechterew's disease, 79
Stump massage, 408
Sulcus, 20
Supportive tissue, aging, 49-51
Syndactylia, 24
Synovialoma, malignant, 31
  origin, 31
  symptoms, 31
  treatment, 31
Systemic disease, spinal changes, 120-122

T

Talipes planus, 329
  physical therapy, 348-349
Talipes valgus, physical therapy, 348-349
Talipes valgus, planus, transversoplanus, combined, 329-330
  origin, 329
  physical therapy, 348-489
  symptoms, 330
  treatment, 330
Talus, 318
  vertical, 329
Tape recorder, 2
Tendon, 2
  surgical procedures, 357-359
Tendon suture, 358-359
Tendovaginitis stenosans of Quervain, 220-221
Tennis elbow, 211
Tenotomy, 357-358
  closed, 357
  open, 358
Thoracic deformity, 111-115
Thoracic syndrome, 158
  origin, 158
  symptoms, 158
  therapy, 158

Thumb
  evaluation, 213
  sensory function, 215–218
Toe, prosthesis, 385
Torticollis, 106–107
  physical therapy, 107–111
    evaluation, 107
    exercises, 109–111
    goals, 107–108
    techniques, 108–109
Treatment program, 2
Trendelenburg sign, 255
Trochanter reinsertion, 276–277
Trunk, 87–187
Tumor
  benign, 28–31
  chemotherapy, 27
  classification, 28
  clinical manifestations, 27–34
  evaluation, 27–34
  giant cell, 31
    characteristics, 31
    origin, 31
    symptoms, 31
    treatment, 31
  malignant, 31–33
    bone metastesis, 33–34
  physical therapy, 34
  radiation therapy, 27
  semimalignant, 28, 31
    characteristics, 31
    origin, 31
    symptoms, 31
    treatment, 31
  spinal, 184–187
    physical therapy, 187
    primary, 185–186
    secondary, 186–187
    treatment, 187
  surgical treatment, 27
Tumorlike lesion, 28, 31
  origin, 31
  symptoms, 31
  treatment, 31

U

Upright position, 95

V

Varus osteotomy, 256–257, 276
Vertebra, 87
  fissure, 118–120
  sliding, 115–118
  transitional, 105–106
Vertebra plana, 126–127
Video recorder, 2
Vitamin D, 19, 21

W

Walker, 280–282
Walking, amputation, 380
Wrist, arthrosis, 220
  differential diagnosis, 220
  origin, 220
  treatment, 220

About the Editors and Contributors

Horst Cotta, MD, studied medicine in Berlin and Zurich. He received his medical degree from and qualified as a full professor of orthopedics at the University of Heidelberg, where he is currently Director of the Orthopedic Hospital and Polyclinic. In cooperation with a national and international team, Professor Cotta is currently investigating the problems and causes of arthritis and degenerative diseases of the spine.

Lawrence W. Friedmann, MD, is Chairman of the Department of Physical Medicine and Rehabilitation at the Nassau County Medical Center for East Meadow, New York. He is a Fellow in the American College of Angiology, International College of Angiology, and the Nassau Academy of Medicine. He has lectured and published extensively, both in the United States and abroad. Currently, he is an Associate Editor for *Angiology*, a Faculty Senator at SUNY Stoney Brook School of Medicine, as well as a consultant for the Subcommittee for Rehabilitative Engineering Research and Development for the Veterans Administration.

Wolfgang Heipertz, MD, studied medicine at the universities of Tübingen, Vienna, and in Munich, and received his medical degree from the University of Berlin. In 1962, he qualified as a full professor at the University of Heidelberg. Dr. Heipertz specializes in pediatric orthopedics, work-related injuries, sports medicine and sports injuries, physiotherapy, diseases of the spine, and artificial joint replacement. He has been chief surgeon at the Emergency Hospital in Tübingen and is now professor and medical director of the Orthopedic Hospital at J.-W. Goethe University in Frankfurt/Main.

Antje Hüter-Becker, PT, received her training as a physical therapist in Cologne and at the Stoke Mandeville Hospital, England, and obtained her teaching credentials in Cologne. For the past ten years, Ms. Hüter-Becker has directed the training programs at the school for Physiotherapy and at the Center for

Continuing Education for Teachers of Physical Therapy, in Heidelberg. She is the editor-in-chief of the periodical *Krankengymnastik (Physical Therapy)*.

Giesela Koester, PT, has been chief physical therapist at the Orthopedic Hospital of the University of Heidelberg for the past twenty-five years. Ms. Koester received her training at the School for Physiotherapy of the Charité in East Berlin. She specializes in internal medicine, neurology, orthopedics, and rheumatology.

Ernst Günter Marquardt, MD, received his medical degree from the University of Kiel in 1951 and qualified as a full professor at the University of Heidelberg in 1969. For the past eighteen years he has been head of the Department for Dysmelia and Technical Orthopedics at the Orthopedic Hospital of the University of Heidelberg.

Eduard Puhl, MD, studied medicine at the universities of Freiburg and Göttingen and received his medical degree from the University of Marburg. He qualified as a full professor of orthopedics at the University of Heidelberg in 1978. At present he is Medical Director of the Rehabilitation Center and Chief of Medicine at the Orthopedic Hospital and Center for Paraplegics in Ulm.

Gerald Rompe, MD, received his medical degree and qualification as a full professor of orthopedics from the University of Heidelberg. He is currently chief of the Department of Physiotherapy and Sports Orthopedics at the Foundation for Orthopedics, University of Heidelberg.

Anneliese tum Suden-Weickmann, PT, obtained her training as a physical therapist from the University of Leipzig State School for Physiotherapy. She specializes in orthopedics and pediatrics and has worked as both a practitioner and an educator in clinics, rehabilitation centers, and children's hospitals. She has also operated her own private practice. Ms. Suden-Weickmann has served as an editor for the series *Krankengymnastik (Physical Therapy)*.

UNIVERSITY OF RHODE ISLAND LIBRARY
3 1222 00406 2140

DATE DUE

NOV 27 1988			
SEP 5 1989			
DEC 14 1990			
MAR 29 1991			
AUG 31 1991			
DEC 02 1993			

DEMCO 38-297

DISCARDED
URI LIBRARY